INTRODUCTION TO REFERENCE WORK

VOLUME I   *Basic Information Sources*

INTRODUCTION TO REFERENCE WORK

Volume I **Basic Information Sources**

Sixth Edition

William A. Katz
State University of New York at Albany

McGraw-Hill, Inc.
New York   St. Louis   San Francisco   Auckland
Bogotá   Caracas   Hamburg   Lisbon   London
Madrid   Mexico   Milan   Montreal   New Delhi   Paris
San Juan   São Paulo   Singapore   Sydney   Tokyo   Toronto

INTRODUCTION TO REFERENCE WORK, Volume I
Basic Information Sources

1 2 3 4 5 6 7 8 9 0 DOC DOC 9 0 9 8 7 6 5 4 3 2 1

ISBN 0-07-033638-5

This book was set in Baskerville by Waldman Graphics, Inc.
The editors were Judith R. Cornwell and Jean Akers;
the production supervisor was Louise Karam.
The cover was designed by Carla Bauer.
R. R. Donnelley & Sons Company was printer and binder.

Library of Congress Cataloging-in-Publication Data

Katz, William A., (date).
    Introduction to reference work / William A. Katz.—6th ed.
        p.   cm.
    Includes bibliographical references and indexes.
    Contents: v. 1. Basic information sources—v. 2. Reference services and reference processes.
    ISBN 0-07-033638-5 (v. 1).—ISBN 0-07-033639-3 (v. 2)
    1. Reference services (Libraries)   2. Reference books—Bibliography.   I. Title.
    Z711.K32   1992
    025.5'2—dc20   91-9714

ABOUT THE AUTHOR

WILLIAM A. KATZ is a professor at the School of Information Science and Policy, State University of New York at Albany. He was a librarian at the King County (Washington) Library for four years and worked in the editorial department of the American Library Association. He received his Ph.D. from the University of Chicago and has been the editor of *RQ,* the journal of the Reference and Adult Services Division of the American Library Association, and the *Journal of Education for Librarianship.* Professor Katz is now editor of *The Reference Librarian,* a quarterly devoted to issues in modern reference and information services, and *The Acquisitions Librarian,* concerned with collection development. He is the editor of *Magazines for Libraries* and edits a magazine column in *Library Journal.* In addition, he edits a collection, *Reference and Information Services: A Reader,* as well as *The Columbia Granger's Guide to Poetry Anthologies.*

To Linda

CONTENTS

PART III SOURCES OF INFORMATION

PREFACE

The purpose of *Basic Information Sources*, Volume I of this sixth edition two-volume *Introduction to Reference Work*, remains the same as for the previous five editions: to acquaint students, librarians, and library users with various information sources. While written primarily for students of reference service and practicing reference librarians, the book is an introduction to basic sources that can also help laypeople use the library effectively.

NEW TO THIS EDITION

In this sixth edition, virtually only the organizational pattern remains the same; the revision is extensive, with fifth edition material reorganized and updated. Chapter 2, "Computers and Reference Service," is a new chapter added to reflect changes that have taken place in the curriculum. Since the fifth edition was published in 1987, new methods of data storage and retrieval have changed the ways reference librarians assist library users. It is no longer possible to isolate computer reference services in separate chapters, as was done in the fifth edition's Volume II when these systems were new. What was then a limited approach to reference questions has now become an accepted, if not always easy-to-use, method of finding answers. Therefore, in addition to the new Chapter 2, discussions of electronic reference systems, such as online and CD-ROM, are integrated into the analyses of all reference forms. Volume II, *Reference Services and Reference Processes*, expands on computer-assisted reference services, with coverage of searching patterns and additional information on where and how to locate software and hardware.

PLAN OF THE BOOK

Volume I is divided into three parts. Part One (Chapters 1 and 2) constitutes an introduction to the reference process and automated reference services.

Part Two, "Information: Control and Access," consists of Chapters 3 through 6 and covers an introduction to bibliographies, indexing, and abstracting services. Chapters 7 through 12 are in Part Three, "Sources of Information," which include encyclopedias, various ready reference sources, biographical sources, dictionaries, geographical sources, and government documents.

It is as pointless for students to memorize details about specific reference sources, as it is necessary for them to grasp the essential areas of agreement and difference among the various forms. To this end, every effort is made to compare rather than to detail. Only basic or foundation reference works are discussed in this volume. But readers may not find *all* basic titles included or annotated because: (1) There is no consensus on what constitutes "basic". (2) The objective of this text is to discuss various forms, and the titles used for that purpose are those that best illustrate those forms. (3) The annotations for a specific title are duplicated over and over again in *Guide to Reference Books* and *Guide to Reference Materials,* which list the numerous subject bibliographies.

In both volumes, suggested readings are found in the footnotes and at the end of each chapter. When a publication is cited in a footnote, the reference is rarely duplicated in the "Suggested Reading." For the most part, these readings are limited to publications issued since 1987. In addition to providing readers with current thinking, these more recent citations have the added bonus of making it easier for the student to locate the readings. A number of the suggested reading items will be found in *Reference and Information Sources, A Reader, 4th ed.,* published by Scarecrow Press, in 1991. It is beyond argument, of course, that *all* readings need not necessarily be current and that many older articles and books are as valuable today as they were when first published. Thanks to many teachers' having retained earlier editions of this text and the aforementioned Scarecrow title, it is possible to have a bibliography of previous readings.

As has been done in all previous editions, the sixth edition notes prices for most of the major basic titles. This practice seems particularly useful today, since librarians must more and more be aware of budgetary constraints when selecting reference titles. CD-ROMS are listed where available. Prices are based on information either from the publisher of the original reference source or from the publisher of the CD-ROM disc. If a particular work is available online, the gross hourly rate as charged by DIALOG is given for its use. Both this rate and the book prices are current as of late 1990 and are useful in determining relative costs.

Bibliographic data are based on publisher's catalogs, *Books in Print,* and examination of the titles. The information is applicable as of late 1990 and, like prices, is subject to change.

ACKNOWLEDGMENTS

I am grateful to the many teachers of reference and bibliography who through the years have given their advice and help. Thanks are due, too, to reviewers who critiqued manuscript for this and previous editions; most recently they include David Carr, Rutgers University, and Bonnie Baker Thorne, Sam Houston State University. My thanks also go to my students and those in other classes across the country who have given me valuable suggestions.

My particular thanks to Judith R. Cornwell, the patient, imaginative McGraw-Hill editor who did so much to improve the organization and the clarity of both Volumes I and II. I must also thank my meticulous editing supervisor, Jean Akers, for her patience and hard work. It is as pleasant as it is rewarding to work with such professionals.

William A. Katz

INTRODUCTION TO REFERENCE WORK

VOLUME I *Basic Information Sources*

PART I
INTRODUCTION

CHAPTER ONE
THE REFERENCE
PROCESS

What is the reference process? It is the process of answering questions.[1] This simple equation may be quickly analyzed, and the basic factors are listed here:

1. *Information.* This comes in many formats. It may come from a traditional book or magazine or from a book or magazine in machine-readable form, accessible by a computer. There is often too much of it, or not enough. It can be difficult to locate and even more challenging to interpret.
2. *The user.* This is the person who puts the question to the librarian, and often he or she is not quite sure how to frame the query. A basic problem in reference work is trying to determine precisely what type of answer is required.
3. *The reference librarian.* The key individual in the equation, the librarian, is the person who interprets the question, identifies the precise source for an answer, and, with the user, decides whether or not the response is adequate.

Although a simple description of the reference process has

[1]No one would dismiss reference service as simply answering questions. It is much, much more. At the same time the definition offers a good, pragmatic start. As the reader progresses through these volumes, and particularly the second volume, it will become apparent just how complex reference service is and how and why it has been the study of countless researchers in almost as many fields from psychology and medicine to law and history.

been given here, this can never be definitive. Because of the rapid changes occurring in information technology, the reference process will continue to change too. But its goal remains the same: to answer questions.

There are numerous approaches to tackling this information and answer equation, and students know many of them.

Consider cramming, for instance, which requires skills of evaluation, focus, and retention. Learning what information is important, marginal, or useless is an essential part of what colleges teach. Cramming

> is properly criticized as a way of trying to look good academically without long term retention . . . but it also teaches valuable job skills. It teaches crisis management by making every approaching finals week a crisis. It hones the ability to retain information needed only for the short term without cluttering up one's long term memory of important things. This is most valuable in our information overload era, in which a great deal of information is junk.[2]

Relevancy is a major goal of every reference librarian, and while cramming may not be the best training, it does offer numerous lessons applicable to librarians. The point is that so much that occurs in daily life has some reflection in reference service. That is part of what makes it exciting, and contributes to its constant state of change.

Cramming offers another important lesson: learning to evaluate what is and is not important. The problem has become not so much one of locating information as one of being able to sort out what information is relevant. As more than one wag has put it, Americans are lost in a sea of information. The problem is *not* in finding enough material to write a four-page paper on *Moby Dick,* or a dissertation on whales, or a government report on conserving sea life. The real difficulty is in finding a raft to ride out the mass of irrelevant data which turns up when one simply asks about the novel, the whale, or conservation.

More and more the public looks to the reference librarian to save them from the deluge. If anything, this is the primary role of the librarian in the 1990s—not just answering questions, but limiting the response to the individual's special needs. That is why it is important to understand the original question.

The fact is that information is rapidly becoming the nation's

---

[2]Gary M. Galles, "What Colleges Really Teach," *The New York Times,* June 8, 1989, p. A31. The article is a tongue-in-cheek criticism of cramming and of much of modern education. Along the way the author offers numerous truths.

most precious commodity. Thus the individual or company who can gather, evaluate, and synthesize information ahead of rivals will have a competitive advantage. Reference librarians are leading the way in managing the flow of information which, in the 1990s, will dominate national interests.

Information Science

Reference service is a springboard to information science[3] wherein one is involved with all aspects of information, both theoretical and practical. On a given day a study may be launched to explore why a particular catalog entry baffles the average user. Another day it may be a carefully guarded examination of information-gathering skills of both friends and enemies. In between one may be exploring the methods of reference services, management of personnel, search processes, desktop publishing, and electronic archives—to mention only a few fields of interest in information science.

REFERENCE LIBRARIANS

Working at the reference desk is a marvelous intellectual game and can be great fun. Librarians prefer reference services to any position in the library: Year in and year out the graduating library school students rightfully conclude it is a highly desirable role to play in the library world.[4]

---

[3]Lawrence Auld, "Seven Imperatives for Library Education," *Library Journal,* May 1, 1990, p. 57. An educator makes the sensible distinction that information science "is the theoretical study of the life cycle of information," while library science "is the practical application . . . of the information cycle. . . . The problem for librarians is to determine the intersection of library science with information science." There is a massive amount of conjecture and unfortunate prose on what is or is not information science. A few sane voices such as Auld are about. For an objective evaluation of information, knowledge, and the role of the library see Pauline Wilson's excellent summary, "Mission and Information: What Business Are We In?" *The Journal of Academic Librarianship,* May 1988, pp. 82–86. A book-length discussion in clear, easy-to-understand prose is offered by John Olsgaard in his *Principles and Applications of Information Science for Library Professionals.* (Chicago: American Library Association, 1989). Michael Gorman, a frequent wise and witty critic of the passing library scene, takes a dim view of information science: "It's time for us, as librarians, to recognize and proclaim that there is a body of knowledge called librarianship." *American Libraries,* May 1990, pp. 461–462.

[4]William Moen and Kathleen Heim, "The Class of 1988 . . ." *American Libraries,* November 1988, p. 858. Beverly P. Lynch and Jo Ann Verdin, "Job Satisfaction in Libraries . . ." *Library Quarterly,* vol. 53, no. 4, 1983, p. 445.

Some critics see the windup of the twentieth century as the American disaster, the "dumbing down" of the population. More optimistic reference persons disagree. They believe an increasing number of Americans seek to know more about themselves and their society, as well as their historical cultures.

Reference librarians list public service as one of the most pleasurable aspects of the profession. Other sources of satisfaction include meeting people, working with fellow librarians, enjoying the wide variety of tasks and sense of autonomy, problem solving, learning, feeling accomplishments, finding answers, and just being around books. Incidentally, near the bottom of the list, one can cite supportive administration, opportunities to teach, the satisfaction of providing access through cataloging, and spending money.[5]

There are drawbacks. Sometimes the questions asked will be repetitive, dull, or simple, although important to the person asking. Not everyone wants to know either the meaning of art or the best approach to ending the drug problem. In fact, the majority of reference queries of a ready-reference type ("Give me a quick fact-answer") tend to be less world shaking: What is the velocity of a sneeze? (*Answer:* Nearly 85 percent of the speed of sound.) What is the purpose of the half-moons on the base of our fingernails? (*Answer:* Apparently no purpose since they, the lunules, are little more than trapped air.) The most popular question put to *RQ* (a magazine for reference librarians) concerns the history of the peace symbol. (*Answer:* It was originally used by a British group to protest nuclear war in the 1950s.)

A few other job challenges: (1) Staffing remains constant, but the number of requests for help increases. (2) New technologies combine to speed searching and to suggest more complex patterns of service. This causes constant reappraisal of past performance and a need to keep up with almost daily changes in reference services. Although not always a "problem," this process is a constant challenge. (3) Additional expensive reference works are available in both the traditional print and the new electronic form with which the librarian must be familiar. All of the foregoing point to the need for improved collection development and understanding of patron needs.

A director of an academic library takes a cynical view of reference work, and it is one which should be presented:

Actual reference desk work has taken on the flavor of Kitchen Patrol

---

[5]Charles Bunge, "Stress in the Library," *Library Journal,* Sept. 15, 1987, p. 47.

or punishment of some kind, rather than desirable professional activity. Some people (who come to consider themselves martyrs or scapegoats) are asked to spend large amounts of time at the reference desk, in order to free up others who spend large amounts of time and energy on activities such as faculty seminars, committee work, credit courses for a handful of undergraduates, massive workbook projects, and one-on-one database search appointments.[6]

Let another experienced reference librarian and teacher explain the human side of reference services:

In my youth I thought it would be a fine thing to be able to answer any question that was posed. This, in fact, was a major motivation for my entering the library/information field. Information people know how to find answers to anything. They are adept in seeking out information and testing its accuracy. This characteristic seems to me to be fundamental to our profession, inextricably part of our essential identity as professionals. One of the delights in teaching the first reference course to entering MLS students or in teaching bibliographic instruction to undergraduates is their enthusiasm as they become empowered with information-finding, question-answering skills.[7]

REFERENCE SERVICE GUIDELINES

The Reference and Adult Services Division of the American Library Association offers reference librarians a set of guidelines which help both to define their work and to chart, if only in a tentative way, a philosophy of service. The guidelines are called "Information Services for Information Consumers: Guidelines for Providers."[8] Directed to all those who have any responsibility for providing reference and information services, one of the guidelines' most valuable contributions is the following succinct description of a reference librarian's duties.

[6]William Miller, "Cases and Cures for Inaccurate Reference Work," *Journal of Academic Librarianship*, May 1987, p. 72.

[7]Evelyn Daniel, "The Effects of Identify, Attitude, and Priority," *Journal of Academic Librarianship*, May 1987, pp. 76–77.

[8]"Information Services for Information Consumers: Guidelines for Providers," Chicago: American Library Association, 1990. Also reprinted in *RQ*, Winter 1990, pp. 262–265. This is the source of quotes which follow. The statement supersedes the still-valuable: "A Commitment to Information Services: Development Guidelines," *RQ*, Spring 1979, pp. 275–278, first adopted in 1976, and a section "Ethics of Service" adopted in 1979. For a discussion of the new guidelines see James Rettig's "Guidelines: Joy Is Bustin Out All Over," *The Reference Librarian*, no. 33, 1991.

The guidelines address information services from six points of view: services, resources, access, personnel, evaluation, and ethics.

1. *Services.* The primary service is "to provide an end product: the information sought by the user." Furthermore, the library "should provide users with complete, accurate answers to their information queries regardless of the complexity of those queries."

Another major service is instruction in the use of the library or, more particularly, in the effective use of reference sources. "Such instruction can range from the individual explanation of information sources or creation of guides in appropriate media to formal assistance."

There are still other services, from creating bibliographies to the active use of networks, that gain information for the client.

2. *Resources.* As one might expect, this section deals with the various forms of reference works. One of the most important points: "The library should provide access to the most current reference sources available in order to assure the accuracy of information."

3. *Access.* Just how easy is it for the user to find what is needed in the library? That's what access is all about, e.g., "the library should arrange information services according to a coherent plan, taking into account ready accessibility to users. . . . The library should design service points to accommodate the needs of all users."

4. *Personnel.* This section relates primarily to basic common sense about the way librarians work with the public. Also, there is necessary stress upon simple competency: "Personnel responsible for the services should be thoroughly familiar with and competent in using information sources, information storage and retrieval techniques, telecommunications methods, and interpersonal communications skills."

5. *Evaluation.* Concern is with the evaluation of both services and resources.

6. *Ethics.* Here is a brief statement about the American Library Association's Code of Ethics which "governs the conduct of all staff members providing information service." The heart of the code is that it seeks to guarantee equal service to all.

The "services" and "resources" aspects of the policy statement are discussed throughout this volume. The other points are covered in detail in the second volume.

Beyond Questions

As indicated by the guidelines, in an average day the reference librarian does many things. Some of the more common include:

Selection of Materials. This service requires familiarity with the various types of materials needed for adequate reference service including not only books, but periodicals, manuscripts, newspapers, and anything else which can conceivably assist the librarian in giving direct service. Data in electronic form is a major interest. Another aspect of selection is the weeding of book collections and files.

Reference Administration. The organization and administration of reference services will not always involve every librarian, but it will be a major consideration in small-to-medium libraries with only one or two librarians.

Interlibrary Loan. With the emphasis on networks and the recognition that the whole world of information should be literally at the command of the user, interlibrary loan may be categorized as an access activity. It is a major element of reference service. Administratively, some libraries now divorce interlibrary loan from reference and maintain it as a separate division; others consider it a function of the circulation section.

Miscellaneous Tasks. There are a variety of daily "housekeeping" duties: assisting library users with photocopying, filing, checking in materials, keeping a wary eye on reading rooms, and maintaining records, in addition to all the less frequent chores that are the responsibility of any library department, from budgeting to preparing reports and publicity releases. Still other services may include creating reference sources, local indexes, and information and referral sources. The extent of this kind of activity depends to a great degree on the size and guiding philosophy of the library as well as the financial support the reference section receives. The average academic research librarian puts in an average of 13.3 hours each week at the reference desk. Looking back at the previous list of reference librarian duties, it is easy to understand why the librarian is not more often at the desk.

REFERENCE SERVICE AND THE LIBRARY

The reference librarian does not function alone in a library, but is part of a larger unit, a larger mission. Today the library is considerably more than a warehouse of print materials. It is a media resource with promise for almost everyone. As one authority puts it, the library is "a catalyst in community development."[9]

The specific purpose of any library is to obtain, preserve, and make available the recorded knowledge of human beings. The system for achieving this goal can be as intricate and involved as the organizational chart for the Library of Congress or General Motors or as simple as that used in the one-person small-town library or corner barbershop.

Regardless of organizational patterns or complexities, the functions of the system are interrelated and common to all sizes and types of libraries. They consist of administrative work, technical services (acquisitions and cataloging), and reader's services (circulation and reference). These broad categories cover many subsections. Each is not an independent unit but rather a part of larger units; all are closely related. They form a unity essential for library service in general and for reference in particular. If one part of the system fails, the whole system suffers.

Administrative Work. Administration is concerned with library organization and communication. The better the administration functions, the less obvious it appears—at least to the user. Reference librarians must be aware of, and be prepared to participate in, administrative decisions ranging from budget to automation.

Technical Services: Acquisitions. The selection and acquisition of materials are determined by what type of library it is and by its users. Policies vary, of course, but the rallying cry of the nineteenth-century activist librarians, "The right book for the right reader at the right time," is still applicable to any library today, as long as one understands "book" to include nonprint material. Reference librarians are responsible for the reference collection, but their responsibility extends to the development of the library's entire collection—a collection which serves to help them answer questions.

Technical Services: Cataloging. Once a library has acquired a piece of information, the primary problem becomes how to retrieve it from among the hundreds, thousands, or millions of other bits of information. A number of retrieval avenues are open, from oral communication to abstracts; but for dealing with larger information units such as books, recordings, films, periodicals, or reports, the

---

[9]Darlene Weingand, "No Professional Is an Island," *Journal of Education for Library and Information Science,*" Fall 1988, p. 144.

normal finding device is the catalog. The catalog is the library's main bibliographical instrument. When properly used, it (1) enables persons to find books for which they have the author, the title, or the subject area; (2) shows what materials the library has by any given author, on a given subject, and in a given kind of literature; (3) assists in the choice of a book by its form (e.g., handbook, literature, or text) or edition; (4) assists in finding other materials, from government documents to films; and, often most important, (5) specifically locates the item in the library. It is a primary resource for reference librarians, and it is essential they understand not only the general aspects of the catalog but also its many peculiarities.

Most libraries now have replaced or augmented the familiar card catalog with an online catalog. Here the librarian, or user, sits down before a computer terminal and a screen, types in a few key letters or parts of words, and is given immediate access on the screen to the holdings of the library. At the same terminal it may be possible, too, to access holdings of other libraries—regional, state, national, and even international.

Reader's Services: Circulation. Circulation is one of the two primary public service points in the library. After a book has been acquired and prepared for easy access, the circulation department is concerned with (1) checking out the material to the reader, (2) receiving it on return, and (3) returning it to its proper location.

Adult Services: Reference. An important component of reference service in the 1990s is adult services, often used as a synonym for "adult education." This is a specialized area, although in daily work the average reference librarian will be involved in a range of adult services such as giving assistance with job and occupational information or providing service for the handicapped.

REFERENCE QUESTIONS

There are various methods of categorizing reference questions. By way of introduction to a complex topic, we can divide queries into two general types:

1. *The user asks for a known item.* The request is usually for a specific document, book, article, film, or other item, which can be identified by citing certain features such as an author, a title, or a source. The librarian has only to locate

the needed item through the card catalog, an index, a bibliography, or a similar source.

2. *The user asks for information without any knowledge of a specific source.* Such a query triggers the reference interview—an important consideration in reference services which is discussed throughout this text and most particularly in the second volume. Most reference questions are of a general type, particularly those in school and public libraries where the average user has little or no knowledge of the reference services available.

Handling the two broad types of questions may not be as easy as it seems. For example, the person who asks for a specific book by author may (1) have the wrong author, (2) actually want a different book by that author, (3) discover that the wanted book is not the one required (for either information or pleasure), or (4) ask the librarian to obtain the book on interlibrary loan and then fail to appear when the book is received. All this leads most experienced reference librarians to qualify the "known-item" type of question. The assumption made by the librarian is usually correct, and the user really needs more information or help than indicated. Therefore, librarians tend to ask enough questions to clarify the real needs of the user rather than to accept what may be only a weak signal for help.

A more finely drawn categorization of reference questions can be divided into four types:

1. *Direction.* "Where is the catalog?" "Where are the indexes?" "Where is the telephone?" The general information or directional question is of the information-booth variety, and the answer rarely requires more than geographical knowledge of key locations. The time required to answer such questions is negligible, but directional queries can account for 30 to 50 percent of the questions put to a librarian in any day. The percentages given here and in what follows are relative and may vary from library to library.

2. *Ready reference.* "What is the name of the governor of Alaska?" "How long is the Amazon River?" "Who is the world's tallest person?" There are the typical ready-reference or data queries which require only a single, usually uncomplicated, straightforward answer. The requested information is normally found without difficulty in standard reference works, ranging from encyclopedias to almanacs and indexes. Many of these may be accessed via a computer terminal.

Ready-reference queries may be divided and subdivided in

many ways. Crossing almost all subject lines, one can construct a classification scheme similar to the news reporter's five W's. These are (1) *Who?* Who is . . . ; Who said . . . ; Who won . . . , etc. (2) *What?* What is the speed of sound? What are the qualities of a good swimmer? What does coreopsis look like? (3) *Where?* Where is the center of the United States? Where is the earth's core? (4) *Why?* Why does water boil? Why, why, why . . . almost anything. (This, the favored beginning of all children's queries, continues with most of us through life.) (5) *When?* When was *Coriolanus* written? When was the automobile invented? Most of these queries require only a specific piece of data. Also, many might be modified or rephrased in such a way as to get a yes, no, or maybe answer: Is aspirin harmful? Was America discovered in 1492?

It usually takes no more than a minute or two to answer this type of question. The catch is that while 90 percent of such queries are simple to answer, another 5 to 10 percent may take hours of research because no standard reference source in the library will yield the necessary data. Apparently simple questions are sometimes complicated, such as "What are the dates of National Cat Week?" (Answer: Flexible, but usually in early November.) "When and where was Russian roulette first played?" (Answer: Cambridge University in 1801. Lord Byron describes the incident in his memoirs.) Difficult questions of this type are often printed in a regular column in *RQ,* the official journal of reference librarians.[10]

The percentage of ready-reference questions will differ from library to library. In one study it was found that about 50 to 60 percent of the questions asked in a public library were of the ready-reference type. Requests for background information made up the other 40 to 50 percent or so of the queries. Public libraries, which may have a well-developed phone service for reference questions as well as a high percentage of adult users, tend to attract the ready-reference question.

In academic, school, and special libraries, however, specific-search questions may account for a larger percentage of the total.

3. *Specific-search questions.* "Where can I find information on sexism in business?" "What is the difference between the conserva-

---

[10]The column, called "The Exchange," has various editors. It is devoted to "tricky questions, notes on unusual information sources, [and] general comments concerning reference problems. . . ." An index to vols. 1–26 of "The Exchange" will let the reader find out what has and has not been located in the way of answers to puzzling questions. The index ($10) is available from Charles Anderson, 1618 Elder Lane, Northfield, IL 60093.

tive and the liberal view on inflation and unemployment?" "Do you have anything on the history of atomic energy?" "I have to write a paper on penguins for my science class. What do you have?" The essential difference between the specific-search and the ready-reference questions is important. Ready-reference queries usually can be answered with data, normally short answers from reference books. Specific-search answers almost always take the form of giving the user a document, e.g., a list of citations, a book, or a report.

More information is required if the user is writing a school paper, is preparing a speech, or is simply interested in learning as much about a subject as necessary for his or her needs. This query often is called a *bibliographic inquiry*, because the questioner is referred to a bibliographic aid such as the card catalog, an index, or a bibliography. The user then scans available materials and determines how much and what type he/she needs.

Of course, all specific-search questions do not involve bibliographies. At a less sophisticated level, the librarian may merely direct the user to an article in an encyclopedia, to a given section of the book collection, or to a newspaper index. Aside from directional queries, specific-search questions constitute the greatest proportion of reference questions in school and academic libraries as well as in many special libraries.

The time it takes to answer a user's question depends not only on what is available in the library (or through interlibrary loan) but also on the librarian. If the librarian offers a considerable amount of help, the search can take from ten minutes to an hour or more. Conversely, a less helpful or busier librarian may turn the question into a directional one by simply pointing the user to the card catalog.

Some types of specific-search questions are treated by librarians as reader advisory problems. These are questions that, in essence, ask "What is the best source of information for my needs?" Questioners may be seeking everything from fiction and poetry to hobby magazines. Depending on the size and the organizational pattern of the library, their queries may be handled by subject or reader advisory librarians or by reference librarians. In a small library these are one and the same person.

4. *Research* Almost any of the types of questions described in the "specific-search" section above may be turned into research questions. A research query is usually identified as that coming from an adult specialist who is seeking detailed information to assist in specific work. The request may be from a professor, a business executive, a scientist, or other person who needs data for a decision or for additional information about a problem. With the exception of some academic and special libraries, this type of inquiry is a negligible part of the total reference pattern in libraries.

Ready-reference and specific-search queries presuppose specific answers and specific sources, which, with practice, the librarian usually can locate quickly. Research questions differ from other inquiries in that most involve trial-and-error searching or browsing, primarily because (1) the average researcher may have a vague notion of the question but usually cannot be specific and/or (2) the answer to the yet-to-be-completely-formulated question depends on what the researcher is able to find (or not find). The researcher recognizes a problem, identifies the area that is likely to cover the problem, and then attempts to find what has been written about the problem.

There is another useful method of distinguishing types of queries. The first two types of queries (directional and ready-reference) may be classified as *data retrieval*, i.e., individuals have specific questions and expect answers in the form of data. The specific-search and research questions might be classified as *document retrieval* in that the users want information, not just simple answers, and the information is usually in the form of some type of document, e.g., book, report, or article.

Few situations require one or, indeed, even allow opportunity to categorize questions in this manner; and this is just as well. A ready-reference query can quickly turn into a specific-search question, and someone embarked on research may have a few ready-reference questions related to that quest.

The difficulty with the categorization of reference questions is that few are that easy to label. True, when someone asks for the bathroom, this is a simple directional query. True, when another person needs material on the salmon, this is a specific-search question. At the same time, a directional question may turn into a ready-reference query, and a specific-search need may develop into research.

For example, the young person who asks for material on the salmon actually may be interested in knowing where one can catch salmon in the immediate area. Hence a supposed search question is really a ready-reference query. Conversely, someone may ask where to catch salmon, although she really wants to know about fishing conservation. A ready-reference question has been turned inside out into a search or even a research problem.

Who Is to Answer?

The fascinating result of analyses of types of questions is that (1) the majority of queries are directional or ready-reference pure and simple; (2) generally, the queries and sources used are basic and easy to understand; and (3) most questions, therefore, could be answered by a well-trained person with a bachelor's degree.

But that does not necessarily mean that the trained nonprofessional can or should replace the professional librarian for the purpose of answering directional and ready-reference queries. Often the simple questions can develop into complex ones requiring professional aid.

Even where nonprofessionals are used sparingly, the average library can depend on nonreference librarians to help at the reference desk. Technical services librarians, for example, may take a turn at answering questions. In a survey of research libraries, almost 70 percent of survey respondents relied on the assistance of librarians not formally assigned to the reference department.

Does it make any difference whether a professional librarian or a clerk answers a reference question? No—if the question is answered to the satisfaction of the user. Yes—if either the clerk or the librarian fails to follow through with enough of the right information, or totally strikes out. If the clerk is better-educated, more personable and, yes, more experienced than the librarian, it may just well be that the clerk scores higher. Odds are, though, that the professional will do better because of superior knowledge. In fact, "professionals score significantly higher both in information or materials provided and amount and quality of service given."[11] This hardly resolves the problem of using nonprofessionals, but study after study indicates that the trained librarian (like the trained mechanic, doctor, postal worker, or writer) will do better than the casual employee.

Reference Interview

The most common complaint heard among reference librarians about their work is that few people know how to ask reference questions. There are many reasons why the public may not appreciate the need for clarity at the reference desk, and these reasons are

---

[11]"In 20 Academic Libraries Surveyed, Professional Reference Librarians Score Higher . . ." *American Libraries*, September 1987, p. 632. The study is by Charles Bunge and Marjorie Murfin and suggests better methods of employing nonprofessional staff.

considered throughout this text. Here, we consider the dialogue between the user and the librarian, or the reference interviewer, and its several objectives: The first objective is to find out what and how much data the user needs. This should be simplicity itself, except that most people do not know how to frame questions. The child looking for information on horses may be interested in pictures, an encyclopedia article, or possibly a book on riding. No matter what the scope of the query, it probably will come out as "Do you have anything on horses?"

Searching for Answers

Once the actual needs of the library patron are understood, the next step is to formulate a search strategy of possible sources. To do so requires translating the terms of the question into the language of the reference system. If a basic book on gardening is required, the librarian will find it readily enough in the card catalog under a suitable subject heading. At the other extreme, the question may involve searching indexes, such as the *Biological & Agricultural Index,* to find the latest information on elm blight, or perhaps checking out various bibliographies, such as *Subject Guide to Books in Print* or a union catalog, to find what may be available on elm blight in other libraries. Once the information is found, it has to be evaluated. That is, the librarian must determine whether it is really the exact kind and level of information that the patron wants: Is it too technical or too simple? Is it applicable in this geographic area?

Evaluation

The user has some notion of what is wanted, both in terms of quantity and quality. Yet, that same user may be vague about whether or not an article should be used from a particular journal. The qualifications of the author and publisher are better known to the librarian than to the average user. For example, in a string of 10 citations about solar energy, would a high school senior, a college senior, or a layperson be happier with citations from *Time, Reader's Digest,* and *Newsweek,* or from the *Monthly Energy Review, EPRI Journal,* and *Solar Energy?* These fundamental decisions of the librarian will be of great help to the average user.

Here a distinction should be made between consulting (where the librarian actually chooses the four or five best articles) and counseling (where a recommendation is made). In most cases, the librarian will wish to discuss and consult with the user, not dictate the solution.

INFORMATION SOURCES

In day-to-day activities in most reference libraries, the librarian relies on reference books which are carefully identified and assigned to a special section of the library. The reference book is well known to most library patrons, and the dictionary and the encyclopedia are found in many homes. Furthermore, in most libraries many indexes are now available through a computer, and some homes access encyclopedias via a personal computer.

A question of interest for future reference librarians concerns how many titles the new librarian should be familiar with when taking over a reference position. Some would argue that specific knowledge of individual titles is not very important; but that debate aside, several studies at least indicate the degree of disagreement about how many and which titles every reference librarian should know.

There is no end of select lists, which indicate some consensus but do not dictate "basic" reference collections. Much the same is true when one turns to lists of other reference forms, from databases to video. Ultimately the "best" working basic collection is the one which serves the individual librarian and the audience. Determining what this basic list includes is one of the joys of active reference service.

Published in 1990, "Best Reference Books of 1989" (*Library Journal*, April 15, 1990, pp. 32–39) lists and annotates 30 titles which are typical enough of a year's output. These range, for example, from the new edition of the *Oxford English Dictionary* (20 vols., $2500) to a parent's guide, *What to Expect in the First Year* (592 pp., paperback, $9.95). The annual listing of "best reference works" is replicated in other journals, but usually the choices are pretty much the same. A coeditor of the work, Brian Coutts, points out that "quality and the need for coverage of a particular subject" guided his choice of selections—good criteria to apply for the selection of individual works in individual libraries. Other considerations in evaluation, which are covered in detail later in this chapter, include the authority of those involved in producing the book, the way it is organized, the quality of indexing, the inclusion of bibliographies, and the audience for the work.

What types of reference sources most often are used to field responsible, complete replies?

There is no single answer for all libraries. There are too many variables in terms of the sophistication of the users, skills of the librarian, special needs of the community, and the like. For example, a public library may depend on a good, general encyclopedia for quick, easy-to-answer queries. A university library, such as that at Iowa State, relies most heavily on what falls into the "A" section of the Library of Congress classification, i.e., general reference, with particular attention to periodical and newspaper indexes. Here, for a variety of reasons, "patrons use education indexes four and a half times as often as librarians."[12]

The Control-Access-Directional Type of Source

The first broad class or form of reference sources is the bibliography. This form is variously defined, but in its most general sense it is a systematically produced descriptive list of records.

Control. The bibliography serves as a control device—a kind of checklist. It inventories what is produced from day to day and year to year in such a way as to enable both the compiler and the user to feel they have a control, through organization, of the steady flow of knowledge. The bibliography is prepared through research (finding the specific source), identification, description, and classification.

Access. Once the items are controlled, the individual items are organized for easy access to facilitate intellectual work. All the access types of reference works can be broadly defined as bibliographies; but they may be subdivided as follows:

1. Bibliographies of reference sources and the literature of a field, of either a general or a subject nature—example: *Guide to Reference Books* or *The Information Sources of Political Science.*
2. The library catalog or the catalogs of numerous libraries arranged for easy access through a union list—technically, these are not bibliographies but are often used in the same manner.
3. General systematic enumerative bibliographies, which include various forms of bibliography—example: *The National Union Catalog.*

---

[12]Daniel Arrigona and Eleanor Mathews, "A Use Study of an Academic Library Reference Collection," *RQ,* Fall 1988, p. 76.

4. Indexes and abstracts, which are usually treated separately from bibliographies but are considered bibliographical aids—these are systematic listings which help identify and trace materials. Indexes to the contents of magazines and newspapers are the most frequently used types in the reference situation. Examples: *The Readers' Guide to Periodical Literature* and *The New York Times Index.*

Direction. Bibliographies themselves normally do not give definitive answers, but serve to direct users to the sources of answers. For their effective use, the items listed must be either in the library or available from another library system.

These days most access and control sources of reference works are available not only in print, but in machine-readable form. This is not so true for the next form, the source type.

Source Type

Works of the source type usually suffice in themselves to give the answers. Unlike the access type of reference work, they are synoptic.

Encyclopedias. The single most-used sources are encyclopedias; they may be defined as works containing informational articles on subjects in every field of knowledge, usually arranged in alphabetical order. They are used to answer specific questions about X topic or Y person or general queries which may begin with "I want something about Z." Examples: *Encyclopedia Britannica; World Book Encyclopedia.*

Fact Sources. Yearbooks, almanacs, handbooks, manuals, and directories are included in this category. All the types have different qualities, but they share one common element: They are used to look up factual material for quick reference. Together, they cover many facets of human knowledge. Examples: *World Almanac; Statesman's Year-Book.*

Dictionaries. Sources which deal primarily with all aspects of words, from proper definitions to spelling, are classified as dictionaries. Examples: *Webster's Third New International Dictionary; Dictionary of American Slang.*

Biographical Sources. The self-evident sources of information on people distinguished in some particular field of interest are known as biographical sources. Examples: *Who's Who; Current Biography.*

Geographical Sources. The best-known forms are the atlases, which not only show given countries but may illustrate themes such as historical development, social development, and scientific centers. Geographical sources also include gazetteers, dictionaries of place names, and guidebooks. Example: *The Times Atlas of the World.*

Government Documents

Government documents are official publications ordered and normally published by federal, state, and local governments. Since they may include directional and source works, their separation into a particular unit is more for convenience and organization than for different reference use. Examples: *Monthly Catalog of United States Government Publications* (access type); *United States Government Manual* (source type).

The neat categorization of reference types by access and by source is not always so distinct in an actual situation. A bibliography may be the only source required if the question is merely one of verification or of trying to complete a bibliographical citation. Conversely, the bibliography at the end of an encyclopedia article or a statement in that article may direct the patron to another source. In general, the two main categories—access and source—serve to differentiate between the principal types of reference works.

Unconventional Reference Sources

A term frequently seen in connection with reference service at the public library level is *information and referral,* or simply *I&R.* There are other terms used to describe this service, such as *community information center.* Essentially, the purpose of this special reference service is to offer the users access to resources that will help them with health, rent, consumer, legal, and similar problems. Whenever the economic situation is bleak, people are often laid off from their jobs. Libraries can provide free information on sources of new employment. While I&R is discussed in specific detail in the second volume of this text, the beginner should know that in even the most traditional library, it is now common to (1) call individual experts, including anyone from a local professor to a leader in a local special-interest group, for assistance; (2) provide files, pamphlets, booklists, and so on, which give users information on topics ranging from occupations to local housing regulations; and (3) provide a place which active groups in the community may identify as an information clearinghouse for their needs.

Enter the Computer

Today, as in the past, a convenient method of mastering reference sources is to divide them into the aforementioned categories. The computer has changed this. Information may now be stored in such a way that divisions between encyclopedias, biographies, and government documents no longer are needed. A vast electronic database of reference material includes all these. Sitting at a computer, one is able to search not just an index, not just a bibliography, but many forms of reference works at the same time. Some of the possibilities are considered in the following chapter.

Information Chain

If the ideal reference service, to paraphrase André Malraux, is "reference service without walls," the nature of information does impose certain limitations on that service. Aside from asking experts in the community for "firsthand" information, the library generally must rely on published data—data which, because of the nature of publishing, may be weeks, months, or even years out of date. A rough way of measuring the usual timeliness of materials is to classify them as primary, secondary, or tertiary.

   1. *Primary sources* These are original materials which have not been filtered through interpretation, condensation, or, often, even evaluation by a second party. The materials tend to be the most current in the library, normally taking the form of a journal article, monograph, report, patent, dissertation, or reprint of an article.

   2. *Secondary sources* If an index is used to locate primary sources, the index itself is a secondary source. A secondary source is information about primary, or original, information which usually has been modified, selected, or rearranged for a specific purpose or audience. The neat distinction between primary and secondary sources is not always apparent. For example, a person at a meeting may not be stating original views, but may simply be repeating what he or she has read or heard from someone else. A journal article is usually a primary source if it represents original thinking or a report on a discovery; but the same journal may include secondary materials which are reports or summaries of the findings of others.

3. *Tertiary sources* These consist of information which is a distillation and collection of primary and secondary sources. Twice removed from the original, they include almost all the source types of reference—works such as encyclopedias, reviews, biographical sources, fact books, and almanacs.

The definitions of primary, secondary, and tertiary sources are useful only in that they indicate (1) relative currency (primary sources tend to be more current than secondary sources) and (2) relative accuracy of materials (primary sources will generally be more accurate than secondary sources, only because they represent unfiltered, original ideas; but conversely, a secondary source may correct errors in the primary source).

EVALUATING REFERENCE SOURCES[13]

A thorough understanding of the day-to-day sources of answers requires some evaluation of those sources. How does the librarian know whether a reference source is good, bad, or indifferent? A more detailed answer will be found throughout each of the chapters in this volume. Simply stated, however, a good reference source is one that answers questions, and a poor reference source is one that fails to answer questions. Constant use in practice will help in identifying any source (whether a book or a database) with one of these two categories.

What follows is primarily concerned with traditional reference books, but much of it is applicable to other reference forms, including computer/online/CD-ROM records discussed in the next chapter. At the same time these various machine-readable reference sources have their own particular evaluation problems, which are discussed in the second volume.

Because of the expense of most reference sources, the typical practice is to read one or more book reviews before deciding whether to buy them. Large libraries usually request, or automati-

---

[13]Evaluation takes many forms, but for a detailed study of readability see Marilyn White's "The Readability of Children's Reference Materials," *The Library Quarterly*, October 1990, pp. 300–319. The methodology is suitable for adult works. James Rettig is one of the better reviewers of reference works. His column in *The Wilson Library Bulletin* offers an excellent method of keeping up with the more popular, the more regularly used reference works. For his views on the subject see two articles by him: "Every Reference Librarian a Reviewer," *RQ*, Summer 1987, pp. 467–475; and "The Reference Reviewer's Responsibilities," *The Reference Librarian*, Fall 1986, pp. 21–33.

cally, receive examination copies before purchase. Smaller libraries may have no choice but to accept the word of the reviewer and order, or not order, the work. Ideally, the reference source should be examined by a trained reference librarian before it is incorporated into the collection. No reviewer, review, or review medium is infallible.

The librarian must ask at least four basic questions about a reference work: What is its purpose? Its authority? Its scope? Its proposed audience? Finally, the format of the work must be considered.

1. *Purpose* The purpose of a reference work should be evident from the title or form. The evaluative question must be posed: Has the author or compiler fulfilled the purpose? An encyclopedia of dance, for example, has the purpose of capturing essential information about dance in encyclopedic form. But immediately the librarian must ask such questions as: What kind of dance and for what period? For what age group or experience or sophistication in dance? For what countries? Is the emphasis on history, biography, practical application, or some other element?

The clues to purpose are found in the:

a. Table of contents
b. Introduction or preface, which should give details as to what the author or compiler expects this work to accomplish
c. The index, the sampling of which will tell what subjects are covered

A reference book without an index is usually of little or no value. Exceptions are dictionaries, indexes, directories, and other titles where the index is built into an alphabetical arrangement. This system is suitable for the data type of reference work, but not for running prose, and then an index is absolutely essential.

Other hints as to the purpose of a specific work are often given in the publisher's catalog, in advance notices received in the mails, and in the copy on the jacket or cover of the book. Such descriptions may help to indicate purpose and even relative usefulness, but are understandably less than objective.

2. *Authority* The question of purpose brings us close to a whole series of questions that relate to the author:

a. What are the author's qualifications for the fulfillment of his or her purpose? If the writer is a known scholar, there is no problem with authority. The difficulty arises with the other 95 percent of reference works that are prepared by experts but not by those experts who make the best-seller list. Here the librarian must rely on (1) the qualifications of the author given in the book; (2) the librarian's own understanding and depth of knowledge of the subject; and (3) a check of the author in standard biographical works such as *Who's Who* or *American Men and Women of Science.*

b. The imprint of the publisher may indicate the relative worth of a book. Some publishers have excellent reputations for issuing reference works; others are known for their fair-to-untrustworthy titles. Again, the librarian's expertise and experience are important.

c. Objectivity and fairness of a work are important considerations, particularly in reference works which rely on prose rather than simple statistics or collections of facts. Does the author have a bias about politics, religion, race, sex, or the proper type of color to paint a study? No one is totally objective, but those who write reference books must indicate the worth of both sides when there is a matter of controversy.

3. *Scope* Other questions of major importance in selecting a reference work: Will this book be a real addition to our collection, and if so, what exactly will it add? The publisher usually will state the scope of the book in the publicity blurb or in the preface, but the librarian should be cautious. The author may or may not have achieved the scope claimed. For example, the publisher may claim that a historical atlas covers all nations and all periods. The librarian may check the scope of the new historical atlas by comparing it against standard works. Does the new work actually include *all* nations and *all* periods, or does it exclude material found in the standard works? If an index claims to cover all major articles in certain periodicals, a simple check of the periodicals' articles against the index will reveal the actual scope of the index.

a. What has the author contributed that cannot be found in other bibliographies, indexes, handbooks, almanacs, atlases, dictionaries, and so on? If the work is comprehensive within a narrow subject field, one may easily check it against other sources. For example, a who's who of education which limits itself to educators in the major colleges and universities in the Northeast may easily be checked for scope by comparing the current college catalog of P & Q University against the new who's who. If a number of faculty members are missing from the new work, one may safely conclude that the scope is not what is claimed.

b. Currency is one of the most important features of any reference work, particularly one used for ready reference. Data change so quickly that last year's almanac may be historically important but of little value in answering today's queries.

Except for current indexes, such as *Facts on File* and *The Readers' Guide to Periodical Literature*, most published reference works are dated before they are even off the presses. The time between the publisher's receipt of a manuscript and its publication may vary from six months to two years. Thus, in determining the recency of a work, some consideration must be given to the problems of production. Normally, a timely reference book will be one that contains information dating from six months to a year prior to the copyright date.

Again, the ability to put reference works in a machine-readable form often partially answers the problem of currency. One, for example, may sit down at a computer and search *The New York Times Index*, which has been updated in a matter of hours. A printed version means it is months behind.

The copyright date in itself may be only a relative indication of timeliness. Is this a new work, or is it based on a previous publication? In these days of reprints, this is a particularly important question. A standard reference work may be reissued with the date of publication shown on the title page as, say, 1991, but on the verso of the same title page the original copyright date may be 1976. If the work has been revised and updated, the copyright date will usually correspond to the date on the title page. A marked discrepancy should be sufficient warning that content must be carefully checked for currency.

Most reference works, unless entirely new, contain some dated information. The best method of ascertaining whether the dated material is of value and of checking the recency factor is to sample the work. This is a matter of looking for names currently in the news, population figures, geographical boundaries, records of achievement, new events, and almost any other recent fact consistent with the purpose and scope of the work. It is important to remember that no reference work should be accepted or rejected after sampling only one or two items.

If the work purports to be a new edition, the extent of claimed revisions should be carefully evaluated. This can easily be done by checking the work against the earlier edition or by noting any great discrepancy between the dates of the cited materials and the date of publication.

4. *Audience* With the exception of juvenile encyclopedias, most reference works are prepared for adults. When considering the question of audience, the librarian must ask one major question: Is this work for the scholar or student of the subject, or is it for the layperson with little or no knowledge? For example, in the field of organic chemistry, Beilstein's *Handbuch der Organischen Chemie* is as well known to chemists as the "top 10" tunes are to music fans. It is decidedly for the student with some basic knowledge of chemistry. Often the distinction in terms of audience is not so clear-cut.

A useful method of checking the reading level of a given reference work is for the librarian to examine a subject well known to him or her and then turn to one that is not so well understood. If both are comprehended, if the language is equally free of jargon and technical terminology, if the style is informative yet lively, the librarian can be reasonably certain the work is for the layperson. Of course, if the total book is beyond the subject competency of the librarian, advice should be sought from a subject expert. Still, this is an unlikely situation, since reference librarians tend to be experts in fields within which they operate.

5. *Cost* A major factor of frustration in the evaluation and purchase of reference works is the expense involved. There is much talk about the countless new reference sources and resources, but many libraries cannot afford expensive printed works. Also, the new technologies, such as CD-ROM, often are quite beyond the budget of underfinanced libraries. Budget, rather than client need, may determine whether a particular work is purchased.

Reference service, even on a minimum scale, can be a luxury. Approximately 80 percent of the public libraries in the United States serve populations under 25,000. Although not all rural communities are financially starved, the majority are in a bad way. Most, with or without state or federal aid, suffer from a lack of reference materials, and 75 percent lack any user education in reference services.

6. *Format* The questions which have been discussed are essential, but one of the most meaningful questions concerns arrangement, treated here as part of the format. Arrangement is of major importance. There must be a handy way to access the material. Here, the machine-readable record really does differ from the printed work, and what follows is hardly applicable.

Ease of use is important. Too many reference works (e.g., the citation indexes and online databases) are complicated and difficult to use. When this is the case, some librarians tend to avoid them, resulting in poor service to the user as well as a feeling of incompetence on the part of the librarian.

There are some general rules for arrangement which are significant guides to the relative worth of a particular work as a tool in answering questions. Briefly:

a. Wherever possible, information should be arranged alphabetically in dictionary form. The advantage is that there is no need to learn an additional scheme of organization.

b. Where alphabetical arrangement is not used, there should be an author, subject, and title index or an index covering aspects of content. Even with alphabetical order, it is usually advisable to have an index, particularly where bits of information must be extracted from long articles.

c. Where needed (in either the text or the index, or both), there should be sufficient cross-references that lead to other material and not merely to blind entries. For example, a book which refers readers to "Archives" when they look up "Manuscripts" should have an entry for "Archives." This is a simple rule; but too frequently, in the process of editing and revising, the entry for the cross-reference is deleted.

d. In some works another method must be employed, particularly in scientific sources. The classification should be as simple as possible; certainly it should be consistent and logical throughout. If it is difficult to comprehend, this may be a warning about the merits of the work as a whole.

The arrangement can be either hindered or helped by the physical format. Even the best-arranged work can be a nuisance if it is bound so that the pages do not lie flat or if there is no clear distinction between headings on a page and subheads within the page. The apparatuses of abbreviation, typography, symbols, and indication of cross-reference must be clear and in keeping with what the user is likely to recognize. The use of offset printing from computerized materials has resulted in some disturbing complexities of format. For example, it may be impossible to tell West Virginia, when abbreviated, from western Virginia. Uniform lowercase letters would be equally confusing. Lack of spacing between lines, poor paper, little or no margins, and other hindrances to reading are all too evident even in some standard reference works.

A word regarding illustrations: When photographs, charts, tables, and diagrams are used, they should be current, clear, and related to the text. They should be adjacent to the material under discussion or at least clearly identified.

The last word on the subject may sound as cynical or as simplistic as the reader cares to interpret it, but it is this: Trust no one. The reviewer, the publisher, and the author do make mistakes, sometimes of horrendous proportions. The librarian who evaluates reference sources with constant suspicion of the worst is less likely to be the victim of those mistakes. Whenever possible examine and use the work in question. Make your own evaluation!

To Publish or Not to Publish

An evaluative method that is rarely considered is a totally effective one. It is the refusal of a publisher to proceed with a reference work that is found wanting.

Some reference works are not published because they are in bad taste or downright illegal. Case in point: a how-to-do-it crime book. A former debt collector, for example, wrote a guide for con men while in prison: Barry Sussman's book is "I Scam . . . You Scam, Specific Methods for Defeating Bureaucratic Organizations." The book was never published, primarily because it gave advice on such things as how to milk as much as $60,000 from a single fraudulent credit card.[14]

The Reference and Adult Services Division of the American Library Association asked 15 publishers how decisions are made about publishing or not publishing a bibliography.[15] Essentially the decision to go ahead with a particular work is one of determining whether a market for the work exists and whether there is duplication of the proposed effort in another published work. "Perhaps because the market for bibliographies is largely institutional, and libraries are the primary buyers, publishers field test ideas with librarians."[16] If little or no market seems possible, the idea, no matter how useful it may be to a few librarians, is dropped. Exception: if the compiler can find the grant money necessary to pay for publication.

Disinformation

The problem of *disinformation* is not new, although the term is relatively modern. Here the idea is that a government or large corporation blends fact with fiction to create a news story. The idea is to

[14]"Man Is Sentenced in Fraud Scheme," *The New York Times*, Sept. 25, 1988, p. 55.

[15]"David Pilachowski and Noelene P. Martin, "How Do Bibliographies Get Published . . . ?" *RQ*, Summer 1988, pp. 542–545.

[16]*Ibid.*, p. 544. Another aspect of all this is the concentration of book publishing in fewer and fewer firms, i.e., conglomerates now dominate. For instance, R. R. Bowker is owned by Reed Publishing of England; Grolier was taken over by the French firm Hachette, and Gale is under the direction of International Thomson. The effect of the mergers may be good in that they allow for a larger financial base of operation, but they are bad in that few firms are willing to take risks with new reference works.

influence the public in one way or another, but, at all costs, to avoid the real issue, the real truth. All this is made easier by the masses of information which flow from the presses, computers, and television sets. Few have the time to check, and even fewer seem to really care as long as it is a good yarn.

Here are a few examples: In 1989 the Chinese government attempted to persuade the public that dissenters were not killed in Tienemen Square. The Turkish government denies that during World War I hundreds of thousands of Armenians were slaughtered.[17]

CONCLUSION: WHAT IS IMPORTANT TO LEARN

What should one learn in the basic training for reference work, or, for that matter, the profession as a whole?

In all types of libraries (academic, school, public special, and "other"), the librarians queried said the following five competencies are the most important: (1) Knowledge of bibliographic tools—85 percent ranked it first. (2) Interpersonal skills with patrons—70 percent; (3) Selection and evaluation of materials used in the library—65 percent; (4) conducting the reference interview—64 percent; and (5) assisting readers to find what they need in the library—59 percent.[18]

> Even though new and experienced librarians rate most of the same skills as most essential, the percentages of librarians giving these competencies the highest ranking decrease with experience. There is a definite downward shift in ranking the importance of 'knowledge of bibliographic tools.' The significance of effective communication and human relations increases. For example, while 78.6 percent of beginning librarians stress skill in searching online databases, experienced academic librarians do not include this competency in the top five.[19]

The conclusion is not surprising for anyone who has mastered a skill. The beginning driver, for example, cannot always find the brake pedal or recognize the curb line, but an expert parks and

---

[17]Terrence Des Pré, "On Governing Narratives: The Turkish-Armenian Case," *The Yale Review*, October 1986, pp. 517–531. This is a brilliant essay on the function of disinformation in government.

[18]Lois Buttlar and Rosemary DuMont, "Assessing Library Science Competencies," *Journal of Education for Library and Information Science,* Summer 1989, pp. 15–16. The target audience for the survey: the alumni of the Kent State University School of Library Science. See, too, other studies of the same sort which the authors cite.

[19]*Ibid.*

stops without thinking about the process. A new swimmer sinks, but an expert swimmer laps the pool as easily as she walks to class.

Getting to feel at home behind a reference desk is much the same. First the beginner must master the reference works, the bibliographic tools. Next he must learn to feel comfortable at a computer terminal or talking with a less than verbal user who is looking for a jam recipe or a way to get through to the next day.

In time the beginner becomes a veteran. And veteran librarians never quit, or are fired, or die. They simply gain fame as being among the wisest people in the world. One could do worse.

SUGGESTED READING

Breivik, Patricia, and E. Gordon Gee, *Information Literacy: Revolution in the Library.* New York: Macmillan (American Council on Education), 1989. While the focus is on the academic library, the problems (and solutions) associated with information, budget, personnel, etc. are applicable to other types of libraries. If it serves no other purpose, the study shows the importance of information and the need for increased financial support. It is good particularly for the estimate of what is likely to take place in academic/reference services over the coming decade.

Layman, Mary, and Sharon Vancercook, "Statewide Reference Improvements," *Wilson Library Bulletin,* January 1990, pp. 26–31. In an effort to equalize reference services throughout California, the State Library initiated a plan to see that every library had a core reference collection. Librarians are given training in model reference behavior. The description of the process offers a good overview of basic reference sources and services.

"The Publishing and Review of Reference Sources," *The Reference Librarian,* Fall 1986. The entire 336-page issue is devoted to this subject and includes a variety of viewpoints from reviewers, publishers, and librarians.

"Reference Librarian of the Future," *Reference Services Review,* Spring 1991, pp. 71–80. Edited by Ilene F. Rockman, this is a symposium (with four contributors) that examines the next decade. The guests outline those voices shaping the information age and indicate what is to be implied from the echoes.

Reich, Robert, "The Real Economy," *Atlantic Monthly,* February 1991, pp. 35–52. In this lengthy analysis of the next decade's economy, this Harvard professor makes the basic point that providing the right kind of data at the right time may be the most important contribution to a nation's economy. The national wealth now "depends on the development of the skills and insights of our citizens, and on the infrastructure necessary to link them to the new world economy."

Rethinking the Library in the Information Age. Washington, DC: U.S. Department of Education. Office of Library Programs, 1988, 2 vols. The results of a two-year study to assess the library profession and to predict how it is likely to develop in the 1990s. It gives a good overview of research needed and of likely problems.

Rettig, James, "Do Publishers Have Ears?" *Wilson Library Bulletin,* January 1988, p. 15. The reference book reviewer for the magazine examines reference book publishing and decides that many publishers fail to listen to the needs of librarians. Along the way he provides a well-written profile of reference books in America today.

———, "Sources of (A) First (Class) Resort, *Reference Services Review,* Summer 1987, pp. 19–32. Asked which 10 reference works they would take with them to a desert island, 17 teachers and librarians responded in a series which ran over five years. Here the sponsor of the tour summarizes the findings which consist of close to 130 different works. Among favorites: *Encyclopedia of World Art,* Bartlett's *Familiar Quotations, The Oxford English Dictionary, The Times Atlas of the World,* and the *World Almanac.* The list and article are an excellent indication of the difficulty of choosing any "core" list of reference works.

"Rothstein on Reference," *The Reference Librarian,* nos. 25/28, 1990. The 650-page issue of the journal includes: (1) writings by the world's leading expert on the history and function of reference services; and (2) writings by his friends on the same subject. Rothstein should be required reading for any student or working reference librarian. His work is a basic point of departure for a clear, intelligent view of the whole problem of answering questions, whether it be in a small public library or in the largest specialized information center. Of all the readings in this book, let this be the first.

Short, Randall, "You Can Look it Up," *The New York Times Book Review,* January 27, 1991, pp. 1, 16. A popular writer gives an equally popular definition of a reference work and then goes on to discuss the "stranger animals" that make up much of any reference section. "Everything in the world exists in order that it may end up in a book," he says. That fairly well summarizes the scope of the reference library.

Stabler, Karen, "Introductory Training of Academic Reference Librarians: A Survey," *RQ,* Spring 1987, pp. 363–369. In this study of how beginners receive basic training at a reference desk the author points up the various duties involved. For example, although close to 40 percent of the reference librarian's time is spent at the reference desk, instruction, collection, development, and online searching will take, combined, almost as much time.

Stevens, Norman D., "Our Image in the 1980s," *Library Trends,* Spring 1988, pp. 825–851. A highly imaginative, thoughtful and sometimes humorous approach to an old subject. His conclusion: "The old image persists even as a new—and even less desirable—image emerges. As a profession we are no closer to any resolution of how to deal with this professional question than we were in 1876, 1907, and 1962." A best-of-its-type article.

Vavrek, Bernard, *Assessing Rural Information Needs.* Clarion, PA: Clarion University, College of Library Science, 1990. This 40-page, paperbound study nicely summarizes what one might expect in any rural library. "The library is viewed as most important in providing information on best sellers, reference books, how-to-do-it topics, hobby/crafts, national news, health/medical services." This touchstone of everyday reality counterbalances the emphasis placed on information science. Conversely, it is a startling reminder that much of America is information-starved without recognizing the hunger.

White, Herbert, "Libraries and Librarians in the Next Millennium," *Library Journal,* May 15, 1990, pp. 54–55. The hard-hitting library commentator not only explains what the future may be for libraries (computer applications to document reproduction advances) but considers the reaction of librarians to the possible changes. "When it comes right down to it, our future in the 21st century will depend first of all on how we see ourselves."

CHAPTER TWO
COMPUTERS AND
REFERENCE
SERVICE

The days of seeking answers in reference books have not ended, but the process itself has changed. Now a librarian may find the same answers, often with greater speed and usually with considerably less difficulty, by using a computer. Taking only minutes, the librarian can search thousands of periodicals, scores of books, reports, and studies to discover citations about or, in many cases, the full text of the answer.

A searcher may sit at a computer to weigh the implications of the greenhouse effect, determine when the term itself was first employed, and pinpoint who in Washington, D.C., is an authority on the subject. Multiple-entry points allow one to find a person's name, a subject or subjects, key words used in the abstract, and possibly the article itself, as well as the date and place of publication. The searcher may retrieve brief facts, names, headlines, or statistics from the mass of stored material, as well as the complete text of an article, report, or even a book.

The technological alternatives and changes are characteristic of a gradual move from the writing culture to another, which has still to be thoroughly defined and explained. The practice of electronic information accessing has two basic dimensions that distinguish it from the days of the written word, its hard-copy predecessor. The first is an almost unlimited storage capacity which continually expands. For example, in 1985 IBM offered the world's first successful mass-produced 1-million-bit chip (or about 100 pages of double-spaced typewritten text). By the early 1990s it expects to offer a 256-million-bit chip. The 64-megabit chip is the size of a fingernail tip. It stores the text of several good-sized novels. With increased research it is expected to be adopted for pocket computers, which will contain all of the pages of the gigantic New York City telephone book, or three novels, as one wishes. The second aspect is the ability to select only what is needed (if this is known precisely) from the mass of data. Almost instantly one may read the material by showing it on a screen, printing it out, or, in the near future, listening to the computer speak.

Mass storage and specific retrieval is both a wonder and a curse. The wonder is evident, but consider the curse. One may store masses of undifferentiated information. There are now thousands of citations for a given subject. Only few years ago it might have been a few hundred. This may be labeled many things, but "information overload" is one very good definition.

The ability to store data without much evaluation can result in piling up more and more junk, but among the data there may be a gem or two. The problem is finding ways to discover the jewels in the garbage. Here, the reference librarian becomes the trained magician who is able to extract the desired data.

It all adds up to a self-evident truth. Today, we have access to more information, but this does not necessarily mean we have more knowledge. Is anyone any wiser because of the availability of masses of data? The answer depends on the individual, not the computer.

The Computer in the Library

Before describing further the way in which computers are used in reference service, one should consider their more general application. Computers are now found in over half the libraries that serve 25,000 people or more. By the end of the 1990s, it is likely to be closer to 100 percent.[1]

---

[1]"Information Technology," *The Economist,* June 16, 1990, pp. 5–20. The British news magazine presents a special section on various aspects of the computer and how it is used throughout society to gather and understand information. The explanation is geared to the layperson and offers a wide view of the problems and possible solutions for handling the new technology in the home, office, and library. Coverage is international. Torrey Byles, "Academic Computing Comes of Age," *Wilson Library Bulletin,* February 1989, pp. 21–28. In universities and colleges the use of microcomputers doubled between 1986 and 1991 and will probably continue to increase through the 1990s. Growth is slower in public and school libraries but is expected to become faster in the 1990s. The primary focus is on the CD-ROM. The

Today the librarian employs the microcomputer much as it is used by other personal computer users. In the library office one finds a microcomputer and sufficient software for word processing (the biggest single application of the computer in America, both in and outside the library). Word processors are used for everything from duplicating letters to desktop publishing of library reports and magazines.

The personal computer or microcomputer is an essential part of many libraries' acquisitions and ordering programs, used for everything from preparing book orders to sending them to the book dealer. At a more mundane level it is employed to compile lists of everything from periodicals to friends-of-the-library files.

The ubiquitous spreadsheet package is employed for budgets and statistics. Telecommunications capability including interface from the telephone to facsimile sending of material from one library to another is common. The electronic bulletin board, where one may write and receive letters, notes, and other forms of communication at the computer keyboard, is used more by individuals than by libraries, although some libraries sponsor systems.[2]

Once limited only to the card catalog, the computer catalog has all but eliminated the print version in libraries. The computerized system provides users with basic information about the book. In addition, it will often indicate whether the book is in the library, on order, or checked out. The catalog usually is limited to the local collection but may be part of a network and may include millions of other titles from libraries throughout the country and the world.[3]

Often in connection with the online catalog, the library has an automated circulation system. There are many software programs designed for this function, and it is one of the earliest developed in library automation systems.[4]

shift from online searching, to be explained later in this chapter, has meant the layperson now can conduct a personal search. By the mid-1990s it is expected all but the smallest libraries will offer some form of CD-ROM searching.

[2]Danny P. Wallace and Joan Giglierano, "Microcomputers in Libraries," *Library Trends*, Winter 1989, pp. 282–301. This is a history, a survey of current (1989) activities, and a forecast. There are useful sections on selecting hardware and software.

[3]The local library online catalog is sure to be part of an integrated national (international) system by the end of the century. When this happens "the user formulates a request, and then launches it into the network. All bibliographic databases on the network read the query and respond." The Linked Systems Project of the Library of Congress, OCLC and Research Libraries Group is involved with such projects. Torrey Byles, "Academic Computing Comes of Age," *Wilson Library Bulletin*, February 1989, p. 25.

[4]William Saffady, "Library Automation: An Overview," *Library Trends*, Winter 1989,

THE COMPUTER DATABASE

In reference and information services, the computer has affected the format of materials used by the reference librarian.

The database, or the reference work in a machine-readable form, is searched in much the same manner one would look for answers in a printed work. The essential difference is that the technology offers numerous added avenues of searching, which are discussed later in this chapter.

A tremendous advantage to the computer-assisted search is suggested by the fact that many databases now offer the complete text of the indexed article. This is another way of saying that one may read the full magazine or newspaper article at a computer. Books, reports, and almost all other forms of printed works are now available in full text. This hardly means *all* printed works, but the number grows each year, and particularly those in the reference section.[5]

Among other most-often-cited reasons for using the computer is speed of searching. A computer-aided search may take only a fraction of the time needed for a manual search, particularly when it is retrospective and requires searching several years of material. Various studies indicate that, in general, a computer search may be performed in 5 to 10 percent of the time required for a manual search. A considerable amount of time and effort is saved in not having to look up the same term in each volume of the printed service. Another time savings is realized in the printing out of the citations, which sidesteps the need to photocopy or laboriously write out the retrieved data.

Database Types

Databases are generally divided into several broad categories. The familiar bibliographic, abstract, and indexing service online usually is referred to as a "reference" database. This descriptor includes the majority of databases now accessed by librarians, such as the multiple indexes available from the H. W. Wilson Company through Wilsonline.

pp. 269–281. The author opens with a clear discussion of the development of circulation systems and then goes on to other basic automated functions: cataloging, reference services, acquisitions, and serials control. An excellent introduction to the whole subject.

[5]Roger Summit and Ann Lee, "Will Full Text Online Files Become Electronic Periodicals?" *Serials Review*, no. 3, 1988, pp. 7–10. A useful discussion of the pros and cons of full text in machine-readable form.

The other broad category is the "source" database. This is everything outside of the bibliographic, abstract, and index group. Source databases may comprise full text (such as *The New York Times*, which allows the librarian to search and/or read each and every word in the newspaper) or numeric (which consists of information in numbers such as census figures).

The obvious difference between "reference" and "source" databases is that the former normally requires the user to go to a cited source for the necessary information. The latter offers information complete in itself and requires no second steps.

Database Formats

There are different formats for databases. The five most common are CD-RAM, CD-ROM, CD-I, Multimedia, and online. Translation of these abbreviations explains how the information is extracted from the database.

1. *CD-RAM, or compact disk—random-access memory* This is the disk employed in microcomputers, and has the type of memory format familiar to anyone using a word processing system. The disk may be used to record information, and it may be wiped clean and used again. Comparatively few reference works are available in this format. On the other hand, the librarian may use a floppy disk to "download" material from a computer database, i.e., transfer it from one place to another, much as one may transcribe a radio program or a television show onto a tape.

2. *CD-ROM, or compact disk—read-only memory* Most readers are familiar with the CDs which are available for music and have revolutionized the home music business. A variation on this is the CD which is employed extensively in reference services and soon may be a part of most home libraries along with the music CDs.

Specifically, publishers now offer scores of reference works, and particularly the ubiquitous index, on CD-ROM. It has worked the same revolution in libraries that the music disk has in music.

The 4.75-inch disk, which resembles the more familiar music CD, can hold up to 250,000 pages. It is mounted in a microcomputer and read on a computer screen. The message can then be printed on a printer that is usually at the side of the computer.

All basic periodical indexes are now available in this format, and their number increases each day. Furthermore, the full and complete text of many of the magazines indexed are on CD-ROM. The result is that using computer commands, one looks up a required article(s), and with another command either views the article(s), or has it printed out next to the computer.

In addition to the indexes, there are basic reference works from directories and encyclopedias to handbooks and manuals which are available on CD-ROM. One can see that before the decade is out all the basic reference works will be found in this form.

3. *CD–I, or compact disk interactive.* This is a hybrid of (1) and (2), plus video images. In appearance it is the same as the regular CD. By the early 1990s the CD–I guaranteed a multimedia look. There are now several works, from encyclopedias to directories, which not only offer text but include pictures and, in some cases, sound. Furthermore, these can be had at reasonable prices from a low of just under $100 to from $400 to $800 for general encyclopedias. One example: Microsoft Bookshelf offers on one disk the entire contents of *The American Heritage Dictionary, Roget's Thesaurus,* Bartlett's *Familiar Quotations,* the *World Almanac,* the *Chicago Manual of Style,* a spelling checker, the *United States Zip Code Directory* and several other works. The cost is $295, somewhat higher than the printed works, but then the bound versions don't allow one to summon to the screen a particular problem or question for solution, and finding information tends to be much slower than with the CD.

A more impressive, and soon to be common, reference combination on CD-ROM is suggested by R. R. Bowker's *Children's Reference Plus* and *Library Reference Plus.* Essentially, this is the packaging of a group of related materials on a single CD-ROM which is updated once each year. Each features related resources. For example, the children's CD-ROM includes, among other items, *Children's Books in Print,* children's periodicals from *Ulrich's International Periodical Directory,* videos, book reviews, evaluative listings, activity books, and professional resources. One is able to locate and cross-check juvenile materials from titles to price to the precise item suited for a 4-year-old. The cost is $600. The adult package is much the same but, of course, with adult bibliographical material. Here the cost is $700.

There are many advantages to packing data into a small disk, not the least of which is convenience, speed, and ease of use. (Other advantages will be discussed in detail later and throughout this text.) There are drawbacks, too. The first and foremost is cost, although there is every reason to think that today's $300 to $995 reference work in this form will be priced considerably lower by the turn of the century, as will the equipment necessary to operate the disk.

The ramifications of CD-ROM, and variations on the technology which are sure to appear soon, are mind-boggling. One can, for example, see a complete reference library the size of the one at the Library of Congress in medium-size to large libraries throughout the United States, Canada, and the rest of the world. And all this would occupy the same space that is now devoted to small, inadequate reference collections. There is the distinct possibility that CD-ROM will be a part of the home library and that it will certainly play a major role in industry and government.

4. *Multimedia* In addition to the advantage of storage and retrieval of data, one enters the 1990s with the promise of augmenting print with sound and pictures, i.e., multimedia which is rapidly becoming available on CD-ROM. There is a future for the much-abused video-disc and its related formats, which offer numerous dimensions to heretofore conventional reference works. For example, one sits at the computer and asks by computer or vocal command for information on lemons. Not only does the printed history and future of the lemon appear on the screen—and/or is printed out next to the computer—but one is offered a high-quality photograph of a lemon as well as voice-over description of the lemon grower's problems. If carried a step further, one may watch a movie of how lemons are harvested and sent to market.

The multimedia approach will wed known technologies such as print, the computer, the television screen, and audio. What makes it truly remarkable is that one may search through masses of information for a look/read/hear aspect of only one small item. Subjects for search can range from the theory of evolution to a sketch of the world's fastest backward talker. Nothing is too sublime or ridiculous—nothing too arcane or difficult.

The value of this in terms of reference services is evident when applied only to encyclopedias which offer just such paths to information. Other reference works are sure to follow.

5. *Online* The online database is information transferred to magnetic tape or its technological equivalent and "read" by being mounted on a large, expensive mainframe computer. The library accesses the database using a phone line, a modem, a microcomputer, a monitor, and/or a printer. The process explains the term *online,* which means that the librarian is, via the online wires, directly in communication with the computer's database which can be as little as a few miles or as far as a continent away.

There are three advantages to this system. First the computer can store an unlimited amount of information and, more important, can make it readily available to the library in a matter of seconds.

Second, it can search with lightning speed. By contrast while CD-ROM may hold an impressive amount of information, it is still only a tiny part of the capacity of a mainframe computer. And retrieval from CD-ROM, while rapid enough, is much slower than online.

The third advantage of online is that material may be added to the database anytime, by the minute. Normally, additions are made every few days or once a week.

Conversely, CD-ROMs are updated monthly, quarterly, or only once a year. They might be updated more frequently, but the cost, at least as of now, would be prohibitive. Thus, for rapid access to current information, there is nothing to compare with online database searching.

The initial cost of CD-ROM may be more expensive than online, but a minute-by-minute CD-ROM search is cheaper. Once the equipment is in place, one may search for hours at no additional cost. This is its major advantage, particularly when used by laypersons. Also, it is less complex than the online search.

The ideal is to combine a CD-ROM and online search: One may take as much time as necessary to find retrospective material on the CD-ROM, as well as to establish a basic retrieval pattern. Given the data from the CD-ROM, one then switches over, on the same terminal, to the online version of the database. The primary benefit of this is that the most recent entries to a database—usually too new to be included on a monthly, quarterly, or annual CD-ROM—are searchable online. Several services now offer such a combination.

These database forms hardly exhaust the possibilities. One can imagine in the next decade disks or other formats which will hold even more data at less cost. There are videodisks which are coming into their own, and the possibilities are seemingly limitless.

Full-Text Presentation

The real technological revolution of the 1990s will be the increased availability of the full text of the article, book, or report at the computer terminal. This has been available in the past with microfilm, but accessing is far from easy. At the computer one will simply press a key and the text of the article(s) will be available to read on the screen and can be printed out.

While full text has been available online, more and more will be available on CD-ROM. University Microfilms International, for example, allows the librarian or client to search its *Periodical Abstracts Index* for necessary citations to articles. Then one can turn to the companion *General Periodicals Ondisc* to see the article(s). Almost all urban newspapers may be viewed in this fashion, as may several general encyclopedias and reference works. The time is near when most basic reference works will be so available.

There are a few drawbacks to full-text presentation: Cost is sometimes prohibitive (up to $20,000 on CD-ROM for index and full text for a single year). Not all the magazine and book indexes in a single index are available in full text. Multiple CD-ROM disks are required to search retrospectively. There are other technological problems as well as cost considerations.

A real question is just how much is put on the disk. If the number of magazines available in full text is about half those indexed by a single system, can the coverage of the full-text issues really be that complete? Most are not. Producers tend to be selective, using only relevant articles and rarely smaller, shorter articles.

Currency is a major headache. While many newspapers are available within hours online in full text, many of the CD-ROM versions are a month or more behind. The full text of a magazine may be several months behind, in lock step with the CD-ROM index, which can be issued monthly or quarterly.

Aside from indexes and bibliographies which require up-to-the-minute citations, the field for CD-ROM full text is literally unlimited. At least three general encyclopedias (*Academic American, Compton's* and *World Book*) are available on CD-ROM at slightly more than the printed version. Numerous directories are on CD-ROM as are other guides and reference aids. Two examples: *Ulrich's International Periodical Directory* and *Webster's Ninth New Collegiate Dictionary*.

There is promise that hard-to-locate, out-of-print nonfiction and novels will be available in this format. An excellent example: the Library of America has teemed up with Electronic Text Corporation to put most of its works both on videotape and on CD-ROM. A single disk contains 12 thick volumes of print ranging from Willa Cather's early novels and stories to Herman Melville's *Redburn, White-Jacket*, and, yes, *Moby Dick*. All this is on one disk for $500.

Picture-Perfect[6]

A major drawback to online and CD-ROM databases has been a lack of ability to re-create photographs and other forms of illustration.

---

[6]"Picture Perfect Images," *The New York Times*, Nov. 12, 1989, p. D5. See also "Compact Discs Go Visual," *7 Days*, Feb. 7, 1990. Interactive discs (music, sound, visual) are slowly coming into the market. One of the first is *Treasures of the Smithsonian*,

Line drawings, graphs, and related illustrative material have been duplicated with success, but until the close of the 1980s, reproducing the sophisticated graphics appearing in encyclopedias and magazines was not possible.

Today this is changing. *Compton's* and the *Academic American*, for example, now offer a CD-ROM with full illustrations, and there are other reference works which increasingly have modified, or will modify, CD-ROM to include pictures.

Online and the crude computer images of the 1980s are giving way to the creation of images as realistic as photographs. Known as *rendering*, this process has been available only with mainframe computers. But by the mid-1990s it is predicted that it will be a standard feature of most desktop computers. The addition of a circuit board can turn the otherwise pictureless home computer into a source which can generate photolike images.

Given these developments, there is reason to think that the full text available online and on CD-ROM will include illustrations in the near future. Furthermore, all these enhancements are part of a broader movement toward multimedia computing in which images and sound appear on the screen in addition to words, numbers, and illustrations.

Software[7]

The computer's memory is useless without software, i.e., the program of instructions which allows the user to access the database through online searching and word processing. Each so-called application software program performs specific tasks. They can be purchased, at a cost which may be quite high, from various publishers, much as books or periodicals are purchased. This "prewritten application software" has fairly well replaced the earlier programs developed by individual users. One no longer must master the rudiments of programming language, any more than one had to learn how to print in order to read a book: one simply bought the book. Today one simply buys the program.

---

which lets one see 300 exhibits accompanied by a flow of narration. Many more are planned. Again, the problem: first-generation compact disk-interactive players cost over $1000. However, in time, the cost will come down.

[7]See vol. 2 where there is a survey of the various guides to hardware and software.

SEARCHING WITH THE COMPUTER[8]

There are two basic types of searches at a computer. The first is the familiar ready-reference type. The second is the search or research query which requires a good deal of information on the part of the user.

In the past, the search-and-research query has been the most used, and it continues to require the most skill. Here one may be looking, say, for everything on radon gas published over the past six months, or only in the United States, or only by the government, or only on radon gas in residential communities etc. Using print sources is difficult enough, but to use online or CD-ROM requires added skills.

CD-ROM or online search begins with the librarian, or user, sitting down at a terminal and keyboard which is connected to the database. In order to get information from the database the librarian must know a series of commands which allow one to find citations, i.e., needed information. The commands are usually typed. Subject terms and author names are the primary keys to unlocking or retrieving data. There are subtle variations, and the actual search can be a complicated procedure.

When one finds what is needed, a command is typed to view citations or to have them printed out. If the sample is satisfactory, one may then ask for more citations; if it is not satisfactory, one can switch tactics and try a new search pattern.

While the technology of the process is mind-boggling, the actual search and the end result are much the same as those carried on in a traditional way at the reference desk. The two essential differences are that the user gets information not from a printed source, but from data consigned to a computer's memory and that it uses electronics, rather than a hand turning a page, to find the necessary data. Also, it requires mastering searching skills which, while much the same in principle to manual searches, differ in the command structures.

The typical point of entry into any printed reference work is usually (but not always) subject, author, or less frequently, title. Not so with a computer-assisted search. Here one may search by all of these, *plus.* The plus is important because the computer allows one to look for a key word in the text of an abstract, in a title, or even in the full text of the article or book.

---

[8]See vol. 2 for a detailed explanation of both the online and manual search.

For example, a cataloger gives only one subject heading to the article on the history of women in Rome. (The title of the article is "The Mother in Rome as a Manager.") The computer permits one to search the title by key words such as "women," "Rome," "mother," "manager," and any other important word which may be found in the title or any major word in the text of the article itself. All the points of entry ensure that one is no longer confined to a single subject heading, as valuable as that may be, or the author or title. Other tags or points of departure can be language, date, publication, etc. Finally, one can combine these to limit or expand a search.

Currency is another plus because while the printed volumes are usually produced from a modified machine-readable database, the actual database may be ready for delivery weeks or months before the printed version. The time elapsed between indexing and the published index is a constant problem, which can be overcome with the database. For example, *The New York Times Index*, which in printed form is two or three months behind, may be updated daily and weekly online.

COMPUTER-SEARCHING PROBLEMS

As with any technology, there are numerous difficulties with the online or CD-ROM and company search. The basic three are: (1) cost, (2) lack of standardization, and (3) complexity of searching.

The primary drawback for a computer search is the cost. Most librarians think the cost of a computer search is higher than the manual print search. There are so many variables that it is difficult to generalize, but most online searches cost a minimum of $1 per minute. Between the equipment and the database disks, the cost of installation of a CD-ROM setup will be from $4000 to $6000. (After the equipment is purchased, there is an annual cost of disks which may be from $500 to $1400, with a low of only $100 and a high of close to $20,000.)

An example can be found in *The Readers' Guide to Periodical Literature* which is available both online and on CD-ROM directly from the publisher. A subscription to *Readers' Guide* includes the disk, plus quarterly cumulative updates. The cost is $1095 a year, compared with about $120 for the printed version and about $35 an hour online. The opening date for searching the *Guide* is January 1983, both on CD-ROM and online. Retrospective searches must be done with the print volumes.

Another example: *The Physicians' Desk Reference,* or *PDR,* is in the $40 price range for the printed volume which gives information on 3000 pharmaceuticals. Add three equally reasonably priced companion printed volumes, put all four on a CD-ROM and promise two updates. The price is now $595 from the same publisher.

One may argue that the added cost is saved in the time it takes a physician to search for an item, which may well be true, but here we are considering only the basic expenses. And in most cases the printed work tends to be less costly than either CD-ROM, online, or any other form.

There is no absolute saving between CD-ROM and online. Individual searches may cost less with CD-ROM, but the initial purchase and continuing maintenance of the system are likely to cost more, possibly much more, than for online services.

Online costs include the many variables from the monthly charges for the telephone line to connect terminal to database, the hourly use charges, and the cost for citations printed and/or displayed. These average, if an average is at all possible, from about $15 an hour for off-hour or government databases to about $65 an hour. Some cost much more, particularly those scientific databases which can run to over $300 an hour.

What is likely to happen to the cost of computer-assisted searching in the decade ahead? It depends. If the producers of the various services and hardware decide to make an all-out drive to capture a layperson audience, in they decide mass production is in order, then prices are going to come down drastically. This seems true particularly of CD-ROMs. The hourly cost could be lowered to a relatively few dollars, and the cost of the equipment needed to search could be lowered as well. A case in point is *Compton's Encyclopedia,* which on CD-ROM costs only about $100 more to purchase than the in-print version at $895. If the drive to operate the disk could be made less expensive, one could see any wise customer selecting the disk rather than the in-print version.

Thus, if a concerted effort is made by CD-ROM producers to tap the millions in the home market, the price will be lowered. If producers determine that this market does not exist or that it is not large enough, then prices are likely to remain steady or even to increase. Why? Because the primary purchase point will be the library, which, while important, does not offer a very broad economic base.

Much the same may happen for online searching, and the various layperson databases and vendors have shown that there are some lay customers out there. However, many people in the field, including this author, doubt that there are enough to substantially cut rates. For the future, mass production and lower prices are with CD-ROM or its equivalent.

Lack of Standardization

While differing in particulars, the basic organization and retrieval apparatus for most groups of printed reference works may be mastered quickly. The majority of encyclopedias, for example, have alphabetical indexes, and most bibliographies are arranged by title, author, and subject. Unfortunately, this standard approach is foreign to databases. There is no standard, no one single method of digging information out of all databases.

Each database distributor offers a separate program which must be mastered in order to use the system. Furthermore, once the basic commands are understood, then the user has to appreciate that each of the databases has peculiar retrieval problems. For example, on one database an author may be found with one command, on another it will require two, three, or even four commands.

Asked what are the worst problem areas in using databases, reference librarians inevitably point to the necessity for mastering multiple retrieval languages, learning about new databases, and learning the unique features of each database. The consequence of using such a vast number and variety of unique retrieval commands is somewhat predictable. Librarians, and particularly laypersons, who have become familiar with the command structure of one type of CD-ROM or online search tend to use that work first, and often do not go any further, although there may be better databases to search. At best the user may confine searches only to several databases in the single subject area.

What is really needed to make all the databases potentially useful is a common command language, a single set of standards. Master one system and you have mastered them all. A partial answer is found in the gateway front-end software systems.

Gateway Front-End Software

Since 1980 a subcommittee of the National Information Standards Organization has attempted to create a common command language to ease the problem facing searchers of more than one system.[9] Full implementation of the common command language will

[9]Margaret Morrison, "The NISO Common Command Language," *Online,* July 1989, pp. 46–52.

require cooperation from vendors, publishers, and others, but in the meantime there are several alternatives.

These are the alternatives offered by gateway, or front-end software. (This is sometimes called *end user software*, or *user friendly software*.) The purpose is to offer a common command structure which makes it possible, among other things, to search a number of databases without learning the codes for each. While primarily designed for laypersons, many of the systems are employed by librarians to overcome the standardization problem.

Using the menu approach, the systems ask and answer questions which take the user step by step from the problem to the solution. There are now numerous examples of online menu systems, and all the major vendors offer them, usually at a minimum cost.

EasyNet is the most ambitious of the services. Introduced in 1984, it provides a key to the basic systems. It offers a single access point to close to 1000 databases.[10]

Hypertext is another aid for the lay and professional searcher. The term *hypertext* is a synonym for linking similar ideas. Hypertext software connects related ideas in a database, and may permit cross-database searching. It allows, for example, the searcher to ramble through a CD-ROM encyclopedia looking not only for *Moby Dick*, itself, but also for any other factors that might be related to the novel, such as the influence of the nineteenth-century whaling industry, the religious background of the time, and even such minutiae as the type and size of boats that were in use. This type of extensive search can sometimes be combined with graphics as well as voice-over explanations.[11]

The Ultimate Solution

Natural-voice commands or instructions which will activate the computer-searching databases seems the ultimate answer to complex

---

[10]Mick O'Leary, "EasyNet Review cited . . ." *Online*, September 1988, pp. 22–30; See also Emily Fayen's "The Answer Machine," in the same issue, pp. 13–21; and "Carol Tenopir, "A Common Command Language," *Library Journal*, May 1, 1989, pp. 56–57. EasyNet in other forms, but from the same company, is called Alanet Einstein, Easy Search, InfoMaster, IQuest, and a half dozen other names and acronyms.

[11]For a detailed explanation of Hypertext see Myke Gluck *Hypercard, Hypertext and Hypermedia for Libraries and Media Centers.* Englewood, CO: Libraries Unlimited, 1990. There are thousands of uses for such software, including literary criticism where a database stores the various forms of a poet's work, as well as scattered comments and texts. "This database would be accessed through Hypertext programs which would enable the reader to reconstruct any state of any particular text." "Which Yeats Edition," *The Times Literary Supplement*, May 11–17, 1990, p. 494.

searches and confusing standards. At this writing, such a development is still a few years off, but a bridge is offered by "windows of opportunity" which are simply on-screen symbols matched by lists of commands. This menu approach, familiar to MAC and IBM PC users, allows one to use a mouse to move from one command to another. The user simply points the mouse at a picture representing the necessary command which is shown on the computer screen. She presses a button on the mouse to execute her needs. In present nongraphical or character-based systems, the user must memorize and type in many lines of sometimes confusing codes.

Another shortcut will be a system which permits one to use a pen or pencil rather than a keyboard. So-called notepad computers will soon be available. These are lightweight machines that can be operated with penlike styluses, using a flat screen as the writing surface.

There is a need to make software available in a wide variety of formats, from voice to styluses, that can search all databases. The arrival and anticipated success of advanced systems are still years away, but their beginnings are with us today.

DATABASE VENDORS

When one searches online, the cost of the search is billed to the user by a vendor, a private publisher, or the government. It all depends on who has jurisdiction over the database(s) being searched. In the case of CD-ROM, the disk is purchased from the publisher of the printed version or from a second party who is acting for the publisher.

Online Vendors

An online vendor, as the middle person between the library and the database, supplies the larger, more powerful computer, software, and other necessary elements for a search. The library, or individual, pays the vendor for using the system. Individual vendors offer access to scores, even hundreds of different databases.

The amount of payment varies, but usually is based on a set rate per hour of use, and a fee based on the amount of information viewed and/or printed out.

There are over 600 vendors in the world today. In the United States, the two major commercial vendors for general reference services are DIALOG and Maxwell Online. (The latter is owned by

Macmillan and is the result of combining **BRS** and **ORBIT** under a new ownership in 1989.)[12] DIALOG, with over 500 databases, offers a wide spectrum of interests, and there is little subject matter which cannot be found via the system. Maxwell with some 300 databases concentrates on scientific, technical, and medical databases.

Three additional vendors dominate the library information market: the government-owned National Library of Medicine's Medline and more than two-dozen related services; Mead-Data Central with NEXIS and LEXIS; and the legal databases from West Publishing Company, particularly Westlaw. A sixth is Wilsonline from The H. W. Wilson Company.

These same vendors offer lower rates for the use of many, although not all, of the databases by home computers after peak hours. DIALOG, for example, has Knowledge Index which offers basic databases at a low hourly connect rate for use by laypersons. Compuserve and The Source are only two of several independent types of the same service.

Aside from vendors, the next large group of database suppliers are individual publishers. Why, they argue, go through a vendor? Why not use your own mainframe computer and utilize our services? An example of an independent publisher who serves the library with the databases and eliminates the vendor is The H. W. Wilson Company. Many of the most heavily used indexes in the library are those published by this company. Of the some thirty services, by far the most familiar is *The Readers' Guide to Periodical Literature.*

Government is in a category by itself. One may either buy the database directly from the government for use on one's own mainframe computer, or (and this is the more usual case with librarians) access the government database through a vendor. A government

---

[12]In the world of vendors it sometimes is difficult to say who owns what. For example, DIALOG was connected with the Lockheed Corporation from the beginning, but by 1989 had been sold (for over $350 million) to the newspaper chain, Knight Ridder. The parent company offers numerous databases such as Vu/TEXT with over 30 newspapers in full text. See what is now a historical brief study of the subject: Carol Tenopir, "Who Owns What?" *Library Journal,* April 1, 1989, p. 65–66. And "Considerations on the Merger," *RQ,* Fall 1989, pp. 113–119. Viewpoints of various librarians.

The leading online information companies in terms of sales and subscribers are: (1) Mead Data Corporation (LEXIS, NEXIS, etc.) 210,000 subscribers with sales of $307.5 million; (2) DIALOG, i.e., Knight Ridder, 310,000 subscribers, sales of $113 million; (3) Compuserve, a home service owned by H & R Block with 489,000 subscribers and revenues of $86.5 million; and Dow-Jones with 310,000 subscribers and sales of $60 million. Maxwell's interests are not shown. The *Wall Street Journal,* Aug. 2, 1989, p. B1.

agency such as the National Library of Medicine offers direct access to a file, but most use is made of the medical file through a vendor.

Access may be provided to a library by other means by joining a bibliographic utility or local network consortium which provides such services.

Another twist was introduced to the vendor scene in 1988, and promises to be a major consideration in the 1990s. The nation's telephone companies for the first time may now offer online services to customers. At this writing the companies still cannot offer information products as such, but they can provide the link as distributor or vendor.

CD-ROM

It is worth emphasizing again that once the equipment and the CD-ROM disk(s) is purchased, there is no added cost for searching. One may search hour after hour at the same expenditure as for one minute. This contrasts sharply with the practice of subscribing with an online vendor who charges, literally, minute by minute for search.

Disks of various services may be purchased from concerns such as Silver Platter, by 1991 the leading publisher of CD-ROMs, with over 30 different services. The U.S. government, from the Department of Commerce to the Library of Congress, offers CD-ROM. The online vendors are moving into CD-ROMs as well. DIALOG, for example, offers many of its indexes both online and on CD-ROM. The combination of online/CD-ROM searches, as well as sophisticated software, is a leading sales boast of DIALOG.

Guides to sources are considered in the second volume of this text. At the turn of the 1990s there were under 1000 CD-ROMs available in reference services, as compared to close to 5000 online databases. In the years to come, CD-ROM is likely to have many more disks.

Evaluation of Databases[13]

Effective evaluation of databases depends on methods similar to those employed for evaluating printed works. Purpose, authority,

---

[13]See J. A. Large "Evaluating Online and CD-ROM Reference Sources," *Journal of Librarianship*, April 1989, pp. 87–108. While evaluation of all formats of reference sources follows a set pattern, there are differences for computer sources. These

and scope (as considered, often with individual titles, in the first chapter of this text) are to be tested. However, because of the lack of standardization in their preparation, it is even more important to evaluate databases than their print versions.

There are additional considerations. One must evaluate the various formats for the storage of the material in the database. How is the data accessed? Does it meet the specific needs of the average user? How is the work to be updated and how often? What hardware and software is necessary to make use of the database to its fullest?

One must also size up the comparative costs of the different vendors, various formats, and individual database charges against the speed and efficiency of the computer search. One should also scrutinize pricing policies.

THE FUTURE OF AUTOMATION AND REFERENCE SERVICE

Over the past forty years, the experts on the future of libraries generally have been no more accurate than stock brokers, horse experts and weather forecasters. For example, it was predicted that today's society would be a paperless society with all of us reading the newspaper on a computer screen and getting our books on CD-ROM or equivalent. But the reality is that the production of paper has increased and so has the number of books.[14]

Still, it is entertaining and sometimes instructive to try to predict the outcome of the coming years. Here are some of today's common predictions (probably to be trusted only as much as those of the past):

1. In the future there will be less dependence on the library. The individual may tap information sources at home by means of a computer or whatever new technology is around the corner. Although this has been a theme for many years, library use, if anything, seems to have increased. Why?
   a. The cost of online, CD-ROM, etc., is too high for most

differences are spelled out here in enough detail to allow the beginner to appreciate what is involved with evaluation and to better understand the technologies. The article is extremely clear and well written. See, too, the second volume of this text for more on the evaluation of machine-readable records.

[14]Lawrence Fisher, "Paperless Office Evolves with Paper, but Less of It." *The New York Times,* July 7, 1990, pp. 1–30. "Fifty-five million printers and billions of reams of paper (since 1980), the paperless office is still an elusive goal. The moment you put a computer in an office you breed paper." Libraries find this true equally at reference desks.

people. Moreover, they can get the same information at less cost from the library. (Fees, to be sure, often are charged, but they are not as high as home-use charges).

b. Computer searching is not easy. An expert can find data in a sixth of the time (and at less cost) than a lay user. Also, the librarian can differentiate between what is useful and what is not, thus saving the user considerable time and effort. (The exception is when a subject expert searches a database who may be equal in approach to the librarian; but the number of experts is small when compared to the general public.)

c. The most important reason the use of the library will continue to increase is often forgotten because of the technology mania. Many books and magazines are there not only for information and education but simply for fun. Most people read for amusement and aesthetic reasons, or both.

2. Information needs are great and getting greater. They are equally becoming more complex. The result is that the use of the trained specialist in the library is likely to increase, not decrease. More expert reference librarians are going to be needed, not fewer, and this need will be so for all types and sizes of libraries.[15]

3. The cost of gathering information and making it available is growing, too. Sooner than most people expect, the public is going to have to decide whether or not it wants to spend money on information (i.e., on libraries). One hopes that the decision will be a wise one, in spite of the fact that those who have made a living betting on the "dumbing" of America are pessimistic. However, the good news is that librarians are now in greater demand, they are becoming more professional, and in time they will be better paid than ever before.

4. The increased use of databases, and related items for desktop publishing means: (*a*) more and more individualized journals and/or (*b*) access to the increased number of articles using only an online or optical disk type of approach.

---

[15]See for example: Carol Tenopir, "Online Information Anxiety," *Library Journal*, August 1990, p. 65. In her summary of Richard Wurman's *Information Anxiety* (New York: Doubleday, 1989), Ms. Tenopir spells out the problems involved due to too much information and too few librarians; and Diane J. Cimballa, "The Scholarly Information Center: An Organizational Model," *College & Research Libraries*, September 1987, pp. 393–398; and David Lewis, "Inventing the Electronic University," Ibid., July 1988, pp. 291–304.

5. Increased networking and cooperation between libraries and within the library community mean that the distinction between the library and other parts of a university, for example, will rapidly disappear.

   The real challenge of networking is beyond the immediate community and is worldwide. For example, there are plans for a European-managed data network involving all the countries in the 1992 European Market. The increasing links across national boundaries can only mean greater speed access and reliability for online searchers.

   Networking among individuals will increase taking the place of letters, phone calls, and other forms of communication. The library will be part of this informal/formal networking scheme.[16]

6. More emphasis will be placed on new forms of imaging, i.e., making electronic copies of physical documents. Microform will not fade away entirely, but its uses will be more limited. In its place will be online documents, CD-ROM, and similar technologies.

7. Specific standards will be developed for software and other guides to electronic information which will make it possible to turn from one system to another without memorizing a whole new set of instructions. Furthermore, software utilizing "windows" will allow access across the database standards, allowing one to search by simply pointing at on-screen symbols which will be the same for all systems.

. . . And

Books, periodicals, CD-ROM, online, and floppy disks all have their place. It is unlikely that one is going to totally replace the other. Anyone even vaguely familiar with the history of recorded language can shrug off the notion that the printed book will be replaced by an electronic or optical system. Technocrats are fond of sounding the death knell for the printed word. Do not believe them. They have been celebrating the dirge for the past twenty or thirty years. Meanwhile, the number of books produced in America has grown from around 20,000 per year to over 50,000 per year.

[16]"Some Computer Conversation . . ." *The New York Times*, May 13, 1990, p. A1, 20. The growth of computer networks is changing the way Americans work, find friends, and seek information.

SUGGESTED READING

Beiser, Karl, "Database Software for the 1990s," *Database,* June 1990, p. 20. By the end of the decade almost everyone will have access to information via a computer terminal. The hardware and software will be less expensive than today. That's the opinion of the author who concludes: "Selection of software will become more difficult, but also far more enjoyable."

"CD-ROM Issue," *Library Journal,* Feb. 1, 1990, pp. 45–60. In a series of short articles one is given a round-trip understanding of CD-ROM and its place in the library and reference services. Among the authors is Nancy Melin Nelson who gives a fine overview of products available. See, too, Kim Schultz and Kristine Salomon's article, "End Users Respond to CD-ROM."

"Contemporary Technology in Libraries," *Library Trends,* Winter 1989. Ably edited by Beth Paskoff, here is expert advice on everything from an overview of library automation (Bill Saffady) to electronic mail (Becki Whitaker) and F. W. Lancaster's favorite subject, electronic publishing. The information is not likely to date soon, and the issue offers a fine, detailed, easy-to-understand overview of the subject.

Desmarais, Norman, *The Librarian's CD-ROM Handbook.* Westport, CT: Meckler Corp., 1989. While the first five chapters discuss how to select hardware and discs for the appropriate library need, the largest section (pp. 103–140) discusses the basic CD-ROMs available for reference work. These are arranged by subject from business to miscellaneous. While some of this is sure to date, the general view is accurate enough and the overall presentation simple enough to follow. A good beginning book for anyone.

Eaton, Nancy, et al., *CD-ROM and Other Optical Information Systems.* Phoenix, AZ: Oryx, 1989. This is an illustrated tutorial, by a number of experts, on the basics of CD-ROM and other optical disc forms. Written for the beginner, it is a good place to find basic data on all aspects of the issue from the technical to the fiscal.

Foulds, M. S., and L. R. Foulds, "Librarians' Reaction to CD-ROM," *CD-ROM Librarian,* January 1991, pp. 10–14. This is a survey of librarians in the United Kingdom, but much of what was found holds true for North America, i.e., "The staff and patrons . . . embrace CD-ROM technology for both acquisitions and reference as complementary to online." See too, in the same issue (pp. 15–23), a Canadian study on 1990s' use of CD-ROMs.

Glossbrenner, Alfred, *The Complete Handbook of Personal Computer Communication,* 3d ed. New York: St. Martin's Press, 1990. Although written for the layperson, this is an excellent introduction to online standbys from DIALOG to NEXIS. The first part of the book gives a comprehensive overview of the computer which is as easy to follow as it is useful, particularly for beginners.

Hawkins, William J. "CD Libraries: New Power for Home PCs," *Popular Science,* May 1990, pp. 75–78. Complete with illustrations, this is by far the easiest to understand explanation of CD-ROM and family. The article gives details on how CD-ROMs may be used at home, with specific examples. Much of the information, particularly on encyclopedias, is applicable to libraries.

Hunter, Margaret, "Writers Score with Databases," *Folio,* May 1989, pp. 128–135. This is a crash course in how computers are used, not only by writers but by laypersons and librarians. The explanation is simple, direct, and accurate. It is a good beginning point for anyone who is totally unfamiliar with the subject.

Martin, Susan, "Information Technology and Libraries: Toward the Year 2000," *College & Research Libraries*, July 1989, pp. 397-405. The executive director of the National Commission on Libraries gives an easy-to-understand view of current and promised technology which will influence the library and reference services. Most bases are touched from CD-ROM and networking to telefacsimile and the image of the library. A good beginning point for anyone who is curious about the subject.

Miller, Karl, "Music Software," *Notes*, September, 1990, pp. 91–97. In this review of multimedia approaches to Beethoven and Mozart, the University of Texas librarian suggests the numerous aspects of not only the two software packages considered but multimedia in general. He stresses how the media may be employed in teaching and, indirectly, in reference work. Along the way he sets up criteria which might be employed to evaluate any multimedia software.

Miller, William, and Bonnie Gratch, "Making Connections: Computerized Reference Services and People," *Library Trends*, Spring 1989, pp. 387–401. An excellent overview of what the authors call the "technology express: up to 1990." They raise the usual questions about the role of the librarian in the new period of computerized reference services, and suggest a few answers. They say they only know, finally, that the new technologies in reference increase the need for new skills. *Note:* The whole issue of *Library Trends* is devoted to "The human response to library automation," and many of the articles other than that by Miller and Gratch will interest reference librarians.

O'Leary, Mick, "Local Online," *Online*, January 1990, p. 15; March 1990, p. 20. In this two-part article the author offers a current new definition of online which includes CD-ROM and other access technologies. The first article describes the situation, and the second details how the changes have affected how librarians and users find answers to questions.

Patton, Phil, "Steve Jobs . . ." *The New York Times Magazine*, Aug. 6, 1989, p. 23. A discussion of the wonder child of the computer at home and in the office, of the man who promises to put information at the fingertips of anyone with the price of a computer. The popular article goes a long way to explain the competition involved in the home/business information market for computers.

Quint, Barbara, "From the Editor—Numbers," *Database Searcher*, April 1990, pp. 4–5. A brief discussion of online costs and why they are too high. The editor explains the situation in terms anyone can understand. And the high charges all add up to greed.

Steig, Margaret, "*Technology and the Concept of Reference*," Library Journal, April 15, 1990, pp. 45–49. The argument is that no matter how easy it may be to retrieve masses of information—from online, CD-ROM, etc.—a librarian is still required to understand the problem. Furthermore, the librarian is necessary to help the patron—"to direct him to the best source, help him use it, and perhaps to interpret and clarify what he finds." The concepts of service and technology are clearly discussed. A good introductory article for almost anyone.

Stewart, Linda, et al., *Public Access CD-ROMs in Libraries: Case Studies*. Westport, CT: Meckler, 1990. After a discussion of general library experience with CD-ROMs used by the public, the editors examine six academic, two school, one public, and three medical and health science libraries. Beyond that, the selected features of various CD-ROM stations are considered for additional libraries. It is an excellent guide for the beginner as well as the librarian planning to purchase CD-ROMs.

Tenopir, Carol, "The Impact of CD-ROM on Online, "*Library Journal,* February 1, 1991, pp. 61–62. Going into the 1990s, the biggest question in reference services is whether or not CD-ROM will replace online searching in most, if not all, libraries. The expert thinks not, although the heavy use of CD-ROM will shape the services (and costs) of online in the future.

PART II
INFORMATION: CONTROL AND ACCESS

CHAPTER THREE
INTRODUCTION TO
BIBLIOGRAPHY

American publishers issue approximately 40,000 to 50,000 books each year. About the same number are published in England and in some western European countries. The so-called third-world nations do not have such a vigorous publishing program, but they nevertheless add to the international total. The result is a flood of hundreds of thousands of new titles. Add to this deluge of information articles in more than 120,000 periodicals, plus reports, studies, audiovisual materials, software programs, movies, recordings etc., and one gets a graphic idea of what is meant by information overload.

The problem this creates is not new: How does one retrieve from this growing mass of data the precise information needed to solve a particular need? The answer, if only in part, lies in using the bibliography. Whether in printed form, or online, or on CD-ROM, the bibliography gives the vital facts needed to locate X or Y item.

In a broader sense, the bibliography brings order out of chaos. The frightening thing about many libraries is that there appears to be too much of everything. How can one person even imagine the contents of a small portion of this mass of information, delight, and frustration? A partial answer to the query, as well as a method of at least controlling the fear of abundance, is the bibliography.

There are many definitions of bibliography, but no single definition is suitable for all situations. To most people, a *bibliography* is "a list of books." Experts give it a different meaning: the critical and historical study of printed books. In France, particularly during the late eighteenth century, the term emerged as a form of library science, i.e., the knowledge and the theory of book lists. The Americans and the British now tend to divide it into critical, analytical, and historical designations, as differentiated from a simple listing. The definition problem is not likely to be resolved, but for most purposes it is enough to say that when Americans are talking about bibliography they are concerned with the study of books and lists of books or other materials.

A bibliography tells you, among other things, who is the author of a book, who published it and where, when it was published, and how much it will cost to purchase, in either hardback, paperbound, or even another form such as CD-ROM.

Once an item is located in the catalog or bibliography, the user wants to know (1) whether it is in the library and available to be read or (2) if not in the library, whether it is on order or can be obtained via interlibrary loan. The ideal catalog answers all but one of these queries. Consultation will be necessary with a librarian to know whether it can be obtained via interlibrary loan.

Bibliographies are not necessarily confined to books. They may list, too, other forms of communication from films and recordings to computer software and photographs. A bibliography of, say, railroads could well include books about railroads as well as films and photographs of railroads.

If it is what is known as a *national* bibliography and/or a union list, it will tell you, too, which library has the book you need and will give enough information so it can be borrowed from that library.

Bibliography has assumed a major role because of technological developments. Online it is possible to literally view the holdings of not one, but thousands of libraries from the United States to Australia. The proliferation of information, and the ability to locate and acquire such data through bibliography is impressive. One should appreciate (1) how a bibliography is constructed, (2) how a bibliography can be used, and, possibly most important, (3) how to discover among thousands of items the dozen or so which will really assist the user.

SYSTEMATIC ENUMERATIVE BIBLIOGRAPHY

The average librarian, when speaking of bibliography, is probably referring to systematic enumerative bibliography, i.e., a list of books, films, or recordings. An effective bibliography needs several elements if it is to meet the need for control and access adequately.

Completeness. Through either a single bibliography or a combination of bibliographies, the librarian should have access to the complete records of all areas of interest, not only what is now available but also what has been published in the past, what is being published today and what is proposed for publication tomorrow. Also, the net should be broad enough to include the world, not only one nation's works.

Access to a Part. Normally the librarian is apt to think of bibliographies in terms of the whole unit—a book, periodical, manuscript, or the like. But an ideal bibliography should also be analytical, allowing the librarian to approach the specific unit in terms of the smallest part of a work.

Various Forms. Books are considered the main element of most bibliographies, but a comprehensive bibliographical tool will include all forms of published communication from reports and documents to the various types of machine-readable databases.

No bibliography or set of bibliographies has yet met all these needs. At best, a bibliography is a compromise between completeness, access to parts, and various forms.

With the bibliography ready at hand, how does the reference librarian use it on a day-to-day basis? Regardless of form, a bibliography is used primarily for three basic purposes: (1) to identify and verify, (2) to locate, and (3) to select.

Identification and Verification. The usual bibliography gives standard information similar to that found in most catalogs: author, title, edition (if other than a first edition), place of publication, a collation (i.e., number of pages, illustrations, size), and price. Another element added to many bibliographies is the International Standard Book Number, abbreviated as ISBN or simply SBN, which is employed by publishers to distinguish one title from another. The ISBN number usually is on the verso of the title page. A similar system, the International Standard Serial Number (ISSN) is employed to identify serials.

In seeking to identify or verify any of these elements, a librarian will turn to the proper bibliography, usually beginning with the general, such as *Books in Print* or *The National Union Catalog,* and moving to the particular, such as a bibliography in a narrow subject area.

Location. Location may be in terms of where the book is published, where it can be found in a library, or where it can be purchased.

Selection. The primary aim of a library is to build a useful collection to serve users. This objective presupposes selection from a vast number of possibilities. In order to assist the librarian, certain bibliographies indicate what is available in a given subject area, by a given author, in a given form, or in a form suitable for certain groups of readers. A bibliography may give an estimate of the potential use of the particular work for the needs of a reader.

Forms of Systematic Enumerative Bibliography: Universal Bibliography

A true "universal" bibliography would include everything published, issued, or pressed in the field of communications from the beginning through the present to the future. Such universality is today an impossible dream. In practice, the term is employed in a narrower sense. *Universality* generally means that a bibliography is not necessarily limited by time, territory, language, subject, or form. National library catalogs, some book dealers' catalogs, and auction catalogs are the nearest thing to a universal bibliography now available.

Ready access to the world's information is growing closer. If "complete" may never be realized, at least "almost complete" is close at hand. This will be accomplished by having online access to the national bibliographies, which, in turn, are exhaustive listings of information sources produced in one country, plus other nations as well. For example, the *National Union Catalog* from the Library of Congress offers access to millions of books, periodicals, recordings, films, and other materials. When combined with similar national bibliographies from England, Germany, and other world nations online, on CD-ROM, or in other forms, the dream of universal bibliography comes closer to realization.

> An international network has grown up in which magnetic tape versions of the records in current national bibliographies are already being made available to users across national boundaries. . . . [This enables] all potential users of documents to identify, locate and gain access to every document useful for their particular purpose. . . . The day of the published national bibliography is coming to an end, and

the day of the published international bibliography database will soon be here to take its place.[1]

The main problem remains, though, and that is how to ferret out the elusive works from equally elusive sources. One may claim that universal bibliography is a reality today, only to be frustrated by a country, region, or individual who refuses to methodically list what is issued. The day may come when the world, or most of the world, will recognize standard bibliographic procedures to allow for universal bibliography, but that probably is far in the future.

National and Trade Bibliographies[2]

These kinds of works are limited to materials published within a given country. They may be limited in scope to a section of the country, a city, or even a hamlet. For ease of use and convenience, national bibliographies normally are divided into even finer parts.

Time. This is a matter of listing works previously published, works being published, or works to be published. Such bibliographies are normally labeled as either retrospective or current.

Form. This classification may be in terms of bibliographical form: collections of works, monographs, components (e.g., essays, periodical articles, poems); physical form; books, databases, recordings, pamphlets, microfilm; or published and unpublished works (manuscripts, dissertations).

[1]P. R. Lewis, "The future of the national bibliography," *Library Association Record,* October 1987, pp. 516–520. See too: Pauline Cochrane, "Universal Bibliographic Control," *Library Resources & Technical Services,* October 1990, pp. 423–431. There is a "catch" to this vision of bibliographic paradise. UBC (universal bibliographic control) is of little value unless there equally is UAP (universal availability of publications.) Or as Lewis puts it (p. 516): "If the library world is seen as a huge, multi ethnic restaurant, UAP organizes the kitchens and UBC prepares the menus. The diners can only obtain the dishes of their choice by using menus; but if what is on the menu can't be produced from the kitchens, they cannot get their nourishment by eating the menus instead."

[2]*Trade* bibliography is often used synonymously with *national* bibliography. *Trade bibliography* refers to a bibliography issued for and usually by the booksellers and publishers of a particular nation. The emphasis of a trade bibliography is on basic purchasing data. Information for a trade bibliography is gathered from the publishers, and the individual item listed is *not* examined by the compiler of the trade bibliography. A *national bibliography,* which includes additional information (often complete cataloging data) is compiled by librarians. The data is taken directly from the item which is examined by the compiler. Result: national bibliographies are more complete and more accurate than trade bibliographies.

A typical national bibliography will set itself limits of time, form, and, obviously, origin. For example, *Books in Print* is limited to books available for purchase (time); it includes only printed books, both hardbound and paperback, and some monographs and series (form); and it is a trade bibliography, i.e., issued by a commercial organization (origin). There is no limit to the possible subdivisions of national bibliography.

A distinction must be made between national bibliography and national library catalogs. A *national bibliography* often is the product of the government and is an effort to include everything published within the boundaries of that nation. An example is the *British National Bibliography,* which, since 1950, has listed and described on a weekly basis every new work published in Great Britain. The important limitation is that the work must be published in Great Britain. Nothing else is included. A national catalog considerably broadens the scope.

A *national library catalog,* such as our United States *National Union Catalog,* lists all works which are cataloged by the Library of Congress and other member libraries of the system. A national bibliography of this type normally has many books not published in the country of origin. The NUC, for example, lists Chinese, French, Russian, and other foreign language titles as long as they have been cataloged.

Subject Bibliography

The subject bibliography is intended for research workers and others in special areas. Once a subject is chosen, the divisions common to national bibliographies may be employed—time, form, origin, and others. However, unlike most national bibliographies, a subject work may use all the divisions. For example, a definitive bibliography on railroad engines may be retrospective, current (at least at date of publishing), inclusive of all forms from individual monographs to government publications, and reflective of various sources of origins.

Guides to Reference Materials

Theoretically, lists which include the "best" works for a given situation or audience are not bibliographies in the accepted definition of the term. In practice, however, they are normally so considered. They include guides to reference books, special reading lists issued by a library, and books devoted to the "best" works for children, adults, students, business people, and other specific groups.

Analytical and Textual Bibliography

Analytical bibliography is concerned with the physical description of the book. Textual bibliography goes a step further and highlights certain textual variations between a manuscript and the printed book or between various editions. Often the two are combined into one scientific or art form. This type of research is designed to discover everything possible about the author's ultimate intentions; the goal is to recover the exact words that the author intended in expressing his or her work. In achieving this goal, one group of bibliographers may be experts in nineteenth-century printing practices and bookbinding, for example, and another group in paper watermarks or title pages.

There are differences between analytical and textual bibliographies, the most basic being that analytical bibliography is more concerned with the physical aspects of the book and textual bibliography with the author's words, i.e., the exact text as the author meant it to appear in printed form.[3]

Daily Use

Returning to the standard enumerative bibliography, how is this form used in a library? Normally it directs the individual to an item, and it is employed primarily to find X book or Y article. There are two basic approaches to looking in the bibliography for a particular work.

Experts and laypersons who know a subject well look up X or Y by its title or by the author's name. Those who do not tend to use subject headings.

---

[3]For an excellent example of the problems involved with textual bibliography see: "The Continuing Scandal of Ulysses: An Exchange," *The New York Review of Books,* Sept. 29, 1988, p. 80, and "The Scandal of Ulysses" in the June 30 issue of the same publication. This concerns the 5000 corrections or so made by bibliographers in the 1984 James Joyce novel. Some critics claim the corrections are invalid, others say they are necessary, and still others make additional claims. For further discussion, see any issue of *The Times Literary Supplement* for the same period; the letter column is filled with debate on the matter. For an update see "After 2 Steps Forward, One Back for Ulysses," *The New York Times,* June 28, 1990, p. C18. See also G. Thomas Tanselle, *Textural Criticism Since Greg.* Charlottesville, VA: University of Virginia Press, 1987. This covers the controversies dealing with textual criticism over the past 40 years.

The more sophisticated and knowledgeable a person is in any field (whether it be automobiles or psychology), the more likely the individual is to try to search a bibliography by author or by title. This is not only a very precise approach, but very simple, because one does not have to guess the subject headings in the bibliography. For example, is automobile under "Automobiles" or "Cars" or "Transportation"? The most complex search is a subject search.

EVALUATION OF A BIBLIOGRAPHY

When considering the relative merits of a bibliography, one applies the general criteria used for evaluation of all reference works: purpose, authority, and scope. (See the discussion on "Evaluating Reference Sources" in Chapter 1.) Beyond the general considerations, one should evaluate a bibliography in the following manner:

1. *Purpose* It is important that the bibliography fill a real need and that it not be a repetition of another work or so esoteric that it is of little or no value. The subject is stated clearly in the title and well defined in the preface.
2. *Scope* The bibliography should be as complete as possible within its stated purpose. For example, a bibliography of books and articles in periodicals about nineteenth-century American railroads will include contemporary magazine reports about the construction of railroads. Where there are different forms, such as magazines and books, these must be clearly identified.
3. *Methodology* The method of compiling the bibliography should be straightforward and should make clear that the compiler has examined all material listed. The items are to be described in a standard bibliographic style, and include the basic elements of a bibliographical entry.
4. *Organization* The bibliography should be organized in a clear, easy-to-use fashion, and indexes (from subject and author to geographical location) should be included where multiple access is desirable. At the same time, look for material arranged in a logical fashion so that it is not always necessary to use the index, e.g., alphabetical by author, by date, by subject, etc. You want to see that the author offers a clear explanation of how to use the work as well as definitions, a key to abbreviations, and the like.
5. *Annotations and abstracts* Where descriptive and/or critical

notes are used for entries, these should be clear, succinct, and informative.

6. *Bibliographic form* This is a standard entry with the information one needs to identify and locate the item.

7. *Current* The material should be current, at least where this is the purpose of the bibliography. It is conceivable that one would list only eighteenth- or nineteenth-century publications, and in such a case timeliness would not be a factor.

8. *Accuracy* It goes without saying that the material must be accurate. There should be some arrangement, if possible, for corrections to be made after publication, should the need arise.

9. *Format* Is the bibliography available in print, on CD-ROM, online, etc.? If in machine-readable form, is the software adequate to easily retrieve the necessary data? If only in print, is it easy to read?

GUIDES TO REFERENCE BOOKS

The basic purpose of a bibliographical guide to reference material is to introduce the user to (1) general reference sources which will be of assistance in research in all fields and (2) specific reference sources which will help in research in particular fields. These guides take a number of forms, but primarily are either (1) annotated lists of titles with brief introductory remarks before each section or chapter or (2) handbooks which not only list and annotate basic sources, but also introduce the user to investigative tools by a discursive, almost textbooklike, approach.

There are numerous research guides of this latter type, but the most widely useful one is Jacques Barzun and Henry Graff's *The Modern Researcher* (4th ed. New York: Harcourt Brace Jovanovich, 1985, 480 pages). While written for history students, the advice on the research and preparation of a paper is useful for anyone in almost any field. It contains a particularly clear and useful presentation of how to use reference works.

The general bibliographical guide to reference materials is the starting point to answer many questions. There are several guides which are helpful in the selection and use of reference books.

Sheehy, Eugene P. *Guide to Reference Books,* 10th ed. Chicago: American Library Association, 1986. 1582 pp. $65.

Walford, Albert John. *Guide to Reference Materials,* 5th ed. London: The Library Association, 1989–1991, 3 vols. $100 to $120 each.

Wynar, Bohdan. *American Reference Books Annual.* Englewood, CO: Libraries Unlimited, Inc., 1970 to date, annual. $85.

The two basic guides which tell a reference librarian which reference books are basic in all fields are those by Sheehy and Walford. Most librarians refer to them as "Sheehy" and "Walford."

Reviewing the tenth edition of the American Library Association publication, a critic remarked: "No other source does so well in providing access to so many reference sources in so many languages and for so many subjects."[4] A similar comment fits Walford, where concentration is more on England and Europe.

The guides list and annotate the major titles used in reference service. *Guide to Reference Books* includes some 14,000 entries and the British guide about the same. Complete bibliographical information is given for each entry, and most of the entries are annotated.

Their arrangements differ: The American guide, Sheehy, has five main sections in a single volume. Walford, using the Universal Decimal Classification System, divides his work into three separate volumes: science and technology; social sciences; and generalities, languages, the arts, and literature.

Both works begin with a broad subject and then are subdivided by smaller subjects and by forms. For example, *Guide to Reference Books* has a section on economics under the social sciences. This is subdivided by forms: guides, bibliographies, periodicals, dissertations, indexes and abstract journals, dictionaries and encyclopedias, atlases, handbooks, and so on. The economics section is later broken down into smaller subjects and often, within the subject, a further division is made by country, as, for example, in political science. *Guide to Reference Materials* subdivides economics by bibliographies, thesauruses, encyclopedias and dictionaries, dissertations, and so on, generally following the Sheehy pattern. In practice, the arrangement is not really important. Each volume has an excellent title, author, and subject index.

Guide to Reference Books concentrates on American, Canadian, and British titles, and Walford is stronger on British and European titles. In the second volume of Walford, about 13 percent of the listings are from American publishers, 31 percent from Great Britain, and over 50 percent from European and Commonwealth nations.

---

[4]"Guide to Reference Books," *Choice*, May 1987, p. 1361.

The basic problem with *Guide to Reference Books* is the lack of current material. This is overcome, if only in part, by supplements. The next supplement, according to the publisher, is to be available in 1992, or 6 years after the primary work was issued. The supplement will annotate about 4500 titles, principally works published since the closure of copy for the tenth edition in 1984.

With that, the eleventh edition is scheduled for 1995. It also will be in machine-readable form on CD-ROM and online. Once it is part of a computer memory, the hope is to update it quarterly, both with CD-ROM and online and to make the printed volumes available more often.

Incidentally, Sheehy is no longer editor, and as of 1989 the work is under the supervision of *Choice* magazine staff. Robert Balay, a reference editor of *Choice* and former head of reference at Yale University will be the primary editor. After 1995 one will probably refer to the volume as "Balay."

The British *Guide to Reference Materials* (or "Walford") is considerably more current than its American cousin and therefore favored in many larger libraries. The three volumes are under constant revision and are published on a three-year schedule. The fifth edition's first volume, published in 1989, covers science and technology. There are approximately 6000 evaluative annotations, not only of printed books, but of databases, microfiche, and related materials. There is an excellent index.

The high point of the three-volume work is the annotation style. The critical notes are written with a flair which has made Walford famous. They are not only descriptive, but include well-directed barbs and praise when necessary. Most are a delight to read.

While much of the focus in Walford's guide is on British and Continental works, it is broad enough to include the basic American titles as well. This is evident in the second volume covering the social sciences, philosophy, and religion. Published in 1990, it is edited by Joan Harvey and Alan Day. It offers a fine selection of international reference works. The third volume, published late in 1991, covers literature, the arts, and languages.

Ahead of its American counterpart, Walford is in machine-readable form, which accounts for the one-book revision per year until the cycle is complete and the revision begins once again. (By the time the next edition of *Guide to Reference Books* is available, Walford will have gone through two editions). Plans are to have the British work available online and on CD-ROM.

American Reference Books Annual (usually cited as ARBA) differs from both *Guide to Reference Books* and *Guide to Reference Materials* in three important respects: (1) It is limited to reference titles published or distributed in the United States and Canada[5]; (2) it is comprehensive for a given year and makes no effort to be selective; (3) the annotations are written by more than 320 subject experts and are both more critical and more expository than those found in Sheehy or Walford. Depending on the extent of American publishing, the annual volume, usually available in March or April of the year following the year covered in the text, analyzes some 1300 to 1500 separate reference titles. (Since its inception, the service has examined more than 35,000 reference sources.) The work is well organized and well indexed. Every five years the publisher issues a cumulative index to the set, e.g., *Index to American Reference Books Annual* 1985–1989 or 1975–1979 or 1970–1974. Each indexes about 8000 reference works by author, title, and subject.

The January issue of *College & Research Libraries* (Chicago: American Library Association) offers a section of "Selected Reference Books." The 50 to 75 titles are carefully selected, annotated, and arranged by broad subject. This updates the previous edition of *Guide to Reference Books*. While it is helpful, it is hardly comprehensive enough to be a real update.

The Canadian counterpart to the American and British guides is Dorothy Ryder's *Canadian Reference Sources* (2d ed. Ottawa: Canadian Library Association, 1981). Unfortunately, the publisher reports no plans to update the work, and as it is now over a decade old, it is of limited value to any one user except the largest of libraries. It is arranged in much the same way as the British and American guides and has the same type of descriptive annotations. The titles are limited to those published in Canada and reference works about Canada. There is an author, title, and selected-subject index. The work is supplemented annually in a list of Canadian reference sources in the August number of the *Canadian Library Journal*. See also the *American Reference Books Annual* from 1988 to date for a fairly complete roundup of Canadian reference works for the previous year.

Guides for Smaller Libraries

Most libraries are in the small- to medium-size category. The larger guides are too inclusive. A small library needs considerably less ex-

---

[5]Canada was included only from the mid-1980s on, at least in any detail. The change, found in guides from 1988 to date, is an effort to include complete coverage of Canadian reference works of works published in the United States.

haustive works. Although now dated, *References Sources for Small and Medium Sized Libraries* (4th ed. Chicago: American Library Association, 1984) affords a useful list of some 1800 basic titles. The standard titles, from dictionaries to indexes, remain much the same today.

The bibliography may be updated and revised by the annual *Recommended Reference Books for Small and Medium Sized Libraries and Media Centers* (Englewood, Colo.: Libraries Unlimited, 1980 to date). This a cut-down version of the same publisher's *American Reference Books Annual.* The reviews are under four major subject categories, and codes indicate use by academic, public, or school libraries. It includes from 500 to 550 reference works published the previous year which meet the needs of the smaller- to medium-sized reference collection.

Concentrating on encyclopedias, atlases, and dictionaries, *General Reference Books for Adults* (New York: R. R. Bowker Companies, 1988) offers both evaluative and descriptive reviews of more than 200 current reference works in the three forms. Coverage is selective and trustworthy, and the guide is a help in selection. A similar work, but for schools, by the same publisher is *Reference Books for Young Adults* (1988). A third, *Topical Reference Books* (1991), gives data on about 2000 subject titles suitable for small to medium-sized libraries.

The guides differ drastically from standard general bibliographies. First, they are limited to either a few basic forms or a single audience. Second, they have long, discursive sections on the forms as well as the individual reference works. While the discussions are too long for some, they are useful for those seeking detailed comparisons of reference works.

Subject Bibliographies

A cursory glance at any subject area in either *Guide to Reference Books* or *Guide to Reference Materials* will reveal hundreds of subject bibliographies. Most of these follow the Sheehy/Walford pattern of organization and presentation, but are for a particular area of interest.

The various disciplines and large areas of knowledge have their own bibliographies, their own versions of *Guide to Reference Books.* For example: the third edition of Ron Blazek and Elizabeth Aversa, *The Humanities: A Selective Guide to Information Sources* (Englewood, Colo.: Libraries Unlimited, 1988, 382 pages). Here there are close to 1000 entries and annotations to core information sources in philosophy, religion, arts and language and literature. *Information Sources in Science and Technology* (Englewood, Colo.: Libraries Unlimited, 1988,

362 pages), edited by C. D. Huff, is an annotated guide to more than 2000 reference sources. Individual disciplines, from astronomy to zoology are covered in the individual chapters.

Moving from larger to smaller areas, one finds hundreds of bibliographies. A single example: *Music Reference and Research Materials* (New York: Schirmer, 1988, 714 pages) Now in its fourth edition, this is an annotated bibliography of more than 3200 items, both American and international.

There are several specialized annuals of books, which are a mix of reference works and standard titles. The most useful is *Science and Technology Annual Reference Review* (Phoenix, Ariz.: Oryx, 1989 to date, annual). This follows the ARBA pattern. The science reviews are by 73 experts and vary in length and style. Most, but not all, are evaluative. The 600-plus titles are arranged by subjects such as computer science and mathematics. And there are the usual indexes. This differs from ARBA in that the reference net is extended to include textbooks, how-to-do-it titles, and more ephemeral materials such as guides on how to take a test. Consequently it can be used in conjunction with ARBA. There is some overlap, but so little as to make it a valuable addition to the reference collection of most libraries.

CURRENT SELECTION AIDS

Librarians who want to build collections in given subjects need only consult their preferred guides for basic titles, but they will run into the problem of currency. The reference librarian with an interest in current titles must study reviews in periodicals. Most of the periodicals also review books ranging from fiction to technical publications.

The selection of reference sources is a highly individualized process. The character and distribution of the elements which constitute the needs of users differ from library to library. Consequently, the first and most important rule when considering the selection of reference materials, or anything else for the library, is to recognize the needs, both known and anticipated, of the users.

How is a satisfactory selection policy reached? First and foremost, there must be a librarian who has some subject competence; that is, one who knows the basic literature of a field, or several fields, including not only the reference works but also the philosophy, jargon, ideas, ideals, and problems that make up that field. There is no substitute for substantive knowledge. Second, the librarian must be aware in some depth of the type of writing and publishing done in that special field. Where is there likely to be the best review? Who are the outstanding authors, publishers, and editors in this field? What can and cannot be answered readily?

Selection is charted, rather than dictated, by the following:

1. Knowing as much as possible about the needs of those who use the reference collection.
2. Calling upon expert advice. In a school situation the expert may be the teacher who is knowledgeable in a certain area. In a public library it may be the layperson, skilled practitioner, or subject specialist who uses the library. Most people are flattered by a request that draws upon their experience and knowledge, and one of the best resources of reference materials is the informed user.
3. Keeping a record of questions. This is done to determine not only what materials the library has but what it does not have. Most important, a record of *unanswered* queries will often be the basis for an evaluation of the reference collection.
4. Knowing what other libraries have, and what resources are available. For example, the small library contemplating the purchase of an expensive run of periodicals or a bibliography would certainly first check to see whether the same materials may be readily available in a nearby library.

These four points only begin to suggest the complexity of selection. Many libraries have detailed selection policy statements that consider in depth the necessary administrative steps which are merely hinted at here.

Reference Book Review

Choice. Chicago: American Library Association, 1964 to date, monthly.

Library Journal. New York: R. R. Bowker Company, 1876 to date, semimonthly.

RQ. Chicago: American Library Association, 1960 to date, quarterly.

"Reference Books Bulletin," in *The Booklist.* Chicago: American Library Association, 1905 to date, semimonthly.

Wilson Library Bulletin. New York: H. W. Wilson Company, 1914 to date, monthly.

Reference and Research Book News, Portland, OR: Books News, Inc., 1985 to date, bimonthly.

Under the able editorship of Stanley Whiteley, "Reference Books Bulletin," a center section in the twice-a-month issue of *The Booklist,* is the single most important place for a librarian to turn for accurate, current, and in-depth reviews of general reference works. Each section is prefaced by a series of notes about publishing, reference services, and new works. This is followed by unsigned reviews. The names of the members who write the reviews and serve on the committee (librarians and teachers) are given in each issue.

In the course of a year, the service reviews about 100 to 150 major works, and about double that number of more conventional, less expensive titles. From time to time a whole issue, or a good part of an issue, is dedicated to an overview of encyclopedias, dictionaries, children's reference works, and the like. The reviews are cumulated in a separate publication each year.

Reviews appear no more than six months after publication of the reviewed book, and sometimes even sooner. Although hardly timely, this is an improvement over the 10-month to even 3-year gap of earlier times.

There are detailed reviews, as well, of CD-ROM and other forms of databases most likely to be used in the average library. The analysis is useful particularly for the person who wishes to learn the good and bad points about searching for the layperson. In fact, the reviews of databases are among the best now available.

Other current sources are:

1. *Choice* While specifically geared to college libraries, this professional journal evaluates a number of reference titles of value to all libraries. These are listed under "Reference" and in addition to the printed sources, often include one to four reviews of databases (including CD-ROM), Also, from time to time bibliographical essays in the front of the magazine highlight reference titles. There are approximately 6800 reviews a year, of which about 500 cover reference books. The reviews are usually 120 to 500 words in length and are signed. Almost all reviewers make an effort to compare the title under review with previously published titles in the same subject area, a feature which is particularly useful but rarely found in the other reviews. When budgets are tight, when choices must be made, it is of great importance that comparisons are available.

2. *Library Journal* Again, the general book review section leads

off with "Reference." (To be more precise, it follows "The Contemporary Scene" section.) There are about 450 reference reviews each year. These are 100 to 150 words long, usually written by librarians or teachers, and all are signed. Also, *School Library Journal* includes reviews of reference titles.

3. *RQ* The last section of this quarterly is given over entirely to the review of reference books. A few other related titles are considered, but, unlike *Library Journal* and *Choice, RQ* makes no effort to review general books. About 140 to 150 reference titles are considered each year. Reviews average about 200 words each.

   In addition to the section on "Reference Books," four to five databases (including CD-ROM) are evaluated. These are excellent, critical reviews which consider the most often used online services. Finally, "Professional Materials" are considered in another part, i.e., usually about ten to twelve books for librarians of interest to those in reference work.

4. *Wilson Library Bulletin* One section is devoted to "Current Reference Books," and has the distinction of being the only series of reviews by an individual. James Rettig covers about 20 to 30 current titles each month. Most of these are suitable for the general reference collection in public, academic, and school libraries. The reviews are both descriptive and evaluative, although Rettig tends to select only books he can recommend. The reviews are current, and help the librarian to decide immediately whether or not to purchase the work.

   Norman Stevens of the University of Connecticut, critically reviews professional books for the librarian, and often these are of value to the reference person. Signed reviews of software and nonprint sources may be useful, too.

5. *Reference and Research Book News* This work does not concentrate entirely on reference works, but includes many of them under the main Library of Congress subject areas, which is the basic form of arrangement in each 36- to 40-page issue. For example, under "General Works" two reference titles are listed with full bibliographic information and a short (35- to 70-word) descriptive annotation. No effort is made to be critical, and so this is an alerting service and not a review. The same publisher issues *SciTech Book News* (1978 to date monthly), which follows a similar approach, but is limited to books in science, technology, and

medicine. Again, it serves primarily as a method of keeping up with new titles, and is not a review source.

There are other approaches to reference works and news of the reference and information services field. One leader is *Reference Services Review* (Ann Arbor, Mich.: Pierian Press, 1972 to date, quarterly.) This does not so much review new books as offer a dozen or more bibliographies. These may include an annotated listing on AIDS or one on the joys of mountain climbing. All the authors/compilers are experts in their respective fields. From time to time, too, there are general overviews of reference services.

While there are no reviews, *The Reference Librarian* (New York: Haworth Press, 1981 to date, quarterly) features 25 or more articles on a single subject of interest to reference librarians. The topics may range from online searching to ethics to the publishing of reference works. The authors are working librarians who offer a unique approach to a subject of interest to reference librarians everywhere.

American Libraries, the monthly magazine of the American Library Association, does not regularly review reference books, but it does have an annual feature of interest: The "Outstanding Reference Sources of 19–." Appearing in the May issue, it is a compilation of the best reference titles of the year selected by the Reference Sources Committee of the ALA. *Library Journal* offers a competitor, "Reference Books of 19–" with titles selected by its book review editors. This appears in the April 15 issue which is devoted almost entirely to reference services.

Five of the titles—*Library Journal, Choice, Booklist* (i.e., "Reference Books Bulletin"), *Reference & Research Books News,* and *Sci-Tech Books News*—are available on a CD-ROM disk as part of the R. R. Bowker "Books in Print with Book Reviews Plus." This is discussed in the next chapter.

INDEXES TO REVIEWS

Book Review Digest. New York: H. W. Wilson Company, 1905 to date, monthly. Service. Author/title index, 1905–1974, 4 vols. $275; 1975–1984, 1488 pp., $65 (Wilsonline, $25 to $45 per hour.)[6]

---

[6]Here and throughout the two volumes of this text, machine-readable reference services are noted by giving the name of a primary vendor and the price per hour of usage or per CD-ROM disc. Almost all vendors include other charges, but these vary. The hourly rate gives an approximate notion of cost as compared with the printed version. No effort is made to indicate that databases are available from many vendors.

Book Review Index. Detroit: Gale Research Company, 1965 to date, bimonthly, $175. Cumulation, 1965–1984, 10 vols. $1250. (DIALOG file 137, $55 per hour.)

The titles considered here are specialized because their sole purpose is to list reviews. They are used by students and others seeking background material on a given work as well as by the reference librarian on the lookout for notices about specific reference books.

The major indexes in this field—*Book Review Index* and *The Book Review Digest*—rely on author or title entries. In addition, the librarian must know the approximate date that the book was published. The fastest method is simply to search *The Book Review Digest Author/ Title Index, 1905–1974.* For reviews published after 1974, one needs to go to the annual index volumes or other services. If the date cannot be found in these indexes, the librarian should turn to the card catalog where the title may be entered or to one of the national or trade bibliographies such as *Books in Print.* Another possibility is to search for a title by using a bibliography.

Book Review Index seeks out reviews from about 475 periodicals, and is published every two months. In addition there are annual cumulations published at year's end. The reviews are listed in two sections; the first by author, and the second by title. Unfortunately, there is no subject approach. On an average, about 75,000 books are covered each year, with about one to two reviews per title. This contrasts sharply with the other basic key to reviews, *The Book Review Digest.* Here one finds only about 6000 titles considered.

A useful index feature for the reference librarians is that all reference works are marked with an "r." Thus one can look through the bimonthly issues for updated information on new works otherwise missed. Other codes include a "p" for a periodical review; and a "c" and a "y" for children and young people. (See the introduction of *The Book Review Digest* for a full explanation.)

The Book Review Digest (BRD), however, has a distinct advantage and one which makes it preferable to *Book Review Index.* Not only does it list where a review may be located, but it excerpts enough from the review to give the reader a notion of what the contents are and whether the book is favored by the reviewer. With this, the user does not have to consult the reviews but can make judgments about a title by merely reading *BRD.* Found in almost every library, the *BRD,* going back to 1905, often serves the scholar as an invaluable key to contemporary reviews.

The catch is in the limitations exercised by the *BRD.* It analyzes only 80 periodicals, and, even more unfortunately, it includes reviews of nonfiction only when there have been a minimum of two reviews, and of fiction only when four or more reviews have appeared. The result is that the *BRD* is a bastion of conservatism and is probably the last place anyone might hope to find a review of a book by a beginning author.

Both the book review services are available online. Wilsonline offers its own *Book Review Digest,* but this only goes back to 1983 and is of limited value, except for the annotations. *Book Review Index* is online from 1969.

A problem with using these otherwise excellent guides to the "best" in new reference works is apparent to any working librarian. This is succinctly explained by St. Louis Public Library reference people:

> Reviews can never really predict how valuable a reference tool will be in a particular library setting. Many times librarians concentrate on "comprehensiveness" and "accuracy" as desirable features, forgetting to evaluate the user-friendliness of an item, which often plays a substantial role in the ultimate usefulness of a source. It is sometimes frustrating to see the same publications reviewed over and over especially when they are expensive. One begins to wonder how many potential reference items are overlooked or whether there are less expensive substitutes for a particular need."[7]

BIBLIOGRAPHY OF BIBLIOGRAPHIES

Bibliographic Index: A Cumulative Bibliography of Bibliographies. New York: H. W. Wilson Company, 1937 to date, triannual with cumulations. Service. (Wilsonline, $38 to $40 per hour).

A bibliography of bibliographies is, as the name suggests, a listing of bibliographies. One may find a bibliography on dogs at the end of an article in a periodical, at the conclusion of an essay in an encyclopedia, or as part of a book on pets. If one lists these three bibliographies and adds from a dozen to a thousand more, one has a bibliography of bibliographies—in this case, a listing of bibliographies from various sources about dogs. (In turn, each of the individual bibliographies constitutes a subject bibliography.)

The primary example of a bibliography of bibliographies is *Bib-*

---

[7]Catherine Alloway, Celia Bouchard, and Brenda McDonald, "Field Tested Reference Works . . ." *Wilson Library Bulletin,* January 1989, p. 37. This is an annotated listing of works found useful day by day in St. Louis and other libraries polled throughout the country.

liographic Index. Under numerous headings, one may find bibliographies about subjects, persons, and places. The entries represent (1) separate published books and pamphlets which are normally bibliographies in a specific subject area, e.g., *East European and Soviet Economic Affairs: A Bibliography . . . ;* (2) bibliographies which are parts of books and pamphlets, such as the bibliography which appears at the end of David Kunzle's book *The Early Comic Strip;* and (3) bibliographies which have been published separately or in articles in approximately 2200 English and foreign-language periodicals. Emphasis is on American publications, and to be listed, a bibliography must contain more than 50 citations.

The inevitable catch to many reference works is applicable here: (1) the bibliographies are not listed until six months to a year after they are published, and (2) although books, and to a lesser degree pamphlets, are well covered, the index cannot be trusted to include many periodical bibliographies. Why? Because over 65,000 periodicals are issued, often with bibliographies, and the index includes only 2600.[8]

BIBLIOGRAPHIES: NONPRINT MATERIALS

"Nonprint" is not a precise description. It has come to mean any communication material other than the traditional book, periodical, and newspaper. Machine-readable records discussed in the second chapter are by far the most pervasive type of nonprint reference material. At the same time, materials such as recordings and videos are the most popular nonprint materials for laypeople. Nonprint materials are an essential part of reference service, particularly in school libraries or, as they are called, "school media centers" or "learning centers."

When working with resources other than books, the reference librarian functions much as she would when working with the traditional media:

1. In schools, universities, and colleges, the librarian will be

---

[8]When a bibliography is published separately as a book, it is picked up through Library of Congress copy. If the bibliography is published as part of a periodical index, it may be identified by the various Wilson indexers when they are going through the periodicals for indexing. "If the bibliography is published as part of something else, the author should send a copy of the bibliography to *Bibliography Index* for possible listing. This is the only way *Bibliographic Index* will know about the bibliography's existence. . . .", *RQ,* Fall 1982, p. 32, Appendix.

called upon by the classroom teacher for information on
media which is available in the library and which may be
ordered, or even borrowed, from other libraries.

2. The students will want information and advice about multimedia for the primary learning process.

3. The layperson's needs will be somewhat similar, although
here most of the emphasis is likely to center on advice about
the library's films, recordings, and so on, which may extend
knowledge (or recreational interests) beyond the traditional
book.

The reference librarian should be conversant with at least the
basic bibliographies and control devices for the media. Knowledge
of bibliographies and sources is important for answering questions
directly dealing with audiovisual materials: "Where can I find [such
and such] a catalog of films, records, tapes?" "Do you have anything
on film that will illustrate this or that?" "What do you have on
recordings or film pertaining to local history? In large libraries, such
questions might be referred to the proper department, but in small-
and medium-size libraries, the questions usually will have to be answered by the reference librarian.

See the second volume of this text for a discussion of the various bibliographies employed to locate databases, software, and
other nonprint materials closely associated with reference services.

Guides and Bibliographies

National Information Center for Educational Media. NICEM
Media Indexes. Albuquerque, NM: Access Innovations, 1967 to
date. Various services, prices. CD-ROM publisher, annual, various prices. (DIALOG file 40, $70 per hour.)

The Video Source Book. Detroit: Gale Research Company, 1978
to date, 2 vols. annual with two supplements. $210.

Bowker's Complete Video Directory. New York: R. R. Bowker Company, 1986 to date, 2 vols., annual with one supplement. $169.
CD-ROM, publisher, 1989 to date. $395.

Opus. New York: Schwann Publications, 1949 to date, quarterly.
$20.

On Cassette. New York: R. R. Bowker Company, 1986 to date,
annual. $110.

There are no entirely satisfactory bibliographies for all nonprint materials—no *Books in Print,* no *Cumulative Book Index,* no *Na-*

tional Union Catalog. And even the by-now-standard bibliographies leave much to be desired in organization and coverage. Lacking overall bibliographical control, the materials are difficult to track. The lack of such tools accounts in no small way for the development of media experts who are familiar with the many access routes.

The closest thing to *Books in Print* for audiovisual materials is the *NICEM Media Indexes*. The purpose of these indexes, which are really bibliographies, is to provide noncritical information on what is available in nonprint materials. And, although directed at elementary and secondary school needs, a good deal of the data is applicable to other types of libraries. Hence it can be used to answer such queries as "What transparencies are available for geography?" "What educational films are there on animals?" "On environmental studies?" And so on.

The *NICEM Indexes* are really a series of individual indexes, *not* a single work. In 1991 the combined indexes included over 1 million items. Each item is briefly annotated, but only as description, not evaluation. Full information is given as to cost, rental (when available), and necessary bibliographical information for identification and order. Almost all types of audiovisual materials are covered, from overhead transparencies and films to video cassettes. Available online, the file is much easier to search because one does not have to go through each of the multiple volumes.

NICEM's online database, "AV On-Line" offers relatively recent titles as it is updated quarterly. Unfortunately, the CD-ROM version is updated only once a year and is quite expensive, costing between $799 and $1199.

The basic work for locating films is the *Film & Video Finder*. A merger of two previous indexes, it gives basic information on thousands of items, particularly those suitable for schools. Published irregularly since 1987, it is $295 per year; but for most, the online access is probably better and less expensive.

There are two major media areas where the primary audience is the adult, not the student: films and recordings.

In most libraries videocassettes have replaced the traditional 16-mm films.[9] And while films are still important for groups and for classroom use, the VCR is the most popular general tool for film viewing. There are now numerous guides to the best and better films

---

[9]Ray Serebrin, "Video: Planning Backwards into the Future," *Library Journal*, Nov. 15, 1988, pp. 33–36. This is a good introduction to video lending problems and solutions in public libraries. A useful guide for collections in this area: James Scholtz, *Developing and Maintaining Video Collections in Libraries*, Santa Barbara, CA, ABC Clio, 1988.

on disks and tapes, as well as by subject, age interest etc., as well as selected lists of the "best" movies for home entertainment.

The Video Source Book has listings, a wide variety of approximately 60,000 video programs on videotapes and disks. It is the only one of the guides which includes both popular entertainment videos and educational units. Arrangement is alphabetical by title with full bibliographic information and numerous indexes. Titles are assigned one of eight main categories from "Children" and "Business" to "Movies/Entertainment." Within these large groups are over 400 smaller subject divisions which are noted for each entry. Complete information is given including such details as running time, price, and producer. By far the most comprehensive index of its type, it is a basic necessity for any library with a large video collection. A CD-ROM version of the service is promised, as is an online service.

Bowker's Complete Video Directory gives necessary information on the 62,000 movies now available on video and other forms of disks and tapes. The first volume includes 28,000 entertainment films, while the second concentrates on 34,000 educational, professional videos. Arrangement offers quick access by title and by subject, and there are numerous indexes to everything from awards and directors to producers and distributors. This is a midyear supplement, and additional supplements are planned.

The CD-ROM version, *Bowker's Complete Video Directory Plus,* is distributed by Bowker. Here one is offered access to the information by at least 24 possible points of reference.[10]

Although not that well known to librarians, an excellent current source of videos is the commercial *Videolog* (San Diego, Calif.: Trade Service Corporation, $212). The weekly loose-leaf service for video stores provides information about many popular titles which will be of interest to the average viewer.

The "books in print" of recorded sound, Schwann's *Opus* offers a listing of CDs, records, and cassettes. The paperback guide is well known to music lovers, and anyone who has ever wandered into a music section of a store. Listings are under various headings from

---

[10]A selective guide, including 1000 films with brief annotations, is edited by Sally Mason and James Scholtz. The latest edition was published in 1988 by the American Library Association for only $14.50. It is the *Video for Libraries: Special Interest Video for Small and Medium Sized Public Libraries.* Another useful guide in a field of many is *The Bowker Librarian's Guide to Home Video,* New York, R. R. Bowker, 1989. The publisher promises to update as needed. For a comparison of the various video guides, see Joseph Palmer, "Bibliographic Control of Videos," *Public Libraries,* January/February 1990, pp. 36–41.

"Classical" to "Spoken Word." Enough information is given for each recording to permit purchase.

The family of Schwann catalogs also offers: (1) *Artist Issue* is an annual which lists the artists rather than the composers. There are cross references to *Opus*. (2) *Spectrum* covers popular music from folk to rock and jazz, and comes out quarterly. (3) *In Music* is a monthly which covers all categories (and artists) and updates the other catalogs. A library should have all these works as they are used equally by the librarian and the public.[11]

Limited to the spoken word, *On Cassette* lists some 40,000 titles. Each has a descriptive annotation, but is in no way evaluative. There is an excellent subject index which helps locate material in hard-to-find areas, as well as title, author, and producer access points. A similar work, *Words on Tape* (Westport, Conn.: Meckler, 1989 to date, annual) lists 20,000 audiocassette titles. Arrangement is by title and author with a subject index. The essential difference between this and the Bowker title is price. The Meckler work is $35 as compared with $95 from Bowker. Only the largest of libraries would need to spend the added money for the somewhat more expensive Bowker title.

Librarians trying to locate a particular film or video in another library or collection will turn to the *Educational Film & Video Locator* (New York: R. R. Bowker, 1980 to date). The 1990 fourth edition lists 52,000 items which may be found in 46 geographically dispersed libraries. The first volume lists titles, with full bibliographical data, under some 630 subject headings. The second volume lists the titles alphabetically.

An often-overlooked resource is the network system, OCLC (discussed later). This online union catalog offers bibliographic information on numerous audiovisual materials.

Indexes to Reviews

AudioVideo Review Digest. Detroit: Gale Research Company, 1988 to date, quarterly. $145.

Media Review Digest. Ann Arbor, MI: The Pierian Press, 1970 to date, annual. $245.

The *Audio Review Digest* indexes reviews of audiovisual materials

---

[11]Bruce Connolly, CD Collection, *Library Journal,* May 15, 1989, pp. 36–42. This offers a brief, thorough coverage of the subject and is a fine guide to everything from basic bibliographies to magazines and newsletters.

which have appeared in some 600 periodicals. Published quarterly, it is cumulated in an annual volume. The result is a relatively up-to-date reference work to locate sometimes hard-to-find reviews of audio and videocassettes, films, filmstrips, and spoken word recordings. For each of the 3000 or so titles in a typical issue there are excerpts from the reviews which are long enough to indicate content. The publisher carefully indicates what is recommended or not recommended. As one might expect, most of the reviews are of videocassettes. There are various indexes, including a subject index.

Media Review Digest analyzes reviews of the media appearing in over 140 periodicals. The 40,000 or so reviews are then indexed, with full citations, by type of medium. Some excerpts from reviews are given and an evaluative sign shows whether the comments were favorable or not. A librarian can use it in almost the same way as the indexes to book reviews, i.e., to check reviews, probably for purposes of buying or renting a given item. The information provided is full, and often includes descriptions of the material as well as cataloging information.

Beginning in 1987 the service included a great many more videocassettes than before and promises to include even more in the future. A most useful feature are the codemarks which give a quick summary of the review as being favorable or unfavorable. In some cases, too, there are brief quotes from the reviews.

Microform

Guide to Microforms in Print: Author-Title. New York: R. R. Bowker-Saur, 1961 to date, annual, 2 vols. $150.

Microform is used in libraries to preserve space, to keep bibliographies and other reference aids relatively current, and to provide easy access for users. Microfiche is probably the most familiar type of microform.

Microform exists in two formats: the roll and the flat transparency or card. The familiar 35-mm reel or roll has been in libraries for so long that many librarians and users think only of this form when microform is mentioned. The flat microform comes in several basic varieties or types: (1) Microfiche, or fiche, is available in different sizes, but the favored is the standard 4 by 6 inches, with an average of 98 pages per sheet. Various reductions may either increase or decrease the number of pages on a sheet. (2) Ultrafiche, as the name implies, is an ultrafine reduction, usually on a 4- by 6-inch transparency. One card may contain 3000 to 5000 pages. (3)

Micropoint is a 6- by 9-inch card which contains up to 100 pages of text in 10 rows and 10 columns.

For purposes of storage and convenience, most libraries with substantial holdings in periodicals and newspapers store them on microform. Books, particularly those hard to locate or out of print, are on microform as are various other printed works, from reports to government documents.

The equivalent of *Books in Print* for microform is the ever-expanding *Guide to Microforms in Print*. It lists alphabetically over 100,000 titles from some 500 publishers, including international firms. Arranged by title and author in one alphabetical listing, the guide lists books, journals, newspapers, government publications, and related materials. Sixteen different types of microform are considered, and the types, with explanation, are listed in the preface. Not all materials on microform are listed, including for example, theses and dissertations. Another approach by the same company is *Guide to Microforms in Print: Subject* which lists the material under 135 broad Library of Congress headings. Certain types are classified by form, i.e., government documents, manuscripts, and so on.

Microform is employed in a library for many reasons, one of the most frequent being its use as a substitute for books or other forms of printed material which are no longer in print, no longer available from a used-book dealer, or so prohibitive in cost as to make microform preferable. It would require a whole chapter to explain how librarians find out-of-print materials.[12]

The Future

Some people argue that microform is a thing of the past, that it will be replaced by CD-ROM and other new technologies. Nevertheless, this author believes that microform has so much in its favor that it is unlikely to disappear soon. Microform allows the librarian to purchase sometimes hard-to-find materials in a relatively inexpensive format. It is used extensively as a method for library users to quickly locate magazine articles.

True, microform may have its limitations, but so do other tech-

[12]Among numerous aids for finding out-of-print books is, fittingly enough R. R. Bowker's *Books Out of Print* (discussed in the next chapter). This includes names of companies and other resources likely to assist the librarian in finding an elusive out-of-print title.

nologies, and it is questionable whether any one storage form will ever be a total replacement for previous forms.[13]

SUGGESTED READING

Barker, Nicolas, *The Butterfly Books.* London: Rota, 1988. A study in the best tradition of textual and analytical bibliography, this work explores pamphlets produced by the American poet and novelist Frederic Prokosch. Apparently pamphlets dated prior to World War II are suspicious because paper, type, printers, etc., came into existence much later than the time they are said to be employed in the prewar works. The investigation follows the pattern of the classic, *An Enquiry into the Nature of Certain Nineteenth Century Pamphlets,* by John Carter and Graham Pollard (1934) which exposed the T. J. Wise forgeries.

Carpenter, Michael, "Organization and Use of Large Scale Bibliographic Databases," *Cataloging and Classification Quarterly,* vol. 8, nos. 3/4, 1988, pp. 1–14. "The advent of online databases has provoked a literature proclaiming their many capabilities," notes the author. He then proceeds to examine the hopes and the actual results of such databases and how they are employed.

Gray, Richard, "Reviewing Reference Publications," *Reference Services Review,* Spring 1990, pp. 7–16. Drawing upon review errors, an experienced reference editor points out the danger of trusting reviews. "The assumption that librarians as librarians possess an unquestionable competence to evaluate certain categories of reference books" is challenged. And while some of Gray's criticism is querulous (particularly about the *Guide to Reference Books*), most of what he says makes great sense.

Grogan, Denis, *Bibliographies of Books.* Chicago: American Library Association, 1988. This is one of six volumes which is devoted to case studies. The reference interview, the search and, of course, the actual bibliographies used to answer the query are explained. A minor problem: Grogan is British and some of the cases reflect British rather than American library experience.

Harmon, Robert, *Elements of Bibliography.* Metuchen, NJ: Scarecrow Press, 1989. This is a revised edition of a basic guide to the fundamentals of bibliography for beginners. It is particularly good in its discussion of the often-used enumerative bibliographies. Some attention is given to the electronic forms of bibliography. A good text for those who want an in-depth coverage of the subject.

Henige, David, "When Bad Is Good Enough: The Lowest Common Denominator in Reference Publishing and Reviewing," *Reference Services Review,* Spring 1991, pp. 7–14. An African specialist uses a less than perfect reference work to test what reviewers have to say about the book. Most find it acceptable. Much the same is found for other titles tested. He concludes the reviewers are not given adequate space for reviews and/or are often not qualified in the subject area. "Perhaps what is needed is a new serial publication dedicated to providing analyses of the worst reference books."

---

[13]Susan A. Cady, "The Electronic Revolution in Libraries: Microfilm Déjà Vu?" *College & Research Libraries,* July 1990, pp. 374–386. The author gives a brief history of microform in libraries and warns that its demise is not any more certain than its earlier promise to take over the library by replacing the printed word.

Landau, Herbert, "Microform vs. CD-ROM: Is There a Difference?" *Library Journal,* October 15, 1990, pp. 56–59. The question is answered in the affirmative. However, the author believes there is a place for both forms in the modern library. The article stresses the importance of different types of formats for data.

Spencer, Michael, "Thoroughness of Book Reviewing Indexing: A First Appraisal," *RQ,* Winter 1986, pp. 188–199. A critical study of how indexing journals and other services take notice of book reviews. It is uneven and the author makes the point that in certain areas, in certain journals, "it might be worth checking the magazines themselves for book notes not cited by book review sources that deal with the book in question."

Stevens, Norman, "Thoughts on Information, Knowledge, and Music Research Guides," *Annotations* (a publication of Indiana University's Music Department), Fall 1989, various publishers. A witty, informative article focusing not only on music research guides but on aspects of proper bibliographic form. Stevens, the critic and librarian, concludes that true knowledge comes from proper use of reference works and a dash of common sense.

Stokes, Roy, *A Bibliographical Companion.* Metuchen, NJ: Scarecrow Press, 1989. This is a dictionary of terms employed in bibliography. The descriptions, terminology, and general approach are as literate as they are a delight to read. Highly recommended for both beginners and would be experts.

Sweetland, James, "Errors in Bibliographic Citations. . .," *The Library Quarterly,* October 1989, pp. 291–304. The author finds a high percentage of errors in citations used in many scholarly works. "Such errors can be traced to a lack of standardization in citation formats." And there are other reasons, but the failure to standardize procedures goes a long way to explain the problems librarians have with bibliographies. If anyone thinks this a passing problem, see the 63 references at the end of the article.

CHAPTER FOUR
BIBLIOGRAPHIES: NATIONAL
LIBRARY CATALOGS AND TRADE
BIBLIOGRAPHIES

A common problem concerns the person who wants to know just how much is available on a given subject, such as eighteenth-century gardens or nuclear-waste dumping facilities. One searches the library and may even tap other resources by a computer, but even the most refined search inevitably ends with the question: "Yes, but is that all?" Furthermore, is what was found the best available information for the query?

Matching total retrieval with total relevancy is close to impossible, but bibliographies offer a workable compromise.

There is a type of coordination, a kind of fitting together of different pieces of a puzzle, which allows an overview of what is available from many parts of the world. The procedure is to consult various national library catalogs. This procedure is quite comprehensive for specific books and, for that matter, nonprint materials such as databases and videodisks.

Since a national library catalog is not limited by time, territory, language, subject, or forms of communication, it does come close to the ideal universal bibliography. And although none of the national library catalogs claims to be universal in scope, collectively they do offer a relatively comprehensive record of international publishing. The Library of Congress, for example, catalogs materials from around the world, and a good proportion of its holdings consists of books, magazines, music, and the like from international publishers. Numerically, an idea of the scope of the Library of Congress holdings may be gathered from the fact that the Library contains more than 130 million discrete items and, on the average, adds from 5 to 6 million new items each year. Comparatively speaking, the average number of books published in America each year hovers around 50,000 titles, a small part of the overall annual acquisitions of the library's net, which sweeps in titles of books as well as other published items from around the world. Quite similar figures apply to the British Library.

In order to be properly qualified as a national bibliography, the system must have two elements: (1) It needs a legal deposit system which ensures that the national library receives a copy of everything to be listed in the bibliography; and (2) the records must be from direct examination of the materials, not from the publisher or author. Most western countries now have depository/direct examination as a foundation for national bibliography.

National bibliographies are connected to and are part of a national library. In western countries the two are almost synonymous, but this is not so everywhere. "The priorities for national library functions differ from country to country, not only in scale but in importance. For example, the creation of the national bibliographic record is an important but very small function for a small less-developed country, but leadership, training and planning of the nation's library system must be regarded as both important and major functions."[1]

Form

Bibliographies and other reference works are no longer limited to print. The majority may be accessed online, through CD-ROM or microfiche. Today the online/CD-ROM approach is favored. It will lead to two results:

1. By the end of this century, few national or general bibliographies will be available in print. The majority will be accessible only in an electronic form, which is not only cheaper but allows for faster updating of material and for easier searching.
2. There will, however, be some printed bibliographies. These will be detailed scholarly works dealing with a specific subject. It is unlikely that analytical or textual bibliographies will be limited to electronic access because they are less fre-

[1]Maurice B. Line, "National Libraries in Time of Change," IFLA Journal, 14(1988)1, p. 26.

quently used and may be less costly to produce in print form.

Meanwhile, one must learn about the printed versions of bibliographies. Why? Although the form may be transferred to an electronic system, the content is similar. The method of compilation and the problems involved are the same. The basic theory behind the intellectual approach to bibliography does not differ. What is more important to consider, no matter in what format, is that the bibliography has definite uses, uses which can only be understood when one appreciates the scope and purpose of a particular type of bibliography.

UNION CATALOGS

A term associated with national catalogs is *union catalog,* for example, the Library of Congress's *National Union Catalog.* A union catalog indicates who has what. A fuller, often-repeated definition is this: "an inventory common to several libraries that lists some or all of their publications maintained in one or more orders of arrangement." The user turns to a union list to locate a given book, periodical, or newspaper in another library, which may be in the same city or thousands of miles away. Given the location and the operation of an interlibrary loan or copying process, the user can then have the particular book or item borrowed from the holding library.

National Library Catalogs[2]

U.S. Library of Congress. *The National Union Catalog: A Cumulative Author List.* Washington: Library of Congress, Card Division, 1956 to 1983. Nine monthly issues and three quarterly cumulations. Ten- and four-year cumulations from 1956. Price varies.

————, *Library of Congress Catalogs: Subject Catalog.* Washington: Library of Congress, 1950 to 1983. Three quarterly issues with

[2] *The National Union Catalog* is employed by most libraries today online or on a CD-ROM disk. This is discussed in the next section, but before one can approach the daily use of the online *NUC,* it is necessary to appreciate the printed version, i.e., what is involved in compilation. The services mentioned here are only a few of many. For a complete catalog of works (and prices) request the annual "Access" catalog of publications from the Library of Congress.

annual cumulations. Four-year cumulations from 1950. Price varies.

————, *The National Union Catalogs in Microfiche.* Washington: Library of Congress, January 1983 to date. Monthly issues and quarterly cumulations: (1) *NUC Books.* $580. (2) *NUC Audiovisual Materials* (quarterly). $95. (3) NUC Cartographic Materials (quarterly). $175. (4) NUC Register of Additional Locations (quarterly). $295. The National Union Catalog in part is available online from 1968 to date as MARC (machine-readable cataloging) from the Library of Congress and other sources. DIALOG file 426 is $45 per online hour. It is available, also, from numerous publishers on CD-ROM.

————, *The National Union Catalog: Pre-1956 Imprints.* London: Mansell, 1968–1981, 754 vols. $35,000. Microform: $11,750. Much of the pre-1956 imprints is available online as REMARC (retrospective machine-readable cataloging).

What is the scope of *The National Union Catalog?* One will note that each page photographically reproduces catalog cards, the same familiar cards found in most libraries. Each card represents an item cataloged by the Library of Congress or by one of more than 1,500 libraries in the United States and Canada. This feature makes it a union catalog in that it shows the holdings of more than one library.

What is cataloged? Almost every communication medium. In this case, the entries are primarily for books; maps; atlases; pamphlets; and serials, including periodicals.

The ongoing book catalogs of the Library of Congress are essentially no different from the familiar catalog found in the local library. This is important to recognize. Sometimes the imposing sets, as well as the databases and microfiche, intimidate the novice. Before turning to the microfiche and database formats consider the general scope, purpose, and use of the service.

The printed volumes are arranged alphabetically by author or main entry. Generally, the heading of a main entry is an author's name, but lacking such information, it may be a title. It is never both author and title. There is no subject approach in the main *National Union Catalog* and cross-references are minimal. (A subject approach is offered, but in another set to be discussed.)

The reproduced card varies in quantity and type of information given, but in almost all cases it includes the typical bibliographical description in this order: full name of author, dates of birth and death; full title; place, publisher, and date; collation (e.g., paging, illustrations, maps); series; edition; notes on contents, history; tracing for subject headings and added entries; the Library of Congress and, usually, the Dewey classifications; and The International Standard Book Numbers.

How is *The National Union Catalog (NUC)* used in reference work?

1. Since this is a union catalog that shows not only the holdings of the Library of Congress but also titles in over 1500 other libraries, it allows the reference librarian to locate a given title quickly. Hence users who need a work that is not in their library may find the nearest location in *The National Union Catalog.* For example, the first edition of *I Remember,* by J. Henry Harper, is identified as being in eight other libraries. Location symbols for the eight are: OOxM, TxU, OCU, OCL, MnU, NIC, ViBibV, and WU. The initials stand for libraries in various parts of the country and are explained in the front of cumulative volumes. Depending on the policy of the holding library, the librarian may or may not be able to borrow the title on interlibrary loan. Failing a loan, it may be possible to get sections copied. All titles without indication of a contributing library are held by the Library of Congress. (The symbol of the Library is DLC.) After 1973, the bulk of location reports are not found in the *NUC* main set. One must turn to the *National Union Catalog—Register of Additional Locations* for such information. Books are listed chronologically by the Library of Congress catalog card number.

2. *The National Union Catalog* amounts to virtually a basic, full author bibliography. Anyone wanting to know every book (magazine articles and other such items aside) that author X has published has only to consult the author's name under the full *NUC* set.

3. The complete cataloging gives details on a book (e.g., when it was published, by whom, and where) and helps the reference librarian to verify that it exists—an important matter when there is a question as to whether a particular publisher actually did publish this or that. Verification, however, is even more important when the reference librarian is attempting to straighten out the misspelling of a title or an author's name. In other words, the *NUC* sets the record straight when there is doubt about the validity of a given bit of information.

4. In terms of acquisitions, particularly of expensive or rare

items, *NUC* permits a library to concentrate in subject areas with the assurance that the less-developed areas may be augmented by interlibrary loan from other libraries.

5. In terms of cataloging (which is basic to reference service), the *NUC* offers a number of advantages. The primary asset is central cataloging, which should limit the amount of original cataloging necessary.

6. The sixth advantage of *The National Union Catalog* is as much psychological as it is real. Its very existence gives the librarian (and more-involved lay users) a sense of order and control which would otherwise be lacking in a world that cries for some type of order.

When one is seeking a book by subject, rather than by author, one turns to the *Library of Congress Catalogs: Subject Catalog.* However, there is one important catch. The subject approach can be used only for material published since 1945. (The set begins in 1950, but cataloging goes back to books published in 1945.) Prior to that date, there is no subject avenue to *The National Union Catalog* titles.[3]

So far, the discussion has concerned only ongoing issues of *The National Union Catalog,* i.e., those published monthly and cumulated annually. But how does one locate a title published, say, in 1950 or, for that matter, any one of the 10 million retrospective entries not in the current *National Union Catalog?* The answer requires a brief historical sketch of a monumental undertaking.

The National Union Catalog began in card form in 1901. By 1926, the *NUC* had over 2 million cards, physically located in the Library of Congress. Anyone who wanted to consult the *NUC* had to query the Library of Congress or go there in person. The problem was solved, or so it was thought, by sending duplicate cards of the *NUC* to key research libraries throughout the United States. This procedure proved as costly as it was inefficient. Beginning therefore, in the early 1940s, work started on the printed-book catalog; the individual cards were reproduced in the familiar *NUC* book form instead of being sent to libraries card by card. However, it was not until January 1, 1956, that it was decided that the book catalogs should be expanded to include not only Library of Congress holdings but also the imprints of other libraries.

What was to be done with *The National Union Catalog* prior to 1956, that is, with the card catalog in the Library of Congress which

---

[3]An online search of REMARC (REtrospective MARC) does enable a limited subject approach in that one may search for key words in the title of a book.

was not in book form? The answer came in 1968 when *The National Union Catalog: Pre-1956 Imprints* began to be published.

The *Pre-1956 Imprints* is a cumulative *National Union Catalog* up to 1956. The more than 11-million entries represent the *NUC* holdings prior to 1956 and take the place of other sets.

The rapid development of technology, from microfiche to online catalogs, makes it unlikely that there will ever be another printed bibliography of this size. (Balanced one upon the other, the 13.6-inch-tall volumes in a single set would stack higher than the Pan American Building in New York.) Future catalogs, if there are any of this size, will be in another form, probably on the order of the microfiche edition of the *NUC.*

NUC in Microfiche

The ongoing familiar printed-book form of *The National Union Catalog* gave way to microfiche in 1983, and is now issued only in this format. The reasons for the change were many, but primarily they involved cutting costs.

Essentially, this version has the same information as the book form, but it is presented in a different order. The main set, *NUC Books,* averages about 340 fiche a year. (*NUC U.S. Books* is limited to American publications; it offers 128 fiche a year, but follows the same procedures as the larger set.) It is subdivided, each on a separate series of microfiche, by author, title, subject, and series. This allows a new title and a new series entry into the holdings, but it has some drawbacks in terms of rapid use.

In order to locate the full Library of Congress entry one must have the register number, found in the lower right-hand corner of the author, title, subject, or series entry, right after the Library of Congress catalog card number. One then turns to another sheet of microfiche *(NUC Books Register)* where the numbers are in order. When the number is located (in the upper left-hand section of the main entry), one has the complete cataloging information. Actually, the author, title, or subject entry may be enough in that each gives the author, title, publisher, date, and Library of Congress classification. Conversely, if one wants to know the number of pages in the book, its size, or find tracings or the Dewey Decimal Classification, one must turn to the *NUC Books Register.* This two-step process can be confusing, particularly if one needs data on a series of books.

The same process is followed when one is looking up audiovisual materials in the *NUC Audiovisual Materials,* or is seeking information from the *NUC Cartographic Materials.*

There is even a third step involved. If the user wants to find what other libraries may have a copy of *The Journey of a Librarian,* it is necessary to (1) locate the Library of Congress catalog card number at the bottom of the author, title, subject, or series card and then (2) locate that number in the *NUC Register of Additional Locations.* Here additional libraries holding the book are noted as *NUC* symbols.

Another drawback to the microfiche system is that a mechanical viewer must be employed, and that can break down. Also, only one person at a time may search each microfiche. None of this is a major barrier to use, but it will be inconvenient for those accustomed to the printed form or rapid bibliographic information at the computer terminal.

NUC Divisions

The *NUC* is composed of numerous divisions. It includes media other than books, but these are beyond the scope of this text. One example, however, will indicate how material other than books is treated. The printed *National Union Catalog and Manuscripts Collections* (1959 to date) lists some 60,000 collections in over 1300 libraries. The entries are complete in that they give the name of the person(s) involved with the manuscripts, the title of the collection, a description of its size (in feet), and the like. There are geographic, name, and general indexes, as well as a contributing list of depositaries. What may be confusing is that the collections are listed as received and not in any particular order. The use of the indexes is absolutely essential. An *Index to Personal Names in the National Union Catalog of MS Collections 1959–1984* (Alexander, Va.: Chadwick-Healey, 1988, 2 vols.) is self-explanatory. One finds, for example, Gibbon, Edward, 60-1579. The number refers to the entry number in the set.

NUC ONLINE AND CD-ROM

The awesome number of volumes, as well as the forms in which the *National Union Catalog* appears, gives one pause. But one's timidity in approaching the *NUC* can be tempered by a computer terminal.

Many librarians and certainly the majority of reference librarians today turn to the *NUC* online or on a CD-ROM disk. The microfiche or the bound volumes are used on occasion, or where the library cannot afford online services, but, for the most part, they are an anachronism.[4]

The *NUC* is referred to online in two parts:

1. MARC, an acronym for *ma*chine-*r*eadable *c*ataloging, has reference to the *NUC* from 1968 through to today, and now consists of over 2.5 million records. It is updated monthly with about 15,000 new records a month.
2. REMARC, an acronym for *r*etrospective *ma*chine-*r*eadable *c*ataloging, or retrospective MARC. This has reference primarily, although not exclusively, to many of the records in the *Pre-1956 Imprints* set.

There are at least two different ways in which these records may be viewed, aside from using the printed and microfiche versions.

Online via OCLC and/or RLIN. Although acronyms, OCLC (Online Computer Library Center) and RLIN (Research Libraries Information Network) are used so often in libraries as names of bibliographic utilities or networks that they are enough in themselves. Essentially both systems allow member libraries to share cataloging information. This information includes the basic Library of Congress cataloging on MARC tapes. They provide additional services discussed in the second volume.

The utilities are used by the majority of American libraries. They offer catalog/reference information for about 25 million works.

Through a series of simple commands, the searcher may locate a record by author or by title, and by subject as well. There are other avenues of approach. The utilities not only allow one to find complete information on a given book, periodical, or recording but also indicate which libraries have the material. Needless to say the systems are used extensively in interlibrary loan and by reference librarians in locating and verifying titles.

In addition, one may access the two online versions of the *NUC*: (1) by accessing them through a commercial vendor such as DIALOG, (2) by obtaining them from an individual library which may have one or both of the systems as part of the online library

---

[4]Actually any library large enough to use NUC regularly probably has the funding and the know-how to handle online or on CD-ROM disks. As will be shown, even small libraries may now access *NUC* online at probably less cost than the printed and microfiche works.

catalog, or (3) by simply buying the tapes as issued by the Library of Congress for various uses, private and public.

CD-ROM Disks. The cost of accessing the *NUC* online may be so high (it varies from service to service but is now around $50 an hour) that the library finds it more economical to get the same data on a CD-ROM disk.

There are several commercial firms which offer MARC or RE-MARC, or both, on CD-ROM. Turn to any of the CD-ROM guides described in the second volume of this text for publishers, or consult advertisements and mailings which inundate libraries each time a new service is made available by a publisher of CD-ROM. Here one example will suffice.

Bibliofile. This is published by the Library Corporation and distributed by the well-known book dealer, Brodart. The entire MARC database is on three disks. It is updated and published monthly (at about $1500 a year) or quarterly (at about half that price). The system operates with a CD-ROM disk drive and a standard microcomputer. The cost for equipment varies, but runs from $3000 to $5000.

MARC is at the heart of national and international online bibliographical searches, but there are numerous other bibliographies now available at a terminal. These are mentioned throughout this text. One example is the familiar *Books in Print,* discussed in the next section, which allows the reference librarian to verify the most recent publication's date, price, and author.

United States Retrospective Bibliography

For most purposes the *National Union Catalog* offers the average individual all the information needed about published books. Still, there comes a time when more detail is required, when an item is so scarce, so elusive, and so esoteric that it may not be fully described (particularly in terms of its importance in the development of a subject) in *NUC.* At this point the search leads toward one of numerous retrospective enumerative, analytical, or textual bibliographies.

The basic bibliographies of this type are dutifully listed in both *Guide to Reference Books* and *Guide to Reference Materials,* as well as in specialized bibliographies dealing with everything from the history of printing to the history of medicine. Retrospective bibliography is hardly limited to the United States. In fact, it is found where there is any type of developed bibliographic system.

NATIONAL BIBLIOGRAPHIES OUTSIDE THE UNITED STATES

European national libraries follow much the same pattern as the Library of Congress. Each nation has its own bibliography. These are listed in detail in the *Guide to Reference Books,* and can only be suggested here. Today all are in several forms from the traditional printed book to online and CD-ROM.

Thanks to machine-readable-capability there is an increasing drive to combine the various Western bibliographies. For example, the British Library and the French Bibliothèque Nationale launched an effort in the late 1980s to produce CD-ROM disks with bibliographic data from both libraries.

Meanwhile, the Canadian and the British national bibliographies are put to great use by students. The reason, of course, is that they primarily are concerned with books in the English language. Scholars and those with knowledge of other languages turn to the other bibliographies.

National Bibliography in Canada

> *Canadiana.* Ottawa: National Library of Canada, 1960 to date, monthly with annual cumulations. Prices on request. CD-ROM, publisher, weekly, various prices.

There are now over 5 million records in the Canadian national bibliography. This represents the holdings of the national library as well as approximately 300 libraries throughout Canada. The format is much the same as that for the Library of Congress and includes all MARC English language files since 1965.

About 45,000 serials (i.e., journals and magazines) are in the social sciences and humanities, as well as close to 70,000 in science, and a wide variety of other materials are dutifully cataloged.

Through the online service DOBIS one may search the files in the standard way, as well as by Library of Congress numbers. A private firm, Utlas International, offers similar online searches through UTLAS. Here, too, one has the available records from the Library of Congress, as well as records of The British Library, the Library of Medicine, and several other sources for a total of some 45 million records. The same company offers the system on CD-ROM disks.

The National Library of Canada offers CANMA (Canadian Machine-Readable Cataloging) on CD-ROM, which includes *Canadiana* and several related bibliographic databases. Monographic coverage is from 1973 to date, while music and sound recordings are from 1986 to date. Updatings are weekly for most of the data.

National Bibliography in Great Britain

British Library, Department of Printed Books. *General Catalogue of Printed Books.* London: Trustees of the British Museum, 1959–1966, 263 vols. *Ten-Year Supplement,* 1956–1965, 1968, 50 vols. *Five-Year Supplement,* 1966–1970, 1971–1972, 26 vols.; 1971–1975, 1978–1980, 13 vols. Prices on request.

————. *The British Library General Catalogue of Printed Books to 1975.* New York: K. G. Saur, 1979 to 1983, supplement, 1976–1982, 256 vols. plus 50 additional vols. Prices on request. (CD-ROM, Chadwyck-Healey Inc. Price on request.)

The British Library is roughly equivalent to our Library of Congress, and its various catalogs are similar in purpose (if not in scope) to *The National Union Catalog.* The essential differences are that

1. The British Library is much older than the Library of Congress and has a considerably larger collection of titles dating from the fifteenth century up to the 1960s when the Library of Congress moved to embrace all world publications. The Library of Congress bibliographies, for the past thirty or so years, are suitable for all but the most esoteric study. Only scholars are likely to consult other sources in order to avoid any gaps in research.
2. The British Library's catalog is not a union catalog and shows holdings only of the British Library.
3. The data for titles are somewhat briefer than those in *The National Union Catalog.*
4. Larger amounts of analytical material and cross-references are included. For example, considerable attention is given to the analysis of series, and there are numerous cross-references from names of editors, translators, and other names connected with a title.
5. Key-word title entries are used, and in some ways this approach is useful because of the lack of satisfactory subject catalog. The problem, of course, is when the title does not reveal something about the contents.
6. Whereas *The National Union Catalog* can be considered very

much a current bibliographical aid, the *General Catalogue,* because of its approach and infrequent publication, is more retrospective.

How much duplication is there between the massive British catalog and *The National Union Catalog?* Walford did a sampling and found that 75 to 80 percent of the titles in the British work are not in the American equivalent, and for titles published before 1800 that number increases to 90 percent. Some experts estimate that there are from 900,000 to over 1 million titles in the British Library catalog not found in other national bibliographies. With increased interest in capturing worldwide titles in *The National Union Catalog,* the amount of duplication is bound to increase in the years ahead. Meanwhile, no large research library can afford to be without the British Library's *General Catalogue.*

Just as *NUC* has its massive *Pre-1956 Imprints,* so the British Library has an equivalent in the *British Library General Catalogue.* The set incorporates the *General Catalogue of Printed Books,* plus the supplements.

The British Library's holdings may be searched online through a number of systems, including the aforementioned UTLAS (which concentrates on Canadian holdings as well). One British Library online source is BLAISE-LINE, which is more limited in that it includes only monographs published since 1980 and available on interlibrary loan from the British Library center at Boston Spa. Three CD-ROM disks (published from 1989 through 1991) have the holdings of the *British Library General Catalogue* to 1975. The cost of the set is approximately $16,000; it is published by Chadwick-Healey.

TRADE BIBLIOGRAPHY

Most of the enumerative bibliographies found in libraries can be classified as national or trade bibliographies. The distinction between the types is not always clear, if indeed there is a distinction. There are numerous definitions and possible combinations. The important consideration is not so much where the bibliography falls in the sometimes esoteric reference scheme but, rather, how it is used.

The pragmatic function of a trade bibliography is to tell the librarian what was, what is, and what will be available either by purchase or by possible loan from another library. The bibliographies give necessary bibliographical information (e.g., publisher, price, author, subject area, and Library of Congress or Dewey numbers), which is used for a number of purposes ranging from clarifying proper spelling to locating an item by subject area. Also, the trade bibliography is a primary control device for bringing some order to the 50,000 or more books published in the United States each year, not to mention similarly staggering figures for pamphlets, reports, recordings, films, and other items.

The process of compiling trade bibliographies differs from country to country, but there is a basic pattern. An effort is made first to give a current listing of titles published the previous week, month, or quarter. These data are then cumulated for the annual breakdown of titles published and beyond that, those which are in print, those which are out of print, and those which are going to be published. (The same process applies to forms other than books.)

United States Trade Bibliography: Annual and Biannual

(All titles listed below published by the R. R. Bowker Company)

Books in Print, 1948 to date, 8 vols., annual. $350.

Supplement, 1973 to date, 2 vols., annual. $175.

Subject Guide to Books in Print, 1957 to date, 5 vols., annual. $240.

Paperbound Books in Print, 1955 to date, 3 vols., biannual. $290.

Publishers, Distributors and Wholesalers of the United States, 1986 to date, annual. $110.

Note: As with the *National Union Catalog,* many libraries use these bibliographies online or from a CD-ROM disk. The electronic versions are discussed in the next section.

These bibliographies list the books that can be purchased from American publishers (i.e., are in print), in what forms (hardbound, paperback), and at what prices. Depending on the individual trade bibliography, additional information is given as to the date of publication, the number of pages, the subjects covered, and other data necessary for proper and easy use of the bibliography.

The most frequently consulted titles are *Books in Print (BIP)* and the *Subject Guide to Books in Print.* More than 800,000 in-print books of all kinds (hardbounds, paperbacks, trade books, textbooks, adult titles, juveniles) are indexed by author and by title in *Books in Print.* (*In print* is a term which indicates the book is still available from a publisher. If not available, it is called "out of print.") The eight-volume set is in four parts: (1) authors, (2) titles, (3) O. P. (out of print), and (4) the eighth volume, publishers. Actually, the last volume may be used independently, as noted later, as a handy guide to publishers.

Besides telling the user whether the book can be purchased, from whom, and at what price, the trade bibliography also answers such questions as: "What books by William Faulkner are in print, including both hardbound and paperbound editions at various prices?" "Who is the publisher of *The Old Patagonian Express*"? "Is John Irving's first novel still in print?"

Issued in October of each year, *Books in Print* is supplemented by two volumes in April of the following year. Here publishers list some 250,000 titles newly published, or with price changes and not included in the basic BIP, as well as titles which are out of print or which are to be issued before the next annual *BIP* volumes. These listings are arranged by author and by title as well as by subject; thus the *Books in Print Supplement* is also a supplement to *Subject Guide to Books in Print*. The *Supplement* includes an updated list of all publishers, with any address changes. For normal purposes, *BIP* is enough for most questions. When the original publishing date is more than one or two years old, when there has been a spurt of inflation, or when the librarian cannot find a title, a double check in the *Books in Print Supplement* is wise.

The majority of titles listed in *BIP* are similarly found in *Subject Guide to Books in Print*. In the subject approach, no entries are made for fiction, poetry, or bibles. (Note, though, that the guide does list books *about* fiction under the name of the author of the fiction; criticism of the works of Henry James, for example, is found under James.) The use of the subject guide, which virtually rearranges *BIP* under 65,000 Library of Congress subject headings, is self-evident.[5] It not only helps in locating books about a given subject but may also be used to help expand the library's collection in given areas. If, for example, books about veterinarians are in great demand, the guide gives a complete list of those available from American publishers. An important point: The list is inclusive, not selective. No warning sign differentiates the world's most misleading book about veterinarians from the best among, say, 20 titles listed. The librarian must turn to other bibliographies and reviews for judgments and evaluations of titles in any subject area. Beginning in 1990–1991, some of the entries include brief annotations supplied by the pub-

[5]Library of Congress subject cataloging is used only as a guide, and Bowker or the publisher frequently assigns modified Library of Congress headings. This, coupled with only about 1.1 subject headings per book, results in less-than-satisfactory retrieval. Often, too, a vast number of titles may be assigned under a heading so broad that a search is almost impossible.

lisher. These are descriptive, not evaluative. Also, with the 1990–1991 edition, a fifth volume was added—this is a subject thesaurus that lists and cross references all headings from the *Subject Guide.* The fact that sometimes the inquiry cannot be answered is not always the fault of the questioner's incorrect spelling of the title or of the author's name. *Books in Print,* through either filing errors or misinformation from the publishers, may fail to guide a user to a title which the user knows to be correct.

Almost every entry in *BIP* includes the author, coauthor (if any), editor, price, publisher, year of publication, number of volumes, Library of Congress card number, and the International Standard Book Numbers (ISBN).

Over the past 40 years *Books in Print* has grown from one volume and 85,000 titles to well over 850,000 entries by the early 1990s. While the population has increased about 60 percent from 1948 to 1990, the number of U.S. published titles has jumped over 900 percent. One explanation: the increase in publishers from approximately 350 in the late 1930s to well over 32,000 today. Incidentally, less than 2 percent of the publishers are responsible for two-thirds of all books published.

As all this data is on a computer memory, it hardly takes great skill to divide and subdivide it for other types of bibliographies. For example, *Paperbound Books in Print* takes the paperbound titles out of *Books in Print* and, again, arranges them by author, title, and subject. The end result is a separate work with about 365,000 in print titles. It has two distinct advantages over its parent volumes: (1) It is updated twice each year, i.e., spring and fall. The 1990 spring update, for example, included 25,000 new titles, plus 100,000 entry updates. (2) It is limited only to paperbacks and therefore removes any confusion about the various forms in which the title may appear. A third advantage is that titles which may not appear in *Books in Print,* if only because they are published after the master volumes are out, can be found here.

Using the same set of tapes for *Books in Print,* although often adding newer titles or giving the user additional features, the publisher issues *Children's Books in Print,* which is an author and title listing of close to 50,000 books. The unique feature is the third volume in the set, *Children's Books in Print: Subjects.* Here there are subject headings to the 50,000 or so titles in the two-volume main work. The headings are for those working with children, and include Sears as well as Library of Congress listings; and, most important, has a fiction category for a limited number of subject headings.

There are other spin-off works from the basic *Books in Print* computer memory, e.g., *Scientific and Technical Books and Serials in Print;*; *Medical and Health Care Books and Serials in Print, Large Type Books in Print,* etc. Note that two of these titles include magazines and journals as well as books. Again, the periodicals are lifted from tapes used to publish serial directories by the same publisher.

While many of these are questionable purchases, there is one R. R. Bowker spin-off which will be of great help to almost all libraries. This is *The Complete Directory of Large Print Books & Serials* (1970 to date, annual). At only $90 this guide includes approximately 7000 books arranged under twenty-four broad subject categories. There are numerous indexes, including title and author. The newspapers and periodicals are divided according to interest to various age groups.

In the 1990 publicity release, the publisher notes that "eight major publishers are providing almost 1200 titles per year, while smaller publishers account for another 200 titles per year." The extremely small number involved with the valuable project explains why there are so few large print books. As the population ages, this may change, but for now the number of available titles is a critical problem for many libraries.

R. R. Bowker distributes similar bibliographies for other countries. For example, *British Books in Print* is available, which has over 400,000 titles from about 10,000 publishers, and then we also have *Canadian Books in Print.* There are French, German, Italian, and other foreign language equivalents published by firms in various countries.[6]

For a broad view there is *International Books in Print* (1979 to date, Munich and New York: K. G. Saur, 2 vols.) which has around 170,000 books published outside of the United States and Canada. Note that this only includes English language works. About 6000 publishers from 120 countries are represented. In addition to the author and title approach there is a subject entry, too.

Books in Print and Online/CD-ROM/Microfiche

Books in Print, and its many cousins, offer an example of the four basic forms in which many reference books are now available. A fifth, which reacts to voice commands, is likely before the end of the 1990s. One may (1) purchase *Books in Print* in printed form; (2)

---

[6]Most are in as many forms (online, CD-ROM, microfiche, etc.) as *Books in Print.* For example, *Les Livres Disponibles* (French Books in Print) offers a six-volume basic set, plus a microfiche edition and is available online.

access it online;[7] (3) access it through a CD-ROM disk; or (4) access it on microfiche. .

Aside from its intrinsic value, the primary value of understanding *Books in Print* in various forms is to appreciate what is likely to be the situation for thousands of other works in the same formats. For the future, it appears that many publishers will offer reference works online, on CD-ROM, and possibly microfiche. Other formats will be employed as they are developed.

Online. The by-now obvious relationship between the various R. R. Bowker bibliographies makes them ideal for online searching. DIALOG's database, which goes back only to 1979, not to 1948, when *Books in Print* was first published, includes almost all of the approximately 1 million works from the basic listing. Although there are many advantages to this approach, including multiple points of access, probably the biggest advantage is the time factor. As the file is updated by around 6000 entries each month, it is considerably more current than printed sources.

Standard search patterns of DIALOG are followed. One may locate a title by having one of the primary elements in the printed work such as author, title, publisher, publishing date, or ISBN. Possibly the greatest advantage for the reference librarian is the ability online to search by key words, both in terms of author, subject, and in the title. Thus, someone with only a vague notion of the name of a book may be satisfied by being offered not one, but sometimes a half dozen or more closely related titles for consideration. Specifics are imperative; if one only enters basic words such as *economics*, the search result may show 3000 or more such words used in a title. This problem can be overcome by using multiword titles and phrases.

Searching for an author, the prefix "AU" is employed: S AU=James, Henry. As in most search patterns it is essential to follow precise instructions: It is necessary not only to enter the symbol, but to be sure there is a comma and space between the last and first name. Where variations exist in the first or last name, a shortcut may be to expand the name: ?E AU=James, J?

Complementing *Books in Print* online, one may use *Publishers, Distributors, and Wholesalers* as well. This is DIALOG file 450, which

[7]The online version is offered by numerous vendors and some book dealers in various forms. DIALOG (File 470, $65 per hour) is typical. Online includes the following printed sources: *Books in Print, Subject Guide to Books in Print, Books in Print Supplement, Forthcoming Books, Books Out of Print, Paperbound Books in Print, Children's Books in Print, Subject Guide to Children's Books in Print, Scientific and Technical Books, Medical Books, Business and Economics Books, Religious Books.*

includes everything found in the printed volume as well as all the publishers listed in the seventh volume of *Books in Print.* There is a total of some 65,000 names, almost all of which include full data, from address to telephone number. The file is updated monthly and the connect time runs $66 an hour.

CD-ROM: *Books in Print with Book Reviews Plus,* (monthly, $1395). The latter includes the *Books in Print* set,[8] as well as reviews, taken quarterly, from *Publishers Weekly, Library Journal, School Library Journal, Choice, Booklist, Reference and Research Books News,* and *Sci-Tech Book News.*

The monthly update means that the user has some 25,000 book reviews from 1987, plus new reviews as added. In addition, as the main part of the system, are the nearly 840,000 entries in *Books in Print* and its cousins.

Thanks to a series of easy-to-follow menus (i.e., directions) which appear on the computer screen, one may search the file with a minimum of difficulty. As in the printed version, the usual search is by author, title, or subject. But as in online, searching capabilities are added, such as by an ISBN number, a publisher, or, most important, by key words. One can modify the quest by stipulating a given price, audience, with or without illustrations, date of publication, and the like.

Again, and this is worth stressing, as with the online version, the reference librarian can use the system to find a work using an incomplete or incorrect title. If the user can give one or two key words, say, from the title, these entries may be searched for the proper title.

The publicity, for once, is nearly correct. According to the publisher, "Users can browse through the databases much like looking through a bound paper volume, or they can conduct sophisticated searches just like using an online computer database."

The CD-ROM version and the online access helps to speed along book orders. Many book dealers (Baker & Taylor, Ingram Book Company, Brodart, etc.) allow the library to transmit information found in *Books in Print* directly to them. With a push of a few computer keys, the order is electronically moved from the library to the book wholesaler. This saves the laborious typing of multiform order slips and is much faster and likely to be more accurate.[9]

---

[8]The CD-ROM "family" is not as extended as the online version, but does include: *Books in Print, Subject Guide to Books in Print, Supplement to Books in Print, Forthcoming Books, Children's Books,* and *Children's Subject Guide.*

[9]*Books in Print Plus* does not include the book reviews. It has monthly updates. For

Microfiche

Less extensive, and even less expensive is the microfiche edition of *Books in Print*. Published quarterly for $625, each quarterly edition is a complete revised version of the basic set. Not only does it record new prices, out-of-print books, and other changes, it includes forthcoming titles for the next six months. There are separate author and title indexes for each entry, albeit no subject approach. While primarily used in acquisitions, the microfiche can be a useful ready-reference aid. The frequent updating makes it an exemplary work for information currency.

WEEKLY AND MONTHLY BIBLIOGRAPHIES

Cumulative Book Index. New York: H. W. Wilson Company, 1898 to date, monthly, with three-month, annual, and two- and five-year cumulations. Service. (Wilsonline, $37 to $50 per hour.)

American Book Publishing Record. New York: R. R. Bowker Company, 1961 to date, monthly. $90. (annual cumulation, $150). Cumulations: 1876–1949, 15 vols.; 1950–1977, 15 vols.; 1980–1984, 5 vols.; microfiche edition, 1876–1981 (annual cumulations). $999.

Weekly Record. New York: R. R. Bowker Company, 1974 to date, weekly. $110.

Forthcoming Books. New York: R. R. Bowker Company, 1966 to date, bimonthly. $175.

Published since 1898, the familiar brown-covered *Cumulative Book Index (CBI)* is to be found in almost all libraries, as are its monthly and annual cumulations. It has the advantage of being well known, accurate, and easy to use. Annually about 50,000 to 60,000 books are listed in one alphabet by author, title, and subject. The author, or main, entry includes pertinent bibliographic information, as well as useful data for catalogers and acquisitions librarians. The subject headings, which follow those established by the Library of Congress, are exhaustive. Although fiction is not included as a subject, one does find headings on science fiction, short stories, mystery

two of many evaluations of the system see: Dalia Hagan, "The Tacoma (Washington) Debut of Books in Print Plus," *Library Journal,* Sept. 1, 1987, pp. 149–151; and "Books in Print Plus," *Technical Services Quarterly,* vol. 6(2), 1989, pp. 69–74. *Books Out of Print Plus* is a separate disk (for $400 a year) which gives the user out-of-print data.

and detective stories, and so on. There is also a good directory of publishers.

The publisher of *CBI* is able to list new titles monthly because "most publishers in the United States and Canada send copies of their books to the H. W. Wilson Company promptly," to quote a Wilson brochure, "and these are processed quickly and appear in the earliest possible issue of *CBI*. Therefore books are frequently listed in *CBI* before they appear in any other major bibliography." There is an understandable "sales pitch" here which is of interest because *CBI*'s rival, *American Book Publishing Record (ABPR)*, does much the same thing in terms of listing new titles each month. One would not want to argue that *CBI* is faster to the mark with new titles than the *ABPR*, but only that the librarian who cannot find a title in one has the advantage of being able to check the other.

ABPR covers much the same ground as *CBI*, but differs in that (1) it limits listings to titles published in the United States and includes from 40,000 to 55,000 entries, the number depending on how many books are published or distributed in the United States the previous year, (2) it is arranged by the Dewey Decimal System, that is, by subject, and has an author and title index, and (3) it includes separate sections on juvenile and adult fiction and paperbacks.

There is basic cataloging information for each entry. Although the data come from the Library of Congress, much of it is updated and refined. All entries include, at a minimum: title; subtitle, if any; author; publisher; date and where published; collation; series statement, where applicable; general notation, and the Library of Congress classification and subject tracings. The full entry makes it an invaluable aid.

There are two cumulations, which cover the years 1876–1984. One is multiple-print volumes available from the publisher. The other, and now most favored, is the microfiche set which has about 2 million author/title and subject entries of books published in the United States.

The monthly issues of *ABPR* lead back to another service, the *Weekly Record*. Although more important to catalogers and acquisitions librarians, the *Weekly Record* is interesting to reference librarians because it records, on a weekly basis, what is published in the United States. About 600 to 700 new titles are listed each week by author. Full bibliographic information is given for each, including Dewey Decimal and Library of Congress classifications and, often, descriptive cataloging notes. Most of the data is furnished by the Library of Congress and supplemented by the staff at Bowker. In advertising for the *ABPR*, the publisher claims that "approximately 80% of all entries have been significantly supplemented with revised and updated publication information, verified prices, and other essential data *not* included in the MARC tapes." One suspects that this is much the case with the publishers of the *CBI*.

The author arrangement limits the use for most reference purposes. However, every four weeks the contents of *Weekly Record* are rearranged by subject and cumulated as the aforementioned *ABPR*.

As in the *Books in Print* series, all Western countries have much the same system for keeping track of weekly, monthly, and annual titles published. In England, for example, there is the well-known *Whitaker's Cumulative Book List* (London: Whitaker, 1924 to date, quarterly) which is then cumulated annually. The annual volume, distributed by R. R. Bowker, has about 60,000 titles arranged in one alphabet, as is the CBI, by author, title, and subject. Each entry is brief, but with much the same data as in the *CBI*.[10]

For Canada there is *Canadian Books in Print* (Downsview, Ont.: University of Toronto Press, 1967 to date, annual). This is in two volumes. The first covers author and title; the second, subjects. A microfiche edition of the author-title volume is issued each quarter.

As a running record of what is going on in publishing, *Publishers Weekly* (New York: R. R. Bowker Company, 1872 to date) is required reading for reference librarians. This is the trade magazine of American publishers and, in addition, often contains articles, features, and news items of value to librarians. It is difficult to imagine an involved reference librarian not at least thumbing through the weekly issues, if only for the "*PW* Forecasts." Here the critical annotations on approximately 50 to 100 titles give the reader a notion of what to expect in the popular fiction and nonfiction to be published in the next month or so.

A more definitive approach to what is going to be published is found in *Forthcoming Books*. Again, this periodical is likely to be of more value to acquisitions and cataloging personnel than to refer-

---

[10]Publishers are now working on electronic ordering which bypasses the jobber or middle person. *Pubnet*, for example, is sponsored by the Association of American Publishers and allows the bookdealer or librarian to order directly from individual publishers. The database is electronically updated daily by each publisher to reflect price change and availability. "Bookstores Look to Instant Ordering," *The New York Times*, Jan. 2, 1989, p. 33. Weekly titles are found in *The Bookseller*, which is both a record of new titles and publishing news. Monthly listings are in *Whitaker's Books of the Month and Books to Come* (London: Whitaker, 1970 to date monthly). As the title suggests, it is, too, another version of *Forthcoming Books* and has works two to three months in advance of publishing date.

ence, but it does answer queries about a new book or possibly about a book which the patron may have heard discussed on a radio or television program before it is actually published. The bimonthly lists by author and by title books due to be published within the next five months. Each issue of some 85,000 titles includes a separate subject guide. This is too general for most purposes and where subject is a factor, one should really not count on *Forthcoming Books.*

Note, too, that the service is bimonthly, at least in print. If one takes it as part of the CD-ROM *Books in Print Plus,* it is a part of the quarterly database, hence is later than the in-print version.

INFORMATION ABOUT PUBLISHERS

Where does one find a publisher's address? The quickest way is to consult the eighth volume of *Books in Print* which is devoted to "Publishers." This includes some 25,000 names, distributors as well as publishers.[11] There are numerous other sources.

Publishers, Distributors and Wholesalers of the United States (New York: R. R. Bowker, 1988 to date, annual) offers convenient access to 50,000 publishing companies in one alphabet. Basic data include names of primary personnel, telephone number, address, as well as names of subsidiaries, various divisions, and imprints. The ISBN prefixes assigned the publisher are indicated as are any acronyms or abbreviations. There are some 4000 publishers of software (which, of course, include some book publishers) as well as distributors and wholesalers.

At one time the *Publisher's Trade List Annual* (New York: R. R. Bowker, 1973 to date, annual) offered complete publishers' catalogs and could be employed to find additional information about a publisher and the company's books. No more. Due to a change in policy and procedure, fewer and fewer catalogs are now part of the four-volume set. In fact, several major publishers no longer bother sending in catalogs. The result is a four-volume work of only about 800 catalogs and listings from a field of over 25,000. Most of the major publishers are found here, though. Also, it can be useful because of two indexes: a subject index to publishers and an index to publishers' series. One can never be sure who is or who is not included. By 1990 R. R. Bowker was making a major effort to improve the work,

---

[11]The eighth volume stands by itself in that it is a listing of publishers represented in the first seven volumes. These are arranged alphabetically with addresses and phone numbers.

but at close to $200 it is hardly worthwhile for most situations. If it improves, then it must be reevaluated.

Publishing Directories

Three related directories from R. R. Bowker are more likely to be used by librarians and book people than by laypersons. These are:

1. *American Book Trade Directory* (1915 to date, annual) which lists booksellers, wholesalers, and publishers state by state and city by city, with added information on Canada, United Kingdom, and Ireland. The 1991 edition included over 26,000 retail book dealers and wholesalers.

2. *The Bowker Annual: Library and Book Trade Almanac* (1965 to date, annual) is a related work which includes basic information on publishers and publishing. It particularly is valuable for the statistics on publishing for the previous year. In addition, as the title suggests, there are review articles and summaries of the year's past activities in various types of libraries. Other information includes updates on salaries of libraries, organization reports, product and supply directories, networks and consortia, award winners, and news. Again, statistical data are supplied.

3. *Literary Market Place* (1940 to date, annual), the standard in the field, gives directory-type information on over 12,000 firms directly or indirectly involved with publishing in the United States (about 2500 publishers are listed). It furnishes an answer to a frequently heard question at the reference desk: "Where can I get my novel [poem, biography, or other work] published?" Also, it is of considerable help to acquisitions librarians, as it gives fuller information on publishers than do bibliographies such as *Books in Print* or the *Cumulative Book Index*. Beginning in 1990 approximately 300 major small-press publishers were added, i.e., those who issue no more than three titles a year. Standard data, from address and fax number to names of primary personnel, are given for each publisher. It also has sections on marketing and publicity; book manufacturing; and sales and distribution.

The *Literary Market Place* includes names of agents whom the writer might wish to contact. However, it presupposes some knowledge of the publisher and fails to answer directly the question: "Does this publishing house publish fiction or poetry, or other things?" For this, the beginner should turn to *Publishers Trade List Annual*, or several much-used allied titles, such as *Writer's Market* (Cincinnati, Ohio: Writer's Digest, 1929 to date, annual), with a section on book publishers that includes not only directory-type information but paragraphs on types of materials wanted, royalties paid, and the manner in which copy is to be submitted.

4. *CD-ROM*   By mid-1991 R. R. Bowker offered many of its publisher guides on CD-ROM. Called "Library Reference Plus," the $695 annual disk includes: American Book Trade Directory; Publishers, Distributors and Wholesalers of the United States; Literary Market Place; International Literary Market Place; The Bowker Annual: Library and Book Trade Almanac; and the American Library Directory, discussed later in this text. Ease of use, relative low cost, and a single source of much information makes this a best buy for many libraries.

Book Prices

> *American Book Prices Current.* New York: Bancroft Parkman, 1895 to date, annual. $95.

> *Book Auction Records.* Folkestone, England: Wm. Dawson & Sons, 1903 to date, annual. Price varies (approximately $175).

> *Bookman's Price Index.* Detroit: Gale Research Company, 1965 to date, annual. $180.

The average layperson's contact with retrospective bibliography is indirect, usually taking the form of trying to find a long-out-of-print book or, more likely, the answer to a question about the value of a book printed years ago. "What is my book, map, or broadside worth?" is a familiar question in many libraries. The three guides listed here are the most often used for an answer. The larger library will have them, not only to help the user but to assist in acquisitions when a question about a used-book dealer's asking price arises. Should the library pay X dollars for a title which last year cost Y dollars less at an auction? There are many variables for both the user and the library, but the guides indicate the logical parameters of pricing.

American Book Prices Current and *Book Auction Records* are collections of book prices paid at various auctions. The third, *Bookman's Price Index,* is based on prices garnered from antiquarian dealers' catalogs. The two first titles are frequently indexed over a period of years. Hence, it is not always necessary to search each volume for a given title.

The American work lists items sold for $100 or more and includes books, serials, autographs, manuscripts, broadsides, and maps. Arrangement is alphabetical by main entry with cross-references. Each of the forms is treated in its own section. Sales run from the fall to the spring, hence each volume is usually numbered with two years, e.g., 1990–1991. Fourteen or so major auction firms, from Parke-Bernet Galleries to Christie, Manson & Woods Ltd., are included, as are a number of large individual sales of private libraries. The entries are cumulated about every five years.

Book Auction Records is the English equivalent of the American title, and although it duplicates some of the information found in that work, it includes a number of European auctions not covered elsewhere. Arrangement and form are similar to the *American Book Prices Current,* and there are periodic cumulations. Both titles suffer a time lag and normally are at least one year, and usually two years, behind the sales reported.

Bookman's Price Index differs from the other two titles in that it includes prices in catalogs of at least 60 booksellers. Entries are listed in a standard main-entry form. Volume 30, issued in 1985, includes over 45,000 titles—almost twice the number found in the auction price lists. It also has the advantage of representing retail prices which may be somewhat higher than those at an auction where book dealers themselves are bidding.

The guides give only relative indications of price. The price requested by a book dealer or sold at an auction often represents the maximum. Someone selling the same copy of the book to a dealer must expect a lower price in order for the dealer to realize a profit. Other variables, such as condition and the demands of the current market, enter into pricing. On the whole, a librarian should refer such matters of pricing to an antiquarian book dealer. The most the librarian should do is show the price lists to inquirers, who can then reach their own conclusions.

Frequently the price of a book will turn on whether it is a first edition or whether it has some other peculiar feature which sets it apart from the thousands of copies printed over the years. There are numerous guides, as well as detailed explanations of what constitutes a first edition, although the most valuable are the individual author bibliographies which give detailed information on such matters. These bibliographies are listed in the standard guides, from *Guide to Reference Books* to the *American Reference Books Annual.*

READER'S ADVISORY SERVICES

Reader's advisory services are common in public libraries and are often a part of reference services. They are defined succinctly by the Free Library of Philadelphia as "reading guidance, selection of materials to meet a particular interest or need, aid in identifying the best sources of information for a given purpose, instruction in the use of the library or a particular book, seeking an answer from or referral to other agencies or information sources outside the library".[12] Actually, most libraries are somewhat more limited in their definition, and define the descriptive phrase as helping people find books they wish to read, as well as assisting in the purchase of those books.

In one sense, the reference librarian is constantly serving as a guide to readers in the choice of materials, either specific or general. This is particularly true as an adjunct to the search-and-research type of question. Here the librarian may assist the reader in finding a considerable amount of material outside the reference collection or may suggest the right book in that collection as an aid in searching.

At an informal stage, particularly in smaller and medium-sized libraries with limited staff, the reference librarian may help a patron select a title. For example, someone may wander into the reference room looking for a good historical novel or a nonfiction work on the siege of Troy. The staff member will assist in finding the desired material, usually in the general collection.

Reader's Advisory Aids

Fiction Catalog, 11th ed. New York: H. W. Wilson Company, with four annual supplements, 1986–1990. $80.

Public Library Catalog, 9th ed. New York: H. W. Wilson Company, with four annual supplements, 1989–1992. $180.

The Reader's Adviser, 13th ed. New York: R. R. Bowker Company, 6 vols., 1986–1988. $375.

The Reader's Catalog. New York: Random House, 1989, 1500 pp. $24.95.

Of lists there is no end, and one of the more popular types centers on "best" books for a given library situation. The lists, despite certain definite drawbacks, are useful for the following:

1. Evaluating a collection. A normal method of evaluating the relative worth of a library collection is to check the collection at random or in depth by the lists noted here.
2. Building a collection. Where a library begins without a book

[12]The Free Library of Philadelphia, "Policies & Procedures," 40B (rev.), Sept. 15, 1979 (processed), p. 5.

but with a reasonable budget, many of these lists serve as the key to purchasing the core collection.

3. Helping a patron find a particular work in a subject area. Most of the lists are arranged by some type of subject approach, and as the "best" of their kind, they frequently serve to help the user find material on a desired topic.

The advantage of a list is that it is compiled by a group of experts. Usually there is an editor and an authority, or several authorities, assisting in each of the major subject fields. However, one disadvantage of this committee approach is that mediocrity tends to rule, and the book exceptional for a daring stand, in either content or style, is not likely to be included.

Used wisely, a "best" bibliography is a guide; it should be no more than that. The librarian has to form the necessary conclusions about what should or should not be included in the collection. If unable to do this, the librarian had better turn in his or her library school degree and call it quits before running a library. When any group of librarians discuss the pros and cons of best-book lists, the overriding opinion expressed is that such lists are "nice," but highly dubious crutches.

Another obvious flaw, in even the finest special list, is that it is normally tailored for a particular audience. Finally, despite efforts to keep the lists current (and here Wilson's policy of issuing frequent supplements is a great aid), many of them simply cannot keep up with the rate of book production. No sooner is the list of "best" books in anthropology out when a scholar publishes the definitive work in one area that makes the others historically interesting but not particularly pertinent for current needs.

For a number of years the Wilson Company, with the aid of qualified consultants, has been providing lists of selected books for the school and public library. The consultants who determine which titles will be included are normally drawn from various divisions of the American Library Association. Consequently, from the point of view of authority and reliability, the Wilson lists are considered basic for most library collection purposes.

There are five titles in what has come to be known as the Wilson "Standard Catalog Series." They follow more or less the same organization, differing primarily in scope evident from the title, e.g., *Children's Catalog, Junior High School Library Catalog, Senior High School Library Catalog,* and *Public Library Catalog.* The *Fiction Catalog* crosses almost all age groups, although it essentially supplements the *Public Library Catalog,* which does not list fiction. All the other catalogs have fiction entries.

Typical of the group, the *Public Library Catalog* begins with a classified arrangement of 7250 nonfiction works. Each title is listed under the author's name. Complete bibliographical information is given as well as an informative annotation. Except for an occasional few words of description added by the compilers, the majority of the annotations are quotes from one or more reviews. The reviews are noted by name, i.e., *Choice, Library Journal,* etc., but there is no further citation to year, month, or page. Quotes are selected to indicate both content and value, but the latter is anticipated in that only the "best" books are chosen for inclusion.

From the point of view of partial reference work, the librarian may make a selection of a title by reading the annotation, or invite the inquisitive reader to glance at the description. Further access is provided by a detailed title, author, and subject index.

In order to keep the service updated, a softcover volume of new selections is published each year until the next edition is issued—in this case, in 1992. This method of updating is employed by Wilson in all of the standard catalog series.

The *Fiction Catalog* follows the same format as the public library aid. In it there are 5056 titles with critical annotations. An additional 2000 titles will be included in the supplements. It is particularly useful for the detailed subject index which lists books under not just one area but numerous related subject areas. Furthermore, broad subjects are subdivided by geographical and historical area, and novelettes and composite works are analyzed by each distinctive part. Most of the titles are in print. Anyone who has tried to advise a user about the "best," or even any, title in a given subject area will find this work of extreme value.

Many guides, including those listed here, normally include fiction. In addition there are specialized titles to use with *Fiction Catalog.* A single, good example: Barbara Davis, *Read All Your Life* (Jefferson, N.C.: McFarland, 1989). Divided by nearly 50 subject sections, the guide lists about 500 novels which are suitable for book discussion groups. Further, typical discussion questions are noted.

The Reader's Adviser is among the best known of scores of general listings of "best" books. Planned originally for the bookseller seeking to build a basic stock, the three-volume set is now used extensively in libraries. Close to 40,000 titles are listed.

There is a title, author, and subject index for each volume, but for libraries the essential volume is the sixth which offers a complete index to the five-volume set.

Arrangement in each work follows a set plan. First there is a general introduction to the topic, then an annotated listing of basic reference works for that subject, and, finally, biographies and bibliographies for individual authors within the given area. The five volumes move from "the best in American and British fiction, poetry, essays, literary biography, bibliography and reference" in volume 1 to "the best in the literature of science, technology and medicine" in the fifth volume. Each section is compiled by a subject expert, and the work is fundamental for anyone seeking basic titles.

Note, too, that the inclusion of reference works for a subject may be useful for reference librarians seeking to expand upon what is available, say, in *Guide to Reference Books.*

Developed from a need to serve people who do not have a bookstore handy, *The Reader's Catalog* is the brainchild of Jason Epstein, the editorial director of Random House. The 1500 pages is a type of Sears catalog for those who wish to order books. Of the 40,000 titles, many but not all are annotated sufficiently to give an idea of content. The titles represent approximately 200 subject categories from anthropology to zoology. Each section has a short introduction, and most have numerous illustrations taken from the books considered. One major fault: many entries do not give either pagination or publication date. This fits in nicely with *The Reader's Adviser*—it is nowhere as expensive, or as exhaustive, but it is in a format accessible to most laypersons. The publication will probably be updated each year or so.

The obvious problems with *The Reader's Adviser* and the other guides are their expense and bulk. For individuals, nothing quite measures up to *Good Reading* (New York: R. R. Bowker, 23d ed., 1990). This bibliography is familiar to many laypersons as it is limited to 2500 of the "best" books arranged by broad subject. Each is annotated briefly, and the work covers all possible topics, including fiction from the Sumerians to modern times. Selection and notes are by 34 experts. And each section opens with a brief introduction. The style is commendable throughout, as are most of the choices. It is an ideal list for the would-be well-read individual. The guide is $40. That's not cheap, but it is less costly than the others.

BIBLIOGRAPHIES: PERIODICALS AND NEWSPAPERS

To this point, the primary focus has been on books, but national and trade bibliographies are also concerned with other physical forms of information. Library materials include not only books but periodicals, recordings, films, and databases.

Periodicals

Ulrich's International Periodical Directory. New York: R. R. Bowker, 1932 to date, annual, 3 vols. $319. (DIALOG File 480, $65 per hour. CD-ROM: Ulrich's Plus, 1988 to date, quarterly. $375.)

The Serials Directory. Birmingham, AL: Ebsco Publishing, 1986 to date, annual, 3 vols. $349. (CD-ROM, publisher, 1988 to date quarterly, $495.)

The Standard Periodical Directory. New York: Oxbridge Communications Inc., 1964 to date, biannual. $425.

Magazines for Libraries, 6th ed., edited by Bill and Linda Sternberg Katz. New York: R. R. Bowker, 1989, 1160 pp. $125.

When librarians talk about magazines, they usually refer to them as part of a larger family of serials. A *serial* may be defined in numerous ways, but at its most basic it is a publication issued in parts (e.g., a magazine which comes out weekly) over an indefinite period (i.e., the magazine will be published as long as possible; there is no cutoff date). Serials may be divided in several ways, for example: (1) *Irregular serials:* There are many types of these, such as proceedings of meetings which may come out only every third or fourth year. "Irregular" means that there is no fixed publishing date. (2) Periodicals: (*a*) journals, from the scholarly and scientific to the professional; (*b*) magazines, such as those found on most newsstands; and (*c*) newspapers. Some would not subdivide journals and magazines, while others would offer more esoteric subdivisions.

Ulrich's International Periodical Directory[13] is a guide to periodicals from the United States and all global points. It comes in three volumes and includes about 120,000 titles. These are arranged under approximately 600 broad subject headings, and there is a title index. "International" is a true indication of content in that the 62,000 publishers are from 197 countries.

It is extremely easy to use. Say for instance, one looks up a periodical under the subject of architecture. One finds the title and basic bibliographic information from the year it was first published as well as the frequency of publication (monthly, quarterly, etc.) and price. The address of the publisher is given, as is the name of the

[13]Beginning with the 27th edition in 1988, the publisher incorporated the volume *Irregular Serials and Annuals* (with between 35,000 and 40,000 titles) into the main set. Up to that time it had been published as a separate volume. *Irregular* is used to mean any publication such as a report, handbook, review, or proceedings which is published from time to time without any definite schedule. Also included are standard annual publications such as almanacs, yearbooks, and the like.

editor, and there are indications of content, in a 10- to 20-word descriptive line for about 12,000 of the more popular titles.

Of particular interest to reference librarians: (1) The primary places where a periodical is indexed are given. (2) There is often a circulation figure which is a rough idea of popularity. (3) Enough bibliographical data are given to allow either the librarian or the layperson to verify and order the periodical from a dealer; (4) Periodicals available online or in CD-ROM are listed.

All this is updated by a printed "Ulrich's Update," which comes out quarterly. It is included in the price of the main set. An average issue will have 1200 to 1500 changes and additions.

As with most of their bibliographies the R. R. Bowker Company makes Ulrich's available both online, via all the basic vendors, and on a CD-ROM disk. The online version is updated every 6 weeks with about 1000 to 2000 revisions and new records. The CD-ROM is revised quarterly, and adds and updates about 6000 titles each year.

Direct competition with the long-term *Ulrich's* came in 1986 when the nation's largest vendor of periodicals, Ebsco, published its own guide, *The Serial Directory*.[14] This was developed out of the firm's list of periodicals which it sells, as a middleperson jobber, to libraries, bookstores, and corporations. Although not all the titles in the Ebsco *Directory* are available from the firm, most can be ordered from them.

How does it differ from *Ulrich's?* The number of titles (130,000) listed is about the same, so that there is no real difference. There is a quarterly update. The type of material (from irregular serials to popular magazines) is the same, as is the basic subject approach with a title index. Actually, then, the differences are quite small. The *Directory* indicates major indexing services for each title, but adds dates of coverage of the particular item, although hardly for all entries. It has a listing of 5000 newspapers from around the world, and sometimes the brief descriptions are fuller than in *Ulrich's*.

Given two reference works which are almost identical in purpose and scope, a judgment has to be made about other elements. First and foremost to be considered is the matter of accuracy and complete coverage. Here *Ulrich's* is ahead, possibly for no other reason than that it has been around a much longer time and therefore

---

[14]There are several spin-offs of the basic work, e.g., *Periodicals for Business*, an annual catalog of approximately 21,000 business serials available through Ebsco. Another helpful aid is the *Index and Abstract Directory* discussed elsewhere.

the staff is considerably more experienced. At any rate, the detailed information in *Ulrich's* tends to be more current, more thorough, and more complete in details.[15]

While the *Standard Periodical Directory* has fewer listings than either the Bowker or Ebsco entries (about 75,000), it has both a wider and a narrower scope. It is wider in that it includes not only the periodicals, but many 4- to 30-page newsletters, tabloids, house organs, and social group publications. Therefore, if the librarian is looking for the address of *New World Newsletter,* it is unlikely to be in either Bowker or Ebsco, but certainly would appear in the *Standard.* The scope is narrower, in that coverage is limited only to publications of the United States and Canada.

Arrangement is similar to the multivolume sets, in that it is by broad subject with a title index. Entry information is much the same, too, although not quite as detailed. Better than the others are the brief descriptions of content in the *Standard* which are given for most, although not all, titles.

Considering its wider net, the *Standard* is a useful support bibliographic tool for larger libraries. Its ranking is third, though, if one is considering the three basic guides.

Librarians, laypersons, and advertisers often need more information than is found in any of these guides, and here the publisher of *Standard Periodical Guide's* annual *National Directory of Magazines* is useful. It lists about 17,000 magazines (which are limited to America and include everything from tabloids to house organs). For each entry one finds up to 60 pieces of data, including a 10- to 15-word descriptor of content. All this is to help the advertiser find, for example, the cost of a page or who prints the title. The guide is arranged by subject with numerous indexes.

All these guides are similar to *Books in Print* in that they list what is available, not what is best or better. In order to determine that, the librarian should turn to *Magazines for Libraries.* The sixth edition, as those before it, lists and annotates about 6500 magazines which are considered the best of their type by 140-plus subject experts. The international recommended titles are listed by subject from advertising to women, and there is a title index, as well as a separate subject index. What makes this work different is the effort to annotate each title and give both a descriptive and an evaluative

[15]Comparing the 1986 and 1987 editions, the "Reference Books Bulletin," (*The Booklist* March 15, 1987, p. 1102) notes that "in a sample of 30 periodical titles, 14 entries in *The Serials Directory* lacked beginning dates, while only 3 did in *Ulrich's.* All 30 *Ulrich's* entries showed Dewey numbers, but 10 of the Ebsco entries showed no classification numbers, at all."

summary. The result is an invaluable guide for the librarian or lay-person who must decide whether to select or drop a magazine. New editions are published every three to four years.

A common reference problem is the meaning of a particular set of initials or abbreviations used in footnotes for a periodical title. These are far from standard, and it just may be that an author has a vital bit of information hidden away under a periodical abbreviation which puzzles everyone. The solution is found, in at least 99 percent of the cases, in *Periodical Title Abbreviations* (Detroit: Gale Research Company, 1976 to date, irregular). The frequently updated guide includes close to 118,000 abbreviations. The first volume lists the abbreviation and the full title. The second volume reverses the process. The whole is updated between editions with an annual supplement.

Another pressing question these days: "How do you know if X or Y periodical is available online?" This question can be broken down into two parts: (1) "Which magazine is indexed or abstracted online?" (2) "Which magazine is online in full text so that the total contents of the magazine may be printed out at will or the text may be searched for key words which lead one to the article or section of the article of interest?"

There are several guides. *Ulrich's* includes a section of period-icals online in alphabetical order by title. In *Magazines for Libraries* some, although not all, of the periodicals online are indicated in the individual annotations.

More exhaustive sources are offered in two frequently updated reference works; *Books and Periodicals Online* (New York: Learned Information, 1987 to date) and *Directory of Periodicals Online* (Washington: Federal Document Retrieval Inc., 1988 to date). These list from 7000 to 7700 titles each.[16]

Each year numerous specialized lists of serials are published. Two examples: (1) *From Radical Left to Extreme Right* (Metuchen, N.J.: Scarecrow, 1987). This is the third edition of a basic guide which lists and annotates journals within 21 general subject areas. As the titles are highly controversial, the annotations are sent to the publishers for comments. The problem is that not all such titles are included, and the material is rapidly dated. Still, it affords a unique springboard into an area not covered well elsewhere. (2) *Encyclopedia*

---

[16]A comparison of the two services on CD-ROM is offered by Linda S. Karch, "Serials Information on CD-ROM," *Reference Services Review,* Summer 1990, pp. 81–86. She finds little difference between the two. See also Carol Tenopir's "Database Selection Tools," *Library Journal,* Nov. 1, 1988, pp. 52–53.

of Associations: Association Periodicals (Detroit: Gale Research Company, 1987 to date, irregular). This covers publications of various associations in fields from science and medicine to library science and education. The three volumes offer approximately 12,000 items. While some of these are found in *Ulrich's,* more are included here. Much of the material is so esoteric, however, that it is likely to be a reference work of value only to the largest and most specialized library.

Anyone seeking current information on British journals may now turn to *Walford's Guide to Current British Periodicals in the Humanities and Social Sciences* (London: Library Association, 1985, 479 pp. Distributed here by the American Library Association).

The well-known master of the reference guide uses his skills to cover more than 3000 magazines. Arrangement is by broad area and then by specific subject. A nice added touch: Each section contains well-written and informative introductory material. Descriptive matter usually is limited to outlining contents of a particular issue. There is little evaluation, albeit inclusion is by way of recommendation. Although now somewhat dated, the basic information about content, if not price and address of publisher, is of continued value.

Newspapers

Gale Directory of Publications and Broadcast Media. Detroit: Gale Research Company, 1869 to date, annual, 3 vols. $240.

Newspapers are listed briefly in *The Serials Directory* and found in the other guides, as well. Still, for considerably more complete information, arranged in a standard format, the *Gale Directory*[17] is by far the best. As such, it is a standard item in most reference libraries.

Material is arranged by state (and by province in Canada) and then by city and community. Under city, there are three basic subdivisions—newspapers, magazines, and radio and television.

Basic data are given about each of 1800 newspapers, whether it be a daily, weekly, or monthly. This includes the paper's name, date of establishment, frequency of publication, political bias, circulation, names of primary staff members, and information on advertising rates. A supplement and an updating service are issued during the year.

---

[17]From its inception until the mid-1980s this was known by all librarians as *N.W. Ayer Directory of Publications.* It then changed its title to *IMS Directory of Publications* and in 1987, with a new publisher, became *Gale Directory of Publications.* The new name began in 1990. What next?

In addition to newspapers, the guide includes 10,000 periodicals dutifully listed in the same way as newspapers under place of publication. The information is about the same as that given for the newspapers, but considerably more limited than what is found in *Ulrich's* or the other standard bibliographies. Therefore, while the *Gale Directory* is useful in spotting, for example, how many magazines are published in Albany, New York, it fails to give the detailed information required by most librarians. Thus, under most circumstances, one may discount the reference value of the periodicals listings.

Lack of detail is another difficulty with listings, because they are cited in separate sections by the state and city of the television and radio stations. Here are given call letters, radio frequency, network affiliation, owner, and market served. Advertising rates are included; the same data are found for television.

The *Directory* offers numerous ready-reference aids. Each state, or province section opens with a 500-plus word description of that area's primary attributes from industry to agriculture. There is a handy breakdown of basic statistics such as population, number and type of newspapers and periodicals, population of individual counties, and the like. Also, there is a large map reference section, and after each town and city name there are coordinates which help the user to locate it on the map.

Maps are presented in the third volume with one map for each of the states and Canadian provinces, as well as one for Puerto Rico. This section is followed by telephone numbers and addresses for feature editors. The bulk of the third volume consists of a number of indexes to material found in the first two volumes.

Serials: Union Lists

"Which library has X newspaper or Y periodical?" The question rises often when the librarian or user finds just the right article in a magazine or newspaper, but then discovers that the library does not have the item. Usually it can be ordered on interlibrary loan or on a fax machine if one is available. Also, it just may be that the full text of the magazine article is online, too. At any rate, faxing and the online route are expensive methods, and most people use the standard interlibrary route.

But now it is still necessary to find the closest library with the needed periodical. Here one turns to the same type of union list one consults for books. There are several approximate equivalents of *The National Union Catalog* both online and in print.

Although there are now numerous printed union lists of serials, most larger libraries depend upon what they find online, usually through OCLC, RLIN, and other networks discussed in the section on national bibliography. Here one simply types in the name of the required serial and the standard information is forthcoming, from basic publishing data to, most important, the location of the data. (The publishing data usually refer primarily to the first issue and in no way are as complete or as thorough as that found in the periodical directories.)

The heart of the serials' online union list is called CONSER (Cooperative Online Serials Program) operated by the Library of Congress as an extension of the *National Union Catalog*.[18] In the early years the entire emphasis was on North American publications, but by the early 1980s the scope was extended to international publications. CONSER includes the symbols for reporting libraries, and serials may be listed.

Between CONSER and the MARC (i.e., the online version of the *National Union Catalog* which includes serials) almost all serials may be identified online. Still, there are times when the in-print version is needed, if only to confirm a specific bibliographical detail or some odd item which by a narrow definition of terms, or by accident, may not be online.

Union Lists: Print Format

Titus, Edna Brown (ed.), *Union List of Serials in Libraries of the United States and Canada*, 3d ed. New York: H. W. Wilson Company, 1965, 5 vols. $175.
New Serial Titles. Washington: Library of Congress, 1961 to date, eight issues per year, cumulated quarterly and biannually. $350.

Turning to the print version of where to find what serial, the traditional guide is the *Union List of Serials* and its continuation in *New Serial Titles*. *The National Union Catalog* lists serials, including periodicals, but only those acquired by the Library of Congress. The series of serials is a better guide, if only because more than one source is indicated for location and, more important, because the serials, bibliographies, and union lists are limited solely to that form.

The basis of the American series of union lists is the *Union List*

[18]Linda Bartley and Regina Reynolds, "CONSER: Revolution and Evolution," *Cataloging and Classification Quarterly*, vol. 8, no. 3/4, 1988, pp. 47–66. A good background article on the project.

of Serials in Libraries of the United States and Canada, which includes titles published before 1950. It is continued by *New Serial Titles* which appears eight times a year. *New Serial Titles* is cumulated.

Given the basic volumes and the almost monthly updating (or availability on computer database), the librarian is able to (1) locate in one or more libraries almost any periodical published from its beginning until today; (2) learn the name and location of the publisher; (3) discover the name, and various changes in the name, of a magazine; (4) check the beginning date of publication and, where applicable, the date it ceased publication and possibly the date it began publication again. This information is valuable for interlibrary loan purposes and for determining whether a library has a complete run of a magazine, whether the magazine is still being published, whether it has changed its name, and so on. Full cataloging information is given for each entry.

Newspaper: Union Lists[19]

Who has which newspaper?

The quickest answer, at least for all but the most esoteric titles, is to turn, again, to OCLC or RLIN. Online one may find records of at least 55,000 U.S. newspapers. The file continues to grow, and eventually will include almost all American papers, plus selected foreign titles.

All this is made possible due to over $7 million in grants to the Library of Congress and other libraries from the National Endowment for the Humanities. The project began in 1982 in an effort to trace the whereabouts of the approximately 300,000 papers published in America for the past 300 years or so.[20]

The printed version is the *United States Newspaper Program National Union List* (3d ed., Dublin, Ohio: OCLC Online Computer Library Center, 1989). It gives partial bibliographic information and data on which library has what newspaper(s). It is designed to identify newspapers published in all 50 states, pinpoint the libraries where the newspapers are located, and list the issues held by each of the libraries. Coverage of the 100,000-plus titles is from *Public*

---

[19]Pearce S. Grove, "A Revolution in Newspaper Access," *Resource Sharing and Information Networks,* Fall/Winter 1985–1986. This is a detailed history and study of the U.S. Newspaper Project which hopes to gain total bibliographic control over the nearly 300,000 newspapers published in the United States since they first appeared in Boston 300 years ago.

[20]"What's Unread, Yellow and Stashed All Over?" *The New York Times,* Jan. 29, 1987, p. C9. This is a popular report on the newspaper union list project.

Occurrences (published in 1690) to *The New York Times.* There are two indexes: place of publication (state and city) and language. Numerous cross-references from variant titles makes it easy to use.

The U.S. Library of Congress offers the printed *Newspapers in Microform* which now lists close to 40,000 titles reported by over 1000 libraries. The arrangement is by state and city, with a full title index.

This can be used nicely in conjunction with the printed, often updated *Newspapers on Microform* (Washington, Library of Congress, various dates). In different versions this includes both foreign and American titles. Frequently updated, it offers access to almost all the newspapers employed for research. The reason is obvious: basic newspapers are inescapably consigned to microform, whether they be in the United States or in other sections of the world.

Inevitably record of a newspaper from a small community, or one which was published only for a short time, is not online. If it is available electronically, one may wish to have further information than that found at the terminal. In that case there are two basic guides to employ.

The location of American newspapers prior to 1821 is found in Clarence S. Brigham's *History and Bibliography of American Newspapers, 1690–1820* (Worcester, Mass.: American Antiquarian Society, 1947, 2 vols.). The list is not chronologically complete; where research is being done in a given geographical area, it is wise to check with libraries for local union lists of holdings of newspapers not included in the two major union lists.

The continuation of this is Winifred Gregory's work, *American Newspapers 1821–1936* (New York: The H. W. Wilson Company, 1937). Gregory's list follows much the same procedure as Brigham's. It obviously is very dated, particularly in terms of who has what, but the basic bibliographic data are still valid, still useful.

Beyond online and the printed bibliographies, one must remember that most state and local libraries maintain records of their own regional and city or town newspapers. These usually become part of the online record, but much of this information is printed in more detail in state or local bibliographies of holdings. The programs to store these data often are federally funded and develop into the base of repository collections.

Pamphlets

Vertical File Index. New York: H. W. Wilson Company, 1935 to date, monthly. $38.

The pamphlet is an elusive bibliographical item, although it may appear in numerous indexes such as *Public Affairs Information Services.* Where indexed, it usually is identified as a pamphlet so that the library may have enough information to order. Conversely, it is not a standard item in any of the equally standard bibliographies which draw the line at anything under 49 pages, which is a convenient definition of the form.

Individual libraries classify pamphlets as important to rebind and catalog separately or as ephemeral enough to warrant no more than placement in a vertical file under an appropriate subject.

Recognizing the failure of most general trade bibliographies to list pamphlets, the Wilson Company has a bibliography devoted solely to this form. Issued monthly except in August, *Vertical File Index* is a subject approach to a select group of pamphlets. Selection is based on their probable use for the general library, not for the special, technical library.

Each entry includes the standard bibliographical information and a short descriptive note of content. A title index follows the subject list. Wilson does not recommend any of the works, many of which are distributed by companies and organizations for advertising and propaganda purposes.

One of the headaches of ordering pamphlets is that they must be purchased from the publisher. No general book jobber will bother handling them. A free pamphlet may involve many dollars' worth of paperwork and time on the part of a librarian or clerk.

SUGGESTED READING

Balsamo, Luigi, *Bibliography: History of a Tradition*, POB 5279. Berkeley, CA: Bernard Rosenthal Inc., 1990. In this translation from the Italian, bibliography is traced from its beginnings through medieval development to about 1900. The social/scholarly aspects of the form are stressed. Note, too, the reading list which traces the broad framework of bibliography over the ages. An excellent background work for the serious student and anyone involved with the history of books.

Berman, Cindy, "LaserCat vs. Bibliofile: A Comparison in the Small Public Library," *CD-ROM Librarian*, July/August 1989, pp. 10–16. The two systems, with MARC as the heart of each, are examined. The author finds that Bibliofile is superior for convenience, but its competitor is better in terms of record sources. The analysis is useful as a clear explanation of how much CD-ROMs work in cataloging.

Bills, Linda, and Linda Helgerson, "CD-ROM Catalog Production Products," *Library Hi-Tech*, no. 25, 1989, p. 67. There are now numerous CD-ROM databases which contain MARC records. The authors compare the products of seven vendors and explain the strengths and weaknesses of each. Along the way they give vital information on MARC and on how one evaluates CD-ROM.

Desmarais, Norman, "The Serials Directory/Ebsco CD-ROM," *CD-ROM Librarian*, April 1989, pp. 28–33. A detailed discussion of the serials guide on CD-ROM. The search procedures are explained and the system is analyzed for its good and bad features.

Grogan, Denis, *Periodicals and Their Guides*. Chicago: American Library Association, 1988. This represents a series of case studies which show how the various periodical reference guides are used in the library. Grogan is particularly good at making the situations come to life, and most are based on daily reality.

Harriman, Robert, Jr., "Progress toward a National Union List of Newspapers," *Serial Review*, nos. 1–2, 1988, pp. 15–20. This gives an excellent overview of the topic and reports on both gains and losses in the eternal quest to identify, locate, and save newspaper files. In that same issue, see related articles: Sara Heitshu, "The Case against Union Listing," pp. 95–98; and Cindy Hepfer, "Union Listing: A Literature Review," pp. 99–133.

Krummel, D. W., "The Dialectics of Enumerative Bibliography," *The Library Quarterly*, July 1988, pp. 238–257. An experienced teacher with a respect for writing style, Krummel offers a brief history of the most common type of bibliography used in the library. The background is helpful in explaining what is needed in the compilation of a serviceable bibliography. See the "References" for additional material on the history of the subject.

Lane, David, "Your Pamphlets File Supports Apartheid," *Library Journal*, September 1, 1990, pp. 174–177. The former Kansas City Public librarian points out the flaws in free material from pamphlets to periodicals. He uses South Africa as a point of departure, but the same methodology might be employed in other controversial areas covered by such material.

Patterson, Charles, "Origins of Systematic Serials Control: Remembering Carolyn Ulrich," *Reference Services Review*, nos. 1–2, 1988, pp. 79–92. The woman behind *Ulrich's International Directory of Periodicals* was a Californian, born in 1880, who attended the Albany (NY) summer library school in 1907. After that . . . well, Patterson tells all, not only about the elusive librarian, but how she constructed what is now a standard guide that is now a legacy.

Puccio, Joseph A., *Serials Reference Work*. Englewood, CO: Libraries Unlimited, 1989. A member of the Library of Congress has written the best current book on serials for reference librarians. In 16 concise chapters he covers every aspect of the subject from defining a serial to "the future of serials reference work." (It looks bright.) The book is particularly valuable for the numerous annotations of reference works used with serials as well as for the comparisons of similar titles. A must for any reference librarian working with periodicals beyond last month's *Reader's Digest*.

Richler, Mordecai, "From Beowulf to Tom Wolfe," *The New York Times Book Review*, Oct. 8, 1989, p. 7. The Canadian author takes a critical look at *The Reader's Catalog* and finds much of it wanting. Although only a review of this single work, it demonstrates the points to look for when evaluating any bibliography, particularly one devoted to listing books.

Tabachnick, Sharon, "Reviewing Printed Subject Bibliographies: A Worksheet," *The Journal of Academic Librarianship*, November 1989, pp. 279–284. What information do librarians expect to see in a review of a bibliography or, for that matter, any standard reference work. The author offers worksheets, i.e., various points which the reviewer/librarian should check to see whether the bibliography has been adequately evaluated.

Upham, Lois N., *Newspapers in the Library.* New York: Haworth, 1988. This is a broad survey of issues and trends in newspaper management and includes a collection of papers by various authors. About one-quarter of the contributors discuss the U.S. Newspaper Project, but there is much on public and technical services as well.

Walters, Jaclyn, "EBSCO's Serials Directory. . . ," *The Serials Librarian,* vol. 17, 1/2, 1989, pp. 81–99. What is the best way to get the information out of the EBSCO directory—CD-ROM, online, or print? The author addresses this major question and finds that for many libraries the CD-ROM version is preferable. The methodology is useful in that it may be applied to numerous other reference sources.

CHAPTER FIVE
INDEXING AND ABSTRACTING
SERVICES: GENERAL AND
COLLECTIONS

An index represents an analysis, usually by name and by subject, of a document. Since most books, magazines, reports, and other sources deal with a number of different things, it is necessary for the indexer to select key terms which are likely to be of most value to the user. The noun *index* is "derived from the stem of the Latin verb *dicare* which means literally to show."[1]

A good index provides enough access points, from author and title to subject to publisher, to allow the user to find precisely what is needed. The index should be current and should be arranged in such a way that it does not take a four-week course of instruction to discover how to find material. Simplicity and ease of use are among the golden aspects of *The Readers' Guide to Periodical Literature*. An example of complexity is *citation indexing* where one usually has to be familiar with an author to find what is needed. In addition, the user must have the work in which the known author is cited. More on this later.

People approach indexes in different ways for different reasons. The typical scholar or researcher is likely to look for the author

---

[1]For a definition and history of the index and related services see the "Index" entry in almost any good general encyclopedia, as for example, *Americana*. The basic text in the field is Donald and Ana Cleveland's *Introduction to Indexing and Abstracting* (2d ed., Englewood, CO: Libraries Unlimited, 1990). Clear explanations are given of methods and procedures, both traditional and electronic. It is required reading for those involved with the subject.

of an article or book. She knows that a particular person is proficient in the field. It is faster to go directly to the source of the information than to approach it by subject. Conversely, the innocent student who knows neither the field nor the authors is more likely to approach a question through a broad subject heading.

There are now about 700 indexing and abstracting services that are used more or less regularly in U.S. and Canadian libraries, and the figure is close to 4000 worldwide. The number of services has increased dramatically over the past twenty years.

To meet the challenge of the increased numbers of indexes, technology has come to the aid of the librarian and layperson. Now the most frequently used services are available in machine-readable form. Many think that the day of the printed index is about over. The online, CD-ROM, or other electronic forms may well replace the miles of printed indexes. There are many reasons why. The computer index, for example, allows for rapid access, more points of access, convenience, and printouts of citations, and a big bonus is that it is current.

With a few keystrokes at the computer terminal (either online or CD-ROM) one can now (1) search a number of indexes and (2) turn from the citations to the full text of the articles. This virtually eliminates scrambling about the library looking for separate volumes of the index, not to mention trying to locate elusive copies of a periodical or newspaper. Although the operation may be carried on either online or on a CD-ROM, the future of most libraries is with CD-ROM, at least for the layperson audience. Professionals, and those with the necessary income to cover the cost of online searches, will prefer online because it is more sophisticated and, at least for now, more up to date.

CD-ROM VERSUS THE PRINTED INDEX

The CD-ROM index/abstracting service cannot be overestimated. Laypersons, and particularly younger people, often will only use an index in this form. They avoid the printed format not only because they simply don't understand how it is used but because it fails to offer a printout of what they find.

Granted, there are numerous problems with an automated index. The searching patterns by laypeople tend to be simplistic and often result in finding too little or too much. This is of little interest to most, who prefer to take their chances with a computer terminal with which they feel comfortable.

The 1990s are likely to offer even more sophisticated hardware and software for searching; and the considered use of CD-ROM with current online data will become more common. The real question, then, is, Is the printed index dead? The answer, at least for general indexes and the highly specialized (well-financed) ones is a resounding "yes." Although this will take a bit of time, it is likely to be the situation by the turn of the century, if not sooner.

TRADITIONAL INDEXES

Even with the wonders of technology available, users are most likely to be concerned with the following types of traditional indexes:

1. *Periodicals*
   a. General indexes cover many periodicals in a broad or specific subject field. *The Readers' Guide to Periodical Literature* is the most widely known of this type of index.
   b. Subject indexes cover not only several periodicals but also other material found in new books, pamphlets, reports, and government documents. The purpose is to index material in a narrow subject field. Examples of this type of index are the *Applied Science & Technology Index* and *Library Literature*.
   c. Indexes to single magazines. Very few are now being published, although before the mid-1940s it was a favorite way of indexing. Today the outstanding single index is the *National Geographic Index* covering 1888–1988 (Washington: National Geographic, 1989). The 100-year index includes maps, as well as articles and TV programs.

2. *Newspapers*
   There are numerous newspaper indexes in the United States. The best-known newspaper index is *The New York Times Index*. Today, most services offer several indexes to newspapers. For example, *The National Newspaper Index* includes five newspapers which may be searched simultaneously.

3. *Serials*
   There are indexes to reports both published and unpublished and government documents; proceedings of conferences and congresses as well as continuations; and other materials which can be defined as serials, i.e., any publication issued in parts over an indefinite period of time. Many

of the subject periodical indexes include some of these forms, whereas other indexes such as *Resources in Education* are limited to indexing only reports.

4. *Material in collections*

These indexes cover collections of poems, plays, fiction, songs, and so on. The *Speech Index* and *Granger's Index of Poetry* are examples.

5. *Other indexes*

Here one might include everything from concordances to indexes of various forms: from *Book Review Index* to collections of quotations to indexes to patents or music. Scientific searching may include indexes which have specifications, formulas, standards, and prospectuses. Machine-readable databases may deal exclusively with numerals or their equivalent. Usually these indexes are treated by reference librarians in terms of the subject covered rather than as indexes per se.

Abstracting Services

Abstracting services are an extension of indexes; they perform the same function in locating and recording the contents of periodicals, books, and various types of documents. They differ from indexes in that (1) by definition, they include a summary of the material indexed, (2) they tend to be confined to relatively narrow subject areas, and (3) the arrangement rarely follows the single author, subject, and sometimes title alphabetical arrangement of indexes.

The abstract provides a clue to the relevance of the material and helps the user to determine whether he really wants the particular article, report, or book. An index gives only a key to where the material is located and rarely indicates relevancy.

Many abstracting services aim at relatively complete coverage of a narrow subject area.[2] Coverage tends to be worldwide, with abstracts of foreign language articles in English.

The format varies from abstract to abstract, although normally the issues are arranged under broad subject headings, with appropriate author and subject indexing. The arrangement by broad sub-

[2]Technically, there are two types of abstracts. The *indicative* abstract indicates the type of article and the author's approach and treatment, but does not usually include specific data. The *informative,* and most often used in works described in this text, summarizes enough of the data and findings to relieve the reader of the necessity of always reading the article. In neither case does the abstractor make any critical assessment.

ject classification sometimes confuses beginners, but it is a blessing to experts who need only turn to the classification section of interest. The traditional index uses the specific rather than the broad approach, thereby often requiring the searcher to go back and forth in the index to run down related subject headings. Most abstracting services have limited author and subject indexes. The librarian unfamiliar with the subject will save time by turning to the annual cumulated index to discover the subject classifications under which this or that specific subject is likely to appear in the monthly abstracts.

By the 1990s, more and more general indexes (*Readers' Guide, Magazine Article Summaries,* etc.) offered abstracts. In fact, students and laypersons are now so used to abstracts that they prefer, where possible, to use only indexes which have this feature. The general abstract-indexing services tend to be in alphabetical order, and so avoid the problem of the subject-arranged format. Also, most of these can be searched on CD-ROM or online.

Searching an index or abstracting service online or with CD-ROM eliminates the problem of arrangement, which can be a major headache in the printed version. One simply seeks an author, subject, or title on the computer screen. How the information is arranged in the file is of no interest as long as it is easy to retrieve on the computer.

SUBJECT HEADINGS AND THE SEARCH

In searching most printed indexes, one has to match the search subject or concept with those used by the indexer. If the indexer, for example, uses the term *dwelling,* the user will find nothing if a search is made for *home,* albeit in many cases there may be a cross-reference under the listing for "Home" which says, "see Dwelling." If there were enough cross-references, there would be no real problem, but there would be a gigantic index. The solution has been to compromise. The indexer scans the text and then tries to assign subject headings which are most likely to be used by a majority of researchers.

Where do the indexers get these terms? They come directly from what is known as "controlled" subject heading lists. Indirectly, indexers are influenced by the key words they see in the text, the depth of the indexing being used, and the type of subject heading list being employed. The end result therefore may or may not be satisfactory.

Searching for the specific subject, indexes rely upon certain reference works and techniques which, in turn, can be useful to the reference librarian seeking the specific subject term:

1. *The subject heading list* Most indexes employ some form of controlled vocabulary. The subject headings are predetermined, and the article is matched against an authoritative list of subject headings. The indexer selects one to three, or even more, terms from the list which best describe the article's contents. The two basic lists of subject headings consulted by reference librarians and catalogers are:

a. *Library of Congress Subject Headings* (Washington: Library of Congress, various dates)   This is the familiar, fat three-volume set, usually bound in red (hence, often called the *red books*). The set lists the standard Library of Congress subject headings in alphabetical order. If one wishes to see how they list the history of England, one turns here, finds "England" and a reference to "see Great Britain—History." That one step gives the user a specific subject heading and saves much time churning about the card catalog looking for nonexistent English history books, at least under that subject heading, and covering all the land area of Great Britain. There are cross-references, synonyms, and other bits of advice and help which assist the user in finding the proper subject heading. (See the explanation of symbols, organization, etc., at the beginning of the first volume.)[3]

The Library of Congress list is updated by new editions, and between editions, by additions and changes in the *Cataloging Service Bulletin.* As more than one critic has observed, the subject headings are a profile of our times, particularly in the past few years as the subject heading experts became more sympathetic with change. For example, a few years back there were no subject headings for such diverse aspects of American life as the bagel, the hot tub, or AIDS.[4]

---

[3] By 1988 the Library of Congress had changed the symbols employed, and the 1989 edition ($150) reflects this. Instead of the familiar "x" and "xx," there are now: UF, used for; BT, broader term; RT related term; SA, see also; and NT, narrower term. At the same time there is a move to make the subject headings into a type of thesaurus. Many are less than satisfied with the changes, and for their point of view see Mary Dykstra, "LC Subject Headings Disguised as a Thesaurus," *Library Journal,* March 1, 1988, pp. 41–44; "Can Subject Headings Be Saved?" Ibid., Sept. 15, 1988, pp. 55–58.

[4] William Benemann, "American Graffiti, Library Style," *American Libraries,* September 1987, pp. 650–651. This is a humorous, although perfectly accurate summary

The "red books" are available on CD-ROM from the Library of Congress. A tremendous advantage is that the service is updated quarterly, and one does not have to thumb through the *Cataloging Service Bulletin* to find changes. The cost is a modest $300 yearly, and the service is a major help to any library where the subject headings are used more than once or twice a week.

b. *Sears List of Subject Headings* (New York: The H. W Wilson Company, various dates)   This is the rough equivalent of the *Library of Congress Subject Headings* for smaller libraries. There are fewer subject headings. Sears represents a much-abridged edition, with changes suitable for smaller collections of the Library of Congress. The thirteenth edition (1986), as with previous editions, reflects the interests of the times in that there are added subject headings which cover current social and political issues, as well as forms of entertainment, and developments in technology. *Note: The Sears List of Subject Headings: Canadian Companion* (3d ed., 1987) includes over 150 pages of subjects which may be of special interest to Canadian public and school librarians. As with the basic set, it is often updated.

2. *The thesaurus* The thesaurus is similar to the subject heading list in that it is a list of terms used for indexing and for searching. These days it is a frequent companion for anyone doing an online or CD-ROM search. The essential difference is that the terms are drawn from the documents themselves, or from similar documents in the subject area. Typically, then, the thesaurus is used only in specific subject fields from education to the sciences.

Another important aspect of the thesaurus is that it shows relationships between terms. One may look up what amounts to broader and narrower concepts within a hierarchical structure built on one or more basic term categories. A term family in reference services, for example, could include terms for different kinds of services. Here one might find the term *reference interview* with the broader term, *information search,* and the narrower term, *verbal cues.*

Cross Reference Index (New York: R. R. Bowker, 2d ed., 1989) Which major subject heading system uses "Baby Foods" as a subheading? One turns to the index and finds that there are three sections ("Cookery," "Food," and "Infants—Care and Hygiene") where it is employed. Furthermore, the *Index* shows which of the eight sources of subject headings uses the term. The eight are the

of how the Library of Congress's subject headings "reflect our society's concerns and crazes."

Library of Congress Subject Headings, Sears List of Subject Headings, Readers' Guide to Periodical Literature, The New York Times Index, PAIS/Public Affairs Information Service Bulletin, Thesaurus of ERIC Descriptors, Thesaurus of Psychological Index Terms, and *Subject Guide to IAC Databases.* This is a case where the publisher's claim is more than valid. The *Index* "helps the researcher navigate through the maze of different and sometimes synonymous subject headings or descriptors, and to arrive at the potentially best sources of information and the precise terms of retrieval."

Computer Searching

An end run around the assigned subject heading is provided with the computer search.

Generally most databases do have assigned subject headings. In this respect they follow the lead offered by their printed versions. At the same time there are numerous other entry points. Thanks to the ability of the computer to search out key words in the title of an article, in the abstract, in the full text (where available), or in numerous other parts (from date of publication to language and publisher), the opportunities to find a needed piece of information are vastly increased.

Using an online or CD-ROM search, one may not be tied to the vagaries of subject headings assigned by someone who may not fully appreciate how people look for information. (Keep in mind though that the use of subject headings almost always improves the ease and the accuracy of searches; and they should be used where possible.) The computer search allows rapid access to new terms, to new and different ways of examining a subject. These subject headings may not become available until months to years later.

Which Index?

Which index should one turn to for the answer to a particular question?

Being able to answer any question quickly is a mark of the professional reference librarian and is not really all that difficult. On a simple level, one turns to the general indexes for typical student and layperson queries; and for more detailed subject questions, one turns to a subject index. Most indexes indicate their scope in the title; for example, it is easy to imagine the contents of *Art Index.* At a more complex level, the librarian becomes familiar with several subject fields and is able to quickly call up names of highly specialized indexes within the subject area.

The computer database makes it all much simpler, particularly at the complex subject level. Each of the major database vendors has a system whereby one need only select a broad subject area or subject grouping, enter a key word, and a listing of indexes where the selected term is shown. Furthermore, it indicates how many times the term appears in each of the indexes. On the other hand, the CD-ROM represents an individual index for a given time period and is selected as is the print version, i.e., primarily by the subject covered. It usually does not have the same word count available as online.

Book Indexes

Although this chapter is concerned with indexes primarily to periodicals and their articles, one should not forget the important individual-book index. Many reference questions are answered by consulting the index in the back of a standard work. This can be frustrating, of course, as one may have to search many books to find the right item(s). Some online computer programs do offer what amounts to combining and interfiling book indexes in certain subject fields, but this availability is far from widespread.

One can see the time when a reference librarian, given a subject or personal name, may simply enter it into a computer index which will (1) indicate the major reference works where the needed information can be located and (2) simultaneously show what periodical articles, reports, or studies are available on the same subject. One, again, might limit the search to one type of material or to one citation, or instead might investigate as many as are available.

Meanwhile, there are three or four basic sources in print to turn to for information about who has indexed what. The most ambitious of these is *The Index and Abstract Directory* (Birmingham, Ala.: Ebsco, 1989 to date, irregular). It gives by subject, with standard bibliographic data, approximately 30,000 serials (primarily periodicals and newspapers) which are indexed in one or more service. Each of the indexes and abstracts is given in alphabetical order, which takes up about one-third of the volume, with a complete list of all serials indexed. There are the usual title and ISSN indexes. This is a spin-off of the same company's three-volume 100,000-plus entry, *Serials Directory*. It, like *Ulrich's International Periodical Directory*, includes indexing information.

A basic source for information is *Magazines for Libraries*, 6th ed.

(New York: R. R. Bowker Company, 1989). The first section is an annotated listing of over 200 basic indexes and abstracting services, and is useful because here one finds the truly "basic" services.

FULL-TEXT AVAILABILITY

The primary drawback to an index is that it is a secondary reference aid. It is only a step toward finding the information, usually in a periodical. In searching, one first has to wrestle with the index and find what is wanted, either by subject or by author. The result is a citation, or group of citations.[5]

With these located one then moves to the periodical stacks and hopes to be able to find the precise item. This presupposes that the library has the periodical. If not, the library can order the article on interlibrary loan (or have it faxed).

If the library has the periodical, the next difficulty becomes: "Yes, but is it available?" "Has it been stolen?" "Has the article been ripped out or mutilated?" "Has the individual issue been lost in the library?" "Is the volume in which it is bound not on the shelves?" And finally, and most often: "Yes, we have it, but it is at the bindery!"

Fortunately for the sanity of both the librarian and the user, these problems do not arise that often, and with average skill and luck one can quickly locate the needed periodical (or book or video). Still, how much easier it would all be if the article(s) were readily available next to the index.

Some indexing services meet the problem by:

1. Offering the full text of the article, report, or study on microfiche. The microfiche has a number which appears with the citation. One simply turns to the number in the microfiche file, and voilà, there is the complete text of the needed material.

2. Offering the full text of the article as part of the online database. This is even faster in that one may switch online from the citation immediately to the article and pick out needed parts or, for that matter, have the whole printed out at the computer printer.

---

[5]Sometimes the citation is enough. It will answer the question: "In which issue of *The New York Times* did that article on wild dogs appear?" And if the service includes short descriptors or abstracts, one can often read the abstract and find the answer, particularly to a ready-reference question, such as: "What state has the most wild dogs?"

3. Offering the full text of the article as part of a CD-ROM or equivalent type of optical disk.

The distinct advantage of the online full text as opposed to microfiche or CD-ROM is that it may be updated minute by minute, day by day, rather than by the month or quarterly as is the custom with the other full-text forms. The distinct disadvantage to all this is the high cost. Cost can be reduced in a number of ways, including using the online system at less expensive times of the day, just as one may save money on a phone call after 10 P.M. Another possibility is more frequently updated CD-ROMs.

Drawbacks to Full-Text Databases[6]

Aside from the obvious drawback of cost, at least for online services, there are several other problems with full-text databases: (1) Not many publishers wish to release tapes of the full text of this or that book, periodical, or newspaper for copyright protection reasons. Therefore, choice is limited. Usually the full-text backup represents from one-third to one-half of the actual items indexed. (2) In practice, the full text is not available because of selective choice. Most services exclude minor articles, fillers, letters to the editor, and even book reviews. (3) Rarely does one find advertising.[7]

University Microfilms International is an example of how full text is matched to the index. They issue three indexes with as many full-text CD-ROM backups. They are (1) ABI/INFORM with full text on *Business Periodicals Ondisc,* (2) *Periodical Abstracts Index* with full text on *General Periodicals Ondisc,* (3) *Business Dateline Ondisc* which is an index of the full text in itself. And other systems are planned. Although they are discussed throughout this section, there are several points about the full text on CD-ROM for all publishers that should be emphasized:

1. Most of the full-text CD-ROM systems are independent of the index. This means, for example, that one can search

---

[6]For a discussion of full text see Ruth Orenstein, "The Fullness of Full Text," *Database Searcher,* September 1989, pp. 21–26.

[7]The lack of advertising online presents a problem to commercial magazines which are made possible by advertisements. To drop them even online is to drop off a considerable amount of revenue. As it is difficult to figure how to include advertising, or at least to guarantee that the user will take the time and expense to look at such ads, the dilemma may be an impossible one to solve. Conversely, most learned journals depend on subscriptions, not on advertising, and they are not influenced by this problem.

General Periodicals Ondisc with standard search keys (from boolean and proximity operators to truncation, etc.), but cannot search the full text for key words and names as is possible with most online full-text services.

2. Searching response can be quite slow, at least compared to online. Some systems, too, limit what can be printed to a dozen or so citations. And there are other "catches" to searching which only experienced searchers will discover.

3. And this brings one to the major drawback, at present, to an index of the full text on CD-ROM: cost. It can run to well over $20,000 a year for a single system such as ABI/INFORM with its full-text support. Unless costs are lowered, this system is not likely to find wide appeal, even though it is likely to prove very effective, particularly for the involved layperson doing his or her own searches.

EVALUATION

Indexes and abstracting services are under constant evaluation. Librarians are primarily interested in the amount of coverage and its cost. The latter is a major consideration, particularly in terms of online and CD-ROM and other electronic forms, which can cost from 30 percent to 130 percent more than the print version. One must of course counterbalance the gross price of the service with whatever savings in time and effort may be realized to arrive at the true cost.

The price of a service now has so many potential variables that the basic cost alone cannot be considered. All other factors must be given due weight, at least where the budget allows. Much of this discussion may be academic if the budget is so small that the only index possible is one or two printed versions. We can hope for change, but there is no question that today the budget constraints more often than not are a foremost evaluative consideration.

With that said, we next go on to the evaluative measures aside from the price of a service. They are given here for the print index/abstract, and where necessary there is an added explanation for the database form. The points enumerated here are to evaluate, only in a general way, the machine-readable databases. A more meaningful evaluation would also include such criteria as the user's acceptance or rejection and the efficiency of the system within the context of the total reference situation.

In addition to the importance of cost, there are six other relative constants in evaluation:

1. The Publisher

The H. W. Wilson Company, University Microfilms, and Information Access Company supply most of the general indexes used in libraries today. They all have excellent reputations. One may disagree with what is or is not included in one of these indexes, but the format and depth of indexing are acceptable to excellent.

At the other end of the spectrum are the publishers of time-tested specialized and technical indexes such as *Science Citation Index.* In between are the publishers about whom the librarian may know nothing and who seem to be offering (1) a duplication of another service or (2) a questionable venture into a new area. The librarian should check out the publisher, preferably by talking to subject experts and to other librarians who may have knowledge of the field and by reading reviews in the various sources discussed in Chapter 3 of this text. Any or all of these safety checks will quickly reveal who should or should not be trusted.

Databases—Online and CD-ROM. Wilson is the publisher of many databases used in the average library, and through its own online and CD-ROM services it offers reliable indexing.[8] Beyond Wilson the strongest competitor is the Information Access Company with *InfoTrac Magazine Index.* They also have a variety of subject indexes.

Here one might ask specific questions about publisher and vendor. The vendor often stands between the publisher and the library as a supplier of the CD-ROM or online service. Do the publisher and vendor supply guides and manuals to assist the user with the database(s)? Are these frequently updated? Related questions: Do the publisher and vendor provide training courses and refresher courses, and if so, at what intervals and at what cost? Does the publisher provide a "hot line" so that searchers can call for assistance with difficult searches? Does the publisher send out a newsletter or other periodic update to inform users of changes? Does the publisher send out a newsletter or other periodic update to inform users

---

[8]For a discussion of the CD-ROM/online offerings of The H. W. Wilson Company, see: "Wilsondisc's Readers' Guide Abstracts," *CD-ROM Librarian,* October 1988, pp. 21–27. See also Colleen Seale, "Getting the Most Out of Wilsonline," *Database,* April 1989, pp. 55–63.

of changes? Does the publisher provide the means for users to suggest changes or to make complaints about features of the databases?

2. Scope

A second evaluative point about an index or an abstract concerns coverage. Here one must consider obvious factors: (1) How many kinds of periodicals are indexed and what kinds of periodicals are they? Is the number adequate for the field, and do the titles represent the best in the United States and, if necessary, abroad? (2) What other material is included, since in some disciplines it will be necessary to consider not only periodicals but reports, books, and monographs.

How can one account for the capricious method of indexing of even the best of services? Most of the carelessness is a result of the rush to meet deadlines, the postal service's failure to deliver a magazine for indexing, and strict adherence to space limits.

The index may say it regularly covers parts of books or related periodicals in the field, but check to see that it follows through on its promise. Columnists may or may not be included, and, if they are, it will usually be without an indication of what the particular column is about. Sometimes, too, a given issue of a magazine on a single topic may be indexed only once instead of article by article.

The solution to apparently nonindexed documents, or indexed trivia has two parts: (1) The searcher will with practice learn which indexes are guilty of one, or both of these mistakes. The index will probably be avoided, and will be used only as a last resource. (2) If the publishers or producers of the index make an effort to learn more about what users wish, they will drop the trivia, and add the essential. Although several publishers such as the H. W. Wilson Company are in the constant process of modification to meet needs of users, others do not survey their users that often.

Databases. Here the questions of evaluation are much the same, but in addition to knowing what is or is not indexed, one should now learn the following about a database:

1. Does the publisher or vendor clearly specify which journals are indexed in depth and which are indexed selectively? Publishers of printed indexes rarely give this information, and database publishers will follow suit unless users insist on receiving it.
2. Are the journals indexed listed with their abbreviations and

preferably with addresses of the publishers? Is the ISSN included? If the result of a search is ever to be used to search a library's holdings records, the ISSN (or ISBN) will be the successful link, since these are also included in MARC records.

3. How much does one database overlap another in its coverage? The general periodical databases have overlaps of from 20 to 30 percent and more. In highly selective and narrow-subject databases, there is much less overlap, if any at all.

3. Duplication and Gaps

A decade or so ago, users complained of the lack of quality indexes or abstracts, but in the early 1990s the same people are complaining about too many services.

Ideally, index and abstract publishers would divide the disciplines in such a way that duplication of titles covered would be limited. They do not. Therefore the librarian must always ask the key evaluative question: How much duplication exists between X and Y service, and is the difference so much (or so little) that X should be chosen over Y?

There is a tremendous amount of duplication in indexing among the 30 basic indexing and abstracting services in the social and political sciences. Approximately 50 percent of the journals are indexed in six or more of the services, and five indexes give access to 78 percent of the journals in the field. Knowing this, users tend to avoid esoteric indexes unless they are absolutely necessary. In the social sciences the experts turn to only 1 or 2 of the 30 available services. And, in fact, 5 of the 30 indexes cover a vast majority of the periodicals.

Databases. The foregoing questions and evaluation apply.

4. Depth of Indexing

The thoroughness of indexing varies considerably, and the publisher of a periodicals index should explain (but often does not) how thoroughly a particular article is indexed.

The obvious—some would say deceptively obvious—way of recovering a maximum amount of information from a given document is to index it in considerable depth. This means assigning a maximum number of subject headings to the document (as well, of course, as author and sometimes title labels). The question is: What is the optimal depth of indexing? To put it more precisely: For a given collection of documents and a given population of users of those documents, what is the best number of index terms to assign to those documents on the average and for any single document? Unfortunately there is no consensus on this, even among experts.

Databases. One of the advantages of the electronic search of a database is that depth of indexing is not necessarily a problem. Where one may search with more than subject headings, with for instance key words in the title or abstract or full text, the ability to find terms overlooked by the indexer is not a major consideration. By combining terms, one can often turn up material which is otherwise lost because the indexer assigned subject headings not apparently relevant to an average search pattern.

There is a major caveat in all of this: One may use key words and end up with not one citation, but rather scores of citations. That may be fine, unless many of the citations are not relevant to the user's need. It is best to start with an assigned subject heading(s), which gives the searcher a precise entry. Only when this fails, or when one wishes to expand the number of citations, should the free-text approach be employed. There are exceptions to the rule, but for beginners it is a solid point of departure.

5. Timeliness of Material

In most situations, the more current the index, the more useful it is. The majority of indexes are issued monthly or quarterly. Only a few are published every week or two weeks.

A common problem is that the printed index or abstract does reach the library within the calendar period announced on its cover, but the material indexed is several weeks or months behind the date on the cover. The lag between the time a periodical appears and the time it is picked up in the index is easy to check. Compare a few dates of indexed articles with the date on the cover of the index or abstract.

How often, if at all, is the index cumulated? Is there an annual volume which cumulates the weekly, monthly, or quarterly issues? Are there five-year, ten-year, or other cumulations? For retrospective searching, the necessity for frequent cumulations is apparent to anyone who has had to search laboriously through, say, the bimonthly issues of *Library Literature* before the annual or the two-year cumulation appears.

Databases. Again, one of the great benefits of the electronic database is that it can be updated minute by minute. Actually, most services tend to do the updates by the week or by the month. But CD-ROM may perform less well here. The typical monthly or quarterly update may be no more current than the printed version of the same index.

Another drawback is that most databases are relatively new and offer little or no opportunity for retrospective searching. One may go back only three to five years, at least on the majority of databases. Obviously, one needs to know the cutoff dates. Does the library have the printed works that precede the database?

6. Format

Employing *format* as a general descriptor, the index or abstract may be evaluated in a number of ways. First, is it easy or difficult to understand? This normally depends on arrangement. The standard alphabetically arranged index is easy to follow. However that may not hold true if the index is arranged by subject or class or if it is a citation type of indexing. Second, how readable is the index? This can be a real problem when it is a computer printout. Third, is the citation complete with enough bibliographical information to identify the material which is indexed? Finally, are the citations and information in the index accurate, particularly in terms of sending one to the proper source, page, or book?

Databases. The format here is most important in respect to what is or is not shown on the computer screen or printed out. These are a few of the related evaluative questions. Others are more technical and have as much to do with the hardware as the software, but at the basic level the following is necessary to know:

1. *The searching patterns* CD-ROM and online offer specific searching patterns which are applicable only to each of them. These are discussed in detail in a chapter in the second volume of this text, but for now it is enough to know the variety of problems which are associated with the computer-assisted search.

The key descriptor here is *boolean logic.* Without getting into the details, it is enough to say that the term allows one to combine words and phrases to either limit or expand the search. Boolean logic is a synonym for sophisticated searching patterns, and may or may not be available on various CD-ROM versions of indexes. Normally, it is a part of almost all online searching patterns.

The ideal system should allow the user to (1) enter a command at any time, (2) retrieve data by date, language, geographical location, or other qualifiers, (3) have unrestricted use of boolean operators and a number of search terms, (4) link search statements and words, (5) query the base in language as natural as possible, and (6) have the use of a thesaurus or dictionary.

A common assumption is that online searches and searching of CD-ROM are the same in that similar search patterns are allowed. This can be, but is not always true. For example, if the H. W. Wilson Company offers sophisticated software for its Wilsondisc system, Information Access Company does not always follow the same pattern. One, essentially, is limited to searching key words. On the other hand, many *InfoTrac* users have no real problem because the publisher offers a liberal use of subject headings and cross-references.

The patterns of search are important because most laypersons who use CD-ROM prefer the simple, direct route. The librarians, conversely, prefer the more sophisticated paths such as provided by boolean logic and its cousins. At any rate, it is of major importance in evaluating a CD-ROM or online index whether it allows the use of boolean logic or is more simplified in its approach.

Other points to consider when evaluating databases include:

2. Is there a specialized thesaurus for the database? The thesaurus usually is required to indicate broader and narrower terms related to the primary subject term. Even with a natural language system, the thesaurus of other databases can be useful for suggesting related terms.

3. Does the database provide only citations, or does it include abstracts? Usually the database duplicates what is offered in the hard-copy version. However, for reasons of economy most online databases allow the user to reject (or accept) the abstract printout. "Rejection" may mean only that the user decides to have the abstracts or the complete list of citations printed offline and sent at a later date. With CD-ROM, and a printer, this is not a problem.

4. If a database contains indexes to more than journals, is there a clear indication of the source of the nonjournal materials, preferably in the citation? Lack of full bibliographic details for such materials makes them virtually worthless. Also, policies regarding indexing of nonjournal materials should be clearly stated.

In order to evaluate an index for inclusion in a library, a considerable amount of time and effort is required, as well as some expertise in comparative analysis. Consequently, the majority of librarians rely on reviews or the advice of experts, or both, particularly when considering a specialized service. The advantages of learning evaluation techniques are as much to show the librarian how indexes or abstracts are (or should be) constructed as to reveal points for acceptance or rejection.

GENERAL PERIODICAL INDEXES

Readers' Guide to Periodical Literature. New York: The H. W. Wilson Company, 1900 to date, semimonthly and monthly, 18 issues a year. $140.

Also available as: (1) *Readers' Guide Abstracts: Print Edition,* 1985 to date, 10 issues per year. $229 (Microfiche: $675). (2) *Wilsonline* (i.e., online), 1983 to date, $20 to $45 an hour. (3) *Wilsondisc:* CD-ROM, 1983 to date, quarterly. $1095 (with abstracts, $1995).

Not too many years ago there was only one general index for the general reader and student: *The Readers' Guide to Periodical Literature.* It remains as a basic reference in small- and medium-size libraries today, but now it has considerable, and welcome competition. The competitors are welcome because they offer not only more periodicals indexed, but also indexes to a wider selection of subject areas than found in the *Readers' Guide.*

Among the active contenders for first place in the library are *InfoTrac/Magazine Index, Periodical Abstracts on Disc,* and *Magazine Article Summaries.* All of these, including the *Readers' Guide,* are on CD-ROM and online. Less ambitious, but equally deserving of attention are *Access* and *Popular Periodical Index.*

The Readers' Guide success is due both to the excellent indexing and the selection of periodicals indexed—a selection which concentrates on relatively high circulation, well-read magazines. There are now about 186 titles indexed by author and by subject. Book reviews are in a separate section and are arranged alphabetically by author. Author and subject entries are in a single alphabet. The subject headings, as in all the Wilson indexes, are consistent and easy to locate. Furthermore, numerous cross-references make the indexes a model for rapid use. Each entry contains all the necessary information to find the article. Abbreviations are held to a minimum, and they are clearly explained in the front of the index.

Selection of periodicals for the *Readers' Guide* (and the other Wilson indexes) is determined by a committee and by polling librarians. When librarians are asked to consider a title to be added or deleted, the publisher reminds users that the purpose of the service is to "index U.S. periodicals of broad, general and popular character." A determining factor for or against inclusion is whether the indexed material will be of any "reference value" to the users. Here *reference* is used to mean a work to assist in both ready-reference questions and, to a lesser extent, specific search queries. The general coverage of essentially popular and semipopular magazines makes it of little or no real use for detailed research questions.

Although the book reviews are clearly set off at the end of each issue, the service includes a number of other reviews which are part of the main index. Each of these is indexed under the heading of the subject and includes reviews of ballet, dance, motion pictures, musicals, opera, phonograph records, radio programs, television, theater, and videodisks.

Fiction, poetry, and short stories included in a magazine are indexed under the author's name. For further information, see the "Suggestions for the Use of the Readers' Guide to Periodical Literature" in the front of each cumulation. With variations, this same system is employed in all of the H. W. Wilson indexes. Librarians should remember that the book reviews usually are found in a separate section at the end of each index issue.

An *Abridged Readers' Guide* which indexes only 68 titles is available, but it follows the same general indexing procedures as the larger version. It is published monthly, rather than every two weeks, and is only about one-half the annual price of the more comprehensive work. Its use in libraries is debatable, in that the larger index, which is more frequent and indexes three times as many periodicals, is much better for even the smallest library.

Online and CD-ROM

The H. W. Wilson Company chooses to manage its own online and CD-ROM services. They, as other companies who eliminate the vendor, believe they can be more profitable and more efficient by dealing directly with the library. Librarians find that this depends on the particular situation. In the case of the H. W. Wilson Company, the direct service seems fine.

Wilsonline is the name of the online services, and the company provides its own software for both simple and sophisticated searching. There are various fee structures for both those who subscribe to the printed indexes and for those who choose only online. Hour-connect time, though, varies from a high of about $65 to a low of $25, depending on the index searched and the contract negotiated.

The company makes tapes for its databases available. These

may be loaded on an institutional computer. A subscription price is charged based on the potential number of users. Variations on the fee schedule result in a small library paying as little as $500 for an index. A large library may pay from $12,000 to $15,000 for much the same service.

The use of computer tapes rather than CD-ROMs is likely to increase. The initial cost may be high, but one is able to store considerably more data than on a CD-ROM or other form of optical disk.

Wilsondisc is the company's CD-ROM service, and, again, most of its printed indexes are available in this format. They are issued annually and updated quarterly. Most go back only to 1984, with a few starting up in 1981. Annual subscription rates run from $1095 to a high of $1995.

Numerous modes are available for searching the CD-ROM disks. Browse, for example, is for beginners, and is limited to simple subject searching. The user types in a subject and the service, as with most CD-ROM services, and indicates the number of citations for that word or combination of words available in the index. A list of other indexing terms follows each of the citations. Problems with Browse include a lack of much variation, little possibility of finding other related topics, and the slowness of it all.

The other search modes grow in difficulty, speed, and accuracy. These range from the menu-driven Wilsearch to the expert mode.

Abstracts

The H. W. Wilson Company offers abstracts for *The Readers' Guide*. The printed version differs from most abstracting services in that it is arranged alphabetically by subject and author and is no more difficult to use than a normal index. Only about 25,000 out of 60,000 articles annually are abstracted. Still, the 70- to 150-word abstracts represent, in the view of the publisher, the most likely items to be used by the student and layperson. The service, according to the publisher, is "selected especially for value to the school, college, and public library audiences."

The catch is that the abstracting service is usually five to six weeks behind the *Readers' Guide,* and it is the last place the user would turn for current articles. It might, for example, take two to three months for an abstract of an article to appear in today's news.

If abstracts to all indexed items are required, then the librarian should turn to the CD-ROM version of *Readers' Guide Abstracts.* This abstracts everything found in the *Readers' Guide,* and is not as selective as the printed version.

Periodicals Abstracts

Periodical Abstracts Ondisc (i.e., CD-ROM). Ann Arbor, MI: University Microfilms, 1988 to date, monthly. $1750.

1. *Resource/One Ondisc,* 1988 to date, monthly. $795.

2. Full text available on *General Periodicals Ondisc,* 1990 to date, monthly. $13,500.

Periodical Abstracts Ondisc abstracts slightly over 900 periodicals, including all found in the *Readers' Guide* and many in *Magazine Index.* It adds about 100 scholarly and professional titles more likely to be found in subject indexes. Coverage began in January 1988. Each citation is given in full and contains an abstract of the article of about 25 words.

The service allows for the use of boolean logic. One is not limited to assigned subject headings, but may search using key words in the title or abstract. It contains more abstracts than either the *Readers' Guide* or *Magazine Articles Summaries.*

A junior service by the same publisher is called *Resource/One Ondisc.* It uses the same searching patterns as *Periodical Abstracts,* but differs in two other important respects: (1) It indexes and abstracts only 130 periodicals; all but 18 are found in *Readers' Guide.* (2) The cost is much lower than the senior service and is therefore an ideal work for libraries with limited budgets.

Full Text. University Microfilms International offers a typical menu of various full text on CD-ROM. Among these *General Periodicals Ondisc (GPO)* may be found. This is the full-text accompaniment to *Periodical Abstracts Index.* One searches the latter index, finds a citation, and then turns to *GPO* for the full text of the article. The database contains more than 150 general titles from *Time* and *U.S. News & World Report* to *Science News* and *Vital Speeches.* More general titles are added from time to time. The service is updated monthly. The cost is high: In addition to the $13,500 annual fee, there is a 10 cents per page printout charge.

Online. As a DIALOG file, the service is named Courier Plus. It includes 25 national and regional newspapers, plus the 300 periodicals found on the disk. Newspaper coverage starts in January 1989, and periodical coverage one year earlier. Unlike the Wilson indexes, here the abstracts are available online as well as on the disk.

InfoTrac (Magazine Index)

InfoTrac (Magazine Index). Foster City, CA: Information Access Company.

CD-ROM offers *InfoTrac* in various forms: (1) *Magazine Index Plus,* 1980 to date, monthly. $3300 to $5150. (2) *TOM* 1980 to date, monthly. $2600. (3) *General Periodicals Index* in two editions—the "academic," 1985 to date, monthly, $7500, and the "Public Library," 1985 to date, monthly, $7500. Online DIALOG file 88, $84 per hour.

Also available: (1) *Magazine Index,* 1977 to date, monthly. $2300. (2) *Magazine Index,* online. DIALOG file 47, $84 per hour. (3) *Magazine Asap* online, 1983 to date. DIALOG file 647, $84 per hour.

InfoTrac (Magazine Index) is one of a family of similar indexes published by Information Access Company, a division of the conglomerate Ziff-Davis. This California-based organization offers indexes in many forms, from online to full text.

InfoTrac is an umbrella term employed by the publisher for all of its CD-ROM products. This includes *Magazine Index* (and its numerous forms) as well as the *National Newspaper Index, Legal Resource Index,* etc. Since many libraries have only *Magazine Index* and/or *National Newspaper Index* loaded in the computer, the user sometimes gets confused when it is all termed *InfoTrac.* It is important to point out just what service is being searched.

InfoTrac (Magazine Index) has several advantages over the printed *Readers' Guide:* (1) It indexes more titles: 435 as compared to 186 in the *Readers' Guide.* (2) There are short, supplementary annotations for articles whose titles do not clearly indicate content. In many cases, additional phrases are added to explain a less-than-descriptive title. (3) There is a built-in consumer feature which makes it possible to quickly locate information about products one might be considering for purchase. (4) The publisher provides full-text coverage, in microform, of the majority of periodicals indexed. (5) Book reviews are coded in the index by the grades A through F. Each grade represents a reviewer's opinion, and it is a simple matter to count the number of A or C grades to ascertain the probable level of acceptance of a given work by the critics. In days past, *The Book Review Digest* used to grade reviews, but the system was dropped. Now it reappears, for better or for worse, in the *Magazine Index*. Note, too, that the same grading system is applied to TV shows, film, theater, restaurant reviews, and so on.

The publisher approaches another matter with skill. Full text of a great number of the magazines indexed is available on microform. "Magazine Collection" is the descriptor for the full text of 280 magazines indexed in the senior index. The service is updated biweekly, and coverage goes back four years or further (to 1980) if one wishes to purchase more retrospective files. The format consists of a carousel with 360 cartridges, each containing as many as 65 periodicals. The user selects the proper cartridge and puts it into a reader-printer. He may either just read or print out the material, which is considerable, i.e., over 400,000 individual articles.

A code number from Infotrac or the microfilm edition ties in the *Magazine Collection* to the index. Also, one may use the *Magazine Collection* without Infotrac. There is a printed "Issue Guide" and "Contents Guide" which lets the user go directly to articles when they know the name of the magazine, issue, or article title.

A similar service is offered for the publisher's *Business Index, i.e., Business Collection,* which covers about 380 titles from 1982. The barrier is cost. *Business Collection,* for example, runs from $10,950 to $16,950 a year, depending on whether a reader-printer is supplied. A similar fee is applied for *Magazine Collection.* The complete package is close to $19,000, although a renewal is less, about $13,000 a year.

InfoTrac (Magazine Index) is similar to the *Wilsondisc* for *The Readers' Guide to Periodical Literature,* and is fast becoming a regular feature in most medium-to-large public, school, and academic libraries. The various titles are somewhat confusing, but essentially *Infotrac* is one general index in an expanded or somewhat-reduced form.

InfoTrac's various packages are: *Magazine Index Plus.* This, as all of the services, is updated monthly. It includes indexing for the same 400-plus magazines found in the microfilm edition. The "plus" signifies, apparently, that *The New York Times* and *The Wall Street Journal* are added, but only for two months of issues. *Magazine Index Select* is the same index, but only for 200 periodicals and two months of *The New York Times.*

A less expensive version of *Magazine Index* is the *TOM* index for schools. Available on CD-ROM or microfilm, it covers about 100 magazines from 1980 to the present, with over 60 available in full text from 1985. (The magazines are on microfiche, not microfilm.) A yearly subscription is much less than for the larger sets, i.e., about $2500. With hardware this goes to $3500.

The price is high, but there are other possibilities, i.e., the cost is less if the library provides its own hardware or votes for a school subscription of only nine months. Still, the cost is, again, higher than the services of a similar nature offered by The H. W. Wilson Company.

An important consideration here is that although the system is extremely easy for a layperson to use, it does not offer the sophisticated points of access found in The H. W. Wilson CD-ROM version of *The Readers' Guide.* No boolean logic search pattern is possible, i.e., one cannot use a number of combinations to find a given subject. The user must search by specific words or phrases in the title or description of the article.

The *General Periodicals Index,* the name given to another *InfoTrac* service index, is an expansion of the basic index. Only available on CD-ROM, it reaches out for 1100 periodicals, almost triple the number in *Magazine Index.* The increased cost parallels the increased coverage, although at only about $2000 more, it is a reasonable increase. Aside from the number of periodicals indexed, it is exactly the same as *Magazine Index.* It comes in two garden varieties. One is more appropriate for public libraries and includes more popular, general titles. One is for academic libraries and embraces academic journals,[9] i.e., *Academic Index,* with the only change being, as one might suspect, in the type of magazines indexed. Both seem to include many of the periodicals in *Business Index.* As such, they both have *The New York Times,* again, though, for only two months.

In addition to the general CD-ROM disks for *InfoTrac,* one may search related indexes at the same terminal. Just as with Wilsondisc, one simply changes the CD-ROM disk to obtain a subject search. The company is adding new subject services each year, but as of 1991 there are 20, including *National Newspaper Index Legal Trac, Health Index, Government Publication Index, Computer Database,* and so on.

Magazine Index on Microfilm

Originally the *Magazine Index* (along with *Business Index* and *National Newspaper Index*) was introduced to libraries on microfilm. It still is found in many libraries. Each month the publisher sends the library an updated reel of film which covers the previous month, plus the

---

[9]Christine Guyonneau, "Magazine Index Plus or Academic Index?" *C&RL News,* July/August 1988, pp. 431–433. The study finds the new index less than satisfactory and calls for a more radical approach of magazines indexed. Early in 1991 the publisher introduced new software for a more sophisticated search pattern of the various *InfoTrac* data bases.

past four years. The reel of film is mounted in a machine, and when someone wants to look up an item, a simple, motorized system makes it possible to view the desired area almost immediately.

This is a great help to many, as one need only consult the appropriate reel rather than search through various volumes. The approach here is much the same as for *InfoTrac,* although the latter is easier to use and more convenient.

Other Magazine Index Forms

The *Magazine Index* comes in a variety of electronic forms. These include:

1. *Online* This is available via DIALOG and other major vendors, and provides coverage from 1959 to date. The service is updated by about 12,000 records each month. The after-hours service of DIALOG (Knowledge Index, which is accessible after 6 P.M., offers about 70 databases at a flat fee of $24) is considerably less expensive than the daytime regular search at $84 a connect hour. *Knowledge Index* is used by people at home, although less so by libraries, as few except the very largest offer extensive in-depth online reference service after 6 P.M.

2. *Magazine ASAP* (online) Provides the full text of about 80 publications back to January 1983. It is updated weekly. There is the usual advantage of being able to search using the words, not only in the title and assigned subject headings, but in the full text.

Available through DIALOG, the search cost is not cheap— about $84 per connect-hour. Also, there is a $7 charge for each record which is typed, displayed, or printed. The file goes back only to 1983.[10]

In searching the *Magazine Index,* how does one know whether the particular periodical is available in full text? The answer is that DIALOG indicates which citation is available in full text. Then, without having to change files, one simply types a command: "Format 9" for the full text.

Because of the effort to include a wide variety of magazines in full text, *Magazine ASAP* sometimes makes it difficult to search. As an experienced librarian puts it:

[10]The publisher, Information Access Company, offers several other similar services: Newswire/ASAP; and Trade and Industry ASAP. Each offers full texts of various business newspapers and business services. *Magazine Index,* too, is the core of a "General Reference Library" offered online by DIALOG. Here one may not only search the index, but several other databases as well, including *NewsSearch Books in Print* and the text of the *Academic American Encyclopedia.*

According to my study of *Magazine ASAP*, the mixture of types of journals sometimes makes good search strategy difficult. The news magazines cause many false drops even when searching for concepts within five or ten words of each other because articles about political campaigns just list many unrelated concepts discussed in a speech. These strategies are often too restrictive to retrieve more factual, lengthy articles found in magazines such as *Psychology Today* or *Science* where paragraph retrieval works better.[11]

Another major drawback of this—and of all CD-ROM and on-line services—is the failure to be able to provide graphics, photographs, or advertisements. This, then, is far from a full text—at least in instances where the illustrations and the ads matter.

Magazine Article

Magazine Article Summaries (Formerly: *Popular Magazine Review*). Birmingham, AL: Ebsco, 1987 to date, weekly. $289.
Also available as (1) Online, Maxwell (BRS) file. $71 per hour. (2) CD-ROM, 1984 to date. Monthly $1600 (quarterly, $800; annual, $400). (3) *Academic Abstracts*, 1991 to date, monthly, $1799.

Another contender in the area of print abstracts of popular periodicals is *Magazine Article Summaries*. It is about the same price as *Readers' Guide Abstracts*, but has the advantage of being published every week, not every six weeks.

As compared to the *Guide:* (1) It indexes over 300 titles, including about 70 which are not in the *Guide*. (2) There is a cumulative subject index bimonthly and a separate index to people mentioned in articles.

The drawbacks include: (1) The subject headings are too broad. (2) It comes in a loose-leaf folder, which can be a bit difficult to use. (3) The indexing is more selective than in the *Guide*. (4) The abstracts are only 20 to 55 words. (5) The bibliographic citation is at the end of the abstract, which can be confusing. (6) Finding an item often requires a two-step procedure.

The company offered *Junior High Magazine Abstracts*, which costs only $140 but comes out only bimonthly and covers 73 magazines. This is equivalent to the *Abridged Readers' Guide*, but has abstracts.

CD-ROM. The CD-ROM version is more satisfactory. The

[11]Carol Tenopir "Searching Full Text Databases," *Library Journal*, May 1, 1988, p. 61.

searching pattern is as simple as one may need, but also employs boolean operators and proximity. Three levels are provided for typing out and creating the bibliographies. In one evaluation it was found that the system "offers a powerful search engine to locate information quickly from several years' of popular periodicals."[12]

Since the beginning of the 1990s, there has been a full-text backup for *Magazine Article Summaries*—but with a difference. Approximately 50 magazines in full text are offered on a single CD-ROM. The searcher is allowed, if she wishes, to search the full text quickly, not, as in other systems, the index first, for the desired materials. *The Academic Index*, on CD-ROM, follows the same pattern as its cousin, but includes 540 titles for academics. A full text of nearly 100 periodicals is offered, and the whole is searched as *Magazine Articles Summaries*.

Comparing Services[13]

The decision as to which of these indexes to purchase is a matter of budget and of individual library pattern use. In terms of print formats, the *Readers' Guide* is a clear first choice. If nothing else, it is a fixture in American libraries and is about as well known to the public as any reference work.

Turning to the various CD-ROM offerings, there are several considerations. The first is with material covered. In summary: *InfoTrac Magazine Index Plus*, 435 periodicals; *Magazine Article Summaries*, 300; *Wilsondisc Readers' Guide Abstracts*, 200; *Periodical Abstracts Ondisc*, 900. There are junior partners for several of these which cost less but which, of course, cover fewer periodicals. Monthly frequency is the pattern for updating the services. Wilson is the exception with quarterly updates.

The secondary considerations concern cost and the ease or

---

[12]Norman Desmarais, "Magazine Article Summaries: An Evaluation," *CD-ROM Librarian*, July/August 1989, pp. 17-22.

[13]Carol Tenopir, "Article Delivery Solution," *Library Journal*, June 1, 1990, pp. 91–92. See also John Jaffe, "For Undergrads: InfoTrac, Magazine Index Plus, or Wilsondisc?" *American Libraries*, October 1988, pp. 759–761. The findings at Sweet Briar College, VA, favored the Magazine Index, although libraries prefer the Wilsondisc. See also Charles Forrest et al., "Periodical Indexing Ondisc: A Comparative Analysis of InfoTrac Use in Three Illinois Libraries," *Reference Services Review*, Spring, 1989, pp. 85–92. "In general patron response to InfoTrac was overwhelmingly enthusiastic (p. 90)." Douglas Ernest and Holly Lange, "InfoTrac and Wilsondisc" *Reference Services Review*, Summer, 1989, pp. 67–75. "Reports . . . indicate Wilsondisc is proving equally as popular with users as InfoTrac" (p. 74).

difficulty of searching. Does one use a sophisticated or a simple search pattern to locate the material?

In this regard, *InfoTrac Magazine Index Plus* (a version of *Magazine Index* and *Magazine Article Summaries*) is easier to use, although it lacks subtle search patterns. *Resource/One* (a junior partner of *Periodical Abstracts OnDisc*) is not as comprehensive, but it offers more search options and is less costly—about $800 a year as opposed to $3200 for *Magazine Index Plus* and $1600 for *Magazine Article Summaries*. All considered, *Resource/One* is a first choice in many small- to medium-size libraries.

One study finds that students and laypersons prefer the CD-ROM *InfoTrac* offered by *Magazine Index Plus*. Why? Their reasons for objecting to other sophisticated systems apply here: (1) Online and boolean searching frustrate the nonprofessional. (2) The multi-disciplinary coverage is easier to use than the different Wilson subject indexes, i.e., *Magazine Index* coverage is twice as great as *Readers' Guide* and is often used in varied subject fields as well as general fields of interest.[14] Much the same argument for ease of use by laypersons can be made for *Magazine Article Summaries*.

Most libraries will want only one general index, no matter in what format. There is too much overlap and repetition among the four to justify purchasing more than one. Hands-on experience (by both librarians and the laypersons likely to use the systems) is strongly recommended before making a choice.

Meanwhile, even today the eminent position in the print market for general indexes is held firmly by *The Readers' Guide*. Beyond that, where a sophisticated package is wanted, the author's choice is *Periodical Abstracts OnDisc*, because of its wider coverage of magazines, abstracts, and full-text capability. A close contender, at least with full text of articles on a single CD-ROM, is *Magazine Articles Summaries* or its companion, *Academic Abstracts*.

Most of the services have online capabilities, too. Here, however, the advantage of one over the other is not so marked. The only real matter of concern, again, is how sophisticated the search patterns may be for this or that service. Also, the comparison is more academic than real. Most libraries will turn to CD-ROM, not online for general indexes. However, for special indexes the reverse is likely to be true, at least where being current is a major concern.

---

[14]On the other hand, some libraries prefer the Wilson indexes for the wrong reasons, i.e. the system offers librarians the advantage of indexing periodicals that are most likely to be in their collections and does not go so far afield as Magazine Index and company.

Other General Guides

Popular Periodical Index. Roslyn, PA: Popular Periodical Index, 1973 to date, quarterly. $40.

Access. Evanston, IL: Access, 1975 to date, three issues per year. $137.50.

Several other indexes augment the *Readers' Guide. Augment* is perhaps the wrong word, as the raison d'être of these indexes is the inclusion of periodicals which for one reason or another have been excluded by the selection committee for the *Readers' Guide.*

The earliest indexes to include the omissions from the *Readers' Guide* is the *Popular Periodical Index,* which includes about 30 titles not found in the Wilson index. The librarian-publisher, Robert Bottorff, includes subject headings for reviews, motion pictures, recordings, and so on. Where a title does not describe the content, the editor often adds a word or a line or two explaining what the article is about. While this is hardly a full abstract, enough information is given to make the index particularly useful.

Access is another general index. It emphasizes works on popular music, travel magazines, science fiction, and arts and crafts titles. It is particularly strong in its coverage of city and regional magazines. Its value to librarians is as a wide net, in the indexing of really popular titles which are not in other general services.

About 125 periodicals are indexed in each issue. The index is divided into two parts. The first section is author, and the second is subject. The index tends to lag behind by as much as six months, although being current is improving and the delay factor is decreased each year. After the paperback issues in June and October there is a cumulative hardback issue in December to round out the year.

While technically one should classify the *Catholic Periodical and Literature Index* (Haverford, Pa.: Catholic Library Association, 1930 to date, bimonthly, service) as a religious index, actually it is much broader in scope. It indexes by author, subject, and title approximately 160 periodicals, most of which are Catholic, but vary widely as to editorial content. In fact, many of the titles could be classified as general magazines. Also, the index includes analyses of books by and about Catholics. There are sections for book reviews, movie reviews, and theater criticism. Although this is of limited value in many libraries, it might be considered for public and college libraries serving a Catholic population.

Retrospective Periodical Indexes

Poole's Index to Periodical Literature, 1802–1906: vol. 1, 1802–1881, Boston: Houghton Mifflin Company, 1981; vols. 2–6 (supplements 1 to 5), 1882–1907, Boston: Houghton Mifflin Company; 1888–1908 (6 vols. reprinted in 7 vols.), Gloucester, MA: Peter Smith Publisher, 1963.

This was the first general magazine index, and the forerunner of the *Readers' Guide.* It was the imagination of William Frederick Poole, a pioneer in both bibliography and library science, that made the index possible. Recognizing that many older periodicals were not being used for lack of proper indexing, he set out to index 470 American and British periodicals covering the period 1802 to 1881. Having completed this work, he issued five supplements which brought the indexing to the end of 1906.

The modern user is sometimes frustrated by the fact that the cited journals do not have a date, but rather are identified only by the volume in which they appear and by the first-page number. For example, the article "Dress and Its Critics" is from *Nation,* 2:10. A "chronological conspectus" in each volume gives an indication of the year.

There is no author approach. Indexing is entirely by subject. The author index to the 300,000 references in the main set and to the supplements was later supplied by C. Edward Wall, *Cumulative Author Index for Poole's Index* (Ann Arbor, Mich.: Pierian Press, 1971, 488 pp.). The index is computer-produced and not entirely easy to follow, but it is a great help to anyone seeking an author entry in *Poole.*

With all its faults, Poole's work is still a considerable achievement and an invaluable key to nineteenth-century periodicals. The last decade of the century is better treated in *Nineteenth Century Readers' Guide to Periodical Literature,* 1890–1899, with supplementary indexing 1900–1922 (New York: The H. W. Wilson Company, 1944, 2 vols.). Limited to 51 periodicals (in contrast to Poole's 470), this guide thoroughly indexes magazines by author and subject for the years 1890 to 1899. Fourteen magazines are indexed between 1900 and 1922.

Canadian and British Reference Index

British Humanities Index, London: Library Association, 1962 to date, quarterly. $428.

Canadian Periodical Index. Toronto, ON: Info Globe, 1938 to date, monthly. $395. (Info Globe, $85 per hour) CD-ROM, publisher. Inquire for price.

Canadian Literature Index. Toronto, ON: ECW Press, 1987 to date, quarterly. $275.

Libraries in Canada and England normally use the *Readers' Guide,* although both have rough national equivalents of it. The *British Humanities Index* is a serviceable and relatively general guide to about 300 British journals covering such subjects as politics, economics, history, and literature. Unlike the *Readers' Guide,* it is of limited use in the area of current materials because it is published only quarterly with annual cumulations. By the time the *British Humanities Index* and the corresponding periodicals reach North America, the timeliness factor is worthless.

The *Canadian Periodical Index (CPI)* is an approximate equivalent to the *Readers' Guide.* It is an author-subject index to about 370 Canadian magazines, including French titles. According to the introduction, there are also "21 American magazines most commonly found in Canadian libraries." The book and movie reviews are listed separately as are poems and short stories. The index follows the same excellent pattern of the *Readers' Guide,* but with a few additions. The French titles, for example, are indexed under English language subject headings, but there are abundant cross-references to these in French translation. The Canadian Library Association has a retrospective volume covering the period 1920–1937. But this includes only 22 of the more popular periodicals indexed by *CPI.*

The online version is supplied by the publisher, and it goes back to 1977. *CPI* Online is part of a larger package of news and events offered online by the publisher. The database is updated weekly instead of monthly, as is the printed version. A printed thesaurus is available.

The CD-ROM version, covering the past ten years, is also available from InfoGlobe.

Although the *Canadian Periodical Index* includes many out-of-the-way titles, it can hardly cover them all. Into the gap comes the *Canadian Literature Index* which while stressing poetry, drama, and criticism, includes relevant general material. Over 100 English and French language titles are indexed, as well as international periodicals and newspaper supplements.

There is another general periodical index which surpasses the American services like a Rolls Royce passes a small Ford. This is a German service that indexes not 180, not 400, not 900, but over

7000 individual periodicals in many languages from every continent and the Pacific. Coverage is truly worldwide. The index is *IBZ* (Internationale Bibliographies der Zeitschriftenliterature) which has been published semiannually since 1965 in West Germany. It costs $2780 a year. Problems with using it include language barriers and the somewhat confusing subject arrangement, but it is worth the effort for the serious researcher.[15]

INDEXES TO MATERIAL IN COLLECTIONS

Essay and General Literature Index. New York: The H. W. Wilson Company, 1900 to date, semiannual. $95.

Short Story Index. New York: The H. W. Wilson Company, 1953 to date, annual. Price varies.

The Columbia Granger's Index to Poetry, 9th ed. New York: Columbia University Press, 1990, 2048 pp. $175. CD-ROM, publisher,[16] 1991 to date. Inquire for price.

Play Index. New York: The H. W. Wilson Company, 1953 to date. (Irregular; basic volume, 1953, plus six additional volumes. Price varies, $12 to $55 per vol.)

Anthologies and collections are a peculiar blessing or curse for the reference librarian. Many of them are useless, others are on the borderline, and a few are worthwhile in that they bring the attention of readers to material which otherwise might be missed. Collections may serve the reference librarian who is seeking a particular speech, essay, poem, or play. In reference, the usefulness of anthologies is dependent on their adequate indexes.

This type of material is approached by the average user in one of several ways. He or she may know the author and want to identify a play, a poem, or other form by that author. The name of the work may be known, but more than likely it is not. Another approach is to want something about a certain subject in a play, poem, or short story.

Consequently, the most useful indexes to material in collec-

[15]C. Boyden, "Metamorphosis of the IBZ Bibliographic Index," *Reference Services Review,* 1987, pp. 81–85. The author traces the history of the index (which actually began in 1896, but was stopped by wars) and how it is used.

[16]Here and throughout this book "publisher" in this context means that the publisher of the index or reference work also publishes the CD-ROM. Where the publisher of the CD-ROM differs from that of the printed work, the name and address are given.

tions are organized so that they may be approached by author, subject, and title of a specific work. Failure to find a particular title in an anthology or collection usually means it has been published independently and has still to find its way into a collective form. The catalog certainly should be checked; if it fails to produce an answer, standard bibliographical tools, such as the *Cumulative Book Index* and *Books in Print,* should be consulted.

Indexes to materials in collections serve two other valuable purposes. Most of them cover books or other materials which have been analyzed; and since the analysis tends to be selective, the librarian has a built-in buying guide to the better or outstanding books in the field. For example, the *Essay and General Literature Index* picks up selections from most of the outstanding collections of essays.

The second benefit, particularly in these days of close cooperation among libraries, is that the indexes can be used to locate books not in the library. Given a specific request for an essay and lacking the title in which the essay appears, the librarian requests the book on interlibrary loan by giving the specific and precise bibliographical information found in the index.[17]

Because they share a similar purpose of locating bits of information from collections, anthologies, and individual books and magazines, all these reference aids tend to benefit the humanities, particularly literature. There is little need for such assistance in the social sciences and the sciences, and where the need does exist, it is usually met by an abstracting or indexing service.

While the four indexes, discussed in this section, are the best known, others appear each year. They include guides to science fiction, information on handicrafts, costumes, photographs, and such. Once the form is recognized, the only basic change in searching is in the topics covered and the thoroughness, or lack of it, in arrangement and depth of analysis.

The single most useful work a library can have as an entry into miscellaneous collections of articles is the *Essay and General Literature Index.* It is valuable for general reference questions, in that the analyzed essays cover a wide variety of topics. There are analytical subject entries to the contents of approximately 300 collected works on every subject from art to medicine. While the indexing emphasis is

---

[17]By the end of the 1980s a new approach to locating the necessary books was evident, but at a fairly high cost. This is "CoreFiche". Books listed in such guides as the *Essay and General Literature Index* or *Granger's Index to Poetry* from the first edition through the 1970s are available on microfiche. The price for 1,000 fiche for covering titles indexed in *Granger's* is $5000, and $3700 for 700 fiche for the *Essay* index.

on the subjects, the index is also useful in approaching an author's work via his or her name as well as in locating criticism of the author's individual efforts. There are regular four-year cumulations issued to the index.

The elusive short story may be tracked down in the *Short Story Index*. Now published annually, the *Index* lists stories in both book collections and periodicals. A single index identifies the story by author, title, and subject. The subject listing is a handy aid for the reference librarian attempting to find a suitable study topic for a student who may not want to read an entire book on the Civil War or life in Alaska. The names of the books and the magazines analyzed are listed. More than 3000 stories are included each year. A basic volume covers collections published from 1900 to 1949, and there are five-year cumulations, or with the 1984–1988 cumulation, a group of nine volumes to search. There is also *Short Story Index: Collections Indexed 1900–1978* which lists the 8400 collections analyzed.

The difficulty with these and other ongoing indexes to collections is that one often may have to search numerous volumes to find the needed item. For example, almost any story of Henry James will be reprinted year after year, and it can be found by looking in the latest *Short Story Index* or, more surely, in the five-year cumulation. Conversely, a short story by Joseph Roth may have appeared in only one collection. But which collection, and what year? It is conceivable that one will have to search all eight volumes before finding what is needed. The same problem presents itself when searching the *Essay and General Literature Index, Play Index,* and all indexes to collections. Unfortunately, laypersons may search only one series, and so fail to find what is needed. What is desirable, of course, is a cumulative index for all such works. This is most likely to be made available when indexes to collections are accessed via a computer terminal, rather than volume by volume.

Indexing both individually published plays and plays in collections, *Play Index* is a standard reference work. The basic part is an author, title, and subject index. According to the publisher, the author entry for a play "contains the full name of the author, title of the play, a brief descriptive note, the number of acts and scenes, the size of the cast, and the number of sets required." Numerous other helpful devices are included that range from symbols for plays suitable for elementary school children to prizes a play has won. A cast analysis, making up the second section, helps the reference librarian locate plays for a given number of players required. The other sections key the plays to collections from which they have been taken.

The current edition of *The Columbia Granger's Index to Poetry* follows previous editions in arrangement and approach. Close to 400 poetry anthologies are indexed. There are four indexes: by first line, author, subject, and title. This makes it possible to use the guide for the obvious purpose of locating a poem in a particular anthology or group of anthologies. In addition, the guide is a great help in tracing elusive quotations, either by subject or by first line. Often these are well known, but may be in a poem, and as such, may not be found in standard quotation books. Also the reference work is of considerable assistance for the individual looking for precisely the proper poem by subject to employ in a paper, speech, or letter.

Granger's Index gives access to over 40,000 poems published in anthologies. While there is some carryover of titles from previous editions, it is wisest to consult earlier editions if a given poem is not found in the latest edition. In fact, each edition is a unique index to poetry collections published for each of the years covered, beginning in 1904.

The *Columbia Granger's Guide to Poetry Anthologies* (New York: Columbia University Press, 1991) is an annotated, descriptive, and critical appraisal of all the anthologies indexed in the ninth edition of *Granger's*. The annotations, prepared by William and Linda Katz, are both critical and descriptive, with attention given to the audiences for the particular works. This is helpful for librarians and laypersons trying to determine which of the 400 anthologies to purchase. A first-time effort, it may be prepared in parallel again with new editions of *Granger's*.

A CD-ROM version of *Granger's* includes the aforementioned *Guide* as well as the contents of both the eighth and ninth editions of the service. Other features make it useful for searching. It will be updated with each new printed edition of *Granger's*.

SUGGESTED READING

Gomez, Louis et al., "All the Right Words," *Journal of the American Society for Information Science*, December, 1990, pp. 547–559. Although a somewhat technical article, the result is clear enough. In the words of the authors: "Don't try to pick only the best words, try to harvest all the appropriate ones. . . . For end users doing interactive searches, a controlled vocabulary would probably be strongly counterproductive. . . . In the same situation, full text indexing appears likely to yield very high success rates." The experiment concerned machine readable databases, but much of the article is applicable equally to print indexes.

Henige, David, "Library of Congress Subject Headings: Is Euthanasia the Answer?"

Cataloging & Classification Quarterly, vol. 8, no. 1, 1987, pp. 7–19. The author cites chapter and verse to indicate that the Library of Congress work is less than current with its approaches to subject headings. See, too, a response from the Library of Congress which immediately follows the article on pp. 20–21.

Joy, Albert, and Nancy Keane, "CDMARC Subjects . . ." *CD-ROM Librarian,* October 1989, pp. 36–45. Not only is this a discussion of the headings on CD-ROM, but the authors include comments about the eleventh edition as well. There are some differences between the CD-ROM and print versions, which are pointed out, as are other aspects about both forms.

Pemberton, Jeffery, "Database Interview Morris Goldstein, President of Information Access Company," *Database,* October 1989, pp. 29–38. The publisher of *Magazine Index* and of both special and general indexes reveals plans for the future of the indexing firm. Along the way the reader learns much about the problems of indexing, particularly in the age of the new technologies.

Reynolds, Sally Jo, "In Theory There Is No Solution: The Impediments to a Subject Cataloging Code," *Library Quarterly,* July 1989, pp. 223–238. Lacking any consensus on the major purpose of subject headings, there is little chance the Library of Congress will ever satisfy everyone with its subject headings. The article concludes with some reasonable paths toward at least a temporary solution to the problem.

Summit, Roger, and Ann Lee. "Will Full-Text Online Files Become Electronic Periodicals?" *Serials Review,* no. 3, 1988, pp. 7–10. Will the rise of the full-text database mean an end to the printed journal? Will online databases change the way information is delivered? The authors believe the electronic journals will supplement rather than supplant the printed works.

Tuttle, Marcia, and Jean Cook. *Advances in Serial Management.* Greenwich, CT: JAI Press, 1987 to date, annual. This is a series which presents a mix of historical and practical articles on serials publishing and management. Articles cover all aspects of the subject, including indexes.

Weinberg, Bella Hass, "Why Indexing Fails the Researcher," *The Indexer,* April 1988, pp. 3–6. "It took five times as long to retrieve the references to document the ideas (of this paper) than it did to write the paper." So concludes the author about her own piece, a piece which makes the simple plea to improve indexing by paying more attention to highly specific aspects of a subject. In so doing, she clearly points out one of numerous problems which face any indexer.

Wellisch, Hans, "The Oldest Printed Indexes," *The Indexer,* October 1986, pp. 73–82. According to the author, the "oldest printed indexes are found in [work] published by Fust and Schoeffer . . . probably in the early 1460s." With that he proceeds to explore the history of that index and what it subsequently meant to all indexing. Well written and a fascinating study of what most people today accept as commonplace.

CHAPTER SIX
INDEXING AND ABSTRACTING
SERVICES: SUBJECT AND
NEWSPAPER

So far we have considered only the general periodical index, but there are numerous other forms of indexes. Let us first look at the more specialized subject index which follows as a natural progression from the general index to the subject index, when the user or the librarian has a question associated with a particular subject and with an index. Yet it is not quite that simple. A high school student who asks for an article on the American Civil War should be referred to almost any year of *Readers' Guide*. The same student or, for that matter, the teacher or subject expert who is doing a detailed paper on the Civil War will require not only more periodicals likely to have such material but also more sophisticated approaches. In this instance the searcher might turn to several indexes, but will more likely be successful with the one which concentrates on American history, i.e., *America: History and Life*. The subject indexes are of major importance in libraries, and it is with examples of these that the next section is concerned.

SUBJECT INDEXES

All the following are published by The H. W. Wilson Company:

> *Humanities Index.* 1974 to date, quarterly. Service (Wilsonline, $37 to $55 per hour). CD-ROM (Wilsondisc, 1984 to date, quarterly. $1295).

Social Sciences Index. 1974 to date, quarterly. Service (Wilsonline, $34 to $55 per hour). CD-ROM (Wilsondisc, 1983 to date, quarterly. $1295). Full text, 1991 to date, monthly. $16,500.

General Science Index. 1978 to date, monthly. Service (Wilsonline, $34 to $55 per hour). CD-ROM (Wilsondisc, 1984 to date, quarterly. $1295).

The H. W. Wilson Company issues three indexes which bridge the general to the specific subject, edited specifically for the student, the average public library user, and the nonexpert who wants more depth in a subject than is found in the *Readers' Guide* but not as much specialization as in the subject indexes such as *Business Periodicals Index.*

The *Humanities Index* analyzes 350 English language periodicals. The single index is by subject and author, with the usual section for book reviews. It has several unique features: (1) Opera and film reviews are listed under appropriate subject headings, i.e., "opera reviews" and "motion picture reviews". (2) Poems may be located both by the author's name and under a section, "poems". (3) The same procedure is followed for short stories. (4) There is a section for theater reviews. Given these divisions, the work is valuable for checking current critical thought on a wide variety of subjects in the humanities—here taken to mean archaeology and classical studies, folklore, history, language and literature, literary and political criticism, performing arts, philosophy, religion and theology, and, according to the publisher, "related subjects."

The *Social Sciences Index* covers about 355 English language periodicals in anthropology, area studies, psychology, public administration, sociology, environmental science, economics, and related areas. There are author and subject entries with a separate section for book reviews.

In the social sciences, as in all areas, there are numerous related indexes which may be more narrow (*Index to Current Urban Documents*) or even broader (*Social Sciences Citation Index*) in scope. Then there are somewhat similar efforts, e.g., ASSIA (*Applied Social Sciences Index & Abstracts,* 1987 to date, bi-m. New York: K.G. Saur/ Bowker). This covers 500 journals, or about 150 more than its rival. More important, each entry has a brief (25 to 35 word) abstract. The dramatic difference is in the price. This costs $790 as compared to a service rate for the H. W. Wilson entry, which is lower.

If, then, at one time the average library simply turned to the H. W. Wilson indexes for assistance, this no longer is the case. There are numerous rivals, some better, some not so good, that must be considered in terms of quality, price, frequency of publication, and applicability to the library and its particular audience.

The third basic subject index issued by The H. W. Wilson Company is the *General Science Index.* About 111 English language general science periodicals are indexed by subject. There is *no* author approach other than that in the citations to book reviews, which are listed by book authors. The subject headings are selected for the nonspecialist, and where specialized subjects are used, adequate cross-references aid searchers. Fields covered range from astronomy to zoology.

The *Applied Science and Technology Index* is a related work by the same publisher. It is considered later in this chapter.

Subject Index Scope

Once a user understands how the average subject index is put together, how it is to be used, and what its possible problems are, he may progress from the Wilson indexes to their numerous other sisters and cousins. To know one is to know, with variations, all. Therefore, the concentration on the Wilson family is not so much an endorsement, although they are very good, but more a primary example of what is available in the whole field of subject indexing.

When considering subject indexes, three facts must be kept in mind:

1. Many are broader in coverage than is indicated by such key title words as "Art" or "Education." Related fields are often considered. Therefore, anyone doing a subject analysis in depth can consult indexes which take in fringe-area topics.
2. Most of the subject indexes are not confined solely to magazines. They often include books, monographs, bulletins, and even government documents.
3. A great number are not parochial but, rather, international in scope. True, they may not list many foreign language works, but usually note anything in English, even if issued abroad.

Because of this wider base of coverage, many libraries are doubtful about including such indexes in their collections. What good is it to learn of a particular article in a specialized journal and then be unable to obtain the journal? However, the library should be in a position either to borrow the journal or to have a copy made of the article. Another possibility—full text on CD-ROM. If the cost is lowered, this may be the saviour of smaller libraries in the decade ahead. At least all popular magazines will then be within easy reach (and indexing) for all libraries.

There is little point in describing each of the Wilson subject indexes. For the most part, their titles explain the scope and purpose of each. Their users may be either a specialist or a generalist—journals and periodicals for both are indexed. Most indexed titles are American, but there are representative selections from other countries in other languages. They each index from 185 to 300 works.

All the Wilson indexes use much the same approach; that is, the author and subject entries are in a single alphabet, and each contains the usual excellent cross-references. (Some indexes, such as the *Applied Science and Technology Index*, have only a subject approach.) Subject headings are frequently revised, and in most services, book reviews are listed in a separate section. Each index has its peculiarities, but a reading of the prefatory material in each will clarify its finer points.

Social Sciences Index/Full Text offers a monthly full-text service. The 350 periodicals in *Social Sciences Index* are on a series of disks. The index is on a separate disk. Actual use is easy enough, despite failure to be able to search the full text, but the cost of $16,500 is prohibitive for most libraries. Still, it is the way the H. W. Wilson indexes and others will go in the years ahead.

Beyond the ubiquitous Wilson indexes, there are three- to four-thousand indexes and abstracting services by almost as many publishers. What follows are examples of subject indexes, including those published by The H. W. Wilson Company. Some abstracting services are listed.

Art

Art Index. New York: The H. W. Wilson Company, 1929 to date, quarterly. Service (Wilsonline $43 to $65 per hour) CD-ROM; publisher, 1984 to date, quarterly. $1495.

Art Index is the only one of its type in the Wilson family, although numerous art titles are covered in the *Humanities Index*. *Art Index* includes indexes of more than 230 periodicals, yearbooks, and museum publications. The definition of "art" is broad and includes such areas as films, photography, architecture, and landscape design.

Other publishers offer several parallel services. Many of these are narrower in scope, but are often considerably more refined.

Some are noted in the section which follows. It is worth noting here that Wilson hardly has a monopoly on the art indexing market. For example, the expert searcher probably will turn to *RILA*: (Art Literature International, Williamstown, Mass.: Clark Institute, 1973 to date, semiannual). *RILA* indexes over 400 journals as well as major catalogs, books, and dissertations, in the field. *Art Bibliographies Modern* (Santa Barbara, Calif.: ABC-Clio, 1969 to date, semiannual) is another service which indexes 500 journals, as well as reports, books, dissertations, and museum catalogs that discuss art from the 1800s to the present. Both services are available online through DIALOG and others.

One aspect of an art index, as well as that for any form other than print, is the indexing of the art itself. There are indexes of art work by the artist, as well as guides on how to index a picture collection. Much the same approach is taken for recordings, films, and other media. Turn to any of the standard bibliographies for indexes to these forms.[1]

Business

Business Periodicals Index. New York: The H. W. Wilson Company, 1958 to date, monthly. Service (Wilsonline, $45 to $65 per hour) CD-ROM, quarterly, 1984 to date, publisher. $1495.

The Business Index. Foster City, CA: Information Access Corporation, 1979 to date, monthly. $2500. (DIALOG file 148, "Trade & Industry Index," $90 per hour.) CD-ROM, publisher, 1990 to date, quarterly, price varies.

Canadian Business Index. (CBI) Toronto: Micromedia, 1975 to date, monthly. $850. For smaller libraries, $275–$400. DIALOG file 262, $72 per hour.

Predicasts F&S Index United States. Cleveland, OH: Predicasts Inc., 1960 to date, monthly, $850. (DIALOG file 98: 1972–1978; and file 18: from 1979 on, $114 per hour.) CD-ROM, Wellesley Hills, MA: Silver Platter, 1990 to date, monthly, $6000.

Predicasts issues a number of business services, including (1) *Predicasts Forecasts.* Cleveland, OH: Predicasts Inc., 1980 to date, quarterly. $750. (DIALOG files 81 and 83 $114 per hour.)

---

[1]Michael Krause, "Intellectual Problems of Indexing Pictures Collections," *Audiovisual Librarian*, May 1988, pp. 73–81. This is a clear discussion not only of the problems involved with indexing a picture collection, but with identifying images in the pictures.

(2) *Predicasts Overview of Markets and Technologies.* 1977 to date, monthly. $850. (DIALOG file 16, $126 per hour.)

ABI/INFORM. Louisville, KY: UMI/Data Courier, 1971 to date, CD-ROM, publisher, inquire, weekly. Full text on CD-ROM: *Business Periodicals Ondisc.* (DIALOG file 15, $114 per hour.) *Note:* There is no print equivalent.

As with many subject indexes, it is deceptive to think that business indexes are limited to business. They can cover almost every human interest, and may be consulted for information on everything from psychology and art to science and prison life. In fact, for a different, broader view of many subjects, the typical business index is a good secondary source.

Business Periodicals Index covers 304 titles with indexed items by subject, not by author. Subjects are so all-inclusive as to make this almost a general index, and it is used as such by librarians who cannot find enough material in the basic services. For example, one may be looking for an article on the relationship between reading and television, only to find that an analysis of the subject (from the point of view of sales of books and television sets) has been indexed in *Business Periodicals Index* while hardly considered in the more likely *Library Literature.* Still, the index is customarily used primarily for finance, business technology, and economics.

The *Business Index* is a specialized version of the *Magazine Index,* and it comes with a reader and a monthly update on computer output microfilm. It indexes some 810 periodicals as well as noting major books, and includes cover-to-cover indexing of *The Wall Street Journal, Barrons,* and the business section of *The New York Times.* Brief annotations are usually included where needed. It is used just like the *Magazine Index,* but for those who wish to refresh their memories, it includes a detailed set of instructions both at the beginning and the end of the file.

As with its companion, *The Magazine Index,* it has the advantage of being updated once a month and allowing the user to search three years of indexing in one place. The disadvantage is that it goes back only three years, and for retrospective materials one must look elsewhere, i.e., in The H. W. Wilson *Business Periodicals Index.*

The publisher also offers the "Business Collection" (similar to the "Magazine Collection") where the full text of about half the periodicals (i.e., 400) indexed is available on microfilm. The cartridges, in a carousel for easy use, go back to 1982 and are updated biweekly. With printer, the user may quickly and for a rather small amount of money, have the needed article in hand. Online this is called Trade & Industry ASAP (DIALOG file 648); and, again, is the business counterpart to the full-text Magazine ASAP for *Magazine Index* online. This is updated weekly.

Business Index is available, too, as part of the InfoTrac group on CD-ROM. This indexes the same material as in the microfilm edition and is used much as one searches the company's *Magazine Index* and other general indexes on InfoTrac. When the service is enlarged, it becomes what is known as the *General BusinessFile* on InfoTrac. This includes the basic index, plus *CompanyProfile* and *Investext,* and other business services. The magazine articles are linked with company directory information as well as analyst reports.

The *Canadian Business Index* (formerly *The Canadian Business Periodicals Index*) is a monthly analysis of periodicals and 10 newspapers published in Canada. In addition to the usual subject arrangement, there is a personal name and corporate name index. Few of the titles indexed here are found in the American indexes.

An important feature of the Canadian index, as in the other business services discussed here is the coverage of trade names and brand names. In standard indexes these are seldom mentioned, although the *Magazine Index* does feature a given number of critical reviews of particular brands. Here, though, the names are used as instant subject headings for relevant material of interest to both business people and consumers.

Predicasts

Predicasts indexes are divided into United States, Europe, and International volumes. One finds current information on individual corporations, industries, and products. Each indexes about 500 to 750 different periodicals, newspapers, and reports. (These are designated in the front of the issue.)

Each work is arranged in a similar fashion and covers the same basic type of data. The first section, "Industries and Products," is a subject-heading approach to a wide variety of topics, from energy to population. Groupings are in a hierarchical system, and automotive brakes, for example, is a subgroup of motor vehicle parts. Fortunately, the major subject divisions are given in alphabetical order in the cumulative alphabetical guide, and each issue has an "Alphabetical Guide to the SIC Code," which allows ready access to the Industry and Product section. Also, there is a "User's Guide" which clearly explains the arrangement.

The second part of the index is alphabetical by the name of the company, and where the company is vast, there are subheadings.

This is easy to follow and presents no momentary problem as does the first section.

Predicasts is really a collection of several databases, each of which serves a specific purpose.[2] The databases are tapped by well-defined thesauruses for products, organizations, events, and geographical locations. The various services index over 3000 domestic and foreign trade journals, business periodicals, government documents, reports, statistical publications, bank letters, long-range forecasts, and a variety of other materials. Although the focus is on business, the subject matter covers millions of records in related areas, from agriculture to education and the social sciences. Coverage is generally from the early 1970s, although this varies with the different databases. Each base must be searched separately, and some files are used for both retrieval and computation; i.e., it is possible to perform algebraic, statistical, and forecasting routines, as well as to enter data.

Both controlled and free searching are possible, but most of the files use the Standard Industrial Classification (SIC) System. This is a numerical hierarchical system established by the United States government to classify the total economy into different industrial segments. Using specific numbers one may retrieve a "needle" from millions of records.

Among related indexes: *Predicasts Forecasts* draws from over 500 periodicals worldwide. The quarterly issues cover thousands of products and the forecast of their success. More important for the generalists are the forecasts of economies, country by country and region by region. There are currently over 1.2 million records available online.

Predicasts Overview, normally referred to by librarians simply as PROMT, offers a worldwide view of business and individual companies. Over 1200 periodicals, books, and reports are searched for material. The online version has about 1.5 million citations. (Daily coverage is offered by a special online service, otherwise the update is weekly.) A great advantage of the online *Predicasts* is that it is updated each week, and, according to the publisher some 2000 new records are added at that time. The emphasis on current data is stressed, and is typical of the reasoning behind almost all business

---

[2]Typical of many business services online, Predicasts is divided into numerous forms. Some notion of what is involved can be seen simply from the names of a few of many databases, e.g., *PTS Aerospace/Defense Markets; Annual Reports and Abstracts; Marketing and Advertising Service,* etc. Online, the most generally used, is *PTS F&S Indexes* which covers both domestic and international concerns and is, in fact, a combination of the three printed services.

services, particularly those online. The publisher's advertisements point out that the service keeps the reader on top of competitor activities, new product development, license agreements, manufacturing methods and similar items—all of which mean financial gain or loss.

ABI/INFORM

ABI/INFORM is not only one of the oldest online bibliographic databases, it is among the few heavily used systems which has absolutely no print equivalent. It must be searched online or on CD-ROM, or not at all.

ABI (Abstracted Business Information) is available on close to 20 systems and is considered one of the most popular of all databases both in and out of libraries.[3] It has more than 400,000 citations to material in some 800 periodicals. Almost all items have detailed abstracts. Coverage is international. Topics move from accounting and auditing to taxation and real estate. Almost any aspect of the business/economic world can be found. It is updated weekly, and in a month adds from 3500 to 4000 new records.

The popularity comes not only because of its ease of use and relatively low cost, but because the term *business* as interpreted here is truly broad. Almost any subject can be accessed, from art to zebra farming. Fortunately, there is an excellent thesaurus which helps considerably in the search.

The CD-ROM version is much the same as the online. It is a favorite in many libraries, again because it includes not only business, but numerous general titles. The software uses boolean logic and other paths to finding citations.

Business Periodicals Ondisc. This CD-ROM backs up ABI/INFORM and provides full-text article retrieval for some 300 titles indexed in ABI. Coverage is about 55 percent of what can be found in the index, and includes business and management journals which

---

[3]Theresa Jehlik, "Putting Knowledge to Work," *Public Library Quarterly*, vol. 9 no. 4, 1990, pp. 13–30. A study of business collections in public libraries, this points out that a core list of at least 156 business titles is needed to support the various indexes. Most queries may be divided into three main categories: (1) selling/marketing information; (2) company/industry information; and (3) miscellaneous. Both ABI/INFORM and Predicasts fill these needs. See also Susan Veccia, "The Ubiquitous ABI/INFORM . . ." *Database*, February 1987, pp. 35–46. The author points out the numerous differences in accessing the database through various systems. The detailed article shows the lack of standard approaches, even to a single database.

are most heavily used. Retrospective coverage begins with 1987 material. A current year includes about 50 to 60 disks. The total package (ABI/INFORM and the full text) makes up about 140 to 150 disks per year. Disk storage carousels overcome some of the problems of using so many disks, but manual handling remains a problem to be solved. Cost: $15,000 for the full text alone, or $20,000 for the full text and ABI/INFORM. In addition, for each page printed out, UMI charges added 10 cents.

University Microfilms offers another related monthly service. This is *Business Dateline Ondisc.* The CD-ROM contains the text of about 190 regional business publications, as well as three wire services and fifteen business newspapers. It differs from the other publications in that it is both an index and a full-text service on a single disk. The software allows one to search the text for companies, people, and events using standard search procedures. It is much more narrow in scope than Business Dateline Ondisc. This accounts for the considerably lower cost of the monthly update: $3000 a year. (A similar version is available online from numerous vendors with a three-to-five-week time lag.)

Much current business news is available through online newspapers, discussed in the last section of this chapter. In fact, this approach often is favored because it is most up-to-the-minute. Beyond the general newspaper indexes are highly specialized services such as the *McGraw-Hill News* online (DIALOG file 600), which transmits news throughout the business day.

Dissertations

> *Dissertations Abstracts International.* Ann Arbor, MI: 1938 to date, monthly. $140 per section.
>
> *Comprehensive Dissertation Index.* Ann Arbor MI: 1973 to date, annual. Inquire for price. The basic set covers 1861–1972; there is a ten-year cumulation, 38 vols., for 1973 to 1982. (DIALOG file 35, $72 per hour.) CD-ROM, publisher, $1695 for 1985–1989. Semiannual update, $995; archival edition, 1861–1984, $5495.

Each year approximately 500 universities submit dissertations to University Microfilms International (i.e., *Dissertation Abstracts*), which adds up to 35,000 doctoral dissertations and master's theses each year. The total, from 1861 to the early 1990s is close to 1 million.[4]

---

[4]Each discipline normally has a journal which reports on completed or ongoing

Most abstracting services not only analyze periodicals and books but often include dissertations. However, only the *Dissertations Abstracts International* concentrates exclusively on the form—a form which covers all disciplines and interests. Dissertations are important for the reference librarian seeking specific, often unpublished, information about a given subject, place, or person. Since most dissertations contain extensive bibliographies and footnotes, they can be used as unofficial bibliographies for some relatively narrow areas. Before a librarian begins a broad search for bibliographies in any area, these lists should be checked. There is a good chance that some student has already completed the bibliography sought or at least has done enough work to indicate other major sources.

A problem with dissertations is that most librarians will not lend them. Policy differs, but the excuse for not lending is that (1) there is only one copy and it cannot be replaced or (2) a microfilm copy may be purchased from University Microfilms, who just happens to publish the index.[5] Actually, most libraries obtain copies through interlibrary loan via networks such as OCLC.

How does one trace the dissertation? The answer is threefold. The quickest and easiest approach is to use a CD-ROM version. Here one may apply boolean logic as well as other search patterns. If one is confined to print, the first place to go is *Comprehensive Dissertation Index*. The index set is divided into the sciences, social sciences, and humanities, and each of these broad categories has subdivisions, for example, biological sciences, chemistry, and engineering. One locates the volume(s) likely to cover the subject and then turns to the finer subject heading to find a list of dissertations by full title and name of author. Entry is possible by author too, i.e., the final volumes of the main set and the supplement are author-index volumes.[6]

After each entry there is a citation to *Dissertation Abstracts*, where the librarian then turns for the full abstract. The citation refers one to the volume and page number in *Dissertation Abstracts*. For example, in the index one finds "Defining the Roles of Library/ Media Personnel . . . " the author's name, degree-granting univer-

dissertations in its given field. For example, *Library and Information Science Research* in each quarterly issue has a section entitled "Dissertation Reviews." Also, dissertations are noted in many subject indexes such as *Library Literature*.

[5]Manuel Lopez, "Dissertations: A Need for New Approaches to Acquisition," *The Journal of Academic Librarianship*, November 1988, pp. 297–301.

[6]Royal Purcell, "Dissertation Abstracts on CD-ROM . . ." CD-ROM Librarian, November/December 1988, pp. 18–20. A useful explanation of how the system works in Indiana University.

sity, number of pages, and then: "43/06A, p. 1733." The reference is to vol. 43, no. 06A of *Dissertation Abstracts,* on page 1733. This becomes confusing, because on the spine of the volume there is the notation for the volume/number (43/06) and then numbers (1322A-2135A) which are the inclusive page numbers. The number system is easy enough to use and it is understood.

Dissertation Abstracts International is a separate set from the index, but is issued by the same publisher. Like the index, it appears in three parts. Until the annual index is issued, the monthly issues of *Dissertation Abstracts* must be searched individually. Each of the three sections has its own index. It is published monthly, and the arrangement by broad subject headings and then by narrow subject areas is similar to that of the index. Each entry includes a full abstract.

The publisher issues a CD-ROM disk series which covers the whole set and replaces all of the bound volumes, e.g., one disk contains (both national and international) 800,000 citations and covers 1861 to 1984. The second disk moves from 1985 to 1989 and has over 150,000 abstracts and citations. From 1989 forward, the bi-annual CD-ROM service includes master's thesis abstracts as well as British dissertations.

The most current approach is to use the online database which is updated monthly.

Education

ERIC: U.S. Educational Resources Information Center. *Resources in Education.* Washington: Government Printing Office, 1966 to date, monthly. $56. (DIALOG file 1, $30 per hour.)

Current Index to Journals in Education. Phoenix, AZ: Oryx Press, 1969 to date, monthly, $207 (semiannual cumulations, $198). (DIALOG file 1, $30 per hour.) CD-ROM: Wellesley Hills, MA: Silver Platter, 1983 to date, quarterly. $750. Retrospective to 1966, 3 disks, $1200.

By the early 1990s, abstracting has moved from the specialized to the general, i.e., The H. W. Wilson Company's offer of abstracts for *The Readers' Guide* and the promise of abstracts for additional indexes from the same publisher. The use of computers for indexing now makes it much more feasible to employ abstracts, if only of a limited scope. One may envision the day, in the not too distant future, when all major indexes will offer abstracts.

Many of the current abstracting and indexing services are only one part of fuller information systems which not only publish indexes and abstracts, but offer other services. This may be illustrated by ERIC/IR, or, in full, Educational Resources Information Center/ (Clearinghouse for) Information Resources. It should be consulted for both original and secondary material on education, as well as related fields from library science to other social science topics.

The system includes (1) an index and an abstracting service available both in printed form and on database for online retrieval; (2) an ongoing subject vocabulary, represented in the frequently updated *Thesaurus of ERIC Descriptors;* (3) a dissemination system which depends primarily on reproducing the material indexed on microfiche and distributing that microfiche to libraries; and (4) a decentralized organizational structure for acquiring and processing the documents which are indexed and abstracted.

The first abstract part of ERIC is *Resources in Education,* which lists reports and associated items and includes for each a narrative abstract of 200 or fewer words. The abstracts are written by the original authors. Approximately 400 to 500 reports are submitted to ERIC each month, but at least 50 percent are rejected, often as much for lack of typing skills as for content. The reports have to be reproduced on microfiche, and if not typed properly cannot be properly reproduced. Hence they are rejected. Selection is made at one of 16 clearinghouses, each of which considers only a particular subject and has experts able to evaluate the submitted material.[7]

About 15,000 items are included and indexed each year. The actual type of material is divided nearly equally among three categories: research and technical reports; published proceedings, dissertations, preprints, and papers presented at a conference; and curriculum guides, educational legislation, lesson plans, and the like prepared for the classroom. The key to access includes both a subject and an author index as well as an index by institution. The index is cumulated semiannually and annually.

The second method of tapping ERIC is through *Current Index to Journals in Education.* This is an index to about 775 periodicals in education, which results in around 1700 citations each month. Although published by a commercial firm, the indexing is provided

[7]Steven Hirsch, "Eric . . ." *Online Review,* no. 5, 1987, pp. 315–322. This is a good overview of ERIC, "one of the most frequently used databases." The author points out that the database contained more than 600,000 items in January 1987 and that the rate of rejection of 50 percent for Resources in Education is comparable to rejection rates of journals. Of course, it is not all typing that accounts for rejections. "The academic credentials of the ERIC reviewers are impressive and they are the final word as to what is accepted or rejected."

by the 16 clearinghouses. The first part of the index is much like *Resources in Education* in form; that is, items are abstracted and arranged numerically by the accession number. The second part is the subject index, which, again, follows the style of *Resources in Education.* There are also an author index and a fourth section in which the indexed journals are arranged alphabetically by title, and the table of contents for each is given, with accession numbers for articles.

One outstanding feature of ERIC, although a usual one among similar documentation systems such as that developed by the National Aeronautics and Space Administration, is that approximately 80 percent of the documents abstracted in *Resources in Education* are available on microfiche. In 350 to 400 libraries, the user finds the required citation in *Resources in Education* and then, instead of laboriously looking for the item abstracted, simply turns to the microfiche collection, where the items are arranged by accession number. This, then, is a total information system and not the normal two-step bibliographical reference quest in which one finds the abstract or the indexed item and then must try to find the document, journal, or book which the library may not have available.

Ideally, the total information system would be offered with the second ERIC finding tool, *Current Index to Journals in Education* (CIJE). It is not. Why? Because here the index and abstracts are for journal articles, and the journals themselves have to be searched. The cost of putting each article on a microfiche card, not to mention copyright problems with publishers, makes the cost of a total information service prohibitive. This may change as more indexing concerns, such as the publishers of *Magazine Index*, make the full text available not only on microfiche but online.

At the same time, the publishers state "that reprints of articles included in approximately 65 percent of the journals covered in CIJE are available from University Microfilms." One knows whether a reprint is available, because "Reprint: UMI" is stated after each citation where the service may be employed. Ordering information is given in the front of each issue.

Many indexes and abstracting services offer this retrieval of articles, and some of these are discussed in the second volume of this text. Here, suffice it to say that in an effort to get around the problem of finding the article after the citation is located, the movement is toward quick document delivery at the computer terminal. (1) The librarian may order the article at the terminal from the publisher or from a representative of the publisher, usually the latter. The publisher can have the article usually within 24 hours. (2) Full text of the article may be viewed online, i.e., one can read the article at the computer terminal and have printed out what is needed. This, as indicated, is the trend. (3) Telefacsimile (an old procedure) is another option by which the required article is requested on the computer, and then later sent and printed out where needed. This has numerous problems, from speed of transmission (it has been slow and uneconomical) to quality of the printout.

ERIC is offered on CD-ROM by several companies. Each of the publishers offers separate software, separate paths to getting the information out of the CD-ROM disk. The obvious difficulty is that no user is going to learn different systems in order to tap the CD-ROM variations. "As many libraries build collections of CD-ROM databases, the importance of common search software will carry increasingly significant weight."[8]

Two basic education indexes should be mentioned. While they do not provide abstracts, they are widely employed by many of the same people involved with ERIC, and particularly CIJE.

Education Index (New York: The H. W. Wilson Company, 1929 to date, monthly) covers some 350 journals. It also analyzes some books, reports, and the like. All aspects of education are considered, and numerous allied fields are touched upon, such as language and linguistics and library science.

Canadian Education Index. (Toronto: Canadian Education Association, 1965 to date, three issues per year including annual cumulation.) This covers both English and French publications and indexes about 230 periodicals. Books, reports, and other materials dealing with education are also analyzed. The author-subject index covers materials which relate only to Canadian educational activities. There is a list of French subject headings with the English language translations.

History

America: History and Life: Part A, Article Abstracts and Citations. Santa Barbara, CA: American Bibliographical Center–Clio Press, 1964. Seven issues per year. Service. (DIALOG file 38, $65 per hour.)

America: History and Life, Part A, Article Abstracts and Citations covers articles on U.S. and Canadian history in 2000 scholarly journals throughout the world. Approximately 5000 to 6000 abstracts

---

[8]"A Producer's Perspective," *Wilson Library Bulletin,* December 1987, p. 26.

are published each year, as well as about the same number of brief descriptions from local and specialist historical publications. The classified arrangement ends with a subject and author index. The "subject profile index" expands the subject approach to the classified abstracts in four areas: subject, geography, biography, and chronology. An article on Cornwallis's campaign for Virginia, for example, would be listed as follows: subject: "Revolutionary War; biography: Cornwallis; geography: Virginia; chronology: 1781." Under these and other headings, the article analyzed appears in the subject index an average of four or five times, providing insurance against a user's not finding a work.

Part B is *Index to Book Reviews* (covering over 130 scholarly U.S. and Canadian journals of history); Part C is *American History Bibliography (Books, Articles and Dissertations)*; Part D is *Annual Index.* This whole series is often simply called *America: History and Life.* All three are available on the online database.

Historical Abstracts has been issued by the same publisher since 1955, and the quarterly follows the same organizational pattern as *America: History and Life.* Here, all aspects of world history are considered, first generally and then by topic, and finally by area of the world and country. About 2000 journals, books and other related materials are abstracted each year. It really is two different services, i.e., Part A is *Modern History Abstracts* and covers material from 1775 to 1914. Part B is *Twentieth Century Abstracts* and moves from 1914 to the present.

Law

LEXIS. Dayton, OH: Mead Data Central, dates vary. Updated as needed. (Publisher, cost varies per hour.)

WESTLAW. St. Paul, MN: West Publishing Co., dates vary. Updated as needed. (Publisher, cost varies per hour.)

Legal Resource Index. Foster City, CA: Information Access Company, 1980 to date, monthly, $1720 DIALOG file 150 $102 per hour. CD-ROM: publisher. $5000.

Index to Legal Periodicals. New York: The H. W. Wilson Company, 1908 to date, monthly. $165. (Wilsonline, $43 to $65 per hour) CD-ROM: publisher. $1495.

Legal questions are difficult in nonlaw offices including libraries. Most questions may be answered using the particular state laws, or city codes, but this requires some specialized searching knowledge. Here LEXIS is a great help. In between are more general queries which often can be fielded using PAIS or even *Readers' Guide* or *Magazine Index.*

Two of the major legal indexes are available only online, i.e., LEXIS and WESTLAW, although both contain individual parts which are found in print. For example, LEXIS includes the H. W. Wilson Company's *Index to Legal Periodicals.* Both of the services tend to be limited to large law libraries and medium to large law firms.

LEXIS and WESTLAW are made up of separate, distinct databases such as Westlaw Admiralty Database to Westlaw Tax Base. In between are over a dozen services. The same is true of LEXIS. Both services are supplied directly by the publisher and not through a vendor. Both have complex charges which depend on which is used and how often it is employed. LEXIS has a word-for-word duplication of cases found in print, e.g., federal and state court opinions, statutes of the United States Code, or decisions of the Supreme Court. Coverage dates vary, and the whole file is continuously updated. The arrangement is "by library"; hence the New York Public Library would have *New York Reports* and *Consolidated Laws* among others. The Federal Tax Library would have the *Internal Revenue Code,* tax cases, etc.

Searches follow the normal pattern, and the material may be searched entirely, that is, not only by title and author, but by words found in the text of the legal material. As there is much data online, the particular problem in searching here is to limit the terminology employed, or one will end up with hundreds of citations to less-than-relevant data. Another difficulty with the full-text search is that in earlier days the recorders were not very careful about how names were spelled, and searches may be incomplete because of an improper spelling.

There is debate whether the lack of assigned subject headings in LEXIS is good or bad. On the good side: It allows the publisher to issue the material faster than its competitor, and it permits end-user searching without requiring subject information. On the bad side: the user may end up with too much material which is not relevant, and the search process is not exact.

WESTLAW is similar to LEXIS in that it offers the full text of various federal statutes, decisions of federal courts, and the like. In addition it covers, as does LEXIS, the various state laws. The two services are obvious competitors, and although they include much of the same material, there is a decided difference in the programs. Some claim WESTLAW is easier to use; others assert that this is the case with LEXIS. Also, of course, there are subtle differences in the types of materials updated which may make one more suitable than the other for certain situations. Still, it is primarily a matter of: (1) deciding which is more convenient to use and (2) establishing the cost.

The Information Access Company (*Magazine Index, Business Index*, etc.) uses the same type of microfilm system with the *Legal Resource Index.* The user receives a monthly reel with a six-year cumulation built in. Approximately 800 journals and law reviews are indexed, and there is partial indexing of 1000 related publications. (A print version of this is available monthly, with quarterly and annual cumulations as the *Current Law Index.*) The law index may be searched online and is available, too, in the publisher's familiar CD-ROM format, LegalTrac.

Index to Legal Periodicals is available in print, online and on CD-ROM. It covers only 500 journals and legal publications. It differs from any of the other indexes in that it analyzes books, yearbooks, publications of various law related institutes, and the like. It has the standard subject and author index but adds an index for law cases, and case notes are found at the end of many subject headings. While a good deal of this is technical, the careful librarian will find material here which is equally suitable for the informed layperson, and it can be of considerable help in almost any field which is remotely connected with the law or a legal decision.

Library/Information Science

Library Literature, New York: The H. W. Wilson Company, 1934 to date, bimonthly. Service (Wilsonline, $28 to $40 per hour) CD-ROM: publisher, 1984 to date, quarterly. $1095.

Library and Information Science Abstracts. London: Library Association, 1969 to date, monthly, $500. (Distributed in U.S. by Saur/Bowker.) (DIALOG file 61, $66 per hour.) CD-ROM: Wellesley Hills, MA: Silver Platter, 1969 to date, semiannual. $995.

Information Science Abstracts. New York: Plenum Publishing Co., 1966 to date, bimonthly. $375. (DIALOG file 202, $96 per hour.) CD-ROM; Wellesley Hills, MA: Silver Platter, 1969 to date, bimonthly. Price varies.

Library Literature offers a subject and author entry to articles which have appeared in about 220 library-oriented periodicals. Coverage is impressive with almost one-third of the entries representing publications outside the United States. (About 30 are non–English language). Books and library school dissertations and theses are included. As with other specialized Wilson indexes, the contents of books are analyzed as are reports or pamphlets, which relate to library science. It gives the librarian a fairly complete view of the subject field, but because of its publication schedule, *Library Literature* lags at least three months, often up to six months, behind in its indexing.[9]

The publisher makes it available both online and on CD-ROM. But here material is included only from 1984, and hardly begins to tap sources which go back to 1934. Still, for current searching either is more than adequate. A good case can be made for the online version in libraries where the index is consulted only rarely, and then by professional librarians.

Of added help, although rarely any more current, is *Library and Information Science Abstracts* (LISA). Whereas *Library Literature* is in the traditional alphabetical subject-author arrangement, the abstracting service depends on a classification system for the arrangement of material. Some journals are indexed, and the service abstracts selected reports, theses, and other monographs. The number of abstracts now runs to well over 4000 each year. Also, the publication is monthly rather than bimonthly. There is excellent coverage of U.S. government reports, primarily because the National Technical Information Service of the United States now allows LISA to reprint its abstracts. There are similar arrangements with other groups which account for the increased number of abstracts each year. On CD-ROM, Silver Platter issues this only twice a year without updates. At $995, it is a questionable purchase.

An even-more-sophisticated approach is offered in *Information Science Abstracts*. The emphasis is on technical periodicals, books, reports, proceedings, and similar materials. And of the some 4500 abstracts issued each year, a vast proportion deal with aspects of automation, communication, computers, mathematics, artificial intelligence, and so on. It is a service particularly suited to the needs of the researcher and the librarian in a large system. Arranged under broad subject headings, the abstracts are well-written and complete. Each issue has an author index, and there is an annual subject index.

It is six months or more behind in publishing, and even when issued, the abstracts and citations may be up to eight months be-

---

[9]Despite the delay, *Library Literature* is still the most current of the group. It is the easiest to use, too. ERIC often is employed for searches in library/information science, and this should be consulted when one is looking for original reports or for more information than is available in the standard indexes.

hind. Given this terrible time gap, it is really of little or no use for current searching (although the online system is somewhat better than the printed version.) One should turn to the much faster, more efficient British abstracting service. Ironically, here one may find American titles abstracted months before they appear in the American service.

Literature

MLA International Bibliography of Books and Articles on the Modern Languages and Literature. New York: Modern Language Association of America, 1922 to date, annual. $750. (DIALOG file 71, $66 per hour). CD-ROM: Wilsondisc, 1981 to date, quarterly $1500, includes online access through Wilsonline.

There is no more comprehensive index for literature than the well-known *MLA Bibliography*. And as literature takes in the interests of almost every discipline and subject, the index may be used for general searching as well. For example, one might turn to *ABI/IN-FORM* for data on the telephone business, and then to the MLA for background on how the telephone changed our view of the world. There is very little which cannot be found in one way or another in the MLA.

Given that, the earlier printed volumes are a nightmare to use. They are divided into five separate subvolumes with additional subheadings. The organization is so complicated that it requires an expert in the field of a given section of literature to use.

Fortunately, with the 1981 edition, things became much easier. A subject index was added. This covers all the categories and the some 3000 journals (as well as selected books) which are indexed.

The real solution, and one by now familiar to many, is to turn to the MLA on CD-ROM or online. Here there are close to 300,000 citations since 1981. One simply types in a subject or an author to get a complete or partial run of citations. By checking the "subjects covered," which comes at the end of each citation, one gets leads for additional related subjects and authors. Unfortunately, there are no abstracts.

Again, the *MLA Bibliography* illustrates the problem of new technology and cost. The printed version is $750 a year, whereas the CD-ROM (which covers more than seven years) is $1500. If one could recoup what was invested in the previous years of the reference work, the CD-ROM would be inexpensive by comparison. But that is not the case, and it is a matter of determining relative value versus the higher actual cost of the disk as compared printed volume. Most research libraries come down on the CD-ROM.

Medicine and Science

Applied Science and Technology Index. 1958 to date, monthly. Service (Wilsonline, $43 to $65 per hour.) CD-ROM: publisher, 1983 to date, quarterly. $1495.

Biological and Agricultural Index. 1964 to date, monthly. Service (Wilsonline, $43 to $65 per hour.) CD-ROM: publisher, 1983 to date, quarterly. $1495.

Index Medicus. Bethesda, MD: National Library of Medicine, 1960 to date, monthly. $179. Annual cumulation, $232. (DIALOG file as MEDLINE, files 152 to 155, $36 an hour.) CD-ROM: MEDLINE, Wellesley Hills, MA: Silver Platter, 1966 to date, monthly. $1750.

Biological Abstracts. Philadelphia: BioScience Information Service, 1926 to date, semimonthly $3650. (DIALOG file as BIOSIS previews, files 5, 55; $87 per hour.) CD-ROM: publisher, 1989 to date, quarterly. $2000.

Chemical Abtracts: Columbus, OH: Chemical Abstract Service, 1907 to date, weekly. $9200. (DIALOG file, as CA Search files 308–312, 399, $110 per hour.)

There are dramatically more print and online indexes available for medicine and the sciences. The reason may be explained briefly. First, there are four to five times as many periodicals in this area as in the humanities or social sciences. A common estimate is in the 40,000 range.

Second, government and business tend to be more willing to fund science than the other disciplines. Science online databases appeared earlier than those for the other disciplines primarily because of interest and good funding.

At the same time, the cost of both the indexes and the periodicals are exceptionally high compared to other areas. To cite an extreme example, a year's subscription to a nuclear physics journal published in the Netherlands is close to $4000. It may have more than 11,000 pages but the price is still steep.

The average library must then subscribe only to basic science indexes, all of which are provided by The H. W. Wilson Company. The primary index is the *Applied Science and Technology Index.* This analyzes about 350 English language periodicals by subject. In addition to the sciences, it covers such areas as transportation, food, and a wide variety of engineering titles. It is augmented by the *General Science Index,* discussed earlier, and the *Biological and Agricultural Index* (1964 to date, monthly, service). Here emphasis is on 226 periodicals in biology and more detailed aspects of agriculture.

The Information Access Company (*Magazine Index, Business Index,* etc.) offers the *Health Index* from 1977 to date. This includes about 100 periodicals, most of which are indexed in the other IAC indexes. As a spin-off, it becomes another member of the CD-ROM InfoTrac series. With monthly updates it is $2000 a year.

Index Medicus is the world's most comprehensive and, probably, best-known medical index. Produced by the National Library of Medicine, and sold through the Government Printing Office, it represents government at its best. Approximately, 2337 English and foreign language journals are meticulously indexed. As well there is selective indexing of reports, letters, editorials, and the like.

Here the subject headings are of utmost importance for the medical profession. They are drawn from a special list: Medical Subject Headings. The monthly issues are arranged by subject and author.

Related indexes include the *Exerpta Medica* (Amsterdam: Elsevier, 1947 to date. Frequency varies). This index abstracts articles from some 3500 journals, and these are published as 44 separate abstract journals or sections. It is primarily for the expert, and extremely costly—about $300 to $400 per section.

This, and two other databases (*Index to Dental Literature* and *International Nursing*) is called MEDLINE (or MEDLARS ONLINE). This contains citations, with abstracts, to articles from about 3400 journals published in the United States and some 70 other countries.[10] Scientific databases are more complex, more comprehensive and more difficult to search than many other types of databases. The possible exception is MEDLINE.

One of the four or five most heavily used databases in all disciplines, it offers users a wide variety of searching options. More important, because of the subject matter, it tends to embrace, literally, the world. It has a broad potential beyond medical literature. Thanks to a file of close to 7 million citations, MEDLINE may be

---

[10]There are numerous combinations and variations on MEDLINE, e.g., DIALOG's Medical Connection is one example. This has MEDLINE at the center, but includes access to some eight related databases such as *Psychological Abstracts.* See Donna Lee, "Medical Databases on CD-ROM," *CD-ROM Librarian,* October 1989, pp. 11–19.

used to find data on such related fields as psychology, education, anthropology, sociology, technology, agriculture, and almost any other area—including politics—which is connected in any way with medicine.

The Silver Platter CD-ROM version (and numerous companies offer this service on CD-ROM) is typical in its pricing structure. The $1750 covers monthly updates, but if one wishes to go back to 1966, the library must purchase several volumes, for a total cost of $3500. A similar approach is now offered for almost all retrospective CD-ROM disks.[11]

The National Library of Medicine backs up MEDLINE with an efficient interlibrary loan procedure. About 1500 requests for materials are received each day. Before requests for material reach the NLM they are filtered through three other possible sources of supply. The librarian may send the request to a local library (say, one which is large or has medical journals); to a resource library, usually at a medical school; to one of 11 regional medical libraries which cover well-defined geographic regions; or finally, if none of these are possible sources, to the National Library of Medicine. In other words, the NLM serves as the final resource after requests are unsatisfied at three previous levels of processing.

The library can fill from 80 to 85 percent of the requests received. The unfilled requests are transmitted by computer to the British Lending Library in Boston Spa, England, and quickly accessed by the British Lending Library, thus often making it possible to receive material more quickly from England than from another part of the United States or Canada.

In late 1990, Ebsco Subscription Services calculated the total cost of the 2337 periodicals analyzed in *Index Medicus*. The budget item for the library that subscribed to all of them would be just over one-half million dollars. This is up 73 percent from 1986 when the cost was about $290,000 for 2140 titles. It is little wonder that most libraries rely on getting individual articles from the National Library of Medicine rather than subscribing to all of the journals.

Aspects of medicine are an important part of the well-known *Biological Abstracts*. Here abstracts from over 9000 journals are included, and among these are biomedicine as well as all the biological and life sciences. As a major indexing and abstracting service,

[11]V. E. Morgan et al., "MEDLINE on Disc," *CD-ROM Librarian*, February 1990, pp. 8–16. See also Beryl Glitz, "Testing the New Technology: MEDLINE on CD-ROM in an Academic Health Sciences Library," *Special Libraries*, Winter 1988, pp. 28–33. The article indicates that patrons like the service, but without care it is likely to be used in such a way that material will be overlooked.

this is as well known in science-oriented libraries as *Index Medicus* and *Chemical Abstracts*. Often the three are worked as a unit, particularly online.

The online version of this service and of related services by the same organization is BIOSIS Previews. Accessing the index by computer has a tremendous advantage in ease of use, particularly when searching for an elusive subject. However, the same drawback exists here as in similar cases: the online system goes back to 1969 and the abstracts only from 1976 on. The CD-ROM is from 1989.

Because of its wide scope, BIOSIS is frequently used to answer many scientific and even social science queries. The printed version is updated twice a month, while the online and work CD-ROM are updated monthly. The publisher claims that the online tapes are "available approximately five weeks before the printed version." The printed volumes and the online and CD-ROM versions employ a subject index that uses key words in context. Topics may be searched as well by broad subject concepts, by genus and species and organism names, by broad taxonomic categories, and by author. The online service offers a master index of key words; the other search elements are much the same as in the printed volumes, but with considerably more variation available, as is true in most online systems.

Chemical Abstracts is one of the largest abstracting services in the world and one of the most heavily used, despite its high price. It abstracts over 14,000 scientific and technical periodicals from over 150 countries. It is provided in many sections, and the one devoted to patents is one of the most used.

As in all services, the abstracts are arranged by subject, but here over 80 subject sections are consolidated into five broad groups. Each issue includes indexes for author, patent, and key-word catch phrases from the abstract and the title. It also contains a most useful "Index Guide" in addition to the numerous other aids and sections.

The service is available online, as well as in microform. Online it is available through STN (Scientific and Technical Network) which furnishes direct access not only to American libraries but to those in Europe and Japan. The system is so complicated and is offered in so many different parts that a successful search can be made only by a subject expert or by a librarian who is thoroughly familiar with the literature of chemistry and related areas.

Another giant in the science field is INSPEC (International Information Services for the Physics and Engineering Communities). This online version corresponds to the printed version of *Physics Abstracts, Electrical and Electronic Abstracts,* and *Computer and Control*

Abstracts, usually described as *Science Abstracts A, B, and C.* Updated monthly, this is an index to over 2000 journals. The file now has well over 3 million citations and is available online from 1969 to date.

Minorities and Alternatives

Alternative Press Index. Baltimore: Alternative Press Center, 1969 to date, quarterly. $100.

Hispanic American Periodicals Index (HAPI). Los Angeles: University of California, 1970 to date, annual. $240.

Index to Periodicals by and about Blacks. Boston: G.K. Hall, 1950 to date, annual. $79.50.

Despite the impressive number of general indexes, only a few deal with magazines from the political left, the social right, and almost any place other than dead center. A library may or may not wish to have such a magazine about, particularly in days of tight budgets and limited readership, but it is a good idea to have a few of their indexes to indicate more than one view of America.

Minority indexes should be a first priority if minorities are a primary or secondary audience served by the library.

The Alternative Press Index has been about for over 20 years, and it faithfully indexes some 220 titles. All of these are to the left of center. The right is not represented because of the editors' opinion, right or wrong, that the right has a large voice in other indexes and other services. Be that as it may, the index serves the splendid purpose of opening new doors on new ways of looking at issues. Arrangement is by subject, and there are book reviews by author and title. Although issued quarterly, the index does tend to lag.

The *Hispanic American Periodicals Index* examines about 250 periodicals, most of which are published in Latin America or by Latin American groups in the United States. While popular magazines are not included, the representative group of other titles does reflect trends and ideas in Latin America and among Hispanics living in the United States.

As stated before, one problem with annual indexes is that they are at least one year, and sometimes two or even three years behind. For example, the 1984 edition of *Index to Periodical Articles by and about Blacks* did not come out until 1988. Lack of finance accounts for this delay, as publication relied on volunteer, or not well-paid, part-time indexers. At any rate, there are 37 popular and scholarly titles indexed in the service for those serving a black community.

Political Science

PAIS International In Print (Formerly: *Public Affairs Information Service Bulletin*). New York: Public Affairs Information Service, 1914 to date, monthly, including cumulations and annual, $495. (DIALOG file 49, $75 per hour.) CD-ROM: publisher, 1976 to date, quarterly, $1600.

Despite the title change, still best known as PAIS, the *PAIS International in Print* offers a general source of information for both expert and layperson. Many librarians consider it the *Readers' Guide* of the political and social sciences. With the change in name, coverage was expanded to include the international scene (formerly found in a separate PAIS service). Here one turns for current information on government, legislation, economics, sociology, and political science. Periodicals, government documents, pamphlets, reports and some books in such areas as government, public administration, international affairs, and economics are indexed. About 1400 journals and some 6000 other items (from books to reports) are indexed each year. Valuable additions are a "Key to Periodicals References" and a list of "Publications Analyzed." Both serve as a handy checklist and buying guide for the library.

The new version of PAIS incorporates the indexing found previously in two separate indexes, i.e., *PAIS Bulletin* and *PAIS Foreign Language Index.* While works analyzed are limited to those in English, coverage is international. Arrangement is alphabetical, primarily by subject. A few of the entries have brief descriptive notes on both contents and purpose.

PAIS on CD-ROM is a good example of the delights and problems of the form. The immediate joy of recognition is dulled by the price, $1600 (1991). This contrasts with $495 for the monthly printed version.

If cost were not enough of a deterrent, the CD-ROM only includes material from 1972, although the printed file has been about since 1914. Also, note, that the disk is updated only quarterly as compared with the more current monthly offering of the printed version and the online work. Incidentally, online one may go back to 1972 for the same material but at a cost of about $1 a minute, plus, to be sure, the added other expenses from equipment to phone connections.

By now it is obvious to anyone that in terms of cost and coverage, nothing quite beats the printed version. So why go on? Well, for the usual reasons. First, many more contact or search points are available on the CD-ROM than with the printed version. And although one must have some familiarity with at least three search modes for the system, the chances of coming up with the needed citations are much better than with the printed works. Remember, too, that one must laboriously search each volume and addition, whereas with the CD-ROM, one can quickly scan material since 1972, if not back to 1915.[12]

Psychology

Psychological Abstracts. Washington: American Psychological Association, Inc., 1927 to date, monthly. $750 (DIALOG file 11, $55 per hour.) CD-ROM: Wellesley Hills, MA: Silver Platter, 1974 to date quarterly. $3995.

Psychological Abstracts is familiar to many people, primarily because, as with a few other subject abstracting services (such as *Resources in Education*), it can be used in related areas of interest. For example, an important section concerns communication which, in turn, includes abstracts on language, speech, literature, and even art. Anyone involved with, say, the personality of an engineer or an artist would turn to this source, as would the better-educated layperson seeking information on anything from why a companion talks in his or her sleep to why people can or cannot read.

The abstracts are arranged under 16 broad subject categories from physiological intervention to personality. This allows the busy user to glance quickly at a subject area of interest without being bothered by unrelated topics. As a guide to the less experienced, there is an author and a brief subject index in each issue. The subject approach is expanded and modified in the cumulative indexes published twice a year. (When in doubt about a subject, turn first to the cumulation, not the individual issues.)

The service indexes over 1400 periodicals from about 50 countries. Still, 90 percent of the material is in English. There are about 3000 abstracts in each monthly issue. As in other services of this type there is cumulative index, but the abstracts themselves are not cumulated.

Psychological Abstracts online (*PsycINFO*) is available from the major vendors. It covers the years from 1967 and is updated monthly, and in addition to the basic features it offers the user several advantages. First and foremost one searching for foreign language materials will find them only in the database, not in the

[12]Debora Cheney (a review of the CD-ROM version), in *RQ*, Summer 1988, pp. 567–568.

printed version. Second, dissertations can be found only online. All this began in 1980 as an effort to strengthen the use of the online service. The result is that today the online service offers from 25 to 30 percent more material than the printed version.

In an effort to be as current as possible, the same publisher offers *PsycALERT*. Here the indexing is the same, but there is no abstract, only the citation. The service is updated weekly, as contrasted with only a monthly update for *PsycINFO*. When the indexing is complete and the abstract added, the file is moved into the main service.

A useful aid is the *Thesaurus of Psychological Index Terms*. As with any really first-rate system, this provides the necessary terminology to aid searching either online or via CD-ROM.

Considering the high price of the service on CD-ROM, (PsycLit) $3995 from 1974 to the present with quarterly updates, one might be better off using online only.

Another added expense here, as with numerous other CD-ROM versions in the 1990s is the additional cost for multiple use. If the disk can be accessed in more than one place (a blessing, of course), the cost from Silver Platter almost doubles, i.e., a single user is $3995, but where more than a single terminal is employed it costs $5995.

Although not precisely an index, *PsycBooks,* by the same publisher, is a five-volume annual which (1) gives complete bibliographical information on approximately 1300 books each year, (2) includes the table of contents of each volume, and (3) publishes enough information from the cover, preface, and foreword to tell the reader what the book is about. All this is arranged by broad and then by narrow subject classifications. More to the point, the fifth volume is a detailed author and subject index to the whole. The result is an effective index to all major psychological books.

CITATION INDEXING

The following are published by the Institute for Scientific Information in Philadelphia.

> *Social Sciences Citation Index,* 1973 to date, three issues per year, including annual. $2700. (DIALOG file 7, $63 to $120 per hour). CD-ROM: publisher, quarterly. $2350.

> *Science Citation Index,* 1961 to date, six issues per year, including

annual. $9000. (DIALOG files 34, 94, and 186, $63 and $160 per hour.) CD-ROM: publisher, quarterly. $5300.

Arts & Humanities Citation Index, 1977 to date, three per year, including annual. $2700. (DIALOG file 439, $65 to $120 per hour.) CD-ROM: publisher, quarterly. $2350.

The three sets may be described briefly:

The Social Sciences Citation Index fully indexes about 1400 periodicals and selectively indexes another 3000. A few (about 250) books are noted. Coverage is of the complete social sciences from anthropology to urban planning and development. Either the on-line or the printed version may be used to answer questions in almost any area. Note it is particularly useful for business and statistical questions as well as for those dealing with community problems.

Science Citation Index is the oldest of the group, and probably the most used, as well as the most expensive. Coverage is from acoustics and aeronautics to surgery and zoology. Not only are scientific topics covered in full, but many related areas are considered, which is to say the index may be used for more than science. Over 3000 journals are indexed in depth, and this is by far the most expensive of the general science indexes.

The Arts & Humanities Citation Index is another multidisciplinary index. Here about 1300 periodicals are indexed in depth, and another 4500 are covered selectively. Coverage is from architecture and art to theater and theology.

Citation indexing is unique in that it employs a different approach to searching. The avenue of access is through references cited in articles, hence the name of the service.

Each issue of all three above is in three parts:

1. The Citation Index, which lists papers cited alphabetically by author. The title of the article appears under the author's name, and beneath each article is a list of those who have cited the author's work. Most of the material is abbreviated.
2. The Source Index, which gives standard bibliographic information for each of the papers in the Citation Index.
3. The Permuterm Subject Index, which indexes the articles by subject, i.e., by significant words in the title.

The system expects that the searcher will be familiar with the name of an author in a particular subject field. For example, someone looking for material on Japanese volcanoes would know that the leading expert on this is Kazuo Iskiguro.

The user would then turn in the Citation Index to Iskiguro,

Kazuo. Beneath his name appears seven names of people who have cited him (and his article or book). The fair assumption is that these seven are writing about Japanese volcanoes, too. Furthermore, by citing Iskiguro, they are familiar with both the man and the field.

One then turns to each of the seven names in the Source Index, and finds seven articles or books by the seven.

Clearly, the obvious "catch" is that one must know an expert in the field in which one is involved. If not, the only solution is to (1) use another index with subject headings or (2) turn to the Permuterm Subject Index.

The uniqueness of this system, as opposed to other retrieval schemes, is that it is a network of connections between authors citing the same papers during a current year. In other words, if, in searching for particular subject matter, one has a key paper or review article in the field, or even an author's name, one consults the Citation Index by author. Beneath the author's name will be listed in chronological order *any* of her publications cited during a particular year, together with the *citing* authors (source items) who have referred to the particular work. If one continues to check the citing authors in the Citation Index, a cyclical process take place, often with mushrooming results. The Source Index is then used to establish the full bibliographic reference to the citing author.

A citation index has a major production advantage which makes it particularly suited for automation. Indexers do not have to be subject specialists, and there is no need to read the articles for subject headings. All the compiler must do is (1) enter the author, title, and full citation in machine-readable form and (2) list all the citations used in the primary article in order by author, title, and full citation in machine-readable form. As a consequence, a careful clerk may prepare material for the computer. This obviously speeds up indexing and also makes it possible to index considerably more material quickly.

The Source Index gives full bibliographic details of items listed. It is arranged by author. The Permuterm Subject Index is an alphabetically arranged (Key-word-in-context) *KWIC-type index:* Subjects are derived from words appearing in the titles of the source articles. Each significant word is precoordinated with other terms to produce all possible permutations of terms.

The heart of the system is the Citation Index, which lists authors alphabetically. It is assumed that the user (1) either knows the name of the author in the subject area of particular interest or (2) lacking the name of the author, finds the subject(s) in the Permuterm Subject Index and from that locates the name of the author(s) for search in the "Citation Index."

A sample search, using *Arts & Humanities Citation Index,* might go like this: (1) I am looking for someone who cited W. H. Auden's poem, "Age of Anxiety." I turn to "Auden, W. H." in the Citation Index and find poems and other cited works by Auden listed under his name. In answer to my quest I find a single name, i.e., "Lehman D., *Shenandoah,* (volume 33, page 73, for 1982)." (2) I then turn to the Source Index to find the full entry for Lehman. Under his name I find numerous articles, but am looking for the key, i.e., *Shenandoah* magazine. When that is found, then I am given the full entry, including the name of the article, the total pages and how many references were cited. Beneath the title of the piece are the references in alphabetical order, and here I find Auden's "Age of Anxiety." I need now only turn to the article for more on the poem and on Auden.

Suppose the librarian wants something on book auctions, but does not have the name of anyone who might be cited, i.e., any expert's name to check out in the Citation Index. He turns to the Permuterm Subject Index: (1) Here, under "Auctions," appears "Book" and two names, one of which is "C. Sammons." (2) The librarian turns to "Sammons" in the Source Index and finds an article, "Book Auctions in the 17th century . . . " with, of course, the full citation of the journal in which the article appeared.

Disadvantages of the printed volumes are numerous: the high price, the reliance on type so small that it makes classified-ad-size type look gigantic by comparison, and confusing abbreviations. The most serious drawback is the lack of controlled vocabulary; when approach is by subject, there is total dependence on words in the title. This may work well enough in science, but it fails when used in the humanities and the social sciences.

The multiple volumes make this a difficult set to use, which is all the more reason for its value on CD-ROM or as an online database. One may search here for the cited author, the name of the person who did the citing, and the subject as well. The result is much quicker than going through one or two or even three volumes. Also, when used only on occasion, the CD-ROM or online index may be less expensive than the printed work.[13]

[13]Typically, though, the publisher cancels out some of the advantage of just using the service online. For example, in the *Arts & Humanities* service, the cost for subscribers is about $65 an hour. Those who choose not to subscribe pay $120 per

The publisher offers versions of the citation indexes on CD-ROM. Each disk has about one-half-year's data, and there are quarterly updates with annual cumulations. Retrospective indexing for the *Social Sciences Citation Index* is available beginning with 1983 and the science index goes back to 1980.

A common CD-ROM approach is to search by subject, i.e., by key words, and then take each person mentioned in the references and look up the articles. A so-called STEM common allows one in BRS to find all the listings of the author and by whom and where the articles are quoted.

Once again, the CD-ROM version is easier to use for most laypersons than the online product. At the same time, the online work is much more current. It is updated weekly, as compared to quarterly CD-ROMs.

Very few libraries, except for the largest can offer all or even a good number of the periodicals indexed in these services. But they can and do use interlibrary loan, and eventually will be able to access the full text of many of the titles online. Until then, the publisher will supply tear sheets of one or a thousand articles needed. The system is known as OATS (original article tear sheet). While service is rapid, from 24 to 48 hours, the problem is cost, with each article running $10 or more.

Retrospective indexing can be costly. The publisher of *Social Sciences Citation Index* ten-year edition of that index covers 1956–1965. The purchase price for the printed set is $17,500. This is higher than most 10-year indexes because of the particular format of the citation indexes, but it gives one a notion of the relative cost of going back and indexing material heretofore not covered.

INDEXES TO CURRENT EVENTS

There are two approaches to indexing current events in libraries. The traditional solution to a question dealing with yesterday's or last week's event is to: (1) turn to a newspaper and go through it page by page, (2) turn to a weekly news magazine such as *Newsweek* and thumb through it, or (3) turn to a weekly service such as *Facts on File,* to be explained below. Even when the event is only a month or so old, it may prove difficult to find printed material, particularly if

---

hour. In either case it is 46 cents per full record typed, displayed, or printed. A similar approach is followed for the CD-ROMs, i.e., the Science Citation Index is $10,200 for nonsubscribers to the print edition. See Barbara L. Burke's "SCI/SSCI on CD-ROM," *CD-ROM Librarian,* October, 1990, pp. 31–40.

an index is needed. Why? The indexes are inevitably late, and even those which come out every two weeks are three to six weeks behind.

The modern solution is to turn to an online database such as *The New York Times* which has yesterday's events online and which is searchable by key words. The problem, as always, is cost. Still, if someone is in a rush and does not have the patience to go through a paper or a magazine page by page, the online search is the answer.

Sources for Last Week's Events

Facts on File, A Weekly World News Digest. New York: Facts on File, Inc., 1940 to date, weekly. $496. (DIALOG file 264, $60.) CD-ROM: publisher, 1980 to date. $695.

Keesing's Contemporary Archives. London: Longman Group Ltd., 1931 to date, monthly. $180.

Essentially, these loose-leaf binder services are objective summaries of the events of the past week or month. They may be used to quickly locate a fact, a date, or a name. *Facts on File* is usually prompt (U.S. mails permitting), and normally only a few days elapse between the last date covered and receipt of the publication. Emphasis is on news events in the United States, with international coverage related for the most part to American affairs. Material is gathered mainly from 50 major newspapers and magazines, and condensed into objective, short, factual reports. The twice-monthly, blue-colored index is arranged under four primary headings: "U.S. Affairs," "International Affairs," "World News," and "Miscellaneous." Then, under these one finds broad subject headings, such as "Finance," "Economics," and so on. This a bit confusing, but, fortunately, every two weeks, each month, and then quarterly and annually, a detailed index is issued which covers previous issues. There is also a *Five-Year Master News Index,* published since 1950.

The subject index (which includes numerous names of people in the news) features the brief tag line name of the item, then reference to the date of the event, the page in the issue of *Facts on File,* as well as the margin letter and column number. For example, under Yugoslavia, one might find, "Austerity measures OKd 5–15" (date, May 15, 1991) "367 page number G3" (the letter on the margin of page 367 and the third column).

The publisher notes a "few ways" the service may be used: Check dates in the index, skim the weekly issues to prepare for current affairs tests, read Supreme Court decisions in the Digest, or scan the "U.S. and World Affairs" column for ideas for short papers.

There are countless other uses, although the most frequent call is for specific current data.

At the end of the index is a "Corrections" section. This gives the correct information by page and column, for example: "148A1 chairman (not president)" and "358D2 Symms (not Simms)." This feature is found in every issue.

The disk service, *"Facts on File News Digest CD-ROM,"* is not the weekly *Facts on File,* but the 1980-to-date compilation of the annual files. That amounts to some 10,000 pages of text, with 500 to 600 line drawings of maps (which can be reproduced on CD-ROM). It may be searched with the standard boolean logic and offers a valuable overview of the news. The initial disk costs $695 and covers the period 1980–1989. The annual updates, which are cumulative (i.e., 1980–1990, 1980–1991, etc.), are offered at $195 a year additional. Subscribers to the printed version are given a price cut of about 15 percent, i.e., the regular price is $795.

The emphasis in *Keesing's Contemporary Archives* differs from *Facts on File* in two important respects. (1) It covers primarily the United Kingdom, Europe, and the British Commonwealth. (2) Detailed subject reports in certain areas are frequently included (the reports are by experts and frequently delay the weekly publication by several days), as are full texts of important speeches and documents. However, *Keesing's* does not cover in any detail many events which the management deems to be "less important," such as sports, art exhibitions, and movies, which may be included in *Facts on File.* Arrangement is by country, territory, or continent, with some broad subject subheadings, such as "Religion," "Aviation," and "Fine Arts." Every second week, an index is issued which is cumulated quarterly and annually.

Newspaper Indexes

The New York Times Index. New York: *The New York Times,* 1851 to date, semimonthly, with quarterly and annual cumulations $565. (NEXIS, $80 to $100 per hour.)

The National Newspaper Index. Foster City, CA: Information Access Corporation, 1979 to date, monthly. $2400. (DIALOG file 111, $90 per hour.) CD-ROM: publisher. $4200.

Newsearch. Foster City, CA: Information Access Co., 1979 to date online only, daily. (DIALOG file 211, $120 per hour.)

Newspaper Abstracts Ondisc. Ann Arbor, MI: Microfilms International, 1984 to date. Monthly, $2950. Also available online. (DIALOG file 603, $84 per hour; file 484, price varies.)

Canadian News Index. Toronto: Micromedia, 1977 to date, monthly. $850, with lower rates ($275–$400) for smaller libraries (QL file).

No matter what its form, the best-known newspaper index in the United States is the one published by *The New York Times.* A distinct advantage of *The New York Times Index* is its wide scope and relative completeness. *The Times* makes an effort to cover all major news events, both national and international. The morning edition of *The Times* is available in all major cities. It is printed not only in New York, but in Seattle, San Francisco, Los Angeles, Chicago, Dallas, and several northeastern cities.

The Times Index provides a wealth of information and frequently is used even without reference to the individual paper of the date cited. Each entry includes a brief abstract of the news story. Consequently, someone seeking a single fact, such as the name of an official, the date of an event, or the title of a play, may often find all that is needed in the index. Also, since all material is dated, *The Times Index* serves as an entry into other, unindexed newspapers and magazines. For example, if the user is uncertain of the day a certain ship sank and wishes to see how the disaster was covered in another newspaper or in a magazine, *The Times Index* will narrow the search by providing the date the event occurred.

The New York Times Index is arranged in dictionary form with sufficient cross-references to names and related topics. Events under each of the main headings are arranged chronologically. Book and theater reviews are listed under those respective headings.

Some libraries subscribe only to the annual cumulated *Index.* This volume serves as an index and guide to the activities of the previous year. Thanks to the rather full abstracts, maps, and charts, one may use the cumulated volume as a reference source in itself. The annual cumulation is fine, but it appears late; normally it is published from six to seven months after the end of the year.

Not being current is the major difficulty with the semimonthly issues as well. They do not appear in a library for two or three months after the period indexed. The hard-copy situation is not likely to improve, but the online service for the index offers 24-hour and one-week indexing of the same material.

The modern index dates only from about 1913 to the present. The earlier indexes, which begin on September 18, 1851, present problems in terms of alphabetizing and location of the issue (date not given) by issue number. There is also great variation in the method of listing other material.

The New York Times online version is similar to the printed one, but with three important exceptions: (1) Since the information is updated daily, one does not have to wait the usual two to three months for the printed index, and (2) the user either may ask for the full entry, which normally includes an abstract, or (3) may call to see the full text of the story on the viewer screen or printed out.

Online and CD-ROM Services

Two services are available both online and on CD-ROM. Today they are of great interest to librarians as both cover *The New York Times*, but are relatively current. These are *The National Newspaper Index* and *Newspaper Abstracts Ondisc.*

Using an approach similar to that of the *Magazine Index*, the publishers of the *National Newspaper Index* offer the service on microfilm, which is updated once a month and loaded into a reader. Thanks to this system, it is not necessary to consult various volumes, supplements, and cumulations, as it is with *The New York Times Index.* In addition to *The Times*, this service includes *The Wall Street Journal, The Christian Science Monitor, The Washington Post,* and *The Los Angeles Times.* A tremendous advantage is that one may search for one item in five newspapers at the same time, e.g., one can see how train wrecks, Giant Pandas, and sporting and political events are handled in all newspapers, not just a single one. The wide indexing makes it easier to locate hard-to-find items which may appear in only one of the newspapers.

The National Newspaper Index does not include the annotations found in *The New York Times*, but it does give the reader access to product evaluation, book reviews, and the like. The monthly *National Newspaper Index* compares with twice-a-month issues from *The New York Times*, but the important difference is that the monthly index is just that: up to date and not two or three months behind publishing schedule. The result, at least as of this writing, is that the *National Newspaper Index* is considerably more timely than its rival.

The *National Newspaper Index* is part of the CD-ROM InfoTrac family, and is precisely the same as the microfilm edition other than being on CD-ROM. Updated monthly, it covers the past three years of news. The $4200 price includes the disks, plus the necessary hardware. It is about $1000 less if the hardware is not included. The searching patterns are helped by the publisher's addition of subject headings, but one cannot use boolean logic or other typical online patterns.

Online the same database includes other services, and particularly it adds *Magazine Index*. The online service is called *News Search* and is as sophisticated as the CD-ROM is simple.

The newspapers online are indexed daily, not monthly as on CD-ROM. The periodicals are indexed as published and take from one to four days after publication date to be available online. The online service allows one to search not only newspapers, but some 2000 periodicals as well.

There is no full-text service (as of 1990) of the newspapers online, but the publisher goes in through the back door with "Newswire ASAP." This includes the full text of three basic wire services which supply many of the business stories to the papers. As DIALOG file 649, one may search these services which are updated daily. Most go back only to 1987. The three wire services include Reuters Financial Report, Kyodo's Japan Economic Newswire, and PR Newswire. The emphasis is on business news, and so while useful, the service is of limited value to someone hunting for typical human-interest stories.

Newspaper Abstracts Ondisc is a CD-ROM and online service which includes indexing of: *The New York Times, Atlanta Constitution, Atlanta Journal, Boston Globe, Chicago Tribune, Christian Science Monitor, Los Angeles Times, The Wall Street Journal,* and the *Washington Post.* These are only nine of the 25 newspapers indexed online. Also, online there is selective indexing of nine Afro-American newspapers. About 10,000 entries are added each week. The CD-ROM version, which is issued monthly, may be subdivided by newspaper. For example, one can get the index to *The New York Times* on CD-ROM for $1500. Additional titles, from the *Atlanta Constitution* to the *Washington Post* and *The Wall Street Journal* vary in price from $150 to $795 each.

Both online and on CD-ROM, retrospective searching is limited to 1985 and the years following, although some begin only in 1989. Searching is relatively simple, and boolean logic may be employed as well as simply searching for subjects and by key words.

An interesting feature of the service is the exceptionally well written set of instructions. Unlike most, they are easy to follow and meet the challenge of the individual who knows little or nothing about the index. Also, "reading the first two pages of the Thesaurus is a good way for new users to learn how to do quick and dirty searches."[14]

---

[14]Charyl LaGuardia, "Newspaper Abstracts Ondisc," *RQ,* Spring 1990, p. 426. See also Marydee Ojala, "Newspaper Databases . . ." *Online,* January 1989, p. 91. This is a good overview of the subject.

Choice

Compared with its rival, which covers much the same material, the UMI product is better for two reasons: (1) It allows more in-depth sophisticated searches which can be quickly mastered thanks to a good menu approach to the search. (2) Possibly of even more interest, abstracts are given which are detailed enough to answer many questions without the need to actually read the newspaper. Then, too, as one can limit the service to a single newspaper, the cost is lower than for *The National Newspaper Index* in this same format.

Full-Text Services

NEXIS. Dayton, OH: Mead Data Central, 1978 to date. Daily. Price varies, approximately $100 per hour.

DOW-JONES NEWS/RETRIEVAL. Princeton, NJ: Dow-Jones, 1978 to date, daily. Approximately $112 per hour.

VU/TEXT. Philadelphia: VU/TEXT Information Services, various dates, frequencies. Price varies.

DIALOG OnDisk/NEWSPAPERS. Palo Alto, CA: Knight-Ridder, 1990 to date, frequency and price varies.

Most general or specialized newspapers in the United States and Canada (as well as Europe) are available for search online. A few are on CD-ROM. The majority may be viewed or printed out in part or in whole at the computer terminal.

Most are updated within 24 hours of publication, and some literally on a minute-by-minute basis. Some may be searched using standard patterns, but others have no indexing. This is important to understand when deciding which database to search or which vendor to consider.

The primary newspapers with full-text service include: *The New York Times,* the *Washington Post,* the *Christian Science Monitor, The Philadelphia Inquirer,* Canadian Press news service, *The Current Digest of the Soviet Press* (another Soviet Press service); *The Wall Street Journal,* and numerous business newspapers such as *American Banker.* These, it should be stressed, are only the primary papers. Over 100 business, local, and subject newspapers are available in full text for search online.

The best-known American news wire service, the Associated Press, offers its own full-text service, AP News (DIALOG et al.). This is available through Mead Data's NewsNet or VU/TEXT. It is updated daily and the files go back as far as 1977 depending on the vendor used. UPI Database, also available from numerous vendors, has full text of United Press International wire service.

Lack of standardization of searching methods and loading the texts results in some interesting consideration. (1) Depending on the newspaper and the writer, copyright considerations may block the electronic version of their story or feature. The text of many syndicated columnists, for example, is excluded. Often this is indicated by the service giving only a citation to the printed version of the story, but not the full text. (2) Various services offer various editions. For example, the Capitol Edition of the *Washington Post* which is online by 2 A.M. is an abbreviated version of the newspaper's other editions.[15] (3) Various vendors and services offering the texts have as many different software entry points which makes searching different for each system. Some vendors, for example, allow one to search the lead (the first paragraph or two in a news story where content is summarized) separately. Others do not.[16]

NEXIS offers *The New York Times* in full text online. In addition to the New York paper, NEXIS offers full text of the *Christian Science Monitor, Washington Post, Financial Times, Manchester Guardian Weekly* and several business publications, including *American Banker* and *Computerworld.* Another service is *The Current Digest of the Soviet Press.* Add to these several wire services (Associated Press, United Press International, Reuters) and the opportunity for finding almost anything about world events is increased considerably.

NEXIS is by far the most ambitious of the various online full-text services. In addition to newspapers, it offers some 150 periodicals, as well as other publications, online in full text.[17] The databases

---

[15]The various editions pose problems for online or CD-ROM searching. For example, the *National Newspaper Index* which includes *The New York Times* has difficulties with the various national editions. To cope with the changes in page numbers, the position of stories, and actual additions or deletion of copy from, say, Seattle to New York, the *Index* advises its readers as follows: "Page numbers of the edition may vary from the edition your library carries. Our research shows that even though the page number for a particular article may vary from edition to edition, the section in which it appears does not. Therefore, we will be adding the section name as a title annotation to our citations. . . . For Example, *The New York Times*, November 15 '89 pB5 (L)." (L) stands for the Living Arts Pages. There are six designations for as many sections.

[16]Susan H. Veccia, "Full Text Dilemmas for Searching and Systems, The Washington Post Online," *Database*, April 1988, pp. 13–33. Here is a detailed analysis of the different vendors and systems and how each has its own search techniques. Result: confusion.

[17]NEXIS offers full text of about 50 popular and about 70 business and technical journals. Among the general magazines are Time-Life Group (*Time, Fortune, Sports*

may be searched as one, i.e., the user may look for a term in all the magazine and newspaper indexes at once, or instead, may select a single newspaper or magazine for a search. Search costs vary. An average search will cost from $40 to $50 and up.

The Dow-Jones News is an umbrella term for four separate databases, including sports and news. The News World Report offers up-to-the-minute news from the Associated Press wire. As this is updated continuously, it can be considered an ongoing newspaper, and differs only from the on-wire service itself in that it extracts only major events. The full text of each article is available. Dow Jones News not only covers newspapers but, for investors, offers Tradeline, an international report on over 25,000 equities on some 90 exchanges in 35 countries outside North America.

There is also a series of databases (DOW-JONES TEXT SEARCH SERVICES) which has the full text of basic business newspapers from *The Wall Street Journal* to *Barrons* and the *Washington Post.* They include the full text of several business magazines and 13 other major, general American newspapers. It is designed to help the business person, but as the coverage is so broad, it offers an in-depth full-text entry for almost any type of query.

Rates are not cheap. They run from 95 cents to $1 or more per minute or connect time, plus added cost for document printouts. Depending on the database, the records may be kept for no more than 90 days.[18]

VU/TEXT[19], the largest of the services, has the full text of around 72 daily regional and local newspapers. Each year it adds new titles, and in 1990 there were an additional 20 in the service. (It includes, too, 180 business publications and various newswires.) As such, it has virtually replaced the indexing found in many city newspapers. Today, most of these papers no longer index their own work, but simply subscribe to the VU/TEXT service. Coverage generally begins about 1978. The cost is high—about $90 to $105 per hour.

Illustrated, Money, Discover, People, and *Life)* as well as the *Scientific American, Consumer Reports,* Congressional Quarterly Weekly Report, *Forbes, Byte, The Economist, Newsweek, U.S. News & World Report,* and *The Washington Quarterly.* Add to this an even greater number of business periodicals (such as *Chemical Week, Coal Age and Electronics)* as well as newsletters, and the service offers a well-rounded group of titles.

[18]Markham Schack, "Lining Your Microcomputer to Dow Jones. . ." *Computers in Libraries,* October 1989, pp. 16–17.

[19]June Holbert and Donna Willmann, "VU/TEXT Information Services, Inc.," *Serials Review,* Winter 1987, pp. 7–14. This offers a detailed overview of the system as well as practical examples of how it is employed.

In addition to the papers, there are wire services, magazines, and some business publications, but what sets the service apart is its emphasis on local newspapers. Many of these are accessible online within 24 to 72 hours after publication. Subscribers also have access to Canadian magazines, business reports, and newspapers including *The Financial Times* and *Tass.*[20]

There are numerous other full-text services for newspapers, and for related magazines. In Canada, for example the *Toronto Globe and Mail* is available in full text via the vendor InfoGlobe, and Infomart covers 15 Canadian newspapers and wire services.

Microform

The high cost of full-text newspapers online ensures that the traditional form of storage of full text will not soon disappear. Most newspapers are available in microform. This is true of the national papers, as well as the local newspapers. Therefore, libraries usually have a special section filled with microform of newspapers.

It is important that the microform or printout edition be the same as the one indexed. All the indexes indicate which edition of a newspaper is used for indexing. For example, in the instructions in the front of the *National Newspaper Index* there is an explanation of the symbols employed to show whether the edition is national, or late city, or whatever. *The New York Times* has a similar explanation for various regional editions.

CD-ROM Full Text Newspapers

Inevitably CD-ROM will challenge microfilm as a method of storing the full texts of newspapers. A case in point is DIALOG OnDisk/NEWSPAPERS. A number of metropolitan dailies are offered by the online firm on a CD-ROM disk(s). It is important to stress two elements about this service: (1) The CD-ROMs include only the text, not the index. (2) In order to find information in the DIALOG disks, one must turn to a separate index. This awkward division of text and index is sure to change, and there will be a combination of both on a single disk. Also, more firms will enter the field, and in the 1990s it is likely that CD-ROM full-text newspapers will be as

[20]Another full-text business service is called *NewsNet* (Bryn Mawr, PA: Newsnet Inc., 1982 to date, daily) *NewsNet's* claim to attention is that it offers full text of close to 350 newsletters and related services, primarily in the business field. It is used to scan for the least information on a particular industrial development or, for the Wall Street watchers, to check on the activities of a given business.

readily available (with a combined index) as newspapers are now online.

Which Is Best?[21]

Given all these possibilities, which is the best newspaper indexing service for the library?

In many libraries it is an academic question because they cannot afford the online or the CD-ROM service. In fact, they will be fortunate to be able to subscribe to the printed index for *The New York Times.*

But for some others the choice depends upon several factors: (1) The number and the type of newspapers indexed. Here *Newspaper Abstracts* is in the lead, followed closely behind by NEXIS. (2) If one has to go back for retrospective searches, then NEXIS is clearly a leader, with some indexing from as early as 1971. (3) For in-depth as well as detailed coverage of abstracts, *Newspaper Abstracts* is ahead, and the *National Newspaper Index* is close behind. (4) Costs vary too much to be balanced, but in general the services are much the same in terms of expense. So which to choose? As one can see, the one answer is not really here, but the criteria for finding that answer are. Much depends on budget and the needs of the individual library. The choice is up to the library.

It seems evident, however, that no matter which service is selected, the library should have an index to: (1) The local and regional newspapers. (2) *The New York Times* and/or the *Washington Post.* (3) *The Wall Street Journal.* (4) And whatever index to a newspaper is required for a particular need.

At one time the library may have indexed the local paper. These days doing so is hardly required, as most newspapers have their own indexes. At any rate, one should certainly inquire.

SUGGESTED READING

DeBoer, Kee, "Abstracting and Indexing Services for Recent U.S. History" *RQ,* Summer 1989, pp. 537–546. How much of the journal literature of history is available in major abstracts and indexes. The author sets out for an answer and finds, to his surprise, that 22 percent of the articles do not appear in any of

---

[21]Russ Lockwood, "Online Finds," *Personal Computing,* December 1989, pp. 79–84. This is a layperson's short directory of business services, most of which include newspapers. They are the most common found in libraries and in special business situations. Per hour costs run from a low of $60 to a high of $195.

the services. Coverage by each of the five services ranges from a low of 15 to a high of 76 percent. The article serves, too, as an example of how to evaluate indexes and abstracting services.

Ensor, Pat, "ABI/INFORM Ondisc: Patron Evaluations in an Academic Library," *CD-ROM Librarian,* October 1989, pp. 25–30. Despite slow response time, librarians generally favor the disk version, and a questionnaire of patrons shows that an average of 80 percent also favor the system. The simple evaluative method is one which might be used to judge other CD-ROM systems.

Leiter, Richard, "A History of Legal Periodical Indexing," *Legal Reference Services Quarterly,* Spring 1987, pp. 35–46. A well-written and sometimes fascinating history of how the law was put under control through indexing. The surprise is how relatively new the indexing services are, and how applicable the rules for them are to most other types of subject indexes.

McClamroch, Jo et al., "MLA on CD-ROM: End-Users Respond," *Reference Services Review,* Spring 1991, pp. 81–86. The measure of success of the *MLA International Bibliography* on CD-ROM is how well it is used by the average individual. It is quite satisfactory, although there are points of difficulty. The short article is not so much a study of one index as it is a method of studying other CD-ROM indexes. See, particularly, the questionnaire.

Morrison, Doreen, "Indexes to *The Times* of London: An Evaluation and Comparative Analysis," *The Serials Librarian,* September 1987, pp. 89–106. This is an excellent analysis of a standard, 200-year-old index. The author considers the index historically and the techniques employed are universal. Also, the author has chosen excellent examples to illustrate her points.

Stieg, Margaret, and Joan Atkinson, "Librarianship Online: Old Problems, No New Solutions," *Library Journal,* Oct. 1, 1988, pp. 48–59. Here is a detailed, exceptionally well-researched comparison of ERIC, LISA, and Library Literature. The methodology is applicable to almost any other set of indexes and abstracts. Most important is a clear explanation of why so much indexing is so capricious. None of the services, for example, is really adequate.

Walker, Geraldene, "Searching the Humanities," *Database,* October, 1990, pp. 37–46. Many indexes (in print or in electronic form) are much broader than their title employs, and they may be used for numerous types of searches. The author looks at about a dozen of the databases in the humanities and explains their content, search patterns and, most important, overlap between one and the other. An extremely useful overview for both beginner and expert. Note, too, the references.

Weinberg, Bella Hassed, *Indexing.* Medford, NJ: Learned Information, 1989. Here are 10 essays from the annual (1988) meeting of the American Society of Indexers. The contributors concentrate on the practical aspects of indexing, not on theory. The essays represent a landmark for the individual who wants to know the basics of indexing. A must for anyone who would understand the subject.

PART III
SOURCES OF
INFORMATION

CHAPTER 7
ENCYCLOPEDIAS: GENERAL AND SUBJECT

Excluding the catalog, *World Almanac,* and *The Readers' Guide to Periodical Literature,* there is no more often used reference work in a library than a general encyclopedia. It is also the number-one reference aid found in half of American homes, rivaled in numbers of copies only by *TV Guide.*

The best general adult multivolume encyclopedias are *The New Britannica* and *The Americana. The World Book* has no competitor for appeal to children and teenagers and is also favored by many librarians to answer adult queries.[1] In between comes the "others" which comprise about a half-dozen sets familiar to anyone who has ever used a library or answered the call of an encyclopedia salesperson at the front door. Among the best: *Academic American Encyclopedia, Collier's,* and *Funk & Wagnalls New Encyclopedia.*

The choice is limited because there are only about 35 to 40 general sets. The basic ones are published by four firms. In the

---

[1]Inevitably, when polled, librarians select the same encyclopedias for the same group of people. The order may change a bit, but usually the *Americana, World Book,* and *Britannica* are on top of any list. Following behind are titles which usually appeal to teenagers and less well educated adults, e.g., *Academic American, Collier's, Compton's,* and *Funk & Wagnalls.* In between are children's sets such as *Merit Students Encyclopedia, New Book of Knowledge* and a few other works of lesser-known quality and use. (See, for example, a detailed poll conducted by the R. R. Bowker Company in *General Reference Books for Adults* (New York: R. R. Bowker Company, 1988) pp. 25–29. Reviews and summaries elsewhere support this same basic list.

home there is more room for choice than in the library, and some will wisely settle for the excellent *Funk & Wagnalls* at about $140 as contrasted with the more scholarly and considerably more costly ($1400) *Britannica.*

Since choice is limited, why, one might ask, should an entire chapter be devoted to an apparently easily resolved question. There are three answers: (1) First and foremost the encyclopedia is among the most frequently used reference works, particularly in school and public libraries, and should be understood as such. There may not be that much difference in quality between, say, the *Americana* and the *Britannica,* but there are subtle differences of content which every working librarian should appreciate in order to answer questions more efficiently. (2) Second, as one of the world's oldest and most pervasive reference works, the encyclopedia early established the pattern of format, scope, and intent which has been so often repeated in other reference works. To understand an encyclopedia is to understand a whole universe of reference and information sources. If one is able to evaluate an encyclopedia, one is usually able to judge with equal skill other reference books (as well as databases) from dictionaries to biographical and government sources. (3) Third, while the general encyclopedia sets are well known, the equally useful subject works, one-volume titles, and foreign encyclopedias are not. They must be a part of every professional librarian's knowledge.

There's a fourth reason to study encyclopedias, and this is the availability of several general encyclopedias on CD-ROM. These range in price from $400 to $800 which can be less than the cost of the printed version. The catch is that one must have the equipment to "read" the disks, but aside from that, the cost of the disks is reasonable. Also, as will be discussed, the CD-ROM format allows various methods of rapid search, not to mention amusement for the younger readers.

Definition and Background

An encyclopedia is an effort to gather together information either from all branches of knowledge or from a single subject area and arrange it in alphabetical order for ready reference. The desire to understand, to describe, to encompass all things known probably goes back to the earliest effort of a Sumerian or an Egyptian to comprehend the world.

Encyclopedia from the Greek "instruction in the circle of knowledge" was first applied to what we conceive of as an encyclopedia by Pliny the Elder (A.D. 23–79). Pliny, who had a remarkable capacity for work, wrote *Natural History*, of which 31 books survive. This vast encyclopedia is shapeless, but in it the Roman deals with everything from the universe and zoology to the fine arts. Most of the material was taken from other works, and Pliny estimated he had gathered about 20,000 facts from 100 authors.

History notes other men and women who followed in Pliny's ambitious footsteps. One classical example is Isidore of Seville (A.D. 560–636), who wrote a history of the Visigoths and composed the *Etymologies*. It is an effort to gather all human knowledge in 20 volumes. Drawing primarily from Greek and Latin authors, he composed what was to be the basic encyclopedia of the Middle Ages. Isidore derived his title for the set from the fact that he gave the origins of names and words he wrote about.[2] In about 1360 the English monk Bartholomew de Glanville repeated the process in 19 books written in Latin, although John Harris of England (1667–1719) was the first to produce an English language work.

The eighteenth century was the Age of Enlightenment, when Diderot, the eternal optimist, believed it possible to capture all knowledge in his great *Encyclopédie*. The Enlightenment, although a landmark in the history of knowledge, remains, as Hugh Kenner has put it, "a mystical experience through which the minds of Europe passed." Kenner then goes on to cleverly summarize the content and purpose of an encyclopedia:

> We carry with us still one piece of baggage from those far off days, and that is the book which nobody wrote and nobody is expected to read, and which is marketed as The Encyclopaedia: Britannica, Americana, Antarctica or other. The Encyclopaedia . . . takes all that we know apart into little pieces, and then arranges those pieces so that they can be found one at a time. It is produced by a feat of organizing, not a feat of understanding. . . . If the Encyclopaedia means anything

[2]The key spokesperson in the development of the encyclopedia in western Europe, Isidore "was constantly writing and compiling compendia of useful information—useful not only to clerics, monks, and other bishops, but also to rulers, administrators, and practical men concerned with mining, medical knowledge or accounts." Judith Herrin, *The Formation of Christendom* (Oxford: Blackwell, 1988), p. 62. Early encyclopedias were not for children and family use, but primarily for people of action, including clerics, intellectuals, and politicians.

The best general, brief history of encyclopedias will be found under that entry in the *Encyclopedia Britannica, Macropaedia.* Here are 27 closely printed, double-column pages devoted to its history. The article is by Robert Collison and Warren E. Preese.

as a whole, no one connected with the enterprise can be assumed to know what that meaning is.[3]

The complaint is common, although in some ways it misses the point of the modern encyclopedia. Today the general set serves a variety of purposes, but its essential one is to capsulize and organize the world's accumulated knowledge, or at least that part of it that is of interest to readers. Through detailed articles and brief facts, an effort is made to include a wide variety of information from all fields.

Encyclopedias may be divided into two or three categories of organization: (1) *by format*—there are the general and subject sets of 4 to 32 volumes (such as the *World Book*) and the smaller works of 1, 2, or 3 volumes (such as the one-volume *New Columbia Encyclopedia*); (2) *by scope*—here the division is either general (the *World Book*) or by subject *(International Encyclopedia of the Social Sciences)*; (3) *by audience*—the general work may be for a child, teenager, or layperson. If a subject set, it is likely that its intention is to appeal to an expert or near-expert in that subject field. There are other methods of dividing and subdividing encyclopedias, many of which will be explained as the reader progresses through this chapter.

Purpose

No matter which type of encyclopedia is published, it usually will include detailed survey articles, often with bibliographies, in certain fields or areas; explanatory material, normally shorter; and brief informational data such as the birth and death dates of famous people, geographical locations, and historical events. This scope makes the encyclopedia ideal for reference work, and the general set is often the first place the librarian will turn for answering questions.

Almost all encyclopedias are ready-reference sources. They are excellent places to turn for quick, accurate answers to fact queries. The exception is when one is seeking an answer to a question involving a current event or involving an event which has taken place since the last edition of the work.

When an overview of a topic is wanted, one will consult the *Britannica's* main articles in the Macropedia (usually via the index), or, at another level, the well-illustrated background pieces in *World Book*. The librarian soon learns which set is best in this area, and

---

[3]Hugh Kenner, *The Stoic Comedians* (Berkeley, CA: University of California Press, 1974), pp. 1 and 2.

"best" usually is determined by the type of user and the depth of information needed.

No one set is best for all uses, although the *Britannica* and the *World Book* come close. Thus the librarian must be aware of differences and of the strong and weak points in each of these reference works.

The bibliographies at the end of articles may help the reader find additional material in a given subject area. Several encyclopedias offer a variety of study guides which indicate related articles, so that with these, a student may put together, a truly creative paper rather than a carbon copy of an encyclopedia article.

It is a common misunderstanding that a general encyclopedia is a proper source of research (but this statement does not apply to specialized works). An encyclopedia is only a springboard. Furthermore, in presenting material with almost no differentiation, the general encyclopedia is not completely accurate or up to date; important facts must be double-checked in another source, if only in a second encyclopedia.

At the child's level, there's another misconception: Remember that an encyclopedia, no matter how good, is not a substitute for additional reading or for a collection of supporting reference books. In their enthusiasm, some salespeople and advertising copywriters are carried away with the proposition that an encyclopedia-oriented child is an educated child.

Publishers

How good is any given encyclopedia? Before focusing on that vital question, as well as on that of cost, one must ask: Just what choice do I have in the purchase of a set? The real, as opposed to the theoretical, choice among various general encyclopedias is radically limited by the number of publishers.

At one given time, there can be between 35 to 45 general encyclopedias in print. Of these no more than one-third can be rated acceptable for library or home purchase. And almost all the passable sets are published by just four firms. With annual sales of over $550 million, these companies control approximately 95 percent of the general encyclopedias published for all age groups in the United States[4]:

[4]The two largest privately held companies (World Book and Britannica) do not report sales volume, but analysts believe Americans spend between $500 and $550 million each year on sets. Add to this worldwide sales, and the total sales figure of about $550 million is a modest guess.

1. Encyclopedia Britannica Educational Corporation. The Chicago-based publisher, largest of the four, issues *Encyclopedia Britannica, Compton's Encyclopedia and Fact Index, Children's Britannica, Compton's Precyclopedia, Young Children's Encyclopedia, Great Books of the Western World, The Annals of America, Britannica Discovery Library, Britannica World Atlas, Britannica Science, Future Library,* and, to top the list, *The Bible* "available in Protestant, Catholic and Jewish versions." They publish numerous other volumes as well. Among their other holdings are G. & C. Merriam Company, publisher of Webster's dictionaries; Frederick A. Praeger, Inc.; and the Phaidon Press, Ltd.

2. World Book. This publisher sells more than one-half of all the encyclopedia units in the United States, and its *World Book* is by and large the most popular among children's and young people's sets. The Chicago-based firm also publishes *Childcraft,* a set for beginning readers but not really an encyclopedia, and the excellent *World Book Dictionary.*

3. Grolier Incorporated. The New York firm publishes *The Encyclopedia Americana, The Encyclopedia International, The New Book of Knowledge, Academic American Encyclopedia,* and *The Catholic Encyclopedia,* and distributes a number of other sets. It also has controlling interest in Scarecrow Press and Franklin Watts. Sales volume is close to the *Britannica.*[5]

4. Macmillan Educational Corporation. Although a large publishing house, it ranks only fourth in sales of encyclopedias. Its only two major sets are *Collier's* and the *Merit Students Encyclopedia.* However, Macmillan publishes a number of related works ranging from the *Encyclopedia of Philosophy* to the *Harvard Classics* and has an interest in Brentano's bookstores, Berlitz language schools, as well as being the parent company of Scribner, Atheneum, Bobbs Merrill, and other publishing firms.

5. Others. Here one might include the one or two firms whose sets are passable, in that they have been approved by librarians and, more particularly, by the Reference and Subscription Books Review Committee of the American Library Association. An example is Funk & Wagnalls (a division of Standard Reference Library), whose *Funk & Wagnalls New Encyclopedia* is an acceptable set.

---

[5]In 1988 Grolier was purchased by the French publishing firm, Hachette S.A. The firm paid $450 million for Grolier which still operates under the American name. In 1986 *World Book* was purchased by Berkshire Hathaway Inc., a diversified company controlled by Omaha billionaire Warren E. Buffett. *World Book* is among the company's fastest-growing divisions.

Then, too, there are the encyclopedias from England which are quite acceptable, e.g., *New Caxton Encyclopedia* and the *Everyman's Encyclopedia,* to name only two.

There are about 20 other general sets which the librarian might consider, but only the basic works by the big four publishers, plus *Funk & Wagnalls,* are acceptable. In fact, the only other set recommended by the prestigious Reference Books Bulletin of the American Library Association is the *New Standard Encyclopedia.* None of the other multivolume general sets has this important stamp of approval.[6] (*Note:* There are some English sets which are equally fine, but these are not normally considered by American libraries.)

EVALUATING ENCYCLOPEDIAS

Most librarians and, for that matter, laypersons will turn to one or two sources for objective evaluations of encyclopedias. These are trusted, tried, and true.

The first choice is Kenneth Kister's *Concise Guide to Best Encyclopedias* (Phoenix, Ariz.: Oryx Press, 1988).[7] This expert considers 33 general American and Canadian encyclopedias in detail. The volume contains brief reviews of 187 subject and specialized works, and an introduction which considers basic questions concerning the evaluation and purchase of an encyclopedia. It has an excellent "encyclopedia comparison chart" which at a glance allows one to see the difference in price, number of volumes, illustrations, and so on. Each set is considered in terms of history and authority, purpose, reliability, recency, objectivity, and all of the major points one would wish to consider in an evaluation of any type of reference work.

In *Reference Books for Young Readers* and *General Reference Books*

---

[6] *The New Standard Encyclopedia* (Chicago: Standard Educational Corporation, 20 vols., $850) is for the middle grades through adults. It claims about 6 million words, 18,000 articles and 12,000 illustrations, a quarter of which are in color. It has a specific entry form, i.e., short, factual articles, and with the 1989 edition three more volumes, including an index. It has a good, basic revision program. While reliable and relatively pleasing to the eye, the set simply is outclassed in terms of price by the equally excellent *Funk & Wagnalls* ($140) for the same audience. *The New Standard* is recommended by the Reference Books Bulletin of the American Library Association, and it is only one of two sets so recommended which is not published by the big four.

[7] The guide is a condensed and revised version of the author's *Best Encyclopedias: A Guide to General and Specialized Encyclopedias* by the same publisher (1986). The earlier version is much larger, and includes 50 general sets as well as 450 subject-oriented encyclopedias.

for Adults (both published by R. R. Bowker in 1988) one finds authoritative, lengthy reviews[8] of the basic sets. The adult volume considers 15 works, while the guide for younger readers has about the same number, with some duplication, but always with an eye on the needs of the level of readers. Each work begins with evaluative suggestions for encyclopedias in general, followed by specific, descriptive comments of 4 to 10 pages per set. As might be expected the evaluation follows the pattern accepted by almost everyone, and except for this or that point, the reviews are in line with the standard comments.

Another basic source of reviews is the well-known Reference Books Bulletin in *Booklist*, which is discussed in Chapter 3 of this text. Almost every or every other issue has a lengthy review either of a general set or, more likely, of a subject encyclopedia. These are detailed, objective, and meticulously documented. The most useful current check for the standard sets is offered by the same service in the October 15 issue. "Annual Encyclopedia Update" includes material previously published about the basic 10 to 12 general sets. There is a succinct summary of the primary points of each work.

The *American Reference Books Annual* is a source of reviews which are as strong on evaluation as on description. Usually each annual considers a half dozen or so general and subject encyclopedias. These are signed by individual reviewers. Also, there are citations to additional reviews in other sources.[9]

How can you determine which of these sources for evaluation are the best? Without doubt the most current and reliable is the annual summary in *Reference Books Bulletin,* as well as the ongoing reviews of new and revised sets that appear throughout the year.

For example, the "1990 Annual Encyclopedia Update" (October 1, 1990, pp. 375–384) covers the developments in about a dozen major adult and children's sets. This and the most current annual article (which appears about the same time each year) are

[8]Subject encyclopedias are discussed in the same publisher's *Topical Reference Books* (1991). As a member of the R. R. Bowker "Buying Guide Series," this covers about 2000 reference works in various subject areas from history and music to science and art. The guide primarily is for school and public libraries, although many of the reference titles, including encyclopedias, will be found in academic libraries. Unfortunately, the guide is a whopping $104.95 compared to $65 for the much more exhaustive *Guide to Reference Books.*

[9]*ARBA Guide to Subject Encyclopedias and Dictionaries* (Littleton, CO: Libraries Unlimited, 1986) includes reviews of about 1300 titles (but not general encyclopedias). Although somewhat dated, the basic information still is accurate, and it is a marvelous source of data on sometimes hard-to-find sets and individual works.

excellent places to turn for the latest information on price, amount of revision, bindings, etc. The first choice for a compilation of data is Kister's *Concise Guide to Best Encyclopedias*. With these volumes in the library, the question of evaluation is answered. If more information is needed, one may turn to the other works previously discussed.

Evaluation Points[10]

Librarians tend to make up their own minds about which are the better encyclopedias. Their decision is based primarily on daily use of the sets, but there are specific points to consider in a systematic evaluation: (1) scope, or subject coverage, emphasis, and the intended audience, (2) authority, which includes accuracy and reliability, (3) writing style, (4) recency, including revision plans, if any, of the publisher, (5) viewpoint and objectivity, (6) arrangement and entry, (7) index with reference to how one gains access to information in the set, (8) format, including the physical format and illustrations, and (9) cost. The presence of bibliographies is considered, too.[11]

Scope

The scope of the specialized encyclopedia is evident in its name, and becomes even more obvious with use. The scope of the general encyclopedia is dictated primarily by two considerations, age level and emphasis.

Age Level. The children's encyclopedias, such as the *World Book,*

[10]Kister and the Bowker series on reference books give useful advice on evaluating an encyclopedia. Another guide covers the same territory. This is the American Library Association's *Purchasing an Encyclopedia: 12 Points to Consider* (2d ed. Chicago: A.L.A., 1988). The 40 pages discuss the critical factors of selection and concludes with reviews of 10 general sets. The reviews are from the Reference Books Bulletin.

[11]When one considers the size of encyclopedias and the various audiences to which they are addressed, no encyclopedia is perfect. This is nicely illustrated in what has become a classic of its type, Harvey Einbinder's *The Myth of the Britannica* (New York: Grove Press, 1964). Although directed to the now supplanted fourteenth edition, the methodology is still valuable. The findings should alert anyone to the problems of keeping an encyclopedia current and objective. The Columbia professor, for example, found more than 600 articles outdated and riddled with error, e.g., the claim that after World War II the population of Warsaw was nearly 30 percent Jewish. In zoology the set offered false information about lemmings, which are not suicidal, to wolves who do not move in packs. And so on.

are tied to curriculum. Consequently, they include more in-depth material on subjects of general interest to grade and high schools than does an adult encyclopedia such as the *Britannica*. Most encyclopedia publishers aim their strongest advertising at adults with children. All the standard sets claim that an audience ranging from grades 6 to 12 can understand and use their respective works. This may be true of the exceptionally bright child, but the librarian is advised to check the real age compatibility of the material before purchase, not merely advertised age level.

There are two consequences of attempting to be all things to all age levels: (1) In many adult-level encyclopedias, when the material is shortened for easier comprehension by a child, the adult loses; and (2) the effort to clarify for the lower age level frequently results in an oversimplified approach to complex issues.

Emphasis. If age level dictates one approach to scope, the emphasis of the editor accounts for the other. At one time, there were greater variations in emphasis than there are today; one set may have been especially good for science, another for literature. Today, the emphasis is essentially a matter of deciding what compromise will be made between scholarship and popularity. Why, for example, in most adult encyclopedias, is as much space given to the subject of advertising as to communism? This is not to argue the merit of any particular emphasis, but only to point out that examining emphasis is a method of determining scope.

One method of testing the scope and emphasis of a set is to take key subjects or persons with whom the reader is familiar and look them up in several sets. For example, consider *encyclopedia*. In the *Americana* the complete entry runs from pages 330 to 335 (1988 edition); *Collier's* handles it between pages 134 and 137; while the *Britannica* is somewhat more concerned and covers the subject in depth from pages 365 to 385. Furthermore, the two consultants for this extensive coverage are Robert L. Collison, a leading expert on the history of sets, and Walter Preece, a moving power on the board of the *Britannica*. Using the single subject as example, it supports the view, with which few argue, that the *Britannica* is by and large the most scholarly, the most concerned with in-depth coverage than the other sets.[12]

Who is the encyclopedia really for, i.e., who is the salesperson

[12]See Kister, The Bowker series and almost any review in the "Reference Books Bulletin" for extensive examples of how a key word or subject is employed to test the in-depth coverage of a given set.

trying to reach? If you believe the advertisements, the answer is: everyone. The problem is evident: Can one set be equally good for children and adults? Of course not, but you'd never know that from the ads. For example, an advertisement for *Britannica* shows middle-aged adults saying about the set, "The only thing it can't tell you is the time." Another ad shows children and the lines: "Curiosity withers in frustration. That can easily happen with school-age children." The emphasis on children is understandable. Most sets are purchased for the children in the family.

Who buys encyclopedias? Primarily people from about thirty to fifty years of age, and particularly those with children. It is little wonder that almost all encyclopedia advertisements indicate that the set is ideal for children. Most purchases are made by middle-class families; single persons and the elderly do not usually buy encyclopedias.

Authority

A major question to ask about any reference book has to do with its authority. If it is authoritative, it usually follows that it will be up to date, accurate, and relatively objective.

Authority is evident in the names of the scholars and experts who sign the articles or who are listed as contributors somewhere in the set. It is also associated with the names of the publishers who distribute the sets. There are three quick tests for authority: (1) recognition of a prominent name, particularly the author of the best, most recent book on the subject; (2) a quick check of a field known to the reader to see whether leaders in that field are represented in the contributor list; and (3) finally, determination of whether a contributor's qualifications (as noted by position, degrees, occupation, and so on) relate to the contribution.

You can get an indication of the encyclopedia's revision policy and age from knowledge about the authors. Some contributors may literally be dead, and although a certain number of deceased authorities is perfectly acceptable, too many in this category would indicate either overabundant plagiarism from older sets or lack of any meaningful revision.

Any encyclopedia unfortunately will contain some errors and some omissions. Most are quickly corrected when brought to the attention of a publisher. The real test, of course, is the number of such mistakes. The sets considered here, while not perfect, can rarely be faulted for more than a few errors.[13]

---

[13]Errors pointed out by the "Reference Books Bulletin," as in other basic reviews,

Writing Style

When one considers the writing style of today's encyclopedia, one notices that none of the general sets is aimed at the expert. As the former editor of the *Britannica* puts it: "Perhaps the most critical editorial policy that was established [was] our absolute certainty that general encyclopedias are inappropriate source books for specialists in their own areas." Therefore, everything should be comprehensible to the person Preece calls "the curious intelligent lay reader." For the *Britannica,* at least, this is an about-face since the time when not only advertising but the articles themselves proclaimed the scholarly and pedantic nature of many of the contributions.

Recognizing that laypeople considerably outnumber scholars and therefore purchase considerably more volumes, encyclopedia firms tend to cater to their market in a relatively standard fashion: Contributors are given certain topics and outlines of what is needed and expected. Their manuscripts are then submitted to the encyclopedia's editors (editorial staffs of the larger encyclopedias range from 100 to 200 full-time persons), who revise, cut, and query—all to make the contributions understandable to the average reader. The extent of editing varies depending on each encyclopedia's audience. It can be extensive for children's works (where word difficulty and length of sentence are almost as important as content), or it can be highly limited for big-name contributors to an adult volume.

Serving as a bridge between contributor and reader, the editor strives for readability by reducing complicated vocabulary and jargon to terms understandable to the lay reader or young person. The purpose is to rephrase specialized thought into common language without insulting that thought—or, more likely, that eminent contributor. In the humanities and the social sciences, this often works, but the contributing scholar must be willing to have his or her initials appended to this more accessible version of the work that may arouse criticism from a peer.

The quality of the set may depend not only on the skills of the editors and writers, but also on the size of the editorial staff itself.

are carefully monitored by encyclopedia publishers, and often within weeks the errors are corrected. So, these are only examples. The careful student may find many more. The larger encyclopedia companies, i.e., the big four, hire librarians as fact checkers. The same librarians often answer questions from purchasers about material not in the set or not clearly presented or not up to date. The fact checkers are supposed to check every name, statistic, and reference. The result depends as much upon the skills of the checker as on the willingness of the contributor or editor to accept any changes.

The *Britannica* has a staff of between 165 and 175 members, and *World Book* and the other major contenders have an editorial force of somewhat the same proportions. But an underfinanced set may receive the attention of no more than five to ten people.

The editors usually are subject experts in two or more fields. All have wide experience in determining the tone, writing style and level, and subject treatment appropriate to the audience(s) for the set. The amount of editing a contributor's copy receives varies, but it is safe to say that the larger-selling sets receive the more extensive editing.

Recency: Continuous Revision

As most large encyclopedia companies issue new printings of their sets or individual volumes each year, they also incorporate updated changes. Word processing and automation procedures make this process considerably easier; editors can enter new materials, delete, and correct without completely resetting the whole article or section.

No matter what the technological procedures employed for updating new printings of an encyclopedia, the librarian should know: (1) Few general encyclopedias use the "edition" as an indication of the relative currency of the work. For example, the *Britannica's* Fourteenth edition was just that from 1929 until the Fifteenth edition in 1974. (2) Most encyclopedias do revise material with each printing, and a printing normally is done at least once or twice, or even more often, each year. (3) The relative date of the printing will be found on the verso of the title page, but this in itself means little because there is no accurate measure of how much of any given encyclopedia is revised with each printing or how often it is done. Most large publishers claim to revise about 5 to 10 percent of the material each year.[14]

The claim to continuous revision is a major selling point for publishers involved with selling sets to libraries. They rightly reason that no library is going to buy a new set of the same encyclopedia (loss or damage aside) unless there has been substantial revision.

Each year *World Book* spends some $3 million and thousands of hours revising its set. The *Britannica* does the same. The others follow to a lesser extent. All this includes additions such as back-

---

[14]The *Britannica* in its advertisements and interviews with the press claims a revision rate of about 12 percent a year. On the other hand, the *World Book*, in its advertisements, indicates that revision is as high as 40 percent.

ground on a new President or a film star, as well as events in the news which are likely to draw attention.

To make room for new subjects and names, *World Book* in 1988 dropped a couple of "World War II generals, a former Arkansas senator, a former United States ambassador and Mount Rosa in the Swiss Alps, among others."[15]

The decision to add or delete is based on whether a person or event will have lasting significance. Many sets include current personalities in order to make the works appealing to younger people and to make them look more current. "While *World Book* treads cautiously in this area, accepting some pop and rejecting most, *Britannica* stands firm on tradition (and) doesn't represent popular culture."[16]

Acclaimed as one of the best revised sets, *World Book* stresses this aspect each year in a battery of advertisements. "You have rated *World Book* the best," the ads read, "so why did we make all these changes?"[17] The rhetorical query needs no answer, but the copy goes on to say "Take a moment to discover the exciting revisions we've made for 19. . . ." No matter what the year, the proclamation goes on to push the new color photographs, better typefaces, at least one-third updated or completely rewritten articles, and "over 70 are entirely new."

Collier's follows much the same pattern, claiming that a certain number of articles are new or rewritten and updated or revised, as well as a given number of new and revised illustrations. Of course, no one but the advertising agency and the publisher know whether the numbers are that precise, but experience indicates they are at least close.

Viewpoint and Objectivity

Since general encyclopedias are published as profit ventures, they aim to attract the widest audience and to insult or injure no one. Despite their sometimes pious claims of objectivity on grounds of justice for all, they are motivated by commercial reasons. Only after many years of active prodding by women did encyclopedia publish-

---

[15]"Sports Tarts Bump Generals from One Index," *The New York Times*, May 28, 1989, p. F15. This is a series of short articles on modern encyclopedias.

[16]Ibid.

[17]Actually "all these changes" was an honest appraisal of the set in 1988, for in that year it did present a radical new face, both in terms of total revision and in the format of the set itself. The 1988 edition represents a vital new approach.

ers respond to this segment of the market and make a conscious effort to curb sexual bias.

Blatant sexual and racial bias has been eliminated from standard, acceptable encyclopedias, but the slate is not completely clean or neutral. Comparing how women are treated in 10 encyclopedias (all of which are considered in this chapter), June Engles and Elizabeth Futas offer a model of how to evaluate viewpoint and objectivity. Briefly, they found that in 1983: (1) men were included more frequently than women; (2) more men than women were included by name when discussing a given topic; (3) few encyclopedias used neutral language and many employed terms which are stereotypically sexist; and (4) illustrative matter was primarily male. The authors conclude that "encyclopedias should perhaps be regarded as an important factor in perpetuating sexism in our society."[18]

Several years later the incidence of sexism remains much the same and in one study was found to be even more blatant for black women. "It was interesting to note that although scant attention was paid to [black women], *Encyclopedia Americana* (among others) found it expedient to provide information on Vanessa Williams, the first Black Miss America. At the same time Marva Collins, educator; Cicely Tyson, actor; and Maya Angelou, writer, are not included."[19] While these omissions were remedied in later editions, there are still numerous others who are overlooked.

There are ways of determining whether an encyclopedia is objective when covering such controversial issues as conservatism or liberalism. One way is to see if the differences are ignored entirely, through dependence on a chronological, historical approach. The other is to see if an effort has been made to balance an article by presenting two or more sides. The reader should expect at least a consideration of different views, either by the contributor or by the editor.

Another way to consider the question of viewpoint is to see what the editor chooses to include or to exclude, to emphasize or to deemphasize. Nothing can date an encyclopedia faster than antiquated articles about issues and ideas either no longer acceptable or of limited interest. An encyclopedia directed at the Western

---

[18]June Engle and Elizabeth Futas, "Sexism in Adult Encyclopedias," *RQ,* Fall 1983, pp. 29–39. The final quote is on p. 37, and there are two pages of references. See also "Letters" in the Summer 1984 issue of *RQ* for responses to the research project.

[19]Henrietta W. Smith, "Missing & Wanted: Black Women in Encyclopedias," *School Library Journal,* February 1988, p. 29. Again, and it is worth repeating, the precise findings are likely to be corrected in later editions of the set, but one will find other errors by simply looking.

reader can scarcely be expected to give as much coverage to, let us say, Egypt as to New York State. Yet, to include only a passing mention of Egypt would not be suitable either, particularly in view of ancient history and the emergence of Africa as a new world force. The problem of assigning the size of one article as opposed to another plagues any conscientious encyclopedia editor, and there probably is no entirely satisfactory solution.

The problem of objectivity attains major proportions when a set is translated into another language and is meant for other cultural or political systems. For example, the *Britannica* is available in numerous languages. But usually these sets are not just a simple translation, but a modification. A case in point, and typical enough, is the 10-volume edition which is a joint project of the *Britannica* and the state-run *Encyclopedia of China*. Over a period of six years 500 Chinese scholars worked on the translation and revision. Published in 1986–1987 the set attempts an objective view of the world. The exception are sensitive political points, e.g., in the Chinese version, Taiwan, which is led by the National Government that fled China after losing the civil war to the Communists, is described as a Chinese province under separate administration. And the entry on the Korean war does not indicate that it was started by the Chinese.[20]

Arrangement and Entry

The traditional arrangement of an encyclopedia follows the familiar alphabetical approach to material, with numerous cross-references and an index. Most major sets follow this tradition. Average users are accustomed to the alphabetical order of information, or the *specific entry*. Here, the information is broken down into small, specific parts.

Index

Most general encyclopedias are alphabetically arranged, and some publishers have concluded that with suitable *see* and *see also* references, the arrangement should serve to eliminate the index.

The strong argument for an index is simply that a single article

---

[20]"The Fight for Objectivity in New Chinese Britannica," *The New York Times*, Sept. 11, 1986, p. C19. Originally the Chinese scholars proposed a Chinese version of 75 volumes. This set, the *Encyclopedia of China*, is still in progress, and in view of the student problems of 1989 one can only hazard a guess at the problems faced by the editor of this set.

may contain dozens of names and events which cannot be located unless there is a detailed, separate index volume. A good index is an absolute necessity.[21]

Format

A good format includes appropriate type sizes, typefaces, illustrations, binding, and total arrangement. When considering format, evaluate the following:

Illustrations (photographs, diagrams, charts, and maps). Nothing will tip off the evaluator faster as to how current the encyclopedia is than a cursory glance at the illustrations. But just because the illustrations are current, they are not necessarily suitable unless they relate directly to the text and to the interests of the reader. The librarian might ask: Do the illustrations consider the age of the user, or do they consist of figures or drawings totally foreign to, say, a twelve-year-old? Do they emphasize important matters, or are they too general? Are they functional, or simply attractive? Are the captions adequate?

The reproduction process is important. Some illustrations have a displeasing physical quality, perhaps because too little or too much ink was employed. Perhaps the paper was a poor grade, or an inadequate cut or halftone screen was used.

Illustrations are particularly useful in children's and young people's encyclopedias. The *World Book,* for example, has a well-deserved reputation for the timeliness and excellence of both its black-and-white and numerous colored illustrations. At the same time, an abundance of illustrations is a tip-off that an encyclopedia is: (1) primarily for children and young people, or (2) primarily a "popular" set or one-volume work purposely prepared for a wide appeal. Neither objective is necessarily invalid, but the librarian seeking an encyclopedia superior for ready-reference is likely to be more interested in the amount of text (and how it is presented) than in the number of illustrations.

Maps are an important part of any encyclopedia and vary in number from 2300 in *World Book* to 1175 in *Britannica* to slightly

---

[21]For aid in checking out the same topic in numerous subject encyclopedias (but *not,* as a rule in general sets), refer to *First Stop: The Master Index to Subject Encyclopedias* (Phoenix, AZ: Oryx Press, 1989, 1600 pp.). The master volume, edited by Joe Ryan, has over 40,000 topics with references to those subjects in 430 "commonly held specialized encyclopedias, dictionaries, handbooks and other reference sources." Note that the work covers more than encyclopedias.

over 73 in the one-volume *Columbia*. Many of the maps are prepared by Rand McNally or C. S. Hammond and are generally good to excellent. In the adult sets, the major maps appear frequently in a separate volume, often with the index. The young adults' and children's encyclopedias usually have the maps in the text, and if this is the case, there should be reference to them in the index and cross-references as needed. The librarian should check to see how many and what types of maps are employed to show major cities of the world, historical development, political changes, land use, weather, and so on. The actual evaluation of the maps is discussed in the chapter on geography.

There is another consideration to illustrations, and that is sales. More and more publishers are taking the lead from television by giving their sets more visual appeal. *World Book* spent millions to redesign its set and now features more color and more graphics that have more general appeal to the younger set.

Size of Type. The type style is important, as is the spacing between lines and the width of the columns. All these factors affect the readability of the work.

Binding. Encyclopedias should be bound in a fashion that is suitable for rough use, particularly in a library. Conversely, buyers should be warned that a frequent method of jacking up the price of an encyclopedia is to charge the user for a so-called deluxe binding which often is no better, and in fact may be less durable, than the standard library binding.

Volume Size. Finally, consideration should be given to the physical size of the volume. Is it comfortable to use? Equally important, can it be opened without strain on the binding?

Cost

Reporting on the average discussion of cost by a salesperson, John Cunningham writes: "There is a sort of mythical snob appeal about the cost (of an encyclopedia). It is rather like a posh funeral: you don't ask about the bill. Britannica salesmen are tactful about it, though quite open, rather in the manner of undertakers leading the bereaved through the types of coffins available, starting at the top with a leather binding and gold lettering."[22]

[22]John Cunningham, "A Britannica a Day Keeps the Recession at Bay," *The Guardian*, Feb. 17, 1984, p. 15. For a detailed review of the revised *Britannica*, see "Reference Books Bulletin," *The Booklist*, Nov. 15, 1985, pp. 472–474.

Not only do prices vary dramatically from set to set, but they can range from under $1000 to several multiples of that figure for precisely the same work. One can buy the *Britannica* alone, but this is not easy. The salesperson will try to have the sale include other Britannica items from *Great Books of the Western World* to junior encyclopedias. The end result is that one can pay from $1500 to $8000 for the *Britannica,* depending on what else is purchased along with the basic set as well as what kind of binding was chosen.

Another cost factor to consider is the library discount. Most publishers grant large discounts to libraries. For example, the *Americana* retails for $1000, but libraries and schools may purchase it for $895. It is good advertising for the publisher to have the set available in a library. (*Note:* Prices given in this chapter are retail, not the library or school discount figure.)

Discount and remainder houses, such as Barnes & Noble, frequently advertise various sets: The *Academic American* can be "only $199" as contrasted with the 1990 advertised price of $720. Only when one reads the small print is the reason for the price cut clear— a 1985 edition is being sold in 1991. Although there may be nothing "wrong" with this, particularly as the year of the edition is clearly stated, the buyer should beware and be aware.

The *Funk & Wagnalls* is often advertised in newspapers, usually with a supermarket's insert. Here the impression given is that each volume is only 9 cents, although when one goes further along one finds that the second volume is 99 cents, while volumes 3 to 29 will be $4.99 each. While this still may be a tremendous bargain, the impression given of cost is slightly deceptive, as are the advertisements indicating this very set (costing around $135 to $165) is "published at $375."

And that's the problem with cost and pricing. Just how much is a set? The publisher, unless forced, rarely will tell. The *Britannica* sends out a letter containing the good news that you can enjoy the set for less "than you thought possible." You can do so "direct from the publisher, at a substantial Group Discount." How much is the discount and what is the price? No indication of that until the form you send in brings a salesperson to your door.

Sales Practices

General encyclopedias are sold either door to door or in bookstores. At one time the front-door sales pitch was the only one used. The practice almost ceased with much stricter Federal Trade Commission rules on sales promises. By the late 1980s things changed once again. The public's buying power produced a boom and the door-to-door salespersons were back. Today *World Book* has over 45,000 people pounding on doors. About 80 percent of these are women working full or part-time. They report taking one order for every four sales calls.

The *Britannica* and the other sets not only have added salespeople, but spend more on advertising. Early in 1989 the *Britannica* raised its advertising budget from $10 to $15 million a year.[23]

In a candid article-interview, a salesperson for *World Book* explains that full-time salespeople usually make between $25,000 and $50,000 a year. But "more industrious ones reach six figures," and the woman interviewed averages $100,000 a year. "In the *World Book* hierarchy, if you sell 100 sets a year, you're a solid performer. If you sell 200, you attract awe. If you sell 300, people wonder if you ever sleep. If you sell 400, the world is yours." The salesperson interviewed moved from teaching school to sales when "she became interested in making more money."[24]

Today sales practices are as diverse as sets. If *Funk & Wagnalls New Encyclopedia* relies on supermarket sales, the *Britannica* counts on people filling out cards in ads—an invitation to have a salesperson call or, in some cases, simply to have the set delivered. Then, too, at bookstores, department stores, shopping centers, and even local fairs one finds a beaming salesperson ready and willing to sell a set to anyone who stops by for a chat.

Working through schools and related organizations is the favored approach. The University of Utah Alumni Association informed its members on its own stationery that discount prices are available for the *Britannica*. The undated letter (in the late 1980s) gives a pitch for the set and includes a card which allows the graduate to ask for more information from the publisher and salespersons. Utah is hardly alone in employing this sales letter. It is common for many other school alumni groups.

---

[23]In a 1989 London (England) newspaper, a *Britannica* advertisement opens with the headline, "Doesn't your family deserve a head start?" In over 1000 words of dense copy there are such sentences as these: "Your children are going to need every inch of the head start you can give them." "Logical, lucid, stimulating and full of facts—facts to help your children succeed." "At first I learned little at school—but then my parents bought a set of Britannica. It taught me that learning can be fun." Other publishers in other newspapers and other places follow much the same pattern. There is nothing precisely false about the ads, but they seem to be an attempt to attract audiences far beyond the scope of the set.

[24]N. R. Kleinfield, "The Cheerful Trudge of a World Book Ace," *The New York Times*, March 6, 1988, pp. 1F and 10F.

Consumer Advice

The librarian can meet the request for information about a given set in several ways:

1. *Give no advice.* Several major public libraries, fearful of repercussions from salespersons and publishers, adamantly refuse to allow their personnel to advise on the purchase of one or another set. This author believes that such a refusal is unprofessional and highly questionable.
2. *Give limited advice.* The librarian can give the inquirer several reviews of the set or sets under question, and leave the final decision to the user.
3. *Go all out with an endorsement or a condemnation.* Privately, of course, many librarians do just this. Such opinionated statements may have some nasty repercussions, particularly when the question is between sets that are approved by the ALA and are more or less even in quality.

Of the three, the second option is best. If the set is not readily recognized either by publisher or by reputation, the librarian should not hesitate to point out that the chances are that it is a poor buy from the standpoint of both cost and quality. The librarian should be prepared to support this statement with reviews; or lacking reviews (either because the set is too new or such a "dog" as not to have been noticed), there should be no hesitation about standing on one's own professional evaluation of the set. The librarian should explain that the opinion may be personal, but the odds are all against the set being of good quality.

Many public librarians avoid recommending their own favorite titles. Instead they refer the person to one of the standard review compilations and to encyclopedias in the library which can be examined. Actually, the presence of a work in the library is a tacit stamp of approval by the librarian. Asked in a survey if they ever recommended "their favorite encyclopedia," 47 replied "never," 20 said "sometimes," and only 2 replied "always."[25] The reluctance to give advice is not so much a decision taken by the individual reference librarian as it is the policy of the library. Many libraries have policy statements which specifically state that the librarian is to give no advice on such matters.

[25]Ken Kister, "Encyclopedias and the Public Library: A National Survey," *Library Journal,* April 15, 1979, p. 893.

Replacement

Most libraries replace an encyclopedia every two to five years. In practical terms this usually means that the one of the most-used sets (*World Book, Americana, Britannica,* or *Collier's*) is replaced with a revised set every two years, the next most used every three years, the next every four years, and so on. Depending on whether the library is medium or large, the two-to-four-year-old sets are sent to the branches, put in the general reading room, or duplicated in heavily used parts of the library, such as the young adult's area. When a set is more than five years old, it should be discarded. The older sets may be quite suitable for home use, but not for libraries, where the reader expects to find the most up-to-date information. Ideally, and where budgets allow, all the four to five basic sets should be replaced every one to two years; but these days that is rarely possible.

Replacement depends upon whether the publisher actually revises the set from year to year. If this is not done or if it is done at a rate of less than 5 percent revision annually, it is pointless to replace the set unless it is worn. You can see why it is important for a librarian to carefully check the amount of continuous revision carried on by the publisher.

ELECTRONIC ENCYCLOPEDIAS

Several of the basic and subject sets are available either online or on CD-ROM disk or both. The situation is likely to change. With the ability to keep prices down, encyclopedia publishers are able to offer a set either in print or on CD-ROM. In addition, the basic encyclopedia has become part of an information package online. It is uneconomical to use the encyclopedia by itself online, but as part of a total reference library it can be a valuable asset to the publisher and distributor.

Online

One set available online is the *New Encyclopedia Britannica.* It is available only through the Mead Data Central online service NEXIS, discussed earlier. Although pictures are not part of the online service, the complete text to the set (plus the yearbook and several other works) may be had online. Using NEXIS one may search the set, plus newspapers and magazines, to get a complete information profile on a subject or individual.

Among general multiple sets, both the *Britannica* and *Academic American* are available online. The 12-volume English *Everyman's* is online, as is the 1-volume *Kussmaul* (which is inadequate). Subject sets available online include the *McGraw-Hill Encyclopedia of Science and Technology.*

There are disadvantages to online use so great that one wonders whether the encyclopedias, at least when used by themselves, will ever be a viable success online. Three problems exist: (1) It is just as quick to search an alphabetically arranged set, or, for that matter, to use the index. (2) It is much less expensive to purchase a set than to use one online if the set is used frequently. If, as in the case of *Kirk-Othmer Encyclopedia* (specialized subject set of chemical technology), it is used only infrequently, then the online search might be more economical. (3) As of this writing, one cannot transmit pictures online. The result is that a good deal of the value of the general encyclopedias is lost. Understandably, librarians and, to a lesser degree, laypersons, are skeptical.

CD-ROM

The CD-ROM encyclopedia has not been popular either. "Few customers have been willing to purchase CD-ROM drives because of their high price, and the dearth of software that works with them. Schools and libraries have been more receptive."[26] The advantage to a library is twofold: (1) the individual volumes cannot be stolen and are always available; (2) several persons at the same time can search the same "volume" electronically. Furthermore, there are all the advantages of multiple entrance points.

The probable future of the online encyclopedia will be to turn toward the use of optical disks or refined CD-ROMs which will be sold to individuals and libraries for immediate access at home or in the library through a computer. While the library may find this an advantage, the cost is still too high for laypersons and will remain so until the disk drive/computer is less expensive. The disk by itself is usually less, or little more than the printed version.

An example of refined CD-ROM is *Compton's Encyclopedia and Fact Index* on CD-ROM. (Technically this is called a CD-I, compact disk interactive, which allows for sound and image. Still, the publisher and distributors tend to call it by the broader CD-ROM. That

[26]"Looking up Africa—By Pressing a Button," *The New York Times,* May 28, 1989, p. F15.

is used here.) Renamed in this format *Compton's MultiMedia Encyclo-pedia*, it is a modest $895 as compared with the $699 for the in-print version. The disk is a breakthrough in that it not only includes the full set's articles, but has all the illustrations, including photographs, charts, and graphs. A bit of a gimmick is about 60 minutes of sound segments which help advertise the set, but are so few as to add little value. At the same time the use of sound heralds the beginning of multimedia (or hypermedia) sets on CD-ROM.

Still another twist is suggested by the Corporation for Entertainment and Learning. They offer what they term a *Video Encyclo-pedia* of the twentieth century. This consists of 75 one-hour video-cassettes that cover major events from 1893 through the 1989 presidential inauguration. Footage from newsreels, television productions, and movies is included. There is a five-volume index with a subject, author, and title approach and 2500 pages of printed reference material, including a list of 8 to 10 stories and books for every day of the 92 years covered. Aside from a VCR, the library needs a good budget. The cost is $10,000.[27]

ADULT ENCYCLOPEDIAS

The New Encyclopedia Britannica, 15th ed. Chicago: Encyclopedia Britannica Inc., 32 vols. $1600.

The Encyclopedia Americana. Danbury, CT: Grolier Incorporated, 30 vols. $1000.

The *Britannica*

The best-known encyclopedia in the Western world is the *Britannica*. First published in 1768, it underwent many revisions and changes until the triumphant Ninth Edition in 1889. This was the "scholar's edition," with long articles from such contributors as Arnold, Swinburne, Huxley, and other major British minds of the nineteenth century. The Ninth was followed, after a lackluster Tenth, by the equally famous Eleventh. After several changes caused by economic difficulties, the set came to the United States and by 1929 appeared as the Fourteenth edition. By that time, the long essays had been reduced and divided, but the set continued to be sold (as it is even today) on the reputation built with the Ninth and Eleventh editions.

[27]"Newest Teaching Tool: A Video Encyclopedia," *The New York Times*, Dec. 25, 1986, p. 34. The article explains the scope and the method of compiling the video work.

In 1974 the entire set was completely revised and the format changed. In 1985 the set was again revised, and additions made, including a two-volume index. The result is:

1. A 12-volume *Micropaedia* which consists of short, factual ready-reference type material arranged in alphabetical order. This is an imitation of the specific entry found in many European works. There are approximately 65,000 separate entries and close to half that number of cross-references. The average length of an entry is about 300 words. (A few—covering countries, outstanding personalities, and ideas—go as high as 3000 words, but these are the exception.) Each serves to summarize and outline the topic. Often, too, more detail is found in the companion set or part, the *Macropaedia.*

As a result of the 1985 revision more attention is given to summary pieces and charts and diagrams. For example, there is a separate 60-plus page section devoted to "Sporting Record" which has statistical data and photographs for 38 sports.

2. The second part of the set, which like the *Micropaedia* may be used independently, is the *Macropaedia.* The 17 volumes follow the nineteenth century tradition of offering long (20 to 100 pages) detailed articles, again in alphabetical order. Each volume has about 40 articles, for a total in the full 17 volumes of only 681. In effect, the reader is offered an overview of a person, field, or idea in each of the essays.

The guide to the detailed examinations is a table of contents at the head of each essay. For example, in the survey of the West Indies, instead of breaking up the various islands alphabetically (as is done in most sets) they are treated as a single unit in the *Macropaedia.* A score of individual parts treat as many of the individual countries and islands, but always within the context of the main article. Thus the major entries have a coherence not usually found in encyclopedias.

3. The two sets are held together by a detailed two-volume index and the *Propaedia,* which is a guide to related items within the two works. Referred to in advertisements as an "outline of knowledge," the single volume is arranged by broad subjects. The idea is to outline human knowledge, to show relationships between ideas, persons, and events. The *Propedia* is a commendable failure because the complexity of knowledge simply does not allow such a simplistic approach. The index, on the other hand, is one of the best for any set and has about 475,000 entries.

As of 1991 only NEXIS offers the *Britannica* online. Eventually, it is likely to find its way to other services. The CD-ROM version was introduced at the close of the 1980s.

Weak Points.[28] The division of the set into two major parts is confusing, and although the format has some benefit for ready-reference work, it is decidedly confusing for laypersons. Another real difficulty is that many of the detailed articles in the *Macropaedia* are highly technical (e.g., see Mathematics) and beyond the comprehension of all but experts. At the same time, the very challenge makes this a refreshing counterpoint to the sometimes too-easy other sets.

The quality of the continuous revision, which the publisher claims is about 12 percent each year, is generally much improved over earlier years. But there are still too many articles and bibliographies which remain dated. The yearbook is of little help.

The small illustrations in the *Micropaedia* are fine, but the plates, while numerous enough, are not always tied to the articles. This seems particularly true in work of specific artists, architects, and others in the graphic arts. The primary article will include two or three illustrations, but others pertaining to the creators may be scattered through numerous volumes. Also, color is used sparingly.

The primary drawback, though, for laypersons is the cost. At $1600 the *Britannica* is $600 more than the *Americana* and almost three times as much as the *World Book.* (Even with a library discount it is $1149).

The *Americana*

The Encyclopedia Americana is based on the seventh edition of the German encyclopedia *Brockhaus Koversations Lexikon.* In fact, the first published set (1829 to 1833) consisted of little more than pirated, translated articles from the German work. It was asserted in 1903 that the *Americana* was a wholly new work, but still many of the articles were carried over from *Brockhaus.* The set was reissued in 1918 with changes and additions, although still with material from *Brockhaus.* It claims to be the oldest "all-American" encyclopedia in existence.

As the title implies, the strength of this work is its emphasis on American history, geography, and biography. The *Americana* un-

---

[28]Many intellectuals, particularly in England, think the work has deteriorated, e.g., see Charles Mosley's "Living on Borrowed Glory," *The Guardian,* June 24, 1988, p. 29. "The decline of the *Britannica* has become apparent to large numbers of educated Britons, though the general public seems unaware of it as yet." The critics points out the "full horrors" of slips in the *Micropaedia* and often "Yankee self-righteousness' in longer articles.

questionably places greater emphasis on these areas than any of the other sets, and it is particularly useful for finding out-of-the-way, little-known material about the United States. However, general coverage of the United States is matched in other major encyclopedias.

A major plus for the set is that it is fairly current. Each year all the primary articles are updated, and new or revised illustrations considered. Bibliographies are frequently updated.

The writing style is clear, the arrangement admirable, the index good, and the general format (including illustrations and type size) adequate. A helpful feature is the insertion of summaries, resembling a table of contents, at the beginning of multiple-page articles. The set is edited for the adult with a high school education. It is not suitable (despite the zealous efforts of copy writers) for grade school children.

The illustrations in the set are passable to excellent, about 22,000, or 16 percent, of which are in color. Most are closely associated with the text. The maps are detailed and easy to follow, although those of detailed city plans are not always the best.

The emphasis is on short, specific, ready-reference entries and is, therefore, ideal for reference work. However, it does contain sometimes much-longer articles, particularly those which cover states, countries, and historical events. The *Americana* is excellent *both* for the concise articles and for the fewer in-depth pieces. Use is made even more effective thanks to a detailed index of 354,000 entries.

Weak Points: Although its performance in revising items and personalities which are likely to be in the news is fairly good, the same is not true in continuous revision of the basic articles. This lack of timeliness in certain sections can be a major drawback, particularly in schools where curriculum is tied to basic knowledge and not the passing scene.

Despite the fact that the *Americana* has many excellent illustrations, many should be replaced with new plates, and there should be a better balance of colored illustrations in the longer articles. (Continual reader-user criticism of the illustrations has resulted in some much-improved revisions, but more still needs to be done to bring the work up to par with other sets of the same price and scope.)

POPULAR ADULT AND HIGH SCHOOL SETS

Academic American Encyclopedia. Danbury, CT: Grolier Incorporated, 21 vols. $720. (DIALOG file 180, $45 an hour.) CD-ROM: publisher, $395. (*Note:* Door-to-door sales, and sometimes through bookstores, the set is called *Lexicon Universal Encyclopedia,* often at a cut rate of about $300 for older editions. Check the copyright date.)

Collier's Encyclopedia. New York: Macmillan Educational Corporation, 24 vols. $1500.

Funk & Wagnalls New Encyclopedia. New York: Funk & Wagnalls, 29 vols. $165.

There are at least three sets which claim to be of equal value to adults and to young people. The reading level is suitable for those from 12 to 18 years of age to adult. *Collier's* and the *Academic American* are better-suited to adults than the *Funk & Wagnalls* but all may be used by teenagers.

All three differ from the *Americana* and *Britannica,* in that they have particular emphasis on popular, concise writing. They are deliberately edited for the adult with a high school education or for the high school or beginning college student. All claim, too, that they are suitable for upper elementary school students, but this is questionable. All are relatively accurate, but vary in their practices of keeping material up to date.

Collier's

Collier's deserves first place because it can be ranked good to excellent in almost all areas of evaluation. It contains contributions of close to 5000 authorities, and most of the articles are signed. The publisher claims a good balance in coverage, e.g., about 30 percent in the humanities, 15 percent in science, 35 percent in geography and regional studies, with 20 percent given over to the social sciences. Also, there are useful, although at times oversimplified, articles of a how-to-do-it, self-help nature.

The writing style may be too bland for some, but it has the advantage of clarity. The articles are extremely well organized and the set is unusual because it stresses long, rather than short, articles that are often accompanied by biographical sketches and glossaries of terms. Pronunciation of difficult words often is given and less common foreign terms are defined.

Some complain that the articles in *Collier's* are too long. In fact, they can run over 40 or even 70 pages for a particular country. At the same time, there is a fine index which has over 400,000 entries—almost double those found in rival sets. Another plus of the final volume is the section on bibliographies. About 12,000 titles are arranged under 31 broad subjects and are subdivided. Most entries are current, and the reading lists offer adults and students a satisfactory choice of supplements to material found in the set.

The 17,600 illustrations, according to the publisher, make up 20 percent of the space. Almost one-half of these are in color. In the revision process, the editors add new, color photographs each year and the general level of the illustrations is improving. The page makeup and general layout are among the best among the sets.

The set manages to eliminate any overt bias in the biographical entries and in the articles. But there could be still-better coverage of prominent modern women. The coverage of minorities is not all it might be, either.

The index of over 400,000 citations is one of the best available, and extremely easy to use. Unfortunately, the publisher does not follow through with enough adequate cross-references within the set itself—a pity because many students tend to avoid the index and rely on such references. A bibliography of 200-plus pages winds up the index volume and offers approximately 12,500 titles under broad-to-narrow subject headings.

Weak Points: While most of the material is under continuous revision, and the "news" items are current, there is evidence that some basic articles are not. Although the quality of the illustrations has been improved, some are still a bit muddy and not related to the subject matter. On the whole, though, it is difficult to fault the set on any of the major criteria.

Cost is another consideration. For laypersons the set is $1500, and if added material is purchased, it can run to $1800. It is about three times more expensive than *World Book*.

Academic American

First published in 1980 by a Dutch firm, and then sold to Grolier, the *Academic American Encyclopedia* is equal to Collier's in many ways, but has less than one-half as many words, 9 million compared to 21 million in Collier's. Note, though, that the cost is about one-half the price of *Collier's*.

As the name indicates, *Academic American Encyclopedia* desires to reflect the curricula of American schools, and to a lesser degree of colleges and universities. The emphasis is on the ready-reference short-entry form. Each page has about three articles, with some longer ones for countries, scientific topics, and other basic subjects.

Grolier has adopted a thorough revision scheme, and the illustrations in the annual update are kept current. The major articles, and particularly those dealing with politics, science, and personalities, are revised regularly. Much of this revision may be due to the fact that the encyclopedia is available online and can easily be updated. Be that as it may, like its cousin *The Americana*, it is one of the most current print sets available.

The emphasis, as in the other sets of this type, is fairly well divided: one-third sciences; one-third social sciences and related areas (places); and one-third arts and humanities.

About one-third of all the articles are biographical. Although the index cannot be trusted entirely for geographical points on the maps, it is generally good. There are also numerous cross-references within the volumes.

When it comes to the writing style and the factual material, this set has few rivals in its price category. The writing, by over 2400 consultants, is particularly good, and most of the material can be easily understood. The short-entry form works well for popular items. *The Academic American* is one of the first places to turn for background information on a topic which may have gained prominence only a year or so ago.

One technique that is used is to define basic terms in the first paragraph of an article and then expand in fairly simple language. If the subject is complex, the article defines additional terms as it goes along. Nevertheless, the summary opening paragraphs usually give enough explanation even for the most unsophisticated reader.

The illustrations (about 17,000 with close to 12,000 in color), consisting of some excellent photographs and plates, take up about one-third of the space. They are current and nicely placed throughout the set. The maps are equally good and as useful. In fact, this is one of the strong points of the set. Note that the three-quarters of the illustrations in color are among the highest proportion for any set this side of the *World Book*. Note also that none of the illustrations are presently available in the electronic form of the set.

With its focus on being a truly popular set, there is considerable emphasis on individuals, with brief entries accounting for more than 35 percent of the total entries. The excellent index makes it easy to find what is needed.

Weak Points: In trying to be all things to all people, the writing style is sometimes too journalistic, too simplistic. But at the same time, thanks to less than firm editorial control, some of the more complicated articles are not that easy to follow. In other words, the presentation is uneven, although generally good enough. The short-entry form is ideal for ready-reference work, but acts as a check on most comprehensive searches.

There may be too much emphasis on being "objective" in that

in the humanities, some of the contributors fail to appreciate the vagaries of human nature. See, for example, the various entries about art and artists. Still, this is really a minor point, and the general objectivity of the set is quite commendable.

Academic CD-ROM. The Academic American (i.e., Grolier) is the first general set to take full advantage of the new technologies, and is to be congratulated for the move. The "New Electronic Encyclopedia" is the description given by Grolier to the CD-ROM version. The single disk contains the whole 20-volume set (plus about 1 million added words from updated material) and a vastly improved index. It may be searched as in online with boolean logic and by at least three easier methods for beginners.

This is another case where the cost of CD-ROM is less than the printed work, i.e., if one does not include the purchase of the necessary disk drive. The disk is $395 as opposed to $800 for the printed version and has the advantage of being updated each year.

With the third edition of the electronic set in 1990, illustrations were introduced on CD-ROM. Unfortunately, only about one-tenth of those found in the printed work are included, and this excludes maps, flags, diagrams of the human body, etc. The publisher claims additional illustrations will be added in the next year or so. Another drawback (as of 1991) is that it does not contain a dictionary for easy reference—a common feature in other electronic encyclopedias.

The publisher plans to extend the technology to include methods that will allow one to play the set through a home television. Meanwhile, the electronic version is a best buy in anyone's language, particularly as the annual updates are a modest $125 (as of 1990).

Online there are numerous vendors and services offering the *Academic American*. In fact, only a few vendors do not offer the set. It normally is part of a larger information database, e.g., it is part of *Genie* which is a full-text general service including data on stock quotes, photography, and computers.

Funk & Wagnalls

Funk & Wagnalls New Encyclopedia has almost the same number of words as the much-better-designed *Academic American*. They are relatively close to covering about the same amount of material, and they are both quite good in their different ways. (There is no comparison here with *Collier's*, which, in terms of in-depth coverage, is almost three times as large as both sets.)

The essential difference between *Funk & Wagnalls* and the *Academic* is price. To laypersons the *Academic* sells for $800, while the competition, which is sold in supermarkets, comes in at a mere $135. It can be said that this is truly a marked-down encyclopedia with first-class content. It is prominently displayed in many supermarkets with usually one-volume free, and subsequent volumes $4.99 or so each. For once, the value is there, and no one can go wrong purchasing the set, either as individual volumes or in total.

Funk & Wagnalls now contains slightly over 9000 illustrations, of which about one-third are in color. Placed next to the relevant text, the pictures are up to date and, in terms of reproduction and subject matter, are good to excellent. Volume 29 is a detailed index, and in the last part of volume 28 one finds bibliographies, reading lists, and subject outlines. The bibliographies are both current and representative of the best material in the field.

The result of the well-written articles and the carefully researched material is that the set is much above average. It is by far the best of the supermarket sets, and a viable alternative to more expensive encyclopedias. It has an active program of continuous revision which makes it one of the more current works.

Weak Points: Understandably, the set with the fewest words cannot hope to brag about in-depth articles—and that can be a major weakness. On the other hand, for its intended audience the short entries are possibly even more useful for a quick, easy-to-understand overview. The format is attractive, but not as inviting as the other sets, and there are fewer illustrations than in the larger works.

Illustrations are not indexed, and some relatively common controversial topics such as gun control and oil spill are not covered adequately. All the bibliographies are in the last part of the twenty-eighth volume, which is a bit inconvenient.

Other Adult High School Sets

The Canadian Encyclopedia. 2d ed. Edmonton, AL: Hurtig Publishers Ltd., 4 vols. $225.

Oxford Illustrated Encyclopedia. Oxford: Oxford University Press, 1985–1991, 9 vols. $350.

Everyman's Encyclopedia. London: J. M. Dent & Sons Ltd., 12 vols. $400.

The 1988 edition of the Canadian set represents a complete revision of the second edition. It is praiseworthy on several counts. First it is current, and reflects the ongoing activities of the Canadian people in all areas of human concern. Second, it has over 2000 illustrations which are clear, nicely placed, and up to date. The maps are superior. About one-half are in full color. Third, the authoritative articles are easy to read and are at about the level of writing style as the *Americana* or *The Academic American Encyclopedia*. In other words it is a set for everyone. Finally, in the second edition the index more than doubled from 200 pages to 470 pages.

Since it only considers Canada and things Canadian, this may be a drawback for some American libraries, but for those which can afford a standard encyclopedia it is a good addition.[29]

The *Oxford Illustrated Encyclopedia* is a nine-volume work which concentrates, as the title suggests, on maps, drawings, photographs, and charts. There is at least one illustration per page, and sometimes more. Most are in color, and they are closely allied to the text.

The focus is on thematic development of general topics. The first two volumes, for example, cover the natural and physical world, while volumes 3 and 4 focus on history up to the present. An additional four volumes (plus an extensive index in volume 9) cover arts, technology, the universe, and human society. This broad approach is not the typical encyclopedia format which moves over the world from A to Z. At the same time, the massive number of illustrations, coupled with an extremely easy writing style, makes it a useful set for background reading. Some complain that the short articles and the rather simple writing make it more suitable for teenagers than adults, but this is beside the point. It is a successful effort to offer the world to the average layperson in a lively format with accurate facts.

The best-selling *Everyman's Encyclopedia* is a 12-volume, well-illustrated set that was directed at the average British student and adult. There is no consistent revision policy, and the set is now out of date. *The New Caxton Encyclopedia* (London: Caxton) is much more ambitious. The 20 volumes are carefully illustrated, and the material is kept relatively current. The combination of excellent illustrations, meticulously written articles, and well-balanced subject coverage makes this a leading set for any library in or out of Great Britain. Unfortunately, for ready-reference purposes, the index is not all that good and cross-references are generally lacking.

---

[29]"The Reference Books Bulletin" goes beyond the four big American publishers (plus two other general sets) when it comes to recommending encyclopedias outside of the United States. They are more selective on what is reviewed. At any rate the Canadian work "is a recommended purchase for all Canadian libraries" *The Booklist*, April 15, 1989, p. 1444.

CHILDREN'S AND YOUNG ADULTS' ENCYCLOPEDIAS

Compton's Encyclopedia and Fact Index. Chicago: Encyclopedia Britannica, 26 vols. $700.

Merit Students Encyclopedia. New York: Macmillan Educational Corporation, 20 vols. $1400.

World Book Encyclopedia. Chicago: World Book, 22 vols. $559.

The New Book of Knowledge. Danbury, CT: Grolier Incorporated, 21 vols. $750.

Children's Britannica. Chicago: Encyclopedia Britannica, 20 vols. $332.

Among the children's and young adult's encyclopedias, there is one clear favorite. The *World Book* really has no competitors. Still, in terms of excellence of presentation, *Merit Students Encyclopedia* is at least in the race. The problem here is that *Merit* is outrageously expensive—twice as much as *World Book.* Somewhat behind the two are *Compton's* and the *Children's Britannica. The New Book of Knowledge,* written for much younger children, is in a different class.

Not only does the *World Book* stand alone, but it has the advantage of price. At $559 it is a bargain. At about $800 more, the *Merit* is an expensive purchase, but there are special price considerations for schools and libraries which make the price more competitive.

The style of writing in the three is graded, i.e., the articles begin with relatively easy material and definitions and grow progressively more difficult. The coverage usually is brief, with particular emphasis on illustrations and cross-references to related pieces. In terms of reading difficulty the sets may be graded as follows from easy (elementary grades) to more difficult (high school): (1) *New Book of Knowledge;* (2) *Children's Britannica;* (3) *Compton's;* (4) *Merit Students;* (5) *World Book.*

World Book

The triumph of the *World Book* is that it is a planned, careful combination of many elements, not the least of which is a nice balance between timely illustrations and text. The clarity of style and the massive number of excellent illustrations put it so far ahead of the other sets that it really has no competitors. Inevitably, critics rank it highly and librarians regularly repurchase. Its popularity, as noted earlier, makes it the best-selling single set in America.

The twenty-second and last volume contains an excellent index of some 150,000 entries. Because the set has numerous cross-references, the index may not be needed for most students, and rarely for ready-reference work.

The most dramatic aspect of the set is the illustration on each and every page. It has more illustrations than any set, adult's or children's, and the 29,000 plates include 24,000 in color. Illustrations take up over one-third of the total space.

While all children's sets are kept current, the degree of revision varies considerably. *World Book* is by far the best in this respect, particularly in that careful attention is given to current events, and biographical data are updated regularly. In the 1990 set, for example, there are 700 new or completely revised articles. The publisher claims that over 12,000 articles (out of approximately 18,000) have been revised in part or totally.[30]

Weak Points: Few of the sets are likely to win applause for challenging the reader to consider controversial issues. *The World Book,* closely tied to the curriculum of the nation's schools, assiduously avoids appearing to endorse anything which may be controversial. At the same time, it is quite objective in handling national arguments from abortion to the place of religion in education. It often fails to indicate that foreign affairs affect American policy. While often nationalistic, the editors at least attempt to give both sides of an argument. For example, in the 1989 *World Book* the Nicaragua debate is given in admirable detail, although not the slightest attempt is made to establish who is morally right or wrong. Perhaps this is the way it must be when trying to please everyone. Even the article on AIDS is balanced, and draws no conclusions.[31]

The advertising for *World Book* may be faulted for indicating it is for younger children. Actually it is for someone at least 9, but probably closer to 10 or 12 in age, up through high school.

CD-ROM Version. Introduced only a few months after *Compton's* CD-ROM set, *World Book* on CD-ROM is called *The Information Finder.*

---

[30]The revision is a bit unusual, even for *World Book.* But during the year 1987–1988 the company spent over $7 million to revise the set, including the adoption of a new format. According to the publisher these revisions are "the most sweeping and comprehensive in over 25 years."

[31]The topic of AIDS is often employed to monitor the level of reporting of an encyclopedia as well as its editorial position. The *Academic American* has little on the subject, but what it has is more pertinent than that in *The World Book.* Early editions of the *New Book of Knowledge* solved the problem by simply not mentioning AIDS. In subsequent editions the topic is included, but primarily in the dictionary entry at the end of the volume. It is not handled as a primary subject.

When purchased with the printed set, the cost is $795 for both, or $550 for the CD-ROM version alone. It contains all the text and tables of the printed set, but none—and this is a major drawback—of the numerous illustrations. On the plus side, the CD-ROM includes the 140,000 word *World Book Dictionary*. On finding a difficult word in the text a user can push a key and learn the definition.

Searching follows standard patterns by key word and by broad topic. A topic search will often present the viewer with an outline of the material covered. Boolean searches are possible, too. All this is carefully explained in an easy-to-understand tutorial.

In addition to the dictionary feature, the CD-ROM has "Quick Fact Tables." One simply types in a general or specific topic and related tables are shown. For example, an entry for Oregon will give tables demonstrating climate, primary events, places to go, and things to see.

Another great advantage, as with all CD-ROM and online searches, is that one is able to print out the desired material. This particularly is valuable when the search involves bits and pieces from a wide variety of articles.

The cross-references and easy-to-follow linkages between topics make the CD-ROM *World Book* easy to use, and it is valuable for browsing. The drawback, which is sure to be overcome in later editions, is the lack of the one-third of the set which makes up the illustrations.

Merit Students

Merit Students Encyclopedia is one of the more attractive of the sets, and in that respect a challenge to its competitor, *World Book*. The 20,000-plus illustrations are nicely done, well placed, and generally (although not always) current. They take up about one-quarter of the space.

The articles are carefully written and easily within the capabilities of the audience—grades 5 and up. Most of the material is objective, but unlike some of the sets discussed in this chapter, the editors do not shy away from controversial matters. For example, the article on sex education is well done, and the contributors are not afraid to take a stand on Star Wars and the tendency of former President Reagan to avoid direct management decisions.[32]

[32]The reviewers in the "Reference Books Bulletin" take exception to these opinions about Star Wars and Reagan and call for more objective treatment. That may be, but the fact remains that both the man and his strategy for "defense" against war

There are useful bibliographies, i.e., "books for further study" which accompany the longer articles. Many of these are given grade levels.

The index is about the same size as *World Book* (approximately 140,000 entries). Bibliographies and recommended reading lists are generally current and appear often following the longer articles.

Weak Points: Although good in terms of revision of items in the news and the curriculum, the set is weak in continuous revision of background pieces. Unfortunately, this lack appears most often in the dated articles most likely to be used to support the curriculum and interests of young people, e.g., many athletes are not covered, and one searches in vain for current data on the environment.

While the black-and-white and color illustrations are a strong point, some are dated items, and certain color plates are in need of clarity and definition.

The publisher, who also issues *Collier's*, has chosen to price the set at over $800 more than the *World Book*. (The cost is about the same for libraries.) This is quite enough to deter purchase by laypersons.

Compton's

Compton's is unique for its "Fact Index" in each volume, with a cumulative fact index, in the final volume, to the whole set. The features serve both as an index to each volume and as a source of ready-reference data for basic queries. There, also, are useful "reading guides" which are edited to suit current curriculum-oriented subjects and give the young reader related materials to consider.

The writing style is passable, and while far from sparkling, it is clear enough. The articles are generally short, although major topics may cover several pages. Controversial topics are handled, but gingerly. There are some 15,000 illustrations of which about one-third are in color.

The set had been much dated, but beginning in the late 1980s a general revision policy was undertaken to bring it up to date. For the 1990 edition, for example, more than 23 percent of the articles were revised. This revision is evident in new illustrations and maps too.

The set is extremely well organized for easy use. Among en-

were *highly* controversial, and this should be indicated. Which seems only to prove the editors of the encyclopedias simply cannot please everyone. ("Reference Books Bulletin," *The Booklist*, Oct. 15, 1988, p. 380).

cyclopedias it is one of the easiest to use, particularly for the audience of upper elementary grade students and high school students. It can also be recommended for general family use.

Weak Points: The often-repeated criticism that the set is dated needs to be reconsidered.[33] While some material remains dated such as lack of current names in many of the numerous sports articles, the set is much improved over earlier editions. See, for example, the revised article on the Union of Soviet Socialist Republics.

Sensitive subjects are overlooked often or simply skated over. The reader may have no idea the topic is controversial. The article on abortion includes only a few words on why someone is for or against abortion. The drug articles are somewhat better, but tend to avoid the arguments on how to solve the problem.

One can recommend the set for most children, although there is little reason for it to win out over *World Book.* The excellent and numerous illustrations make it a good buy for some, but only as a second set in the library.

CD-ROM Version: In 1989 Compton's (i.e., the *Britannica*) introduced the *Compton's MultiMedia Encyclopedia* which is the printed work on CD-ROM. A breakthrough was the inclusion, for the first time in an encyclopedia in this format, of all the illustrations, including those in color. It also contains a 60-minute token amount of sound.

In addition, the disk features the 65,000 word *Merriam-Webster Intermediate Dictionary.* Given this, the user may click on a word from the set for a handy definition. There is an audio glossary with 1500 words which are pronounced and accompanied by a simple definition.

Using a mouse, the viewer can look at a map of the entire world and then move in on a particular country or region, i.e., the area can be enlarged according to the user's command. A menu around the map indicates the related topics which the person at the computer can then call up to view. This includes articles, parts of articles and all 15,000 illustrations, including 45 brief animated sequences showing, for example, how bones are joined and how they move. Elementary perhaps, but impressive to children.

There are numerous ways to look for other types of informa-

---

[33]The publisher reports an extensive revision of the set, but this may not be completed before the early 1990s. The 1989 set did reflect the new revision policy. See "Reference Books Bulletin," *The Booklist,* July 1989, pp. 1875–1878; and Oct. 15, 1989, p. 482.

tion from a capability for scanning the 5000 titles and subjects used in the set to searching for basic ideas. For example, with a click of the mouse at a point on the atlas, an appropriate article will appear. See a good picture? Call up an accompanying article. Related names, places, and events from more than one article may also be obtained in a printout. The search pattern, using the mouse, is quite simple, although just as slow as searches using other methods. Still, for a young audience it is a remarkably easy and effective search method.

The "idea search" allows the user to type in a key word (or words). The screen then shows a list of articles which have the key words. To cut it down to size, the major articles with the key words are starred. Other features include: (1) A title finder which allows the user to scroll through and choose an article. (2) A topic tree breaks down all the articles under 19 broad classifications and into subtopics. One may then broaden or narrow the search by selecting one of the topics. (3) The picture explorer allows one to type in a broad description of what is wanted, and up comes the picture(s). (4) A note system allows one to type in notes and then, or later, to have them printed.

The disk is priced at $795, while the printed set is $700. Whether this will prove profitable for the publisher to move into other CD-ROM encyclopedias remains to be seen. The initial project proved more expensive than first thought, e.g., it took 60 people working full time for 18 months to input and format the data.

One great advantage to users is that the material will be updated annually on the disk, a feature which may overcome one of the basic weak points of the printed set.

New Book of Knowledge

Originally little more than a collection of stories and activities for young people, the *New Book of Knowledge* is now a full-fledged child's encyclopedia. It is written specifically for elementary school children (i.e., grades 3 to 6), and for that audience is by far the easiest of the group to read and understand.

Each volume is in two distinct parts. There are the regular articles and then, at the end of each volume, a "Dictionary Index." This is more than an index in that it contains short entries, and is a good place to check for current biographies and recent events. (With each revision certain items here are dropped, or moved into the main part of the volume).

There are some 23,000 illustrations, most of which are suitable for the audience and are good to excellent.

Within many of the longer articles are charts, graphs, and summaries, such as "quick-reference" materials. These are so numerous as to fairly well include all the material in the text. There are also numerous ready-reference questions with answers in the text.

In addition to the regular indexes at the end of each volume, there is a serviceable index in the final volume of the set. Bibliographies are in a separate paperbound, more for the use of parents and teachers than for children.

The articles are well written, and, in fact, the writing style is better than that found in many of the pieces in *Merit* and *Compton's*. An effort is made to make everything clear, and most of the articles are short with precise definitions and explanations, usually punctuated with illustrations. There are many summary boxes of information. Coverage is quite even and the material is regularly updated.

The Reference Book Bulletin concludes a highly favorable review (*Book List*, March 15, 1988, p. 1228) with the comment that this is "a reliable, accurate, up-to-date encyclopedia. . . . At present *World Book* is the only competing set for this elementary age group."

Weak Points: Considering the age group for which this is designed, and the careful attention to their interests, there is little to fault. It is *not* appropriate, though, as some have suggested for older children with reading problems. While it may be used for teenagers who have reading problems, they may be offended because the level is so obviously geared to younger children.

There is a decided emphasis on such things as the Cabbage Patch doll. In addition the coverage of countries other than the United States is rather simplistic.

Children's Britannica

The new *Children's Britannica* is really (1) a revised version of the quite miserable *Britannica Junior* and (2) a revision of the set now published in England. It is a rival for approximately the same audience as the *New Book of Knowledge*, i.e., ages 7 to 12, and as such the two can be compared; the audiences for the other works are older.

Actually, it is not a real challenge to the *New Book of Knowledge*. While basically sound and relatively accurate, it is drab and lacks the flair of the other set.

According to the publisher, the *Children's Britannica* has some 4000 articles covering about 4000 topics. (Comparatively, its 3 million words are about one-half the number in the aforementioned

New Book of Knowledge). There is a much-improved index volume which includes 5700 brief dictionary entries on topics which are not in the earlier 19 volumes. Thus the index often can serve as a ready-reference aid.

Most of the 6000-plus illustrations and maps are current and in color. An atlas of some 150 pages concludes the nineteenth volume. The only strength of the set is in the illustrations, but they are considerably fewer than the 23,000 in *The New Book of Knowledge*. The print is large and clear and the set is quite easy to read.

Weak Points: The primary weakness, as in the earlier *Britannica Junior,* is the drab appearance. Other weak points: (1) The writing style is generally clear, but many of the sentences and paragraphs are a bit long for the average American child. (2) There is more emphasis on European and British items than may be appropriate for a U.S. audience, primarily because of its base. (Several U.S. presidents have only short entries in the index volume.) (3) There are no bibliographies. (4) Controversial topics are glossed over or ignored. (5) Many of the background articles are dated, and there is a decided lack of attention to current events.[34]

Other Sets

World Book publishes another 15-volume set, *Childcraft,* for preschool children which is really a luxury for both parents and a library. Perfectly suitable, and extremely well illustrated and cleverly laid out, the 750,000 words and 4600 illustrations cost $170. Many volumes give pronunciation for new words and sentences to show how the words are used properly. Articles are arranged by topic, but each volume has its own index, with a general index in the last volume.

The topic arrangement by science, children's literature, social studies, etc., is reminiscent of a shelf in the library trying to appeal to all interests of young readers. Is it really an encyclopedia or a collection of nicely presented fiction, nonfiction, and activities? The latter is the real answer and as such it is of more real value to families than to libraries.

Even more expensive, and of considerably less value for the money is *Compton's Precyclopedia.* This sells for about $250 and offers preschoolers stories, riddles, and television type fare that no self-respecting librarian or parent would give a child. It is virtually worth-

---

[34]An unorthodox review by children and teachers of the new set will be found in the British *New Library World,* Sept. 1988, pp. 165–168. Particularly informative are the comments by children about ease of use of the set.

less as both an encyclopedia and a good reading set. A slightly different verion of this is sold for about $100 less by the *Britannica,* the parent of *Compton's Precyclopedia,* as the *Young Children's Encyclopedia.* Avoid. It is even worse than its companion, in that the material is dated and far from accurate. Further, it is loaded with stereotypes.

A relatively inexpensive set ($253), the *Young Students Learning Library* (Middletown, Conn.: Weekly Reader Books) is a useful work for elementary school children. It offers some 3000 articles in easy-to-read form from 250 to 700 words each. There is great emphasis on geography and on good illustrations. A separate atlas and a separate dictionary are included in the last 2 of the 24-volume set. While this hardly replaces larger sets, it is a useful addition for libraries.

Note: This same set is published by Grolier at $235 for schools, under the name of *The New Grolier Student Encyclopedia.* From 1972 to 1988 they were two different sets. Today they are one and the same except in name.

The Junior Encyclopedia of Canada (Edmonton: Hurtig Publishers Ltd., 1990. $160) is a five-volume set that focuses primarily on the history, personalities, resources, etc. of Canada. In this respect it covers material not available in such depth elsewhere. The same publisher's *Canadian Encyclopedia* of 1985 is the source of much of the material that is updated and rewritten for a younger audience. The children's version includes over 4000 articles, 3000 illustrations, and a marvelous layout, which makes the set extremely attractive. At only $160 it is a best buy for Canadians but, because of its focus, of lesser value to those living outside Canada.

ENCYCLOPEDIA SUPPLEMENTS: YEARBOOKS

There are two basic purposes of the encyclopedia yearbooks.[35] They are published annually to (1) keep the basic set up to date and (2) present a summary of the year's major events. A third, less obvious, purpose is to increase sales: It is comforting for the buyer to hear that the set will never be outdated (a questionable assumption, but the claim is used by almost every encyclopedia salesperson).

The yearbooks are usually available only to purchasers of the

---

[35]There are numerous versions and twists. For example, by the early 1990s Britannica was publishing not only a standard yearbook, but a *Yearbook of Science and the Future, Medical and Health Annual* and *World Data Annual* (filled with useful statistics which is now part of the *Britannica Book of the Year.*) The yearbook is a vital complement to the set, as it is the first place to turn for relatively current statistics and data on news events of the previous year.

initial sets. They are all attractively printed, and feature numerous illustrations.

These supplements are not related to the complete set except by name. The arrangements are broad, with emphasis on large, current topics. Most of the material is not later incorporated into the revised basic sets—a positive and negative consideration. On the positive side, a run of the yearbooks does afford a fairly comprehensive view of the year's events.

The *Britannica World Data* yearbook devotes about 450 to 500 pages to "The Year in Review." Here the data are arranged by subject from agriculture to world affairs. Subsections include biographies, obituaries, and special features such as the presidential election. These are followed by 250 to 300 pages of world data—a useful comparison of language, religion, health services, and the like among major nations. There are 200 or so pages given over to standard national information, country by country. This does little more than duplicate what is found in basic guides such as the *Statesman's Yearbook*.

On the negative side, is the fact that the revised complete set cannot be depended upon to contain the same material, or at any rate, not in such depth. Consequently, someone looking for more than basic facts on a given topic really should search not only the main encyclopedia, but a number of the yearbooks also. The library is therefore well advised to keep a complete run of the yearbooks.

Aside from the age of the audience for which each is prepared, significant differences between the various yearbooks are difficult to discover. In this respect, they resemble the daily newspaper. One reader may prefer the slant or emphasis of one newspaper over another, but both papers are drawing from the same general materials. The analogy is not as far-fetched as it may seem. In the annuals particularly, the predominantly newspaper-trained staffs of the larger encyclopedia firms have free reign. Format, content, and the ever-important emphasis on up-to-date, often exciting events reflect more than scholars behind the final book; they reveal an emphasis on what makes the daily newspaper sell, at least from the standpoint of the ex-newspaper writer.

If more than a single adults' and children's yearbook is to be purchased, the nod will go to the work preferred by the librarian and the patrons of the library. As long as the preference is within the standards set for encyclopedias, it is a matter more of taste than of objective judgment, and any one of the accepted publishers will serve as well as another.

ONE-VOLUME ENCYCLOPEDIAS[36]

The Concise Columbia Encyclopedia, 2d ed. New York: Columbia University Press, 1989, 944 pp. $39.95.

The Random House Encyclopedia. 3rd ed. New York: Random House, 1990, 3000 pp. $129.95. (*Note:* frequently discounted to under $100.)

The Cambridge Encyclopedia. New York: Cambridge University Press, 1990, 1488 pp. $49.50.

For home use, the one-volume works are economical and, compared with multivolume sets in the same general price range, a better buy. The information is exact, well presented, and more reliable than that in the similarly priced "supermarket" sets. Where cost is a factor, the librarian should always inform the prospective purchaser of these one-volume works, encouraging a personal comparison of reviews or of the encyclopedias themselves.

The revised edition of *The Concise Columbia Encyclopedia* claims to be "the best desk encyclopedia." Few would argue. It has over 1 million words, or about one-ninth of what is in the 21-volume *Academic American Encyclopedia.* The arrangement is alphabetical, and there are approximately 15,000 entries which cover the same topics as the multiple-volume works, but in less detail. The revised edition represents a 33 percent update of the material from the original 1983 work. Also, numerous new entries have been added. There are a few charts and tables, and a scattering of line drawings, as well as a center section of full-color Rand McNally maps. Illustration, however, is not this work's strong point. It is best for quick, accurate answers to equally straightforward ready-reference questions. The result is a truly up-to-date, current one-volume encyclopedia for home and for library.

The *Columbia* is also available in a $300 computer format from Franklin Electronic Publishers Inc. The package is about the size of a paperback. One types in key words on the miniature keyboard. A screen, equally small, shows the necessary text. One may search for key words and names among all the encyclopedia entries. The ad-

---

[36]Another excellent one-volume work which is out of print, but still found in many libraries is the *The Random House Encyclopedia* (rev. ed., New York: Random House, 1983, 2, 918 pp., $100). It contains more than 3 million words and 14,000 illustrations. It is presented in two parts: The first is ready-reference material; the second (with most of the colored illustrations) treats topics under themes such as "Man and Machines."

vantage may be there, but does the cost justify it all, i.e., only $40 for the printed version, $300 for the computer?

Transforming reference books into small computers promises to be a large business. Some estimate that revenue will be well over $200 million for publishers. Dictionaries are available in this format, but computerized quotation books, medical references, recipes, etc., are just around the next electronic bit. The high tech may be grand for individuals, but is of little real value in libraries where standard CD-ROM, online, etc., are much superior.

The best of the group is *The New Columbia Encyclopedia*, which is now much out-of-date, but a new edition is promised shortly. If this follows the pattern of the previous four editions, it will have over 6 million words and compare favorably in coverage to many more expensive multiple-volume sets. The quality is about as high as one can expect. The fourth edition was published in 1975 and became an immediate hit with laypersons and librarians alike.

The Random House Encyclopedia also has a distinguished history, although with 3 million words it is only about one-half the size of *The New Columbia*. The strength is in the 13,500 illustrations, the full atlas, and the combination of essay length and short factual articles.

As with the previous two editions, it can be purchased in two volumes, or in one. (The one-volume edition is somewhat less expensive than the two-volume). The first volume is called the "Alphapedia" and has short, useful entries. This is the most updated part of the new edition and may be of value for ready reference queries concerning recent news events and personalities. (I say "may" because most of the data are just as readily available, at less cost, in standard works from the *World Almanac* to a basic encyclopedia yearbook.)

The second volume (the "Colorpedia") is where one finds the majority of illustrations, usually in technicolor, and longer topical essays on everything from the nature of things to world history. It is a visual delight and of some interest to younger readers and adults who enjoy *The National Geographic.*

All and all it is a delightful set, and of some value for the home. Libraries probably will not purchase it as much because of the questionable organization as for the availability of similar data in other encyclopedias already in their library.

Another one-volume work is being prepared by Simon and Schuster, the *Prentice Hall American Encyclopedia.* This is to be published in late 1991 and is based on the English Hutchinson work (no. 2 discussed below).

There are several British one-volume encyclopedias. The best are: (1) *Pears Cyclopaedia* (London: Pelham Books, 1987 to date, annual, $18). This is a venerable work which is as much a part of many British homes as the *Britannica*, if not more so. With over 1500 pages and some 1.3 million words, it is a best buy in anyone's country. While Americans will see it as a type of expanded world almanac, it has enough encyclopedia features, as well as cross-references and an index, to qualify as an encyclopedia. Most of the focus in on England and Europe with long sections on general information, prominent people, political compendium, etc. (2) *Hutchinson Encyclopedia* (London: David & Charles, 1976 to date, irregular). This compares favorably with Pears, but is not as old and is not as well developed. At the same time it offers short, well-written pieces of a general nature on everything from world politics to painters and medicine. The work is particularly strong on the sciences and technology.

Of all British one-volume works, the best for the American public is *The Cambridge Encyclopedia.* The British university publisher issues a number of subject works (from *The Cambridge Encyclopedia of Africa* to *The Cambridge Encyclopedia of Language*). Drawing upon these as well as original work, the volume offers over 30,000 main entries, or almost double those in *The Concise Columbia.* A 130-page supplement at the end of the volume, printed on yellow paper, features statistical data on everything from baseball to politics. Unfortunately, this is not closely tied to the data in the main work. There is a color section with maps and a number of scientific illustrations. In fact, the numerous pictures set this off as a most useful work for younger people 'as well as adults. It is arranged logically with 75,000 cross-references.

A minor difficulty with the *Cambridge* and the other English works is the close tie to British terminology and culture. Sometimes the British spellings are different. More disturbing is the inclusion of data on such things as how to address a member of the House of Lords but nothing on how to address a member of the United States Congress.

FOREIGN-PUBLISHED MULTIVOLUME ENCYCLOPEDIAS[37]

For Americans, most reference questions can be quickly and properly answered by an American encyclopedia, but there are occasions when a foreign language work is more suitable. Obviously, a foreign

[37]Ken Kister, "Foreign Language Encyclopedias," in his *Best Encyclopedias* (Phoenix, AZ: Oryx Press, 1986) pp. 306–311. Here one finds the basic sets arranged by country and language with brief annotations. Kister is one of the few critics who focuses

encyclopedia will cover its country of origin in much greater depth than an American work, including biographies of nationals, statistics, places, and events.

Even for users with the most elementary knowledge of the language, several of the foreign works are useful for their fine illustrations and maps. For example, the *Enciclopedia Italiana* boasts some of the best illustrations of any encyclopedia, particularly in the area of the fine arts. A foreign encyclopedia is equally useful for point of view: Some American readers may be surprised at the manner in which the Civil War, for example, is treated in the French and the German encyclopedias. Further, the evaluation of American writers and national heroes in these works is sometimes equally revealing about the way Europeans judge the United States. More specifically, the foreign encyclopedia is helpful for information on less-well-known figures not found in American or British works, for foreign language bibliographies, for detailed maps of cities and regions, and for other information ranging from plots of lesser-known novels and musicals to identification of place names.

In Europe, as in America, there are only two or three major publishers (including, incidentally the *Encyclopaedia Britannica* which has arrangements for copublishing with the firms). The giants include: (1) Brockhaus and Herder in Germany; (2) Larousse in France; and (3) Garzanti in Italy. When the librarian finds one of these names on a new or revised set, the odds are about 99 to one that the work will be of high quality.

French

> *Grand Dictionnaire Encyclopédique* Larousse. Paris: Larousse, 1982–1989, 10 vols. $1250. (Distributed in the United States by French European.)

The name Larousse is as familiar in France as the *Encyclopaedia Britannica* is in the United States. Pierre Larousse was the founder of a publishing house which continues to flourish and is responsible for the basic French encyclopedias. In fact, *Larousse* in France is often used as a synonym for *encyclopedia.*

Larousse continues with the policy of short specific entries, but it does give some rather extensive treatment of major subjects. For example, the length of articles for countries and leading personal-

on foreign language, general sets. See also the encyclopedia articles in any of the general American sets. Normally they close with brief descriptions of major European works.

ities often equals that found in American works. Returning to an older concept of encyclopedias, the *Grand Dictionnaire* is precisely what the title suggests in that it not only includes specific encyclopedia entries, but definitions of words as well. There is a strong emphasis on brilliant illustrations, usually in full color. Each page includes photographs, charts, maps, diagrams and the like. Regardless of one's command of French, everyone will enjoy the illustrations.

Another major set is often found in American libraries: *Encyclopaedia Universalis* (2d ed., available in the United States from Encyclopaedia Britannica, 1968–75, 1986, 20 vols. $1850). This work is in the fashion of the *Macropaedia*, in that the articles are long, detailed, and scholarly and are extremely well illustrated. The 17 to 18 volumes are a type of ready-reference work with brief entries. The final two volumes serve as a *Propaedia* and index.

German

> *Brockhaus Enzyklopadie*, rev. 19th ed. Wiesbaden: Brockhaus, 1986, 24 vols., $4000. Plus irregular supplements.

First issued as *Frauenzimmer Lexikon* (between 1796 and 1808), an encyclopedia primarily for women, *Brockhaus* got off to a bad start. The original publisher, possibly because of his limited sales, gave up the financial ghost; in 1808, Friedrich Brockhaus purchased the set and issued the last volume. A wise man, Brockhaus continued to offer his volumes not as scholarly works, but as books guaranteed to give the average man (or woman) a solid education. By doing so, he was years ahead of the times, in fact, so far ahead of his American and British counterparts was he that they freely borrowed his text, if not his sales techniques. As noted earlier, the Brockhaus works were the basis for the early *Americana* and *Chambers's*.

Brockhaus extended his popular formula to cutting back articles to little more than dictionary length, and followed the European form of specific entry. Consequently, all the Brockhaus encyclopedias—and there is a family of them—are an admixture of dictionary and encyclopedia. (The family includes the basic 24-volume set, the revised 12-volume set, and a 1-volume work, among others.)

As might be expected, the longer articles, some of them over 100 pages, focus on European countries. In many respects, the *Brockhaus* encyclopedia is considerably more nationalistic than the *Larousse*; and while it is an excellent source of material on German history and personalities, it can be passed up for other items.

Because of its scope, the *Brockhaus* is useful in large research libraries or where there is a German-speaking populace, but it is probably near the bottom among choices of all the foreign language encyclopedias, if for no other reason than the outrageous price of $4000, plus the cost of supplements.

Italy

Enciclopedia Europea. Milan: Garzanti, 1976–1981. Price varies.

This is the most modern of the Italian sets, and is updated from time to time. It is important for three reasons: (1) It has brief, specific entries which afford a marvelous overview of Italian and European history, culture, and science. (2) There are companion longer articles of considerable substance, particularly in terms of coverage of the sciences and social sciences. (3) There are excellent illustrations.

One of the major European records of the arts is the famous *Enciclopedia Italiana* (Rome: Istituto della Enciclopedia Italiana, 1929–36, 35 vols., plus supplements 1958 to date. Price varies). The basic pre-World War II set is found in almost all large libraries because of its superb illustrations and its scholarly and well-documented articles. Although the articles on the government are far from impartial, the general coverage is excellent and the set is one of the best prewar works to come out of Europe.

Japanese

Kodansha Encyclopedia of Japan. New York: Kodansha International, 1983, 9 vols. and supplments. $720.

This is an unusual and superior encyclopedia which analyzes, explains, and even critically assesses Japan, past and present. After 12 years of planning, and an estimated $15 million expenditure, the all English-Japanese encyclopedia represents the work of 1300 scholars from 27 countries, including Japan and the United States. The text was written with the average layperson in mind, although much of the material will interest the subject specialist. The style is much above average. There are about 10,000 entries and 4 million words. The largest single category of entries concerns Japanese history, followed by geography and art. There are slightly over 1000 articles covering Japanese economics and business. The articles are quite objective, and considerable effort was made to ensure that nothing about Japan's past was glossed over or ignored.

While the illustrations are not as numerous as those found in many encyclopedias, they are at least representative of the subject matter. Unfortunately, they are all in black and white. The final volume is the exhaustive index. The 64-page supplement has only 254 entries in 64 pages, but does cover vital happenings in Japan since the initial set was published.

Russian

> *The Great Soviet Encyclopedia,* 3d ed. New York: Macmillan 1973–1983, 32 vols. $1900. (Published in Russia from 1970–1980 as *Bol'shaia Sovetskaia Entisklopediia,* or *BSE.*)

The *BSE* is the basic encyclopedia for the Soviet schools and for families, being somewhat equivalent in scholarship to the older version of the *Britannica.* The entire set has more than 21 million words and over 100,000 articles. Including both the specific-entry and the broad-entry forms, the set is a combination of routine dictionary and gazetteer items, with detailed, lengthy articles covering every aspect of Soviet interest.

Since most American readers will use the English translation, two points are worth making: (1) The index is necessary because of the unusual alphabetical arrangement of each volume, caused by differences between the Russian and Latin alphabets. For example, the first translated volume "A to Z" contains entries for "Aalen Stage" and the "Zulu War of 1879." (2) The quality of the translation is good. The American version differs from the Russian in that cost considerations made it necessary to delete the fine maps in the original Russian version.

Spanish

> *Enciclopedia universal ilustrada Europeo-Americana (Espasa).* Barcelona: Espasa, 1907 to 1933, 108 vols., including annual supplements, 1934 to date. (Distributed in the United States by French and European, $7500.)

Usually cited simply as *Espasa,* the *Enciclopedia* is a remarkable work. First, it never seems to end. Forgoing continuous revision or new editions, the publishers continue to augment the 80 volumes (actually 70 basic volumes with 10 appendixes) with annual supplements which are arranged in large subject categories and include an index. (The term *annual* must be taken advisedly, as the supplements generally are not issued until three to five years after the period covered. For example, the 1981–1982 volume came out in 1985.)

Second, *Espasa* has the largest number of entries—the publishers claim over 1 million. Since they evidently do not count on "authority," none of the articles is signed, although they are signed in the supplements after 1953. Again, as in the German and French encyclopedias, the emphasis is on short entries of the dictionary type. Still, there are a number of rather long articles, particularly those dealing with Spain, Latin America, and prominent writers, etc.

Third, and less noteworthy, it is the highest priced of all the general encyclopedias. Still, considering that it is over 100 volumes, even $7500 is reasonable, i.e., the cost of a single volume is under $75.

One problem, as with most European encyclopedias, is the alphabetical arrangement. Any student who has had a brush with a foreign language realizes that although the Latin alphabet is employed, there are variations in letters; Spanish, for example, has two letters not found in English, "ch" and "ll." There are also marked differences in common names. In other languages, *John* turns up as Giovanni, Jan, Juan, Johannes, or Jehan. Consequently, before abandoning a foreign encyclopedia for lack of an entry, the user should be certain to look for the entry in terms of the language employed.

SUBJECT ENCYCLOPEDIAS

Now that the general encyclopedia seems to be on the decline, the subject work is gaining added favor with both librarians and individual buyers. It is part of a media trend which has resulted in the increased development of specialized periodicals, recordings, and even radio and television programs for narrow segments of the population. The reasoning of publishers and producers is that it is no longer possible or profitable to reach out to everyone. The best approach is to prepare a work for a select group, normally a group with both a high interest in the subject and a medium-to-high income to purchase the book.

Publishers of subject encyclopedias follow the special-audience philosophy. The result generally is encouraging for reference librarians, particularly when (1) a ready-reference question is so specialized or esoteric that it cannot be answered in a general encyclopedia, or (2) a user needs a more detailed overview of a subject than that found in a single article in a general encyclopedia. The more limited the library budget for both reference work and general titles, the more reason to turn to subject encyclopedias. The librarian may have a limited amount of material on, for example, modern China, but many questions can be readily answered with the one-volume *Encyclopedia of China Today* (3d ed. New York: Harper and Row, 1984).

Few months go by that another subject encyclopedia is not published, announced to be in preparation, or revised. Topics cover every conceivable interest.

Today, one may find a one-volume or multiple-volume set in areas from archaeology to zoology. Less traditional subjects are considered, too; e.g., the University of North Carolina Press in 1989 published a one-volume *Encyclopedia of Southern Culture*. It covers "every aspect of a region's life and thought, the impact of its history and politics, its music and literature, its manners and myths, even the iced tea that washes down its catfish and corn bread."[38] While the one-volume subject encyclopedia is favored, there are numerous multivolume sets, too, often costing over $2000. Some of these are considered in this section.

Both the American Library Association and *Library Journal* select the best reference books of each year. Other than those discussed in these pages, they have named *The Encyclopedia of Special Education*, *The International Encyclopedia of Astronomy*, *The RHS Encyclopedia of House Plants*, and *The Encyclopedia of the American Judicial System* to list only a few. There are hundreds of 1- to 20-volume subject sets published by as many publishers each and every year.

Encyclopedias and Handbooks

Such key descriptors as "companion," "handbook," or "dictionary" may indicate a subject one- to three-volume encyclopedia. For example, Oxford University Press is known for its companion series such as *The Oxford Companion to American Literature* and, in a narrower field, *The Oxford Companion to Chess*. There are dozens of these reputable works edited by well-known experts. Inevitably they are alphabetically arranged by subject. The price may range from $30 to $75. The number of entries can be from 2000 to 6000.

One may argue that these are not encyclopedias, but another form of information package. No matter, the point is that the arrangement, scope, and audience for each is such that it fits the

---

[38]"The South from Alligator to Zydeco," *U.S. News and World Report*, Oct. 3, 1988, p. 57. (Publication of this work, slated for 1986, was delayed three years.)

encyclopedia pattern. More important, they often serve as reference sources for quick, often in-depth answers to common questions.[39]

Evaluation

Use the same evaluative techniques for general sets as those used for subject encyclopedias. Even with limited knowledge of the field covered, librarians may judge the set for themselves, although using reviews or subject experts for evaluation of the expensive works may be more likely. Subject sets are evaluated in scholarly periodicals, which discuss them at greater length than standard reviews do.

Once the librarian determines that the encyclopedia is good, he must ask which and how many readers will use the work. The subject encyclopedias will fill gaps in the collection of art, science, or more esoteric subjects. For this reason, a subject encyclopedia is often a better buy for small-and medium-size libraries than multiple sets of general encyclopedias.

CD-ROM, along with pictures and sound, will play an important part in subject encyclopedias in the coming decade. This will be true particularly for more popular works. One example: *Audubon Birds of America* (New York: CMC Research Inc., 1990). This is the 1840 six-volume set with all the full color lithographs and full text. In addition, there are bird calls for 150 of the 500 birds. This is a modest $99. A more traditional encyclopedia is issued by the National Geographic for under $100. Directed to children, it features mammals—an electronic version of the 1980 two-volume set. On CD-ROM one finds not only text, but photographs, motion, and sound. National Geographic plans to develop a complete line of such subject works.

Examples

Space does not permit a full discussion of the numerous, many quite superior, subject encyclopedias. The focus here is on works which are best known and likely to be found in many medium-to-large libraries. Most, although not all, have been published relatively recently. This rather arbitrary approach gives at least a cursory glance at the direction of subject-encyclopedia publishing.

[39]There is a thin line between the subject, or specialized, encyclopedia and the traditional handbook. The *handbook,* as discussed in a later section, is a collection of a miscellaneous group of facts centered on one central theme or subject area, e.g., *Handbook of Physics* and *Handbook of Insurance.* An encyclopedia tends to be more discursive.

Art and Architecture

Encyclopedia of Architecture: Design, Engineering & Construction. New York, John Wiley & Sons, 1988–1990 5 vols. $950.

Encyclopedia of World Art. New York: McGraw-Hill Book Company, 1959–1968, 15 vols. $1500. Two supplements, 1983, 1987. $100 each.

Sponsored by the American Institute of Architects, the five-volume work in their area is much wider in scope than either the backer or the title suggests. Yes, primary architectural subjects and figures are covered in detail. But in addition, the compilers consider related matters which give the set a much broader use, e.g., the role of behavior on architectural planning, problems of pollution, and planning areas for development or nondevelopment. There are more than 3000 illustrations and tables which are well-placed, and a detailed index. As the Reference Books Bulletin put it after the first volume was published, "This is an incomparable reference work. . . . Its coverage of construction technology makes the work valuable both in art and architecture."[40]

The *Encyclopedia of World Art* is the finest set available among encyclopedias devoted entirely to art. It includes art of all periods and has exhaustive studies of art forms, history, artists, and allied subject interests. Arranged alphabetically, it contains many shorter articles which answer almost every conceivable question in the field. The fifteenth volume is a detailed index.

An outstanding feature is the illustrations. At the end of each volume, there are 400 to 600 black-and-white and color reproductions. They, as well as some color plates in the main volumes, are nicely tied to the articles by suitable cross-references and identification numbers and letters.

The supplements are chronologically arranged. They trace new findings in art from prehistory to the present. Extensive bibliographies end each chapter. There is a subject, artist, and title index. Each volume ends with color and black-and-white reproductions.

Economics and Business

The New Palgrave: A Dictionary of Economics. New York: Macmillan Educational Company, 1988. 4 vols. $650.

When is a dictionary an encyclopedia in disguise? Often. An

[40]"Reference Books Bulletin," *The Booklist,* Oct. 1, 1988, p. 223.

excellent example is *The New Palgrave: A Dictionary of Economics.* Actually, the title comes, as it usually does, from the fact that the material is in alphabetical order and some entries are quite brief, although just as many are essay length. As one reviewer put it:

> More an encyclopedia than a dictionary, this work ... attempts to present the state of the art. It not only defines points and concepts, but also gives their origin and their historical development—how they emerged from philosophies and ideologies as well as from techniques. It also profiles 655 people who have shaped the discipline.[41]

The name is derived from Inglis Palgrave's classic *Dictionary of Political Economy,* which was published almost 80 years ago. Actually a few of the essays in the original work (about 45) are revised and appear in the new edition. The value of the work, though, is the close to 2000 entries which represent the best thinking of 900 experts in universities and think-tanks around the world. The publisher points out that 12 of the contributors have won the Nobel Prize in economics.

All areas of the subject are covered, and the entries range from a few paragraphs to 30 pages for "International Trade." Written by experts, most of the material has been carefully edited to be within the grasp of the educated layperson. But not all, and some of the articles require a thorough knowledge of economics jargon as well as a grounding in statistics and mathematics.

There are over 600 biographies, but, as is the rule in works of this type, all of their subjects are dead and hardly in a position to make comment.

The final volume is an excellent subject index.

History

Civilizations of the Ancient Mediterranean: Greece and Rome. New York: Charles Scribner's Sons, 1988, 3 vols., $225.

Dictionary of the Middle Ages. New York: Charles Scribner's Sons, 1983–1990. 13 vols., $950.

Greece and Rome occupy considerable space in any multiple-volume general encyclopedia, but neither is treated in the depth

---

[41]"Economics in 4 Million Words," *The New York Times,* Jan. 17, 1988, p. 4F. Here follows an interview with the compiler of the work, John Eatwell, whose name somehow fits the subject nicely. For a memorable review of the set, see Robert Solow's evaluative description in *The New York Times Book Review,* March 20, 1988, p. 3. Solow is a Nobel Prize winner in economics.

desirable for either the expert, or the would-be expert, who needs to know, for example, how women fared in one or both of the societies during a certain time frame. It is for that type of query that one turns to a subject set such as this, or the numerous other works in the field as the excellent one-volume *Oxford History of the Classical World* (New York: Oxford University Press, 1988).

The three-volume Scribner work covers the sciences, social sciences, and of course the humanities in the two civilizations, but taking a somewhat different approach. Rather than a chronological system, there are 95 individual essays by as many experts. Organized under broad subject headings, each article considers the topic in some depth. Illustrations accompany some of the pieces, and there is a detailed index in the final volume.

History attracts many publishers, but as indicated, the leader in historical sets is Scribner's. For example, between 1983 and 1990 they published the first edition of the *Dictionary of the Middle Ages*. The 13-volume work (including a detailed index) moves from A.D. 500 through to the end of the period in A.D. 1500. There are over 5000 articles by some of the world's leading historians in this area.

One fascinating point about the coverage is the emphasis on daily life of average people. One moves from the monastery to the farm, not just from the castle to the king. In addition, there are biographical pieces on both famous and minor figures. There are some black-and-white and a few color illustrations, but the strength of the set is the text, not the illustrations. The articles are by 1300 scholars from some 30 countries. It can be read as well as used for a reference work—an almost ideal situation.

Library Science

> *The ALA Yearbook of Library and Information Services*. Chicago: American Library Association, 1975 to date, annual. Price varies.

> *Encyclopedia of Library and Information Science*. New York: Marcel Dekker, 1968 to date, 36 vols., plus supplements. $85 each.

The ALA Yearbook is an indexed, close to 300-page double-columned overview of the past year's events. Articles, which vary in length from one column to many pages, are written by experts. After a series of special reports, including biographies and awards, the articles move from abstracting and indexing services to young adults and various state reports. Although this is an annual, not an encyclopedia per se, it serves as such in that it is an informal update to the *ALA World Encyclopedia of Library and Information Services* (Chicago: American Library Association, 2d ed., 1986, 802 pp.). This latter work remains a valuable overview, particularly in terms of fundamental principles and historical and biographical material.

Even though it is controversial for the reasons given here, the *Encyclopedia of Library and Information Science* cannot be faulted for its wide coverage and its ambitious effort. Some think there is too much material; others, that areas are not always covered as well as they might be, particularly by the contributors involved. The set is quite uneven. Some of the writing is excellent, but too much of it tends to be superficial and dated. The supplements, issued approximately yearly, are an effort to keep the complete set current. Actually, the lengthy articles in the supplements tend to be better than in the primary set, and are a good source of information on major trends in library and information work.

Literature

> *Benet's Readers' Encyclopedia,* 3d ed. New York: Harper & Row, 1987, 1091 pp. $35.

There are scores of one- and two-volume guides to literature, most of which are particularly suited for the ready-reference questions: "When was R. R. Boyd born?" "When did she die?" "What did she write?" "How important is her *Tale of Three Horses* among her other works?" And on and on. One finds answers in these guides.

There is no better-known one-volume literature reference than the *Benet's Readers' Encyclopedia.* Named after its first compiler, William Rose Benet, this is an alphabetically arranged, short-entry format of the world's literature and arts. The close to 9500 entries move from biblical personalities to best-selling authors, right up through and including most of 1987. Much of the data are in handy chart or outline form. Not only literature, but the other arts are mentioned from painting and opera to the military. The explanations are usually short, clear, and well written.

Benet, as it is called by librarians, deserves a place on the ready-reference shelf right next to *Bartlett,* the *World Almanac,* and the *Reader's Guide.* It is a most valuable aid, and one, by the way, which can be recommended to almost anyone as the ideal birthday or holiday gift.

Music

> *The New Grove Dictionary of Music and Musicians*, 6th ed. New York: Macmillan Company, 1980, 20 vols. $1900.

Compiled at a cost of over $7 million, the 20-volume *New Grove* is unquestionably the standard set in the field of music. Like earlier editions it is extremely reliable, drawing on the experience and skills of over 2500 contributors.

While of value to reference librarians primarily for the detailed articles on pre-twentieth-century music and musicians, the latest edition now includes detailed information on modern musical life, covering not only the contemporary classical composers and performers, but also those from popular music, including the vast area of folk music.

There are some 22,500 articles with over 3000 illustrations, which, according to the publisher, occupy about 7 percent of the page space. In addition, there are several thousand musical examples.

Of particular value, in addition to the detailed material on music and the long biographical sketches, are the many bibliographies. Not only are these found at the end of articles but in numerous cases they are separate entries, e.g., "Germany and Austria: Bibliography of Music to 1600." There is equal emphasis on lists of works by various composers. Still, there appears a consensus in many reviews of the set that the high points are the biographies. These are the best of their type to be found in any reference source, and a first choice for reference libraries.

The New Grove Dictionary of American Music (1986, 4 vols., $495) is primarily an original work. One may find entries in *The New Grove Dictionary of American Music and Musicians* for the same material but nowhere in such depth as in this new work. For example, "Popular Music" is in the basic set, but here it is expanded to almost 22 pages. When the ads claim that 70 percent of the material is original to this set, they are right. Its primary contribution is the stamp of approval (often in elegantly written essays) given to American music in its many forms from the classical and jazz to folk and rock. It is exceptionally useful for biographical sketches and thoughtful pieces on regional contributions. A related, equally excellent work, again by the same publisher: *The New Grove Dictionary of Jazz* (1988, 2 vols., $350).

Religion[42]

The Encyclopedia of Religion. New York: Macmillan Company, 1986. 16 vols., $1100.

As with many subject encyclopedias, these 16 volumes devoted to religion can truthfully be said to be "monumental." A group of expert editors compiled the work which replaces to a great extent the standard, but dated Hasting's, *Encyclopedia of Religion and Ethics* (New York: Charles Scribner's Sons, 1909–1937, 13 vols.).

Entries are current and arranged in alphabetical order with cross-references and an excellent index. There are superior bibliographies. Coverage is international and the authorities move from Jewish and Muslim history and rites to the beliefs of the Hindus with ease and clarity. There are superior entries for related areas from the occult and alchemy to atheism. Particularly noteworthy is the fine style of writing and editing which opens up the set not only to students of religion, but to casual readers as well.

The field study of religion, as literature, has spawned many one-volume to multivolume encyclopedias. For example, consider: (1) *The Encyclopedia of American Religions: Religious Creeds* (Detroit: Gale Research, 1988, 828 pp., $125). This is a supplement to a basic work by the same publisher, i.e., *Encyclopedia of American Religions* (2d ed. 1986), and includes over 450 statements of creeds by as many American religious groups. The texts are arranged alphabetically by religious groups, and include only those now considered part of modern religion.

Science

McGraw-Hill Encyclopedia of Science and Technology, 6th ed. New York: McGraw-Hill Book Company, 1987, 20 vols. $1700.

Van Nostrand's Scientific Encyclopedia, 7th ed. New York: Van Nostrand Reinhold, 1983, 2 vols. $195.

Thanks to its frequent revision (about every five years), the *McGraw-Hill Encyclopedia of Science and Technology* is considered a basic set for library or home. The 1987 edition has approximatly 7700 articles of varying length, and over 15,000 illustrations. There are

---

[42]See David Gouker, "God Is Alive and Well at the Reference Desk," *American Libraries,* May 1987, pp. 342–343. A brief essay which covers the basic reference sources used to answer most questions concerning religion.

numerous charts, graphs, and summaries which make even the most detailed articles exceptionally easy to follow. Written with the layperson in mind, the encyclopedia can be read with ease even by the most scientifically naive individual. The writing style is directed to teenagers and adults.

The set is ideal for an overview of a given topic, whether it be tube worms or artificial intelligence, and it has an excellent index which makes it suitable for ready-reference purposes. Also, one part of the index is called the *topical* index. It groups all the articles under major subject headings—this for the person who wants to see relationships between various subjects. There are numerous cross-references for ease of use, and current bibliographies.

Published on a five-year schedule, the next edition of the 20-volume *McGraw-Hill Encyclopedia of Science and Technology* is slated for 1992. Meanwhile, issued each fall, the volume *Technology* acts as an update for the basic set. Unlike many yearbooks, it has references from its pages to the encyclopedia, and it can be used in conjunction with the main encyclopedia. For libraries who either cannot afford the main set or do not have much call for such material, there is the useful one-volume edition of the McGraw-Hill set, entitled the *McGraw-Hill Concise Encyclopedia of Science and Technology* (New York: McGraw-Hill Book Company, 1989, $110). The 7700 brief articles, in 2200 pages, cover all the subjects in the 20-volume work, but are shortened considerably. There are numerous illustrations, and a 30,000-plus entry index.

The publisher offers a CD-ROM version of the *Concise Encyclopedia* which includes a dictionary of scientific terms. This is the *McGraw-Hill CD-ROM Science & Technical Reference Set.* Revised every two years, this has the advantage over many CD-ROMs in that it includes not only text, but photographs and other forms of illustration. It is a modest $300 for the disk, but that is still about three times more than the printed version.

The publisher issues other related science titles. Two examples: *McGraw-Hill Encyclopedia of Electronics and Computers* (2d ed., 1988, 1047 pp.); and the *McGraw-Hill Encyclopedia of the Geological Sciences* (2d ed., 1988, 722 pp.). In reviewing these two works, the "Reference Books Bulletin" (*The Booklist*, Oct. 1, 1988, pp. 242–243) noted a common example of a spin-off. The material in both volumes "largely duplicates articles found in the *McGraw-Hill Encyclopedia of Science and Technology.* Thus librarians will have to consider currency, expense, and possible duplication of material in deciding whether to add these spinoffs to their collections." At the same time the group recommended both volumes where there is "a need to duplicate information found in the parent set."[43]

The Van Nostrand work is revised frequently and has two distinct advantages shared by the McGraw-Hill set. First, the articles and briefer entries are written for the teenagers and adults. Although the material can be quite technical, the explanations are exceptionally clear. Second, it has numerous illustrations which help to underscore and clarify the points made in the text. There are about 7000 entries, 3 million words, and over 2500 illustrations. Arranged in alphabetical order, the work includes numerous cross-references. It is an ideal ready-reference source for busy librarians, and a first choice for the home where the McGraw-Hill multiple set is either too costly or too bulky. Actually, it would be useful to present both it and the one-volume McGraw-Hill encyclopedia side by side in the library.

Another highly thought of subject set for younger people is the frequently revised *The World Book Encyclopedia of Science.* (Chicago: World Book, 7 vols.) The set is divided into major areas from plants to the human body and astronomy. Within each broad subject area the organization is topical, and there are numerous illustrations. It is suitable for both young people and adults, and the price is less than $100 for the set.

SUGGESTED READING

Callison, D. R. et al., "Introducing the Electronic Encyclopedia Across The Curriculum," *Indiana Media Journal,* Fall 1989, pp. 18–25. This is a pragmatic view of the electronic *Academic American* set and how it is used in the schools of Perry Township. The editor and others give various viewpoints that indicate the plus and minus aspects of any CD-ROM reference work in a school situation. Also, to a lesser extent, the lesson is applicable to smaller public libraries. See, too, Purcell's view on this same system in *Computers in Libraries,* February 1989, pp. 16–18.

Ferguson, Gary L., "The Domain of Learning and Imagination: William Rose Benet and The Reader's Encyclopedia," *Reference Services Review,* Spring 1990, pp. 31–36. An informative look at one of the basic ready-reference aids, as well as a comparison between it and others of its type, such as Brewer. The RSR

---

[43]A version of the McGraw-Hill encyclopedia is part of a CD-ROM disk package, *McGraw-Hill CD-ROM Science and Technology Reference Set.* For $300 the user receives the content of the *McGraw-Hill Concise Encyclopedia of Science and Technology* and close to 100,000 terms found in the same publisher's *Dictionary of Scientific and Technical Terms.*

regularly runs feature articles on better-known reference works, and this is an excellent example of the genre at its best.

Grogan, Deni, *Encyclopedias, Yearbooks, Directories and Statistical Sources*, Chicago: American Library Association, 1988. This is a set of case histories which help the student in a reference course to better appreciate the day-to-day use of the encyclopedia. Various situations are proposed, and the reader is asked to solve the problem. Since there may be as many answers as questions, it makes for a fascinating learning approach.

Johnson, Julie, "Teacher Union Faults History Books," *The New York Times*, Sept. 14, 1989, p. A20. A report on a study by the American Federation of Teachers about the failures of standard high school textbooks to report properly about significant events in America. The same argument can be made for evaluating general encyclopedias; as one textbook publisher put it, "The challenge is to have as much coverage and be able to go into as much depth as possible and still offer a manageable textbook." Ditto for the general encyclopedia.

Purcell, Royal "User Organization for the Electronic Encyclopedia," *Computers in Libraries*, February 1989, pp. 16–18. A brief hands-on discussion of the *Academic American Encyclopedia* on CD-ROM. The joys and the faults are outlined with questions about the future of this and other electronic sets.

Raitt, D. I. "McGraw-Hill CD-ROM Science and Technical Reference Set,"*Electronic Library*, December 1988, pp. 422–430. While this evaluative review is dated, it is valuable for the approach—which is applicable to other CD-ROM encyclopedias—and the points raised about the differences in various CD-ROM work. The same author has a somewhat different view of the same work in *Online Review*, December 1988, pp. 487–498.

Urrows, Henry, and Elizabeth Urrows, "Children's Encyclopedias on CD-ROM," *CD-ROM Librarian*, February 1991, pp. 9–20. The authors compare the *World Book, Academic American,* and *Compton's* on CD-ROM. They find good and bad features for all, and along the way give the arguments for incorporating CD-ROM sets into the school environment. They find the Compton's entry a winner, "not by several lengths but laps." The conclusion is questionable, but that hardly detracts from the merit of an excellent evaluation. See, too, other issues of *CD-ROM Librarian* for frequent evaluation of both general and subject encyclopedias on CD-ROM.

CHAPTER EIGHT
READY-REFERENCE SOURCES: ALMANACS, YEARBOOKS, HANDBOOKS, DIRECTORIES

What is *ready reference* all about? Mr. Gradgrind of Dickens' *Hard Times* answered this question nicely in the first lines of the novel: "Now what I want is, Facts . . . Facts alone are wanted in life."

Ready-reference questions are fact questions. They are those which may be answered quickly, usually from a single reference source, and succinctly. An experienced librarian can field this type of question with the grace and speed of an expert ball player. The queries range from the meaning of *lucent* to the meaning of a sign pointing to the reference section.

"Who won the Women's Singles at Wimbledon in 1909?" and "What are the rules for tennis?" "At what point should one oil a bike?" "What does 'well oiled' mean?" "Why do clocks run clockwise?" and "What time is it?" and "When was the first clock invented?" "Where do houseflies go in winter?" and "What is the average temperature of Miami Beach in January?"[1]

---

[1]Looking for answers? Try, the largest edition of *Why Do Clocks Run Clockwise?* (New York: Harper & Row, 1987) or the latest edition of the British work, *Enquire within upon Everything* (London: Century, 1856 to date). There are countless fact books which seem to be equally constant best sellers. For what is right or wrong in such popular works, see the critical review of *Panati's Extraordinary Endings* . . . by a fact expert Ed Zotti, in *The New York Review of Books,* Sept. 17, 1989, p. 22.

The importance of ready reference is seen by a regular advertisement in *Library Journal* for Gale Research Company. It is called "Ready Reference" and is a "page of tips, techniques, and rules of thumb contributed by our readers for librarians."

Much of ready reference might be dismissed as trivia, as beneath the dignity of the librarian. Nevertheless, the librarian is urged to treat each question seriously—unless in residence at the Vatican Library, where the guide carries a warning that any reader who asks more than three "senseless" questions will be expelled. (Just who evaluates what is *senseless* is not explained.)

One person's trivia is another's major concern. Looking up a fact about business may help someone decide on the course of an investment or the future of a career. Checking a trend in climate or the amount spent for arms may trigger or settle an argument. The entire course of a meeting or courtship may depend on the turn of a rule of order or the interpretation of a rule of etiquette.

The ready-reference question normally requires no more than a minute or two to answer. But it may develop into an involved question when (1) one cannot immediately locate the source of the answer and must spend much time and effort seeking it out, or (2) the question becomes a search or research topic because the person asking it is really in need of more data than the query implies. For example, someone who wants the address of a corporation may actually want not only that address, but also information on how to apply for a position with that firm, lodge a complaint, find data to prepare a paper, or make an investment. The ready-reference question may be only an opening gambit for the person who uses it to start the interview dialogue.

It is this latter development—the possibility that a ready-reference question may become more complex—which supports the view that professional librarians should be on duty at the reference desk. Although it is true that someone with a minimum of training is able to find a book to answer a question about a title or an address, it requires the expert to know when the query is really an opener for a complex series of other questions on the same or a related topic.

Numerous ready-reference type situations are a regular part of *The Exchange*. The two to four pages of "tricky questions" are those which reference librarians are unable to answer. Most of the cries for help are answered subsequently in later columns. Typical questions range from the origin of the term *frog* for a flower holder, to the history of the wedding ring, to the name of a children's story in which a family named Apple have numerous children, all named after varieties of apples. (These are from *RQ*, Fall 1989, pp. 12–14.) At the end of each column there is a bibliography which lists reference works where answers were found. Some of these questions are basic, but more are unusual. A cursory glance will help the working reference librarian locate sometimes little celebrated yet extremely useful ready-reference sources. One suspects that simply purchasing titles listed over a year or two would make almost any reference desk able to cope with almost any difficult ready-reference question.

Ready-reference works are among the best-selling books in America, particularly in a paperback format. *Publishers Weekly* (March 9, 1990, p. 26) reports the following as among the 10 best paperbacks reference-work sellers in 1989: *The World Almanac, J. K. Lasser Your Income Tax, The Arthur Young Tax Guide, Information Please Almanac, OPG Baseball Cards, Steven Birnbaum's Guide to Disneyworld, The Universal Almanac, Mr. Boston Official Bartender's Guide, 1989 Guide to Income Tax Preparation, Information Please Sports Almanac.* Sales average from over 1 million copies for the *World Almanac* to between 100,000 and 500,000 for other books.

EVALUATION

The general rules for evaluating any reference work, from audience to cost, are applicable to ready-reference titles. Some of these works have specific points to evaluate, and these will be considered as the chapter moves along.

Outside the science community, there are very few "facts" per se. In the humanities and social sciences, almost everything is up for interpretation, debate, and reevaluation. This can be beneficial, but often the so-called facts are what the late Terrence DesPres calls *governing narratives.* These allow us to behold ourselves and make sense of the world in a way that is comfortable.

A case in point is almost any political campaign where each side seems to be discussing an entirely different set of conditions, with almost as many solutions. A more striking example is the denial by some that the holocaust ever took place, that over 6 million Jews in concentration camps were not eliminated during World War II. Stalin, too, denied the murder of millions of fellow Russians with whom he took exception. Then there is the case of the Armenian genocide of 1915 where more than a million people were killed in the space of a year. Again, many now deny what is fact.

In other words the liars establish the so-called governing narrative. This justifies past action without attention to the fine details of true, tested historical fact.

In an immediate way, our conduct is put to the test by this question:

Will the Armenian genocide in Turkey be recognized, or will it go down, with much else, into Orwell's Memory Hole? Or again, at Bitburg in the spring of 1985 President Reagan called upon the world to forgive and forget, to conflate a killer elite with its victims and let the memory of past events fade. Neither history nor conscience was as important to the leader of Western power as a quick fix of relations with German leaders, West Germany being a vassal state to be kept at almost any price. Reagan's symbolic gesture is of course less acute than attempts to cancel the Armenian agony. What needs emphasis is that these separate cases—Turkey's denial, and Reagan's dismissal, of two of the century's worst crimes—are not only related, not only connected intimately, but are identical *as signs* of the narrative of power, in which knowledge serves the state and truth is what world leaders say it is.[2]

Fact or Opinion?

To some extent we all rely on what reference works say a fact is, more or less what politicians claim to be facts. Both should be tested regularly. Is it a fact, or an opinion? Is the fact no longer true, i.e., has it been bypassed by modern findings? For example, what is one to make of the book which states categorically that "babies should be handled as little as possible." A common notion (or fact) in the nineteenth century, this belief has been canceled out by experiment and common sense in the twentieth. Today, that statement would have to be supported with evidence. The sensible critic recognizes such maxims for what they are.

Another example: Faced with 4685 charges of conspiring to deceive the public, Sir Terry Hamster justified his health food claims in a British court. The extracted questions and answers from part of one day's hearing go far to explain how a "fact" may be interpreted or misinterpreted, depending on one's point of view—not to mention interests.

Counsel: I have here another yogurt labelled "Low Fat." Analysis shows that it is 50 percent saturated oils and fats. Can you explain that?

Hamster: Easily. All that "Low Fat" means is that the fat inside sinks

[2]Terrence DesPres, "On Governing Narratives . . . " *The Yale Review,* October 1986, pp. 530–531. See also an advertisement in *The New York Times* (May 10, 1987, p. 42) which literally denies the charge of genocide against the Turks. The advertisement was paid for by "Federation of the Turkish American Societies, Inc.," and is an excellent support for DesPres's arguments that many deny history.

to the bottom. This gives the consumer a choice; he can eat the fat at the bottom or not.

Counsel: May I ask what rises to the top?

Hamster: It's mostly beech mast, fungi, bluebell leaves . . .

Counsel: You seem to put these forest foods in all your products, though you never mention the fact. Can you say why?

Hamster: The British public is slow to catch on to something new.[3]

An invaluable way to quickly check the fact is to see its original source. *World Almanac*, as most ready-reference works, clearly indicates where information is obtained. If a reference work does not, one should be doubly cautious.

Other Points of Evaluation

Other particular points of evaluation for ready-reference works should include stress on

1. *Arrangement* Is the work easy to consult for quick facts? An index is an absolute necessity. The only exception is if dictionary order with brief entries is used, such as in the classic *Brewer's Dictionary of Phrase & Fable* (London: Cassell, 1870 to date). This work has gone through numerous editions and is a core item for checking out odd facts, particularly of a literary nature. Conversely, an index would be most useful for a book of trivia such as the *Reader's Digest Book of Facts* (New York: Random House, 1987). It has no index and only broad subjects. It may be entertaining reading, but it is a headache at the reference desk.

2. *Current information* This problem is overcome by almanacs, yearbooks, and such titles which are updated once each year. Others have semiannual or more frequent additions, as for example, *The Directory of Online Databases* (New York: Cuadra/Elsevier, 1979 to date). This has regular updates. Where data must be minute by minute up to date, there is nothing to compare with the online databases.

3. *Illustrations* Whereas most ready-reference queries are verbal and can be answered the same way, there does come a time when one illustration is well worth the proverbial thousand words. Therefore where appropriate, one should test the ready-reference work for adequate illustrations.

---

[3]Miles Kington, "A Man Who Will Stoop to Any Depth," *The (London) Independent,* May 27, 1988, p. 16.

David Macaulay's *The Way Things Work* (Boston: Houghton Mifflin Co., 1988) is a perfect example of a ready-reference work tied to illustration. The skilled artist uses dramatic, accurate drawings to explain the infinite number of mechanical, electrical, thermal, and other kinds of machines and gadgets with which we are surrounded. There are over 900 entries in the index to basic gadgets illustrated in four main sections. Each item is illustrated with a step-by-step explanation of the way it works.

Who Needs Facts?

Most Americans are not particularly smart about basic facts. Some blame it on education, e.g., a 1987 federally financed study of 7812 high school juniors found "serious gaps in what 17 year olds know about their historical and literary heritage. ... A third of the students, for example, could not identify the Declaration of Independence . . . while more than a fifth thought that the radio, phonograph and telephone were invented after 1950."[4]

Another study, this time by the National Geographic Society, found that a majority of Americans 18 to 24 years old could not locate Central America. "Our adult population," a society representative pointed out, "do not understand the world at a time when we face a critical economic need to understand foreign consumers, markets, customs, foreign strengths and weaknesses."[5]

Facts approach infinity in number, and as any reference librarian will tell you, so do the reference titles which deal with them. So do ready-reference questions, which, mercifully, can normally be answered with half dozen or so of the thousands of possibilities. Answers to fact or ready-reference queries are usually found in the forms to be discussed here: almanacs, yearbooks, handbooks, and directories.

The titles discussed are considered "basic" by reference librarians, although any given library, librarian, or situation may have a different basic list. See, for example, the "Basic Reference Materials List" for a California system (*Wilson Library Bulletin*, January 1990, p. 26). Many of the titles found in this chapter, and throughout the book are noted, but there are others less familiar such as *Bowes and Church's Food Values*.

[4]Stephen W. Rogers, "Did Anything Else Ever Happen on December Seventh?" *Reference Services Review*, Spring 1986, pp. 17–33. This is a detailed analysis of the strengths and weaknesses of books about particular days. Useful charts. Schools criticized on the humanities. *The New York Times*, Sept. 8, 1987, pp. 1 and B8.

[5]"Americans Falter on Geography Test," *The New York Times*, July 28, 1988, p. A16.

The best and most basic are required for home libraries, and hardly an issue of a popular magazine goes by without someone writing a feature article on essential reference works. Example: John Berendt, "The Thirty Inch Scholar," in *Esquire*, April 1990, p. 56. The title refers to the length of space taken up by the books. One finds the usual, and a few surprises, including *How to Flatten Your Stomach.*

In short, there are hundreds of ready-reference works. A few librarians more or less agree on the some that are essential. Beyond that, the specific choices depend on specific needs. Here an effort is made to show the forms with examples.

Although there are numerous specialized ready-reference sources, the librarian should not forget the general places to turn for answers. First and foremost: any good encyclopedia. Encyclopedias, particularly, are good for isolating ready-reference facts. One immediately thinks of the *Micropaedia* of the *Britannica* or the short, fact entries in *The World Book* described in detail in Chapter 7. All too often the librarian may be so anxious to match the specific answer to the specific question as to overlook the obvious encyclopedia.

Then, too, for current data there is no better place to turn than the numerous abstracted newspaper indexes, and particularly those such as the printed version of *The New York Times Index* or *Newspaper Abstracts OnDisc*. The abstract alone may provide the needed answer. *Facts on File* is another excellent source. These and others have been covered in depth in Chapter 6.

Tina Roose demonstrates the tremendous advantage of a computer search for ready-reference work where a newspaper is used. Someone had a recollection of a Chicago storeowner who killed a thief with an electronic booby trap. The key terms had to serve; there was no indication from the person asking the question as to when it took place.

If one used the Chicago newspaper printed indexes, one would have to start a laborious month-by-month, year-by-year search.

A computer search of a full-text database of the *Chicago Tribune* took about one and a half minutes to complete. The full text of the article was found. A manual search might have taken hours with no guarantee of success, even if one looked under the key terms "thief," "murder," "store owner," and "electronic device".[6]

---

[6]Tina Roose, "Computer Indexes vs. Print Indexes, *Library Journal*, Sept. 1, 1987, p. 158. The short article is worth reading to find out what terms were used online, and how these terms were decided upon. The search command was built around the term "booby trap" and was simply "store/15 booby," i.e., look for any story which had these two terms within 15 words of each other.

GENERAL FACT BOOKS

The New York Public Library Desk Reference. Englewood Cliffs, NJ: Webster's New World (Prentice Hall) 1989. 836 pp. $24.95.

The library may have a shelf of mixed ready-reference works which tend to cater to the popular urge to locate masses of unrelated facts. *Why Do Clocks Run Clockwise?* is one of dozens of examples. A more thorough approach is suggested by *The New York Public Library Desk Reference.*

The advertisement for the book reads: "The New York Public Library answers over 5 million questions every year, ranging from 'how do you get a wine stain off a tie?' to 'what are all of the arguments for and against the existence of God?' " Answers are promised within the four-pound volume—at least one million or so facts. One does not find 5 million answers, but then the questions after all are often repeated. Divided into 26 basic subject areas (including "Dates" and the "Animal World" to "Etiquette" and "Religion"), the book casts a wide net, although there are all too many errors to make it entirely reliable, and where a fact counts, it might best be double-checked in another source. It is useful for isolated facts and answers to numerous common questions. On the other hand, as with most books of this type, the majority of questions may be answered in more detail in general and subject encyclopedias as well as in current almanacs and yearbooks.

Although the title gives the impression that it is the work of The New York Public Library (NYPL), it is actually the brainchild of the publisher and a group of writers and editors. They put it together, and aside from the fact it has the endorsement of the NYPL, it has little to do with the real questions put to that library. The NYPL did supervise the answers, however, and receives unspecified royalties from the publisher. The fact book is followed by related titles, *NYPL Encyclopedia of Chronology* and the *NYPL Book on Where & How to Look It Up,* by the same publisher.

Records and Winners

Guinness Book of World Records. New York: Facts on File, 1955 to date, annual, $16.95; paperback, $4.95. CD-ROM: London: Pergamon, 1990 to date, annual. $125.

There are many fact books edited primarily to entertain, to settle arguments, to meet the insatiable needs of trivia collectors, and to provide people with the "first," the "best," and the "worst" of everything. Most of these are at least accurate and provide the librarian with still another entrance into the sea of facts. Of the scores of such titles now available, the ones listed here are representative.

Although the *Guinness Book of World Records* needs no introduction—it is among the top-ten best-selling books of all time, and known to almost all readers—it is worth reminding sport and game fans that it is a reliable place to check records. Divided into broad sections, it includes everything from the final scores of soccer and baseball contests to those of football and tennis. There are illustrations, some of them in color. Also, it features much trivia from the fastest wedding to the record speed for pushing a baby carriage. For example, Bozo Miller ate 27 two-pound chickens at one sitting; while Alan Peterson holds the record for eating 20 standard hamburgers in 30 minutes. It is a place to find information on almost any winner, and the quest is aided by an excellent index. *Note:* This is updated each year, and past editions are useful for sometimes out-of-the-way facts.

A good part of every edition of *Guinness* consists of records set by swimmers, climbers, pilots, runners, and others determined to establish a new test for ultimate endurance and adventure. As there are no physical frontiers this side of space, adventuring today means doing old things in a new way. Some of the adventures may make their way into the *Guinness* reference work. These include a "700 mile solo trek by dog sled from the northermost tip of Canada to the North Pole," a route taken by Pam Flowers who weighs in at 90 pounds. Then, there is "59 year old Joe Kittinger who once bailed out of a plane at 102,000 feet and spent a record four and a half minutes in free fall, achieving supersonic speeds before opening his chute."

Other related, spin-off titles by the same publisher, with self-explanatory titles, updated frequently are: *Guinness Sports Record Book, Guinness Book of Pet Records,* and *Guinness Book of Olympic Records.* There are only a few; there are many, many more.

A breakthrough on CD-ROM prices came in early 1990 when the British publisher of Guinness offered an annual $125 Guinness Disc of Records. Issued each year it covers much the same material as in the printed volume. The point, however, is that the disk is offered at under $150 in the hope of attracting not only libraries but individuals.

The publisher offers a multimedia approach, i.e., the disk has high-quality color photographs to accompany the text, plus limited animation and, yes, music and sound effects. "Are you ready to be amazed?'' reads the advertisements. Yes, seems to be the expected reply of at least librarians, and—the publisher trusts—individuals.

There are several guides to who won what, from sports and literature to million-dollar lotteries. A basic title in this field is *Awards, Honors, and Prizes* (Detroit: Gale Research Company, 1982 to date, irregular). Arranged alphabetically by the organization giving the prize, this describes the honor, but does not give winners. The work is limited to North American awards in the first volume. The second includes international winners. There are suitable indexes in both volumes. The same publisher issues *World of Winners* (1989 to date, irregular), which lists some 75,000 winners of the prizes described in the previous work. Not all award winners are listed, but the major ones are considered. Actually, the works should be combined, but for now they are two separate reference titles.

ALMANACS AND YEARBOOKS

Although almanacs and yearbooks are distinctive types or forms of reference work, they are closely enough related in both use and scope to be treated here as a single class of ready-reference aids. Aside from the general almanac, e.g., *World Almanac,* and the general yearbook, e.g., *Britannica Book of the Year,* the subject almanac and the yearbook are similar and often used for much the same purpose in reference.

Definitions

Almanac. An *almanac* is a compendium of useful data and statistics relating to countries, personalities, events, subjects, and the like. It is a type of specific-entry encyclopedia stripped of adjectives and adverbs and limited to a skeleton of information.

As most special-subject almanacs are published on an annual or biannual schedule, they are sometimes called yearbooks and annuals. Historically, the almanac per se was general in nature; the yearbook and the annual were more specific, that is, they were limited to a given area or subject. No more. There are now subject almanacs and encyclopedia yearbooks which are as broad in their coverage as the general almanac.

Yearbook/Annual. A *yearbook* is an annual compendium of the data and statistics of a given year. An almanac will inevitably cover material of the previous year, too. The essential difference is that the almanac will also include considerable retrospective material, material which may not be in the average yearbook. The yearbook's fundamental purpose is to record the year's activities by country, subject, or specialized area. There are, to be sure, general yearbooks and, most notably, the yearbooks issued by encyclopedia companies. Still, in ready-reference work, the type that is most often used is usually confined to special areas of interest.

Compendium. A *compendium* is a brief summary of a larger work or of a field of knowledge. For example, the *Statistical Abstract of the United States* is a compendium in the sense that it is a summary of the massive data in the files of the U.S. Bureau of the Census. As almanacs and yearbooks have many common qualities, they are sometimes lumped together as *compendiums.*

Purpose

Recency. Regardless of form and presentation, the user turns to a yearbook or an almanac for relatively recent information on a subject or personality. The purpose of many of these works is to update standard texts which may be issued or totally revised only infrequently. An encyclopedia yearbook, for example, is a compromise—even an excuse—for not rewriting all articles in the encyclopedia each year.

Although most almanacs and yearbooks are dated 1990, 1991, etc., the actual coverage is for the previous year. The 1990 almanac or yearbook probably has a cutoff date of late 1989. The built-in time lag must be understood, because if, in middle or late 1990, one is looking for data in a 1991 reference work, it simply will not be there.

Brief Facts. Where a single figure or a fact is required, normally without benefit of explanation, the almanac is useful. A yearbook will be more useful if the reader wishes a limited amount of background information on a recent development or seeks a fact not found in a standard almanac.

Trends. Because of their recency, almanacs and yearbooks, either directly or by implication, indicate trends in the development or, if you will, the regression of civilization. Scientific advances are chronicled, as are the events, persons, and places of importance over the previous year. One reason for maintaining a run of certain almanacs and yearbooks is to indicate such trends. For example, in the 1908

World Almanac, there were 22 pages devoted to railroads. The 1990 issue contained about 2, while television performers rated close to 12 pages. The obvious shift in interest of Americans over the past 50 years is reflected in collections of yearbooks and almanacs.

Informal Index. Most of the reliable yearbooks and almanacs cite sources of information, and thus can be used as informal indexes. For example, a patron interested in retail sales will find general information in any good almanac or yearbook. These publications in turn will cite sources, such as *Fortune, Business Week,* or *Moody's Industrials,* which will provide additional keys to information. Specific citations to government sources of statistics may quickly guide the reader to primary material otherwise difficult to locate.

Directory and Biographical Information. Many yearbooks and almanacs include material also found in a directory. For example, a yearbook in a special field may well include the names of the principal leaders in that field, along with their addresses and perhaps short biographical sketches. The *World Almanac,* among others, lists associations and societies, with addresses.

Browsing. Crammed into the odd corners of almost any yearbook or almanac are masses of unrelated, frequently fascinating bits of information. The true lover of facts—and the United States is a country of such lovers—delights in merely thumbing through many of these works. From the point of view of the dedicated reference librarian, this purpose may seem inconsequential, but it is fascinating to observers of human behavior.

GENERAL ALMANACS AND YEARBOOKS

Canadian Almanac and Directory. Toronto: Copp Clark Pitman, 1847 to date distributed in the United States by Gale Research Company, Detroit). $80.

Information Please Almanac. Boston: Houghton Mifflin Company, 1974 to date. $12.95; paper, $6.95.

Whitaker's Almanac. London: J. Whitaker & Sons Ltd., 1869 to date.= $32. (Distributed in the United States by Gale Research Company).

World Almanac and Book of Facts. New York: Newspaper Enterprise Association, 1868 to date. $11.95; paper, $6.95.

All the titles listed here are basic general almanacs found in most American libraries. For general use and importance, they might be ranked as follows: (1) *World Almanac,* (2) *Information Please Almanac,* (3) and *Whitaker's Almanac.* The order of preference is based on familiarity. Sales of the *World Almanac* (over 2 million copies) now exceed the combined sales of its two principal competitors.

With the exception of *Whitaker's,* all are primarily concerned with data of interest to American readers. To varying degrees, they cover the same basic subject matter, and although there is much duplication, their low cost makes it possible to have at least two or three at the reference desk. The best one is the one which answers the specific question of the moment. Today, it may be the *World Almanac;* tomorrow, *Whitaker's.* In terms of searching, though, it is usually preferable to begin with the *World Almanac* and work through the order of preference stated in the previous paragraph.

All almanacs have several points in common: (1) They enjoy healthy sales and are found in many homes, (2) they depend heavily on government sources for statistics, and readers will frequently find the same sources (when given) quoted in all the almanacs, and (3) except for updating and revising, much of the same basic material is carried year after year.

Of the three works, *Whitaker's,* the British entry, is by far the most extensively indexed (10,000 entries), followed by the *World Almanac* (9000 entries). *Whitaker's* is distinctive in that, as might be expected, it places considerable emphasis on Great Britain and on European governments. For example, the edition has an almost complete directory of British royalty and peerage, with another 150 pages devoted to government and public offices. Other features include an education directory, lists of leading newspapers and periodicals, and legislative data. Each year the almanac includes special sections on items in the news, such as the Falkland Islands struggle, the coal strike, conflict in Ireland, and current exhibitions. Usually from 60 to 75 pages are devoted to this "events of the year section." There are from 250 to 300 pages on Commonwealth nations and their activities, as well as major foreign countries. Other unique features include the only easily accessible list of salaries of the upper civil service, including Church of England stipends for dignitaries. No other almanac offers so much up-to-date, reliable data on Great Britain and Europe.

Whereas there is little real duplication between *Whitaker's* and the American works, the almanacs published on the American side of the Atlantic are similar to one another in scope if not arrangement and emphasis. The cousins of the *World Almanac* feature discursive, larger units on such subjects as the lively arts, science, education, and medicine. *Information Please Almanac* expanded its contents to include medicine, the economy, and political and world developments. It has several pages of colored maps. *Information Please* gravitates more to the methods of encyclopedia yearbooks than to the standard form set by traditional almanacs. The subtitle "yearbook" emphasizes this focus as does the advertising, which stresses that it is the "most complete, up-to-date, easiest-to-use reference book for home, school, and office." While "most" is Houghton Mifflin's claim, it is certainly excellent. Its makeup is considerably more attractive with its larger type and spacing than the *World Almanac*.

The *World Almanac* provides brief, accurate essay pieces on topics of current interest. For example, there are sections on diet and a part devoted to forecasting the future. Still, the real strength of the work is in facts, facts, and more facts. A quick reference index, with 60 to 75 broad subject headings from actors to zip codes, provides access to the work. There is a 16-page section on maps and flags in color.

Now over 130 years old, the *Canadian Almanac and Directory* is an authoritative work about Canada. There are four sections. The first is a directory of full names and addresses of a wide variety of public and political offices and organizations. Another section is a listing of Canadian law firms and lawyers, a third is given over to statistics, and a fourth to more common types of almanac data. Actually, this work falls more in the directory category, although it is usually considered an almanac.

Almost every year another almanac appears. *The Universal Almanac* (Kansas City, Mo.: Andrews & McMeel, 1989–1990) for example is a compendium of information which first appeared in 1989–1990. While somewhat closer to a one-volume encyclopedia than a standard almanac, it has the usual material from awards and prizes to descriptions of federal agencies. One great advantage: the typography and makeup are designed to allow easy reading. While useful, the real question is whether it can outperform the standard almanacs, which is another way of asking whether it will sell. Given the low price ($9.95 paperback), it is worth the gamble for any library.

The almanacs considered here are the basic ones found in many libraries. In addition, there are scores, if not hundreds, of specialized and subject almanacs published each year.

The Negro Almanac (5th ed., Detroit, Mich., Gale Research Company, 1990, 1622 pp.) is a good example of the subject almanac. Although this has gone through several publishers, and the publishing is irregular, it is an impressive work—more than 7 pounds in weight, with 33 chapters covering everything from the "Black Family" to "Subsaharan Africa." Most of the data concerns the American experience. There is an excellent bibliography which concentrates on basic works since 1982.

REPRESENTATIVE YEARBOOKS

There are two types of yearbooks. The first, and probably best-known, is the general work which covers, as the title suggests, the past year's activities. The type found in most libraries is the annual encyclopedia yearbook which is used to check names, dates, statistics, events, and almost anything else which might have been noticed in the past year.

Newspaper indexes, from the *National Newspaper Index* to *The New York Times Index,* often serve the same purpose; as does the weekly *Facts on File.* The latter is the most up to date, and the most satisfying, because of the well-organized format and the brief annotated stories. The publisher, since 1940, has simplified matters for librarians by issuing what amounts to a cumulation in *Facts on File Yearbook* (New York: Facts on File, 1940 to date) which is divided into four or five large divisions. Most of the focus is on the American sector, although foreign events are covered when they are of interest to American policy. It is useful, too, for the objective summaries of everything from the year in crime and sports to what has been happening in the arts.

A related work, but published in Great Britain, is *Annual Register, A Record of World Events* (London: publisher varies, 1761 to date. Distributed in United States by Gale Research). Essentially it follows the same approach as *Facts on File,* but its primary coverage is of the United Kingdom and Europe. There are 16 sections, which are adequately indexed. Americans find it of particular value for the statistical data on European politics and social developments.

Subject Yearbooks

Almost every area of human interest has its own subject compendium, or yearbook. It is beyond the scope of this text to enumerate the literally hundreds of titles. What follows, then, is a representative group and, more particularly, those "basic" or "classic" works which cross many disciplines and are used in some libraries as often as the familiar index, encyclopedia, or general almanac.

Government: International

> *Europa World Yearbook.* London: Europa Publications, Ltd., 1926 to date, 2 vols., annual. $450 (Distributed in the United States by Gale Research Company.)
>
> *Statesman's Year-Book.* New York: St. Martin's Press, Inc., 1864 to date, $65.

It is somewhat arbitrary to separate most of these yearbooks from the "general" category, particularly as they all relate directly to the type of material found in encyclopedia annuals and, for example, *Facts on File Yearbook.* The major difference is in emphasis. The government titles stress the standard, statistical, and directory types of information, which change only in part each year. The aforementioned general yearbooks stress the events of the past year.

Published for over a century, the *Statesman's Year-Book* provides current background information on 166 nations. Along with a general encyclopedia and an almanac, it is a cornerstone for reference work in almost any type of library. It has a distinct advantage for ready-reference work: It is the most up-to-date of the group discussed here and can be relied on for timeliness. It has a superior index. The indexes include a name, place, and product category.

The *Year-Book,* grouping countries alphabetically, begins with comparative statistical tables and information on international organizations. The first section is devoted to "International Organizations" including the United Nations. This includes useful charts of comparative statistics, such as price levels and wheat production.

With the 1978–1979 edition, more effort was made for balance of coverage, with the result that the third-world countries are now better represented than in earlier volumes. Still, the 1990 edition shows a heavy emphasis on England and Europe. The quantity of information varies in proportion not so much to the size of the country as to the definite Western slant of the reference work.

The book arranges the information systematically. Typical subheadings for almost every entry are: heads of government, area and population, constitution and government, religion, education, railways, aviation, and weights and measures. There are excellent brief bibliographies for locating further statistical and general information and numerous maps showing such things as time zones and distributions of natural resources.

The *Europa World Yearbook* covers much of the same territory as its competitor, but it has several advantages. (1) Timeliness is one. Not all the material is updated (an anticipated weakness in yearbooks), but most of it is relatively current, and both volumes begin with a page of late information on election results, cabinet changes, deaths, and the like. The work is almost as timely as the *Statesman's Year-Book*. (2) It leads in the number of words and amount of information. (3) The first volume covers the United Nations; special agencies, and international organizations, by subject and European countries. (4) The second volume covers non-European countries. There is a uniform format throughout. Each country begins with a short introductory survey, followed by a statistical profile, the constitution, government, political parties, diplomatic representatives, judicial system, religion, the press, publishers, radio and television, trade and industry, transportation, higher education, and miscellaneous facts peculiar to that country. This wider coverage, particularly of the media, gives it a substantial lead for ready-reference queries over the other two works. The balance among countries is good.

Europa is far from perfect; the flaws continue despite its long publishing history. For example, the index in the first volume is only for the UN and international organizations. One must turn to the second-volume index for material on Europe. There is no composite index.

There are scores of titles covering much the same territory, although always in a somewhat different way. Europa, for example publishes six related titles, which simply expand on the data found in the basic work, e.g., *Africa South of the Sahara, The Middle East and North Africa,* and *Western Europe.* See, for another example, the data section of *Britannica Yearbook.*

Common parallel reference works found in many libraries include (1) *The International Year Book and Statesman's Who's Who* (London: Reed Information Services, 1953 to date, annual). In addition to the standard data found in the other works, this includes an extensive biographical section with over 10,000 biographies and addresses of prominent individuals from around the world. The cost is high, $230 for some 640 pages. (2) *World Facts Figures* (New York: John Wiley & Sons 1979 to date, irregular) is unique in that it offers comparative charts and text for 218 countries. Although most of the information may be found in the aforementioned guides and almanac, the compendium is a convenient source of comparative ratings about countries, cities, and major geographic features of the world. For example, the Falklands, with 526 passenger cars per thousand inhabitants, ranks just behind the United States in the ownership of automobiles. The gross domestic product is twice as large as any other country in Latin America. (Which is simply proof that you can do anything with statistics.) A related work, covering 128 nations: *Comparative World Data* (Baltimore: Johns Hopkins, 1989).

HANDBOOKS AND MANUALS

The next large group of ready-reference sources consists of handbooks, manuals, and directories.

Because it is difficult to distinguish between the average handbook and the average manual, the terms are often used synonymously, or the confused writers solve the definition problems by again using the term *compendium* for either or both.

Purpose

The primary purpose of handbooks and manuals is as ready-reference sources for given fields of knowledge. Emphasis normally is on established knowledge rather than on recent advances, although in the field of science, handbooks that are more than a few years old may be almost totally useless.

The scientific handbook, in particular, presupposes a basic knowledge of the subject field. A good part of the information is given in shorthand form, freely employing tables, graphs, symbols, equations, formulas, and downright jargon, which only the expert understands. Much the same, to be sure, can be said about the specialized manual.

Scope

With some exceptions, most handbooks and manuals have one thing in common—a limited scope. They zero in on a specific area of interest. In fact, their particular value is their depth of information in a narrow field.

There are countless manuals and handbooks. New ones appear each year, while some old ones disappear or undergo a name change. It is obviously impossible to remember them all. In practice, based on ease of arrangement, or amount of use, librarians adopt favorites.

There are scores of general handbooks and manuals. There are thousands more dedicated to specific subject areas and subsections of those areas. A cursory glance at *Guide to Reference Books* will make the point, and in the *American Reference Books Annual,* many of the subject areas include a section for handbooks. The following representative group was selected because of its wide use in libraries.

Books of Days and Firsts

American Book of Days. New York: The H. W. Wilson Company, 1978, 1212 pp. $75.

Chase's Annual Events. Chicago: Contemporary Books, 1957 to date, annual, 320 pp. $25.

Kane, Joseph N. *Famous First Facts,* 4th ed. New York: The H. W. Wilson Company, 1981, 1350 pp. $70.

Questions such as "What happened on November 23?" or "I am doing a paper on George Washington. Who else was born on his birthday?" "What are the appropriate ways to celebrate Ground Hog Day?" are answered in numerous sources. Encyclopedias and almanacs, for example, list important events by the day of the year and usually give birth dates of important individuals. Some may offer suggestions on how to celebrate National Totem Pole week. An easier approach is to look in one of scores of reference works specifically edited to tell the curious what made this or that day memorable.

A classic example is the *American Book of Days.* Beneath each day of the year is listed what major or minor event(s) took place. Most moments are celebrated with lengthy essays.

Another avenue is opened by *Chase's Annual Events.* Published each fall, it traces the events of the previous year, as well as marks the upcoming year's day-by-day celebrations. For each celebration or event, it gives the name of the sponsor(s). Of special interest is the attention to trivia. For example, January 1 marks a turn in events, but also is the time when there is "announcement of the ten best puns of the year" and it opens "National Hobby Month." It also includes more substantial information, e.g., a good, short biography of E. M. Forster and an accurate account of the anniversary of the Emancipation Proclamation.

Numerous titles in this area range from *Anniversaries and Holidays* (Chicago, American Library Association, 1983) which offers succinct data and additional readings; *Books of Days* (Ann Arbor: Mich., 1987) summarizing primary events and suggesting readings and visual sources of particular use to mark the day's event(s); to *Holidays and Anniversaries of the World* (2nd ed. Detroit, Mich.: Gale Research Company, 1990); and the classic *The Book of Days* (London: W. R.

Chambers, 1864), which is reissued from time to time. This is the earliest of the genre and of value today as much as a curiosity as a profile of Victorian historical and cultural views.

One might wish to add *Famous First Facts* to the list, although this is considerably more general and less concerned with day-by-day activities. Still, it can be used in that way because it indexes events by the days of the month, as well as year by year. (It also contains personal name and geographical indexes.)

Actually, *Famous First Facts,* simply called "Kane" after the compiler, is primarily concerned with American "firsts" in everything from the first toothbrush to a first major discovery. It is arranged in such a way that one may find an umbrella subject area and either browse or seek out the essential first fact. For example, under "Library" one finds the *first* library catalog (Library of Congress); first library chair endowed in a library school (Columbia University); first library periodical (*Library Journal*); first library building (Philadelphia), and so on.

Etiquette

Emily Post's Etiquette, 14th ed. New York: Harper & Row, 1984, 1018 pp. $25.50.

In days past, strict codes of manners and dress concerned everyone except the upper classes who set their own rules and the lower classes who had more vital things to worry about than etiquette. The middle classes and those on the economic-social upswing did need guidance, and a formal approach to everything from how to carry on a conversation to which spoon to use with soup. Emily Post became the standard guide, and even today is considered the judge of good manners. The last revision takes a much more liberal stand on such matters. This is particularly obvious in regard to what women may and may not do in social and business situations. The change comes, of course, from having at least 50 percent of women in the work force. Where an earlier edition warned of the hazards of dressing in the wrong fashion for an afternoon tea, the revision is considerably more concerned with the do's and don'ts of women's clothing in the office.

An author of best-selling books on etiquette including *Miss Manners' Guide for the Turn-of-the-Milennium* (New York: Pharos Books, 1989), Judith Martin offers frequent advice on office manners. (See, for example, her comments in the November 6, 1989, issue of *Fortune* (p. 155) where she answers such questions as when to speak or keep quiet at a meeting and how to explain being late. A typical male question: "Should you offer to carry a female colleague's suitcase to the airport? Answer: If the colleague has just recovered from a heart attack or is overburdened . . . But if the only reason you're doing it is because she's a lady, no."

The 1989 Miss Manners' guide consists of ten chapters arranged in primarily a question-and-answer format. The queries are supposed to be real ones, and most seem probable enough. A good index gives access to the equally good manners together.

Another popular challenge to Emily is Letitia Baldridge's *The New Manners for the 90s* (New York: Rawson/Macmillan, 1990). A practical, current approach to etiquette, this and other volumes by the good manners guru solves such difficulties as what to do when adult children want to move back home or "what to do when your ex-husband and his new wife remain in your social orbit."

There is no end of etiquette books devoted to a single major topic. For example, there are frequent updates and name changes for *Emily Post's Complete Book of Wedding Etiquette* (New York: Harper-Collins, various dates), but the object is always the same: to guide the innocent through a major event or crisis. Detailed information is given on everything from the right accessories to what the best man is expected to do, and when. Again, the bride is the center of attention and the man often seems like a necessary but bothersome addition to it all.

In the reference situation, books of etiquette serve the important purpose of answering ready-reference questions about standard items (forms of address, who sits where at a table, etc.) as well as wedding arrangements. The latter, many librarians believe, is the most frequent use of the well-worn etiquette guide.

Literature

> Magill, Frank N. *Masterplots,* rev. ed. Englewood Cliffs, N.J.: Salem Press, 1976, 12 vols. $425. Supplemented by *Survey of Contemporary Literature,* rev. ed., 1976, 12 vols. $350, and *Magill's Literary Annual,* 1977 to date, annual. $65.

As far back as the Middle Ages, there were so-called cribs to assist students studying for an examination or working on a paper. There is nothing new about the medium and, in its place, it is a worthwhile form of publishing. A reference librarian may have mixed views about the desirability of such works for students, but that is a problem which students, teachers, and parents must work out together. It is an error to deny a place on the reference shelf to valuable sources, regardless of how they may be used or misused.

Students often request plot summaries and other shortcuts to reading. By far the most famous name in this area is Frank N. Magill's *Masterplots,* a condensation of almost every important classic in the English language. Not only are the main characters well explained, but there is also a critique of the plot's highlights and its good and bad points. Somewhat over 2000 books are considered and there is easy reference to about 12,000 characters.

The basic set is supplemented by a whole series of direct and indirect sources. The direct line consists of (1) *Survey of Contemporary Literature,* which includes additional plots for 2300 more books, published primarily between 1954 and 1976; (2) *Magill's Literary Annual* is a continuation of the basic *Survey* set, i.e., from where it leaves off in 1976 to the present. It contains sketches for 200 fiction and nonfiction titles published the previous year.

Beyond these basics there are numerous stepchildren, cousins, and aunts to the main volumes of *Masterplots. Masterplots II* covers books from the nineteenth century through to the 1990s. It is similar to the basic set, but adds women and black and minority authors, a welcome change. Also, it adds books published after the basic work. There is, too, a nonfiction series (*Masterplots II: Nonfiction Series,* 1989) which includes 325 works of twentieth century nonfiction, with a heavy emphasis on quality of style rather than content. Titles assigned in high school or college are usually found in this work. Even the primary set is published and republished in different bindings, numbers, and even titles.[7]

In the "family," for example, one finds (1) *Magill Book Reviews,* a monthly service which includes 50 reviews of best sellers in considerable detail. Much of this is incorporated into the year's-end *Literary Annual,* and it is online as part of the Dow-Jones News/ Retrieval database. (2) *Magill's Survey of Cinema,* and *Magill's Cinema Annual* describes in detail over 3000 films. This is online as DIALOG file 299.

---

[7]For example, the *Critical Survey of Theory* (1988, 4 vols., $300) offers 247 authors from Aristotle to the present. The writers are literary theorists and critics. Each is given at least four pages in which the primary notions of the individual are explained in easy-to-understand language. Then, too, there is the *Critical Survey of Short Fiction,* 1987, etc. All are from Salem Press, and their numbers and coverage will continue to grow well into the next two or three centuries.

For a discussion of *Masterplots* and related works, see "Reference Tools for Literary Criticism: A Selected Guide," in the "Reference Books Bulletin," *The Booklist,* Feb. 1, 1989, pp. 915–918.

There are numerous versions of the plot-character shorthand approach to literature. Most bookstores, for example, have *Monarch Literature Notes* (New York: Monarch Press, various dates). The over 75 titles in this series consist of 35- to 75-page pamphlets outlining the plot, character, and criticism of a particular work or the place of a writer in history. They are closely related to senior high school and college English courses. Teachers frown on such cribs, and few libraries provide this type of service.

Cliff Notes (Lincoln, Neb.: Cliff) are even more familiar study aids. The firm was founded by Cliff Hillegass who mastered the art of condensing books into 70 to 90 easy-to-read pages. About 5 million paperback black-and-yellow copies are sold each year. The publisher offers hardback copies of the works to libraries—a complete set of 24 volumes costs $1500. Individual sections (such as Shakespeare: 26 titles, three volumes, $203) are available.

A *U.S. News and World Report* study (August 21, 1989, p. 66) reported that the greatest audience for the notes are tenth, eleventh, and twelfth graders. Freshmen and sophomores are heavy users in college, but usually break the habit by their senior year. The 10 best sellers, in no particular order, include *The Odyssey, Hamlet, Great Expectations, The Grapes of Wrath, Huckleberry Finn, The Great Gatsby, Julius Caesar, Macbeth, A Tale of Two Cities,* and *The Scarlet Letter.*

Harold Bloom, the critical voice of Yale's English staff, has edited a series of 37 volumes (whose number will grow) covering individual authors and their primary works. They are all under the umbrella title of *Chelsea House Library of Literary Criticism* published by, yes, Chelsea House.

The difficulty with the handbook is determining what is, or is not to be included. For example, the *Dictionary of Cultural Literacy* (Boston: Houghton Mifflin, 1988) is an effort to arrive at an accepted body of general knowledge. Compiled by E. D. Hirsch, Jr., (who deplores the lack of such culture in his now-famous *Cultural Literacy,* 1987), the reference work is subtitled "What Every American Needs to Know." The isolated facts, arranged in broad categories in alphabetical order, mean little in themselves. The author argues that even a superficial smattering of knowledge is better than none. That argument aside, the real debate is over the choices. Evidently determined to put more emphasis on the recent past than on the distant past, the compiler stresses popular culture.

By this stage we are confronted with a situation in which you are judged culturally illiterate if you don't know about James Stewart or

John Wayne or "Star Trek," but culturally literate even if you have never heard of Berlioz or Poussin or Piero della Francesca. Jack Benny, yes; Delacroix, no. Archie Bunker, in; Anna Pavlova, out. And "On Top of Old Smoky" is given a place of honor where Rossini and Dvorak are consigned to outer darkness.[8]

This illustrates the point that no handbook, no matter how carefully thought out, will include *all* basic elements. In evaluation, then, one looks as much for what is not included as for what is included.

Quotations

Bartlett, John. *Familiar Quotations,* 15th ed. Boston: Little, Brown and Company, 1980, 1540 pp. $35.

Stevenson, Burton E. *The Home Book of Quotations, Classical and Modern,* 10th ed. New York: Dodd, Mead & Company, Inc., 1967, 2816 pp. (out of print).

The Oxford Dictionary of Quotations, 3d ed. New York: Oxford University Press, 1979, 907 pp. $45.

Quotations are beloved by everyone, and they pop up everywhere. They may salt an after-dinner speaker's delivery, get a laugh on a late television show, or be enshrined in literature.

If one wished to find the precise source of such a quote, it would be necessary to search a book of quotations. The librarian would hope (1) that it was an actual quote, and not one made up or slightly changed by the seeker; (2) that the wording was approximately, if not precisely, correct; (3) and that the primary actors involved in the quote were accurately named.

Indexing "who said what" is the role of the book of quotations. Actually, these books are not so much indexes as distinctive forms unto themselves, defying ready classification. Having found the quotation, for example, the average user is satisfied and does not want to go to the source, as he or she might do when using the standard index to materials in collections. Be that as it may, the good quotation book will indicate the source of the quote, usually a printed work. Lacking a source, one is left in doubt, particularly when there may be a question about when and just who did say "You dirty rat" or "Eternal vigilance is the price of liberty."

There are times when nothing seems to work, when no source turns up the quote. *RQ,* the American Library Association's official

---

[8]John Gross, "Ins and Outs of Culture," *The New York Times,* Dec. 26, 1988, p. 29.

journal for reference librarians, frequently publishes quotes which stump readers.

How do a phrase or a few sentences become a memorable quote? There are two or three rules governing compilers. First, if the quote is well known and memorable it is automatically included. Shakespeare's "What's in a name? That which we call a rose by any other name would smell as sweet" is found in almost all books of quotations. Second, the quote may reflect current feeling and policy. Here one need only look at the quote of the day in the daily issues of *The New York Times*. Third, it may drive home a point about morals, homespun wisdom, etc.

While the first two rules are applicable to almost all works, the third should be kept in mind as well. For example, Civil War general John Sedgwick's last words fit nicely into a work of last words or "black" humor but not into a book celebrating the skill of generals. The quote is supposedly the general's last comment as he raised his head above the parapet in the Battle of the Wilderness: "Nonsense, they couldn't hit an elephant at this dist. . . ."

Often who said what is really a case of who repeated what. An amusing and perhaps too-typical example is traced in the letters to the editor column of *The New York Times*. President Gerald Ford is quoted as advising future White House aides, "Remember the observation that the higher a monkey climbs, the more you see of his behind." Books of quotations often attribute this quotation to General Joe Stilwell, but observant readers point out that a version of it was first given by Benjamin Franklin. Not so, says another reader; it goes back much further to George Herbert (1593–1633), the English clergyman and poet. Not so, says another, it originated with the thirteenth century theologian St. Bonaventure (circa 1217–74).[9]

By far the most famous book of quotations is Bartlett's (as *Familiar Quotations* is often called). A native of Plymouth, Massachusetts, John Bartlett was born in 1820 and at sixteen was employed by the owner of the University Bookstore in Cambridge. By the time he owned the store, he had become famous for his remarkable memory, and the word around Harvard was, "Ask John Bartlett." He began a notebook which expanded into the first edition of his work in 1855. After the Civil War, he joined Little, Brown and Com-

[9]According to *The New York Times* correspondents, Dec. 18, 1988, p. 22: Franklin said: "We cannot help considering him (a social climber) as a monkey that climbs a tree, the higher he goes, the more he shows his Arse." George Herbert: "The higher the Ape goes the more he shewed his taile." St. Bonaventure: "An example from the monkey: The higher it climbs, the more you see of its behind." Probably one of the first cavepeople made the same observation, but it is not recorded.

pany, and he continued to edit his work through nine editions until his death in December 1905.

The work is updated about every 10 to 12 years, and the fifteenth edition, published in 1980, includes more than 450 new authors. Most of these are contemporary and, thanks to a famous word or two, have made their way to fame in the standard work. A few are historical and represent a new look at history; e.g., the fifteenth edition has several more representatives of the early women's movement than has the fourteenth. The total is now around 2500 individuals, including such new figures as Woody Allen, Pope John Paul II, and a latecomer, George Sand. The number of quotes is claimed to be near 23,000, or about 2500 more than the last edition. As with past efforts, the editors favor establishment figures; e.g., Milton Friedman has a solid page of quotes, but there are considerably briefer entries from Dorothy Parker, Mick Jagger, and the Beatles.[10]

Although Bartlett and the other sources contain similar material, many quotation works are needed; often a specific quote found in one may not be found in the others.

Stevenson's *Home Book of Quotations* is equally famous and is a companion to Bartlett. The quotes are arranged by subject, and there is a detailed author-title index. The subject approach makes it a useful work for the person who is simply looking for "something on politics" or "a suitable quote or two to drop into a love letter." Although there is some overlap between the standard reference works, there is enough difference to make them unique. In fact, it is hard to imagine any library, regardless of library size or type of clientele, without these two essential books of quotations.

The Oxford Dictionary of Quotations is another popular book of this type found in many libraries. The third edition represents the first substantial revision since the original 1941 publication, and of the three basic books of quotations, the Oxford has the advantage of being the most current. According to the admirably written pref-

[10]Mark Starr "Emerson: I Hate Quotations," *Newsweek*, March 12, 1990, pp. 75–76. The 1992 sixteenth edition, edited by Pulitzer Prize winner Justin Kaplan, will have less emphasis on early American quotes, and more from world leaders. About 3000 new quotes are added from 300 new sources. About as many are to be deleted. Kaplan plans to add a few quotes with heretofore-forbidden four-letter words and give speech writer Peggy Noonan credit for most of Ronald Reagan's comments as well as early ones by George Bush.

Locating quotes where the subject is clear is made even easier by Patricia Bee and Walter Schneider's *Quotation Location*. (Chicago: American Library Assn., 1990). This is a listing of over 900 quotation books and sources, and there are entry points via subjects, fables, aphorisms, etc. Originally published in Canada, this is distributed in the U.S. by the ALA.

ace, selection is based on what is most familiar to a majority of people, and in this case, while the bias is British, most of the quotations represent a considerably more international tone and will be equally well known to educated Americans.

Each year there is another book or two of quotes. Outstanding examples: (1) Simon & Schuster in 1990 offered: *A Dictionary of Business Quotations, A Dictionary of Military Quotations, A Dictionary of Religious & Spiritual Quotations.* (2) *Simpson's Contemporary Quotations* (New York: Houghton, 1988, 495 pp.) which provides basic quotes since 1950. Close to 10,000 quotations are arranged alphabetically by speaker under broad subject headings. Everyone is here from Woody Allen and President Reagan to Jorge Amado. (3) *The Concise Columbia Dictionary of Quotations* (New York: Columbia University Press, 1989, 343 pp.). This work is strong on relatively contemporary quotations under subjects, with the usual indexes.

Concordances

There is one other form of index which is "basic" in most libraries, and that is the concordance. A *concordance* is an alphabetical index of the principal words in a book—or more likely, in the total works of a single author—along with their contexts. Early concordances were limited to the Bible; a classic of its type, often reprinted, is Alexander Cruden's *Complete Concordance to the Old and New Testament . . .* , first published in 1737.

The laborious task of analyzing the Bible word by word, passage by passage, is matched only by the preparation of early concordances of Shakespeare. Fortunately, the advent of the computer considerably simplified the concordance effort (for both editorial and production purposes). Today there are concordances not only to the Bible and Shakespeare, but to almost every major writer. Examples include concordances to F. Scott Fitzgerald's *The Great Gatsby,* James Joyce's *Finnegans Wake,* the complete poetry of Stephen Crane, and the plays of Federico García Lorca. *Books in Print* lists columns of such reference works from a *Concordance of Ovid* to *Concordances to Conrad's The Rover.* Thanks to computer programs, the number of titles increases each year.

A concordance is used in a library for two basic purposes: (1) to enable students of literature to study the literary style of an author on the basis of the use or nonuse of given words; and (2) more often, to run down elusive quotations. With one or two key words, the librarian may often find the exact quotation in the concordance. This approach presupposes some knowledge of the author.

Occupations

U.S. Department of Labor. *Occupational Outlook Handbook.* Washington: Government Printing Office, 1949 to date, biennial. $22.

Current Careers and Occupational Literature. New York: The H. W. Wilson Company, 1978 to date, irregular, $35.

Although vocational guidance is not usually a part of the reference service in larger libraries, it is very much so in medium-size and small libraries, and certainly in schools. When occupational and professional advice is given to students by trained counselors, there inevitably is a fallout of young men and women seeking further materials, either for personal reasons or in the preparation of class papers. The rush has grown so that even the smallest library is likely to include a considerable amount of vocational material in the vertical file.

When working with students or, for that matter, with adults, a certain amount of probing and patience is normally required. Users may have only a vague notion of the type of information they desire, and may be quite uncertain about their particular strengths and the possibility of turning those interests into a channel of work. Here the *Occupational Outlook Handbook* is especially useful. Close to 700 occupations are discussed in terms likely to be understood by anyone. Each of the essays indicates what a job is likely to offer in advancement, employment, location, earnings, and working conditions. Trends and outlook are emphasized to give the reader some notion of the growth possibilities of a given line of work. Unfortunately, the writers are often no more accurate in their predictions than economists and racehorse touts. An effort to update the title is made through the *Occupational Outlook Quarterly* (Washington: Government Printing Office, 1957 to date, quarterly). The periodical contains current information on employment trends and opportunities.

Massive amounts of material are published each year concerning occupations and professions. Much of this, in pamphlet and other ephemeral forms, is often difficult to locate. A great help is *Current Career and Occupational Literature,* ably edited by Leonard Goodman. The first part is an annotated listing of both books and pamphlets, with an asterisk denoting the recommended titles. The second part is a group of materials simply labeled "books and pamphlets describing more than one occupation." The last section gives the full names and addresses of many elusive publishers of this type of material. As a companion to *Occupation Outlook Handbook,* the bibliography is a required item in almost all libraries where vocational advice is a service.

Software packages, as well as CD-ROM disks, are available in the occupational field. A single example: *The Perfect Career* (Northbrook, Ill.: Mindscape $50). This leads the young person through a series of steps which indicates interests and experience and projects probable success in a given type of employment. The final result is a list of suggestions from a database of 615 occupations. There are references, too, to basic books in the area.

Science

> *Handbook of Chemistry and Physics.* Boca Raton, FL: Chemical Rubber Company Press, 1913 to date, annual. $59.95.

Considered the bible of chemists and physicists, the *Handbook of Chemistry and Physics* is, as the subtitle explains, "a ready-reference book of chemical and physical data." The data are readily accessible, as they are organized in a way that groups similar and related materials commonly needed in research. Much of the information is in tabular form and, like the rest of the annual, is constantly updated to include reference material in such developing areas as solar radiation and cryogenics. Although using it requires some basic knowledge of chemistry and physics, it is as familiar to beginning students as to experienced researchers.

ADVICE AND INFORMATION

A common problem that arises in reference service is when to give information, when to give advice, and when to give neither. Normally, the emphasis is on information, not advice. The distinction is important, because in some librarians' minds, advice and information are confused when medicine, law, or consumer information is sought by the layperson. Most librarians are willing to give consumer data, even advice (as this author believes they should about reference books and related materials), but some hesitate to give out data on medicine and law.

There is no reason not to give information about law or medicine. This does not mean the librarian is giving advice. The trend today is to welcome legal and medical queries. Still, doubts may arise in the following forms:

1. "I will feel that I am practicing law (medicine) without a license.'' The answer is that there is no case of a library or a librarian being named a defendant in a legal suit on this ground. The librarian has no liability to fear. Of course, the librarian should not try to diagnose the situation or offer treatment (legal or medical), but simply provide the information required, no matter how much or in what form.

2. "I don't know enough about law (medicine) to find required information.'' The answer is that there are now numerous books, articles, pamphlets, and television and radio tapes available for the layperson. These are reviewed in most of the standard reference review media. Furthermore, as with any subject area, the librarian soon becomes familiar with ways to evaluate a title for reliability, currency, or style of writing. As for finding the data, again this is not difficult when one becomes accustomed to using a few basic reference works.

The sections which follow, on medicine, law, and consumer advice, point up specific problems and reference works. At the same time, it is good to remember that many basic questions about everything from medicine to law may be answered by consulting equally basic periodical indexes. The *Reader's Guide* and *Magazine Index* cover both general and some specialized magazines of interest to laypersons concerning consumer, legal, and medical problems. This equally is true when one turns to features in newspapers via, say, the *National Newspaper Index* or *NEXIS*. And, of course, one should never forget some quite excellent overviews offered in the encyclopedias.

Computer software offers another avenue for advice. There are scores of programs which give general and specific answers to medical, legal, business, educational, and other types of problems. For example, the Hyatt Legal Services' Home Lawyer (Berkeley, Calif., 1990) offers the user a series of questions on a computer screen. When the questions are answered, and the interview is complete, the computer prints out a will. Home Lawyer relies on on-screen interviews to put together and print out a variety of other legal documents such as residential leases, promissory notes, and bills of sale.

This, and other types of ready-reference software, are now found in many libraries. They can be used at the reference desk or checked out to take home. Most of the software is inexpensive— under $100.

Medicine

Physicians' Desk Reference to Pharmaceutical Specialties and Biologicals. Oradell, NJ: Medical Economics Company, 1947 to date, annual. $42. (Online: publisher, rate varies.) CD-ROM: publisher, $595.

The Merck Manual of Diagnosis and Therapy. Rahway, NJ: Merck and Company, 1899 to date. $45.

Scientific American Medicine. New York: Scientific American, 1978 to date, monthly, $245.

Today, there is an active movement among public, school, and even some college and university libraries to develop community health information centers, health lines, or whatever they may be called. At the same time, continuing education about various health sources and services is pursued by many librarians. Although there is consensus that librarians should neither interpret nor analzye medical advice, it is equally true that the library should be scrupulous about reference sources purchased.

The user must be able to understand the books concerning consumer health information. This can be ensured by (1) purchasing books written for laypersons, (2) purchasing medical dictionaries which give solid, clear definitions, and (3) purchasing or providing access to technical information which is not beyond the understanding of the better-educated or the more involved layperson.

In addition to the volumes listed at the beginning of this section as being appropriate for a library, there are a number of standard medical dictionaries; among those most often found in libraries is *Dorland's Illustrated Medical Dictionary* (Philadelphia: W. B Saunders Co., 1900 to date). Frequently revised, this is the work of over 80 consultants, who review all entries and the numerous illustrations. *Stedman's Medical Dictionary* (Baltimore: Williams & Wilkins: 1911 to date) is another often-revised work which has some of the more up-to-date entries.

Somewhat more than a dictionary, *The American Medical Association Encyclopedia of Medicine* (New York: Random House, 1989 to date) has about 5000 entries with half as many two-color illustrations. Definitions may be only a sentence or two, but sometimes run three pages in length. The dictionary section is preceded by an essay describing current medical techniques and advances. And the latter part of the work includes a Drug Glossary which describes 2500 generic and brand name products.

The AMA also issues a useful handbook. This is *The American Medical Association Handbook of First Aid & Emergency Care* (New York: Random House, 1990). The main sections are divided by subject with each following a set pattern of information. The paperback, 350 pages, is only $8.95.

With sales exceeding 1.5 million, the *AMA Encyclopedia* has few rivals. It remains to be seen whether another general medical guide will be as popular. This is the *Mayo Clinic Family Health Book* (New York: William Morrow, 1990). At $34.95 it is somewhat more expensive than the AMA entry ($29.95), but it claims to have 780,000 words as compared to only 350,000 for its rival. At the same time it has only about one-third the number of illustrations as the AMA guide, i.e., 550 versus 1350. The title comes from the fact that the editor is "a widely respected Mayo Clinic physician." It is a welcome companion in libraries to the AMA guide.

The Wellness Encyclopedia (Boston: Houghton Mifflin, 1991) is edited at the University of California and offers, in five sections, current and accurate data on longevity, nutrition, self-care, exercise and environment, and safety. There are excellent illustrations and highlights boxed in the text.

Several directories and bibliographies assist the librarian and layperson. An annual feature of *Library Journal,* usually in November, is "Best Lay Medical Books for Public Libraries." About 30 titles are suggested, and each is annotated briefly. "Medical Reference Tools for the Layperson" is an ongoing selective list published by the "Reference Books Bulletin." The annotated work "emphasizes authoritative materials that can be used by the general public." It is updated every two or three years.[11] Another guide has a similar approach, but this time by the head of the reference department at the New York Academy of Medicine. The annotated listing offers many of the same titles in the "Reference Books Bulletin" choice, but adds just enough to make it worthwhile.[12] The librarian might check the current books on health and medicine in any medium to large bookstore to gain an idea of ongoing interests by laypersons.

The best-known and most often found pharmacology work in a library is the *Physicians' Desk Reference.* Frequently referred to as the *PDR,* it provides information on close to 3000 drug products. The pubisher notes that "the information is supplied by the manufacturers." At the same time, the Food and Drug Administration has

[11]Susan Hagloch, "Best Popular Medical Books for Public Libraries 199 . . ." *Library Journal,* November 1, 1990. This annual feature offers some 30 titles, nicely annotated, which are equally useful in many academic and school libraries. See, too: "Medical Reference Tools for the Layperson," in "Reference Books Bulletin," *The Booklist* Dec. 1, 1988, pp. 620–623. This updates a similar listing in February 1985. For more detailed data see the annual "Selected List of Books and Journals for the Small Medical Library," *Bulletin of the Medical Library Association,* various issues.

[12]Claudia Perry, "Patron Medical Queries: A Selected List of Information Sources," *Library Journal,* Nov. 1, 1988, p. 45–50.

approved the material sent by the manufacturer. Brand, generic, and chemical names are given, and so, with a little experience, one can easily check the content of this or that drug. (A generic and chemical name index is a major finding device.) For each item, the composition is given, as well as such data as side effects, dosage, and contraindications. One section pictures over 1000 tablets and capsules, with product identification. The neatly divided six sections are arranged for easy use.

Each annual volume may or may not have a supplement. According to the publisher, "the supplement is published when necessary during the year to provide . . . important revised information, as it becomes available, on products described in this volume." It is important to check to see whether a supplement has been issued. The obvious reason: between the annual volume and the supplement, discoveries may have been made which will show side effects, even fatal dangers, in drugs otherwise approved in the main volume.

The *PDR* comes in another version, i.e., the *Physicians' Desk Reference For Nonprescription Drugs* (1980 to date, annual) which considers some 1000 over-the-counter products. Arrangement and content is much like the basic volume, including a section with photographs of actual tablets and packages. Updated each year, it is particularly useful for an objective analysis not only of what the drugs promise but of any bad side effects.

Online the *PDR* is available at an annual subscription of $300, plus the normal fee for citations and full text. The service has the advantage of being updated every two months. In the CD-ROM format, three companion volumes are part of the package, including the *PDR's Drug Interactions and Side Effects Index.* The service is updated twice each year.

There are several variations on the theme: (1) the *American Medical Association Guide to Prescription and Over-the-Counter Drugs* (New York: Random House, 1988). This is in layperson's language, and the five sections explain in full everything most people will want to know about the subject. The "A to Z of Drugs" covers most of the volume and is literally that, giving data on 320 common generic drugs. (2) *The Essential Guide to Nonprescription Drugs* (New York: Harper, 1983 to date, irregular). This is particularly useful as a guide to what the advertisements say and to what actually happens when one takes the drug. Ingredients are discussed. The handbook is updated irregularly. (3) The same publisher issues the equally excellent *Essential Guide to Prescription Drugs.* The 1989 edition fully describes 200 drugs.

There is considerably more to health information than simply selecting the best books and having current reference works available. The whole process of the reference interview may be quite different from the usual question-and-answer encounter. In fact, many librarians feel slightly uncomfortable because they think the type of information required is more personal than usual. Then, too, there are other problems that range from offering "bad news" about a particular disease to the user who wishes to talk at great length about a personal difficulty. Nevertheless, the librarian is morally bound to remain objective, to give the right information, and to refrain from making judgments either about the patron or the advice given in a particular source.

A much-used basic work, technical, although suitable for certain library situations, is the *Merck Manual of Diagnosis and Therapy*. Published for many years as a manual for physicians, it is equally clear to laypersons with patients and a medical dictionary at hand. Illnesses and diseases are described in relatively nontechnical language, symptoms and signs are indicated, and diagnoses and treatments are suggested.

In addition to Merck are scores, if not hundreds of volumes dedicated to informing the layperson, not simply the doctor. These can be found on newsstands and in bookstores. Their number and titles change each month, and while many are indifferent, others are at least passable.

The Consumer Health Information Source Book (3d ed. Phoenix, Ariz.: Oryx Press, 1990) by Alan M. Rees and Catherine Hoffman is an excellent guide to 750 books, 79 popular magazines and newsletters, pamphlets, toll-free hot lines, organizations, etc. The book is divided logically by subject with a detailed index. Essential works are so designated. Each title is annotated with descriptive and evaluative comments. The material is for the layperson, and it is by and large the best, single bibliographical aid for all types and sizes of libraries seeking a basic medical collection for the public. It is updated every five to six years.

The librarian should look for current reviews in the *Library Journal, Choice,* and *The Booklist* where particular care is taken to point out flaws and the general reliability of the manual.[13] The reviews are important if only to help the librarian keep a current collection, e.g., *The AIDS Benefit Handbook* (New Haven, Conn.: Yale University Press, 1990) is an invaluable guide, but not the type of

---

[13]The "Reference Books Bulletin," for example, suggests: *The American Medical Association Family Medical Guide, Columbia University . . . Complete Home Medical Guide, The Patient's Guide to Medical Tests,* etc.

book reviewed in the general press. It was widely noticed in the library press, as, for example, in the May 1, 1990, issue of *Library Journal,* p. 82.

How else does the librarian and the layperson keep up with the latest medical advice and research? One can always turn to *Index Medicus,* but this is much more than the average individual needs. The best solution for many is *Scientific American Medicine.* The monthly service updates what is found in two basic loose-leaf volumes. There are 15 well-organized chapters on everything from infectious diseases to psychiatry. Exercise and health and related topics are covered, too. Each month several of the chapters are replaced with updates and the extensive index is revised. There are excellent illustrations and most of the text is within the understanding of the average layperson.

Annual advice and notes on medical progress will be found in *The World Book Health & Medical Annual* (Chicago: World Book, 1988 to date, annual). While prepared for young people, the book is divided into logical sections with numerous illustrations. This is suitable for adults as well, although the latter may prefer what is found in the equally good *Encyclopaedia Britannica Medical and Health Annual* (Chicago: Encyclopaedia Britannica, 1986 to date, annual).

The Atlas of Human Anatomy (West Caldwell, N.J.: Ciba-Geigy, 1990) is one of countless diagrams of the human body, but quite superior in that it represents the life work of Frank H. Netter. The artists' diagrams are exquisitely detailed and may be as instructive to physicians and laypersons as they are pleasing to examine. The 83-year-old's drawings are gathered here in 514 beautiful plates.

Law

> *The Reader's Digest Legal Question & Answer Book.* New York: Random House, 1988, 704 pp. $29.

Legal questions are similar to medical queries in that they require more than an average knowledge of the field. This side of the professional law library, most librarians consult general works as well as specific laws of the state, city, and region. The section on law on the discussion of indexes indicates the basic places to turn for current data, both specific and general. Here the focus is on one-stop guides which are much easier to use, if not as current or as exhaustive.

Who asks what? In one survey of public libraries it was found that "the people asking legal questions include students, and business people. People want to know about divorce, wills, tax laws, and immigration procedures . . . and they want up-to-date materials in languages they can understand."[14]

There are several helpful guides for the nonlawyer, but the best and by far the most consulted is Miles Price and Harry Bitner, *Effective Legal Research* (various publishers and dates). Often updated, it offers an easy-to-understand, jargon-free approach to the literature of law. Important sections on basic reference works are of particular value. Referred to as "Price and Bitner," it can be both a starting point and a constant companion for the librarian.

The Encyclopedia of Legal Information Sources (Detroit, Mich.: Gale Research Company, 1988) lists close to 20,000 sources under around 460 broad subjects. The legal sources cover everything from books to periodicals and research centers.

Although primarily for the librarian, *The Encyclopedia of the American Judicial System* (New York: Charles Scribner's Sons, 1987) is a three-volume set with close to 90 essays on all aspects of the American legal system.

Among guides which are written for laypersons, the *Reader's Digest* entry (distributed by Random House) is one of the best. Some 2000 typical legal questions are listed from alimony to zoning. After each, an answer is given in legal-free jargon. There are not as many legal guides as medical aids, but from time to time such lists are published in library periodicals.[15]

Kessinger Publishing (Kila, Mont. 59920) offers reliable current guides to common questions about state laws. The volumes, $35 to $45 each, focuses on state law governing such entities as marriage, divorce, notary publics, and child custody. Some of these are individual volumes for individual states, i.e. *Divorce Laws: Alabama*; while others cover all states.

Consumer aids

Consumer Index Ann Arbor, MI: Pierian Press, 1973 to date, quarterly with annual cumulations. $180.

[14]Patricia Dewdney et al., *Legal Information Services in Ontario Public Libraries,* Canadian Library Journal, December 1988, pp. 365–371. There are several guides, for example, to marriage and divorce which can be used in a library. *Marriage Licensing Laws: A State by State Guide* (Boise, ID: Kessinger, 1990); *The Encyclopedia of Marriage, Divorce and the Family* (New York: Facts on File, 1990).

[15]See, for example, the section on "legal aids" in Nancy Spillman's "I'm Providing Personal Economics: Personal Finance and Law Books," *Library Journal,* Nov. 1, 1988, pp. 40–44. The column is an annual feature that appears under different names, e.g., on Nov. 1, 1989, it appeared as "Pieces of Today's Money Puzzle" with both law and consumer books annotated.

Consumer's Resource Handbook, 5th ed. Pueblo, CO: U.S. Consumer Information Center, 1990. Free.

Trade Names Dictionary, 7th ed. Detroit, MI: Gale Research Company, 1984, 2 vols. $320. Trade Names Dictionary: Company Index, 1989, 2 vols. $320.

The reference librarian is usually asked one of three questions about products and consumer protection: (1) "What is the best product for my needs?" (2) "To whom can I complain, or to whom can I turn for information about a product or service?" (3) "How can I protect myself from poor-quality products or services?" No one reference source answers all queries, although several are of particular value in locating possible sources. The best product answer may be found in numerous places, including articles indexed in *Reader's Guide* and *Magazine Index.*

Given the popularity of consumer type information, and the various reference works it crosses and recrosses, many public and school libraries meet the problem by establishing special consumer collections or sections. These may include the whole range of Dewey numbers, and everything from books to magazines and video. The collection is used both for reference and for circulation, particularly when there is more than enough material to cover popular topics.

Speaking for the American Library Association's members, the "Reference Books Bulletin" observes: "Consumer information is a prime example of the library's commitment to providing material that has a direct, practical application for users."[16]

One typical consumer guide is *The Complete Car Cost Guide* (San Jose, Calif.: IntelliChoice, Inc., 1987 to date, annual). The work is reliable and uses charts and brief descriptions which cover 500 to 600 vehicles. Figures are given for dealer costs, options, state taxes, warranty, and maintenance. Both domestic and foreign cars and trucks are examined. It is in the words of many librarians, "an indispensable consumer guide." It is issued each year, and in 1989 a new title by the same publisher joined the list: *The Complete Small Truck Cost Guide.*

Current Consumer Material

Anyone buying this or that wants the latest information, the latest product. Or as the Reference and Subscription Books group puts it:

---

[16]"Consumer Information Sources," Reference Subscription Books Bulletin, *The Booklist,* July 1988, p. 1791. This is an annotated listing (pp. 1791–1807) of basic reference works used to answer consumer questions. (See also footnote 15 above.)

"In a society that places an almost obsessive emphasis on the new and improved, rarely will product evaluations older than a few years accurately describe the choices available.[17] Actually, "a few months" is much more accurate. At any rate, for up-to-date material, the librarian will turn first to magazines.

The Consumer Index covers 130 magazines. Its advantage is twofold. It comes out quarterly and is well organized. Here, under 17 broad, and then narrower, related subject headings, one finds quick access to products, manufacturers, and related areas. Many of the items include short descriptions, and there is an excellent index. The major drawback is typical: The index is up to six or more months behind. Issues are not received for several months after the cover date.

The librarian may wish to try a somewhat more limited, but more up-to-date, index: *Consumer Companion* (Chico, Calif.: CaBer Enterprises, 1986 to date, quarterly). This covers only 40 periodicals (but is only $29 a year as compared with $179 for its rival). It gathers material under six subject headings, provides comments from the reviews or notes, and contains a good index.

Infotrac/Magazine Index

Infotrac provides information on products from the 400 or more magazines it indexes and publishes a quarterly service that is free with a subscription to the primary index. This is *Product Evaluations,* a loose-leaf paper affair with an index for types of products, not for brand names as found in the other two works.

There are two basic periodicals, one of which is known to most quality-conscious Americans. This is *Consumer Reports* (Mount Vernon, N.Y.: Consumer Union of the United States, 1936 to date, monthly) which has objective test reports on about 10 to 12 items each month. These may range from a deluxe automobile to an inexpensive toothbrush. The National Information Services Corporation offers the magazine on CD-ROM which allows one to search the contents from 1985 to date. The annual disk, plus the retrospective full-text material is $445 to $695. Convenient, to be sure, but one must weigh the cost against an annual subscription which is $34.

An equally good, but not as well-known monthly is *Consumers' Research Magazine,* formerly *Consumer Bulletin* (Washington, N.J.: Consumers' Research Inc., 1931 to date, monthly) with reports of

[17]Ibid.

the same type. Both magazines issue annual summaries in paperbacks which should be kept near the reference desk. The best known of these is *Consumer Reports Buying Guide*, issued by Consumer Reports since 1936.

The question "To whom can I complain?" may be answered in many ways. At the local level, a call to the Better Business Bureau may serve the purpose. When one is trying to contact the manufacturer of the product, often a careful look at the container will give the address. If this fails, or if more information is needed, then the *Trade Names Dictionary* is most useful. In one alphabetical sequence one finds the trade names of over 250,000 different products. After the name is a one- to three-word description of the product, and the name of the company or distributor. Another section includes addresses of the manufacturers. An annual supplement, which provides about 20,000 new names, keeps the basic work current until it is revised about every two or three years. The Company Index volume is a reverse index in that one finds the name of the company and under it the trade name or names. Approximately 45,000 different firms are listed.

Published free by the U.S. Government, and updated about every four or five years, the *Consumer's Resource Handbook* opens with an explanation of what to do when a product or an individual backfires. This is followed by a listing of names and places where one may complain and get assistance. It is a good place to start, and it is often enough for most people. Beyond this, one may turn to the equally often updated *Consumer Sourcebook* (6th ed., Detroit, Mich.: Gale Research Company, 1989) which is not free, but $175. Under 26 subject headings one finds listings of consumer-related agencies, often, but not always, with a few words explaining what each does.

DIRECTORIES

Directory-type information is among the most often called for in libraries, particularly public libraries. People often try to locate other people, experts, and organizations through addresses, phone numbers, zip codes, correct titles, correct spelling of names, and so on.

Staff-produced directories can be found in almost all libraries, augmenting the standard reference works, from the city and telephone directory to the zip code directory. Here are such items as frequently requested phone numbers, the names of individuals and agencies in the community, sources of help for difficult questions, often-requested names of state and federal officials, and a wealth of other miscellany. The Chicago Public Library reference staff, for example, listed the staff-produced files as the most useful source of data for daily reference work, matched only by the *World Book Encyclopedia* and the *World Almanac*.

Definitions

The *A.L.A. Glossary of Library Terms* defines a directory as "a list of persons or organizations, systematically arranged, usually in alphabetical or classed order, giving addresses, affiliations, etc., for individuals, and address, officers, functions, and similar data for organizations." The definition is clear enough for a directory in its "pure" form; but aside from the directory type of information found in biographical sources, it should be reiterated that many other ready-reference tools have sections devoted to directory information. Yearbooks and almanacs inevitably include abundant amounts of directory-type material.

Purpose

The purpose of directories is implicit in the definition, but among the most frequent uses is to find out (1) an individual's or a firm's address or telephone number, (2) the full name of an individual, a firm, or an organization, (3) a description of a particular manufacturer's product or a service, or (4) the name of the president of a particular firm, or the head of a school, or the person responsible for, say, advertising or buying manuscripts.

Less obvious uses of directories include obtaining (1) limited, but up-to-date, biographical information on an individual, whether still president, chairperson, or with this or that company or organization; (2) historical and current data about an institution, a firm, or a political group, such as when it was founded, how many members it had; (3) data for commercial use, such as selecting a list of individuals, companies, or organizations for a mailing in a particular area; e.g., a directory of doctors and dentists serves as the basic list for a medical supply house or a dealer in medical books; and (4) random or selective samplings in a social or commercial survey, for which they are basic sources. Directories are frequently employed by social scientists to isolate certain desired groups for study. Because directories are intimately concerned with human beings and their organizations, they serve almost as many uses as the imagination can bring to bear on the data.

Scope

Directories are easier to use than any other reference tool, chiefly because the scope is normally indicated in the title and the type of information is limited and usually presented in an orderly, clear fashion. There are many ways to categorize directories, but they can be broadly divided as follows:

Local Directories. There are primarily two types: telephone books and city directories. However, also included in this category may be all other types issued for a particular locality—for example, directories of local schools, garden clubs, department stores, theaters, and social groups.

Governmental Directories. This group includes guides to post offices, army and navy posts, and the thousand and one different services offered by federal, state, and city governments. These directories may also include guides to international agencies.

Institutional Directories. These are lists of schools, foundations, libraries, hospitals, museums, and similar organizations.

Investment Services. Closely related to trade and business directories, these services give detailed reports on public and private corporations and companies.

Professional Directories. These are largely lists of professional organizations such as those relating to law, medicine, and librarianship.

Trade and Business Directories. These are mainly lists of manufacturers' information about companies, industries, and services.

Format

The CD-ROM format is suited to directories which need to be updated monthly or once a quarter or once a year. For example, the U.S. Postal Service's national address file with 109 million delivery addresses, New York Telephone now has its 10 million telephone directory listings in Boston and New York City on CD-ROM, and there are numerous telephone directories in this format.

Numerous directories are also available online. This format is particularly valuable to the library which may need to consult the directory only a few times a month or year. It not only saves purchase money, but it saves space and time in the library.

Additional Directory-Type Sources

The almanac and the yearbook often include directory-type information, as do numerous other sources of directory information:

1. Encyclopedias frequently identify various organizations, particularly the more general ones which deal with political or fraternal activities.
2. Gazetteers, guidebooks, and atlases often give information on principal industries, historical sites, museums, and the like.
3. A wide variety of government publications either are entirely devoted to or include directory-type information. Also, some works are directories in name (*Ulrich's International Periodical Directory*, for example) but are so closely associated with other forms (periodicals and newspapers) that they are usually thought of as guides rather than as directories.

The basic listing of directories is the *Directories in Print* (formerly: *Directory of Directories*. Detroit, Mich.: Gale Research Company, 1977 to date). The annual publication (augmented by a semiannual supplement) lists more than 10,000 new or revised titles under about 16 broad subject categories from business to professional and scientific. There is a detailed subject index and a title index. Information for each entry includes the name of the directory, the publisher, address and phone number, and a full description of the work. A separate volume arranges alphabetically the names of over 7000 publishers or directories with necessary information from address to telephone number. There is a geographic approach to states, and there are other helpful indexes. A related work by the same publisher is *City and State Directories in Print*. As a companion to *Directories in Print* it lists and describes 4500 directories, guides, and rosters from small towns, cities, and every state.

City Directories

The two most obvious, and probably the most-used, local directories are the telephone book and the city directory. The latter is particularly valuable for locating information about an individual when only the street name or the approximate street address is known. Part of the city directory includes an alphabetical list of streets and roads in the area, giving names of residents (unless it is an apartment building, when names may or may not be included). The resident usually is identified by occupation and whether she or he owns the home. Some city directories, but not all, have reverse telephone number services, i.e., a "Numerical Telephone Directory." If you know the phone number, you can trace the name and address of the person who has the phone.

The classified section of the directory is a complete list of businesses and professions, differing from the yellow pages of the telephone book in that the latter is a paid service which may not include all firms. Like the telephone book, city directories are usually issued yearly or twice yearly.

Most city directories are published by the R. L. Polk Company of Detroit, founded in 1870, which issues over 800 publications. In addition to its city directories, it publishes a directory for banks and direct-mail concerns.

A number of ethical questions arise regarding the compilation and use of the city directories. For example, bill collectors frequently call large public libraries for information which can be found only in the city directory, such as reverse phone numbers and addresses and names of "nearbys," that is, the telephone numbers of people living next door to the collector's target. Some librarians believe such information should not be given over the telephone. They argue that this helps the collectors in an antisocial activity and invasion of privacy.

This policy may be commendable in spirit, although questionable in practice, as it simply makes it more difficult, but not impossible, to use the directories. The author of this text would say the librarian is there to supply information, not to question how or by whom it is used. Several large urban libraries are currently examining their policy in this regard, and most now do give the information over the phone.

Telephone Directories

With enough telephone directories, many of the specialized directories might be short-circuited. A telephone book will give the address of a friend, business contact, hotel, and so on, in almost any community. Using the familiar yellow pages to find the location of potential customers or services is a frequent purpose. And from the point of view of a historian or genealogist, a long run of telephone books is a magic key to finding data on elusive individuals.

CD-ROM and other formats come to the rescue. Silver Platter, for example, publishes Disc Northeast, with over 12 million current names, addresses, and telephone numbers for the area covered by New York Telephone, New England Telephone, and other regional sources. Searching can be done by name, address, telephone number or zip code. Cost: $3500 to $6500, depending on which of the options reflecting different geographic areas is selected, e.g., price depends on annual subscriptions with no updates or with only monthly updates, and regional versions are available, such as New York City or New England other than Boston, etc.[18]

Another way of expanding the telephone book collection without the concern of high cost or shelf space is offered by Phonefiche. This is a service of University Microfilms. The microfiche may be purchased in several categories. Prices vary, but if the library wants only directories from cities of 1.5 million it is $310 a year, as opposed to $6650 for all directories covered by the publisher. The drawback is that fiche is sometimes confusing to use, and no matter who is at the machine, it takes longer to locate a number than in the printed work.

Still another approach, which may be used alone or in conjunction with the telephone book collection, is to purchase the annual *National Directory of Addresses and Telephone Numbers* (Detroit Mich.: Gale Research Company, 1985 to date). This has over 115,000 numbers of businesses and government agencies across the United States. Fax numbers, addresses, and zip codes are given. It includes, too, all four-year American universities and colleges, toll-free numbers, and 1200 leading foreign corporations. It is available on CD-ROM from the publisher for $195, but the printed version at a modest $50 is a best buy.

Silver Platter offers a more comprehensive service—10 million names, addresses, and phone numbers on a CD-ROM. Coverage is national. Updated semiannually, it costs between $2000 and $5000, depending on coverage.

Considering how relatively easy it is to encode telephone numbers, names, and addresses, it is not surprising that numerous firms now offer, telephone directories on CD-ROM. The two following are only a sample. (1) *NYNEX Fast Track* (New York: NYNEX, 1989 to date, monthly, $9500). By far the most expensive of the services, this has the advantages of over 10 million listings and of being updated

---

[18]Disc Northeast competes with NYNEX Information Resource Company's Fast Trace CD-ROM, which has a subscription price of $8000 to $10,000. As time goes on there will be other competitors, and eventually the price will come down for libraries.

monthly. It includes over 300 directories, or all businesses and residences served by New York and New England Telephone companies. At the other cost extreme is (2) *The National Directory of Addresses and Telephone Numbers* (Marina Del Ray, Calif.: Xiphias, 1989 to date, annually, $195.) This offers 195,000 listings of U.S. businesses, organizations, and government agencies. Besides these two services are several others that range in cost from a low of $200 to $500 to many thousands of dollars.

While the fax numbers given in the *National Directory* are enough for most purposes, there are special guides to fax numbers alone. *The National Fax Directory* (Detroit, Mich.: Gale Research Company, 1989 to date) is a good example. This has 80,000 major business and organizational fax numbers under approximately 150 subject headings. Listings are arranged alphabetically by name and by area.

Associations and Foundations

Encyclopedia of Associations. Detroit, MI: Gale Research Company, 1956 to date, annual, 3 vols. $220 to $240 each. (DIALOG file 114, $99 per hour). CD-ROM: publisher, 1989 to date, semiannual. $1495. CD-ROM name: *Gale Global Access.*

The Foundation Directory. New York: Foundation Center, 1960 to date, irregular, $125. (DIALOG file 28, $55 per hour)

Searching directory is not the most scintillating reference work. Still, given a bit of imagination, it has promise. Consider the *Encyclopedia of Associations* which lists and dutifully describes over 25,000 groups. Divided by broad subjects, with detailed indexes, this is a profile of American realities and dreams. It goes from the "American Association of Aardvark Aficionados" (600 members who love the animals) to the "Zippy Collectors Club" ("philatelists interested in the collecting of zip code and other marginally marked material").

A typical entry covers 15 to 20 basic points about each of the organizations, whether it has a half dozen members or many thousand, whether it be deadly serious or just deadly, e.g., see "The Flying Funeral Directors of America" (who "create and further a common interest in flying and funeral service"). This catalog of organizations brings the often arid landscape of American commerce to multifarious life. The same inventory that includes the

Financial Accounting Federation also yields up the Electrical Women's Round Table and the Pressure Sensitive Tape Council.[19]

Information for each entry includes the group's name, address, chief executive, phone number, purpose and activities, membership, and publications (which are often directories issued by the individual associations). There is a key word alphabetical index, but the second volume is really an index to the first in that it lists all the executives mentioned in the basic volume, again with complete addresses and phone numbers. A second section rearranges the associations by geographical location. The third volume is issued between editions and keeps the main set up to date by reporting, in two issues a year, on approximately 10,000 changes in the primary set. With this set, the librarian can easily retrieve information by subject, by the name of the association, and by the name of executives connected with the association, and generally can keep up with name changes as well as new organizations. One other volume, while useful, is not essential to the main set. *International Organizations* covers groups outside the United States not found in the first volume.

The edition is updated every few years, as is the custom with most works of this type. Another habit of directory publishers is to develop "spin-offs." A case in point: *Encyclopedia of Associations: Regional, State and Local* (Detroit, Mich.: Gale Research Company, 1988, to date.) First published in 1988, with promises of frequent updates, this follows the pattern of the major set, but is limited to 50,000 local, state, and regional associations. There are five volumes (at $450). If there is humor and pathos in the directory of national organizations, one can only imagine what can be found in the entries which are arranged here alphabetically: first by state, then by city and town, and finally by the association name. The subject index is little more than a key word approach, i.e., it lifts the key words from the title, and if these are not explanatory of subject matter, one is lost. True, the editors do add subjects, but not enough.

Another problem too often found in reference works is highlighted by the review in the "Reference Books Bulletin":

> A hallmark of the *Encyclopedia of Associations* has been a conscientious effort to base entries on data received directly from associations them-

---

[19] "Banana Club Meets Electrical Women," *The New York Times*, Aug. 11, 1986, p. A19. See another feature article on the same subject in *The Wall Street Journal*, Oct. 29, 1986, p. 23, "A Book for the Joiner in All of Us," and "Encyclopedia of Associations Expands Online Reach," by Mick O'Leary in *Database*, October 1989, pp. 59–61. This is a book which invites editorial comment, over and over and over again.

selves. This standard has been abandoned in this work, which relies heavily on secondary sources: "local telephone directories; newspapers, magazines, and other periodicals; state and local chambers of commerce; and, most importantly, national organizations. . . . Questionnaires were mailed selectively." Despite obvious efforts to gather data, it is very difficult to predict which organizations will be included and which will not. Local chapters of the Medical Library Association are included, but not those of the Special Libraries Association or the American Society for Information Science.[20]

The publisher, Gale Research, has yet another spin-off. In 1987 they published *Organization Master Index* which is an alphabetical listing of about 150,000 organizations. The user finds the name of the organization and then is directed to go to one of 45 sources for more information. The index often generates several places where one might discover outline information on the Central Intelligence Agency or the Dog Food Club of America. Actually, a trained reference librarian rarely needs such a second partner in the quest for an association. It is much simpler to turn to a specific source such as, yes, the *Encyclopedia of Associations.*

Although costs run over $100 an hour to use the directory online, it may be cost-effective for the library which consults it four, or fewer, times a year. Certainly more costly is the CD-ROM version, which runs almost $1500 per year, although this is less than the printed versions, which with additions is close to $2000 a year. (The CD-ROM has the basic set, plus three other related databases). The advantage is that it has a semiannual update. It is called "Gale Global Access: Associations," and includes the *International Organizations* volume, as well as data in other "family" members of the group.

As is often the case, the CD-ROM offers added features such as a system whereby one may print mailing list formatted labels. A modem allows the user to immediately access a given organization.

Most Western countries have the equivalent type of directory. For example, in Canada there is the *Directory of Associations in Canada* (Toronto: Micromedia, 1978 to date, irregular) which includes data on over 10,000 organizations.

A number of associations are foundations, but the seeker of information on foundations and more particularly on their grants should turn to *The Foundation Directory.* The 1990 edition lists over 5000 foundations by state, with their purpose and activities, administrators' names, and any grants available. Only foundations with

[20]"Reference Books Bulletin," *The Booklist,* Sept. 15, 1988, p. 134.

minimum assets of $1 million and total grants of $100,000 in the last year of record are listed. (Individual grants are usually less than $100,000.) There are five indexes, including subject, by cities, by donors, and by foundation name.

Education

American Council on Education. *American Universities and Colleges,* 13th ed. New York: Walter deGruyter, 1987, 2024 pp. $119.50.

Comparative Guide to American Colleges, 14th rev. ed. New York: Harper & Row, 1989, 704 pp. $35; paper, $17.95.

Lovejoy's College Guide. New York: Monarch Press, 1940 to date, biennial, paper, $18.95.

A standard work in the field, *American Universities and Colleges* is the first place to turn for detailed information on over 1900 institutions. One finds answers to questions ranging from what is taught by whom, to the number of students, to the shape of various graduate and professional education programs. Schools are listed by state and by city, and there is a detailed index as well as several appendixes which list ROTC schools, dress codes, etc.

Among hundreds of such single-volume guides, it provides the details most students and parents are seeking. Consider, for example, the faculty. It is shown here by number as well as by sex and rank. But there is a drawback: Usually the statistical data is three to four years behind the date of the latest edition. And editions come out only every four or five years.

While *American Universities and Colleges* lets the reader draw conclusions about "best" and "better" by simply weighing the data, other guides are not so subtle.[21] Opinions can be as much based on statistics as on personal reaction to a campus. For example, the often-updated *Comparative Guide to American Colleges* explains the best school for the person looking for the best in social activities or academic excellence, or both. Everything from admission requirements and the racial composition of the student body to the amount of

---

[21]"College and University Rankings" *RQ,* Spring 1986 to date. This is a critical, annotated listing of reference works (as well as articles) which help the student pick the best university or college. The first listing included 83 items and the 1989 coverage included 56 new books and articles. See also: "Best of the College Guides," *Changing Times,* December 1988, pp. 63–65. Although for laypersons, the brief article is of help to libraries.

social life is considered in a standard form for each institution. It answers such questions as how many full-time men and women are on the campus or what percentage of students go on to graduate work. Many students have found it to be remarkably accurate over the years. The listings are by the name of the academic center, and at the end of the book there is an index by subject from accounting to library science and zoology.

There are several less specialized, less detailed directories, particularly of a popular type found in most bookstores and even on newsstands. The best-known is *Lovejoy's College Guide* which outlines, state by state, the various requirements, offerings, and so on, of American schools. There are also Lovejoy guides to vocational schools and prep schools. While uneven in presentation and arrangement, the various guides are at least as popular to many students as are those published by Barron's and Peterson's.

These are only examples in a field for which numerous publishers offer guides. There is no shortage of choices, and the librarian should check with experts in education, including faculty where available, for ultimate selection. For example, Peterson offers a dozen or so different works which can be useful in particular library situations. These range from *Guide to Four-Year Colleges* to *Summer Opportunities for Kids and Teenagers*. Most are updated annually.

The British-published *World of Learning* (London: Europa Publishing Company, 1947 to date, annual) gives data on educational institutions throughout the world, including the United States. The first volume begins with a discussion of international education and of scientific and cultural organizations and continues with the country-by-country listing, completed in the second volume. There is a good index. Standard information (address, function, and so on) is given for each country and institution, here interpreted to mean not only universities and colleges but libraries, research centers, museums, art galleries, and even learned societies. There is a listing of professors at all major universities. This is more of a directory, not a discursive discussion of world education, but informative and considered "basic" in most larger libraries.

Inevitably, the more detailed guides will find their way to CD-ROM format. A case in point: "Peterson's College Database" which draws upon several of the publisher's college printed guides. It offers profiles of 3100 accredited, degree-granting colleges in the United States and Canada. There are numerous points of entry into the full-text database. An annual disk, it costs $595, which, although not expensive for CD-ROM formats, is quite costly in comparison to the printed guides.

Libraries

The American Library Directory. New York: R. R. Bowker Company, 1923 to date, annual, 2 vols. $190. (DIALOG file 460, $75 per hour).

Directory of Special Libraries and Information Centers. Detroit, MI: Gale Research Company, 1963 to date, biennial, 3 vols. $290 to $350 each.

The American Library Directory is included here to indicate that there are directories for virtually every profession. Published since 1923, it provides basic information on 35,000 public, academic, and special libraries in the United States and Canada. Arranged by state and city or town, the listings include names of personnel, library address and phone number, book budgets, number of volumes, special collections, salaries, subject interests, and so on. It has many uses, from seeking addresses for a survey or for potential book purchasers to providing necessary data for those seeking positions in a given library. (Information, for example, on the size of collections and salaries will sometimes tell the job seekers more than can be found in an advertisement.) There is a separate section on interlibrary loan and a bimonthly updating service ($65) which keeps one current with changes in staff, funding, etc. Unfortunately, the online version is updated only once each year.

Special libraries receive much more detailed treatment in the *Directory of Special Libraries and Information Centers.* This work lists over 18,000 units which are either special libraries or ones with special collections, including a number of public and university libraries. Arrangement is alphabetical by name, with a not-very-satisfactory subject index. (Subject headings are furnished by the libraries, and as there is no one standard listing, it tends to be erratic.) The second volume is the geographic-personnel index, and the third is a periodic supplement covering new material between editions. A spin-off of the basic set is the *Subject Directory of Special Libraries and Information Centers,* a five-volume work which simply rearranges the material in the basic set by subject area.

World Guide to Libraries (New York: K. G. Saur, irregular 1978 to date) lists more than 37,000 libraries in 160 countries. Arrangement is by continent and country. Within each section the library is listed by type (academic, federal, public, etc.) and then by city. Often revised, it is a systematic source of information which is quite reliable.

SUGGESTED READING

"Action Exchange: City Directories: Public Information or Invasion of Privacy?" *American Libraries,* May 1990, p. 409. Of three responses to this query, one says that the librarian should give the information, while the other two say to give partial or no such data.

Glazer, Sophie, "Missed Manners," *Boston Review,* December 1990, pp. 17–19. In this review of several etiquette books, including *Miss Manners' Guide* and *The Lady's Guide to Perfect Gentility* (1856), the author questions many of the assumptions behind books of etiquette. Still, she favors "embracing the invigorating world of the well mannered."

Havener, W. Michael, "Answering Ready Reference Questions: Print Versus On-line," *Online,* January 1990, pp. 22–28. Using 12 social science questions and trained librarians, the author seeks to find whether online or print is the most efficient method of fielding ready-reference questions. It is a tie vote, although online does seem faster and more efficient in many cases. An excellent article as much for the findings as the methodology.

Hodges, Deborah, *Etiquette.* Jefferson, NC: McFarland, 1989. This is an annotated bibliography of 1075 book and magazine articles dealing with etiquette and etiquette guides published in English in the United States, from 1900 through 1987. If there is a piece about the subject which the author did not find, it is not a breach of either etiquette or hard work. See, too, the introduction for a brief history of American manners in the twentieth century.

Legal Reference Services. This quarterly journal is edited for law librarians, but often there are articles which will be of considerable assistance to the librarian who needs a few basic lessons in legal bibliography, e.g., in one recent issue (vol. 9, nos. 1/2, 1989) legal research guides as bibliographic efforts are nicely explained by Richard Surles.

Patterson, Charles D., "The Name behind the Title: Joseph Whitaker—Still an Annual Affair," *Reference Services Review,* Spring 1987, pp. 67–69. A brief history/ biography of the son of a silversmith who became a publisher and whose name is a key word in the world's most famous almanac title.

Roberts, Kay, "BARC: A Brief History . . . " *Wilson Library Bulletin,* January 1990, pp. 32–35. BARC (Bay Area Reference Center) had a reputation for superior reference services to member libraries. Looking back over the history of the organization, the author explains the delights and sorrows of networking. The system ceased and a new plan was put into operation during 1990 and 1991, but the lessons are good for students and experts alike.

Shipps, Anthony, *The Quote Sleuth.* Champaign, IL: University of Illinois, 1990. A librarian at Indiana University offers a guide which compares various, basic books of quotations and related works from the OED to concordances. Along the way he explains the best way to use these works to find elusive quotations. Good advice on how to use internal evidence in a quote to find its original source.

Warner, Marnie, and Kathleen Flynn, "Legal Collections in Small and Medium Sized Public Libraries," *Collection Building,* vol. 8, no. 2, 1987, pp. 25–33. Divided between words of advice on how to establish a layperson's collection (with the problems and some solutions) and an annotated bibliography of basic titles. For a discussion of the problems involved with legal reference work see: Michael E. Rice, "Reference Service versus Unauthorized Legal Practice," *Legal Reference Services Quarterly,* vol. 10, no. 2, 1990, pp. 41–56.

CHAPTER NINE
BIOGRAPHICAL SOURCES

The writer Edmund Gosse once described biography as "a study sharply defined by two definite events, birth and death." In the words of another author commenting on the problem concerning biography, it "will always remain an imprecise form: by means of some peculiar alchemy a jumble of facts and impressions is transformed into a life, resurrecting the dead."[1]

The quest for information about the living and the dead has made numerous publishers, compilers, and biographers (not to mention those quite living celebrities penning their autobiographies) the richer. Whether the massive numbers of biographies issued each year has made the reader or the librarian the richer is another question.

How does the librarian know if a work is truly legitimate, i.e., authoritative and based on an accurate, relatively objective selection policy? A rule of thumb will do in most cases: If the title is not listed (or minimally praised) in any of the basic bibliographies, such as Sheehy, Walford, *American Reference Books Annual,* or the current reviewing services, then there is the possibility that it is a worthless volume.

The publisher's name is another indication of authority. Five publishers are responsible for a large number of available biography titles. They are the Gale Research Company, The H. W. Wilson Com-

---

[1]Stanley Olson, "On Biography," *Antaeus,* Autumn 1982, p. 168.

pany, St. Martin's Press, Marquis Who's Who Inc., and R. R. Bowker Company. It is no surprise that most of these are major publishers of other standard reference works. Trade publishers, from Random House to Harper & Row, publish biographical sources, but they tend to be of more popular figures. At any rate, if the librarian does not recognize the publisher, and particularly if it is not one of the major five, then the warning flag should be out to do further checking.

SEARCHING BIOGRAPHICAL SOURCES

The first problem in researching a life, with all but the very well known, is to locate a biography of the individual. Fortunately, this is now relatively easy. One need only turn to *Biography and Genealogy Master Index* for an alphabetical listing of names and some 7.5 million citations where information can be located. This is not to suggest that *all* the names one is searching for will be found in this index, but it is at least a major point of departure.

In determining which biographical source to search, the librarian will work from two basic beginning queries: How much of the history of an individual life does the user require, and what type of data is required? (This query is usually appropriate for a ready-reference question about address, profession, and so on.) At what depth and sophistication should the answer be to a more involved question? This can be determined by the education and needs of the individual user. The quantitative question will require either a silhouette or simple data or an essay form of answer.

The data type of question is by far the most common in the ready-reference situation. Typical queries: "What is the address and phone number of X?" "How does one spell Y's name?" "What is the age of R?" "When did Beethoven die?" Answers will be found in the familiar who's who directory-biographical dictionary sources. Approach varies with each title, but all are consistent in listing names alphabetically and, at a minimum, in giving the profession and position (with or without claim-to-fame attributes) of the individual. At a maximum, these sources will give full background on the entry from birth and death dates to publications, names of children, and so on. The information is usually, although not necessarily, in outline form. It is rarely discursive or critical. The data are all.

The second major type of biographical question comes from the person who wants partial or relatively complete information on an individual. The questioner may be writing a paper, preparing a speech, or seeking critical background material. Typical queries: "How can I write a paper on Herman Melville?" "What do you have on [X], a prominent American scientist?" "Is there a book about George Washington and the cherry tree?" Answers will be found in reference sources with an emphasis on essays (300 words to several pages in length).

In addition to using the standard biographical guides, one may search for information on an individual with the aid of a computer. The guides themselves are found usually online and on CD-ROM; and one can also look for information about an individual in a particular subject area. For example, if John P or Mary R are known to be experts on full-text online reference sources, one might seek out additional data by searching computer science periodical indexes online (or on CD-ROM) as well as in the standard library science indexes, such as *Library and Information Science Abstracts*. The same path can be followed for any profession or interest.

A standard bibliography such as *American Reference Books Annual* will indicate the wide variety of reference works in biography published each year. An impressive reminder of just how much is involved will be found in *Biographical Dictionaries and Related Works* (Detroit, Mich.: Gale Research Company, 1986). Here are some 16,000 entries, and then only of biography compilations which have at least 100 entries.[2]

How many biographical reference works would one find in the average medium to large public or academic library? Guesses vary but some say from 200 to 500. Actually, many small- to medium-size libraries might get along with even fewer reference books. Large libraries will number their collection in the thousands.[3]

Discussion here is limited to reference books. If the circulation of biography were included—since biography is at least as popular as fiction in many libraries—the numbers of individual volumes would be considerably greater.

[2]In itself the *Biographical Dictionaries . . .* is a useful reference work. Each title has a brief (10 to 50 word) explanation of content. The listings are primarily in two sections, national biography and the second part, biography by subject. A third, much smaller, section lists the works by *universal biography*. The second volume, of the two-volume set, includes three indexes: subject, author, and title. New editions are planned about every seven or eight years.

[3]*Biographical Sources* (Phoenix, AZ: Oryx Press, 1986) provides descriptions of 700 reference biographical sources, including indexes and collective biographies. It indicates a compromise number of biographical reference sources for an average library of more than modest size.

Genealogy

A major interest of many library clients is genealogy. It is defined by one expert as "the making of a human pedigree through the linkage of basic biological data found in records with names, dates and places." The quest for a family history fascinates and confuses. As a result it tends to be the province of experts, but there are numerous basic handbooks and guides which may be used by the librarian (and layperson) to launch and complete a genealogical project. And while genealogy is not considered in this chapter, a good beginning (as well as the source of the definition cited above) will be found in "Genealogy Reference Books," in "Reference Books Bulletin" (*The Booklist,* April 15, 1990, pp. 1652–1658). Another excellent source is Val D. Greenwood's *The Researcher's Guide to American Genealogy* (2d ed., Baltimore, MD: Genealogical Publishing Co., 1990.)

EVALUATION

How does the librarian know whether a biographical source is reliable? There are a number of tests.

Selection. Why is a name selected (or rejected) for the various biographical reference aids? The method for the several who's who entries is discussed later, but the process is relatively easy to describe for biographical aids limited to given subject or profession: the compiler includes all the names that qualify for the scope of the work, as in *American Men and Women of Science* or *World Authors.* In both cases, the widest net is cast to include figures and authors likely to be of interest. There are limitations, but they are so broad as to cause little difficulty for the compiler.

All the editors of reputable works do, however, establish some objective guidelines for inclusion; e.g., *Who's Who in America* features many people "arbitrarily on account of official position." This means that a member of Congress, a governor, an admiral, a general, or a Nobel Prize winner, is automatically included; and people in numerous other categories, as well, are assured of a place in the volume only because of the position they hold. The *International Who's Who* is certain to give data on members of all reigning royal families. The *Dictionary of American Biography* takes a more restrictive approach: one must first be dead to be included; after that requirement is met, the editor begins making selections.

Then, too, there are some automatic exclusions. In the case of subject biographical reference works, the exclusion is usually evident in the title: one does not look for poets in *Who's Who in American Art* or *American Men and Women of Science.*

There are levels of exclusiveness; it may be somewhat more difficult to get into *Who's Who in America* than *Who's Who in American Art.* For the former listing, it is a matter of "Don't call us, we'll call you," and inclusion depends on some public achievement. Being listed in other reference sources may depend only on membership in a group or profession; it is difficult to stay out of such titles as *Who's Who in the United Nations* if one happens to work there, or *Who's Who in Golf* should one be a professional or a well-known amateur. A listing in a given title depends on one's filling out the proper forms. Failure to do so may mean failure to be included unless one is such a famous U.N. employee or golfer that the editor digs out the information.

A publisher may apply automatic standards of selection or rejection in a biographical source. Briefly: (1) the person must be living, or dead; (2) the individual must be a citizen of a given country, region, or city; (3) the person must be employed in a specific profession or type of work; (4) the individual must be a given sex or age. One or more of these measurements may be employed in any given reference work.

Although the *Dictionary of American Biography* now includes a few outstanding criminals, many biographical sources restrict selections to everyone from popular entertainers to sports figures. Some counter that any person of importance, respectable or not, should be included. In the past, admission to a biographical reference book was seen as a sign of moral approval, and this is still true for many works today. This author believes that such a policy is highly questionable. A more mature editorial policy would include everyone the broad public wants to know about—a policy now followed by *The New York Times Biographical Services* as well as *Current Biography.*

Audience. The majority of reference works in biography are published for adults, although there are some (particularly concerning books and writers) for younger people. For the adult searcher, works can then be divided by purpose, education level of the user, etc. Obviously, the lines here are not all that clear, and an adult may well refer to a child's reference work (such as the *World Book* biographies).

Length of Entry. Once a name is selected, a question is: How much space does the figure warrant? five or six lines? a page? The purpose and scope of the work may dictate a partial answer. The who's who data calls for a relatively brief outline or collection of facts. The biographical dictionary may be more discursive; the essay type of work will approach the same entry in a way particular to its form. Regardless of approach, the editor still has to make decisions about balance and length.

Authority. Biography began as an accepted form of approbation; e.g., *Ecclesiastes* has the famous line, "Let us now praise famous men"; and this was the purpose of biography until well into the seventeenth century. After a period of relative candor, including Boswell's famous *Life of Johnson* and Johnson's own *Lives of the Poets,* the form returned to uniform panegyric in the Victorian nineteenth century. With the Freudian influence in the twentieth century, unabashed praise once more gave way to reality. The fashion today is for truth in biography, and many famous people have stipulated that no biography should be written about them.[4]

The development of authoritative biography is relatively recent, and the librarian must beware (1) Victorian, i.e., nineteenth and early twentieth century, standard biographical works which took more pride in painting everything with rosy colors than in delivering the truth and (2) modern biographical outlines or even essays where the author is so devoted to the subject that the evaluation is suspect.

A third category is described by Joyce Carol Oates as "pathography." Here the personal involvement is so strong that the result may be entirely out of focus. Oates describes this method as concentrating on "dysfunction and disaster, illnesses and pratfalls, failed marriages and failed careers, alcoholism and breakdowns and outrageous conduct. Its shrill theme is failed promise if not tragedy." Examples: Jean Stafford by David Roberts and Albert Goldman's study of John Lennon. Both are highly suspect.[5] "All biog-

[4]Book-length biographies present other authoritative problems. Here "truth" depends upon the skills and interpretive powers of the biographer. A single example: In 1974 a historian at the University of California, Fawn M. Brodie, published a life of Thomas Jefferson, *An Intimate History.* The best-selling biography claimed that Jefferson maintained an intimate thirty-eight-year relationship with one of his slave women. By 1987 another historian, Sidney Moss, asserted that the Brodie biography drew upon false evidence. According to Moss, the story was a myth created by an unfriendly newspaper, although Ms. Brodie interpreted it as the truth. Who is correct? For more see "Jefferson and His Slave . . ." *The New York Times,* Nov. 22, 1987, p. 42.

[5]James Atlas, "Speaking Ill of the Dead," *The New York Times Magazine,* Nov. 6, 1988, p. 40.

raphy is lies," said Aneurin Bevan, an outstanding English Prime Minister. He may have been right. Sensational, muck-raking lives of famous people have become big business.

Source of Information

Today the question about authority must begin with another question: Who wrote the biographical entry—an editor, the subject, an authority in the field, a secretary? In preparing almost any material except statistical information, the person who penned the entry will have had either conscious or subconscious biases. Even in a straightforward presentation of data, if the biographical subject supplied the information (the usual case with most current biographies), there may be slight understatements or exaggerations concerning age (men more often than women lie about this), education, or experience. Biographical sources relying almost entirely on individual honesty cannot be completely trusted. This leads to the next query: Have sources of information other than the subjects' own questionnaires been cited? The preface should make these two points clear.

In the *Who's Who* series, someone may conceal age, education, experience, etc. This is petty. On a larger scale, others have literally built lives which are completely false but which are dutifully documented in reference sources. A single example will make the point. In 1989 *The Times* of London wrote a long obituary about Sir William Stephenson who died at age 93. A former British intelligence chief, he had claimed that he had the confidence of Winston Churchill. Actually, Stephenson had been a British agent in the United States, and never knew Churchill. He also had claimed he had much to do with the breaking of the German code, but there is no evidence linking him to this event. He was an intrepid fraud, and the astonishing thing is that even before his death he had been exposed in, among other places, *The Churchillians* (1981).[6]

Some think the directory approach is critically flawed in that the subject supplies the material. *Who's Who* (for example) is not so much a biographical reference work as an autobiographical one—a crucial distinction. This may not automatically lead to the telling of outright untruths, but it does promote the suppression of facts embarrassing to the author. This leads the critic, who may just as

---

[6]"Death of an Intrepid Fraud," *The Sunday Telegraph* (London), Feb. 12, 1989, p. 13. The story documents the various lies which Stephenson told during his lifetime.

well have been talking about the thousands of other similar biographical directories, to comment

> Show business is a field where it is possible to check *Who's Who*. The process doesn't inspire one with great confidence in *Who's Who* . . . Roy Boulting appears from his *Who's Who* entry to be neither married nor a father. In reality he has had seven children. . . . Vanity can lead to too much information as well as too little. *Who's Who* acquiesces in the writing by Barbara Cartland of an epic entry, extending to one-and-a-half columns. She lists the full title of every shop girl romance she has ever written. The *Who's Who* spokesman defended this on the grounds that it constitutes a useful record. How sad that such trivia are given space seemingly at the expense of any mention of Muriel Spark's birth date (1918).[7]

Equally, it is useful to know whether the biography was prepared completely by the publisher's editorial staff, whether it was simply slightly edited by that same staff from information received from the subject, and whether it includes sketches written by outside experts. The last is the usual procedure for essay-length biographies.

When the source of the information is questionable, it should be verified in one or more other works. If a serious conflict remains which cannot be resolved, what should be done? The only solution is to attempt to trace the information through primary source material, such as newspapers, contemporary biographies, or articles about the individual, or through his or her family or friends. This undertaking involves historical research. An excellent example can be found in the recurrent arguments concerning the details of Shakespeare's life and times or the famous attempt to straighten out the facts in the life of Sir Thomas Malory, author of the stories of King Arthur and his knights.

Frequency. Most biographical reference sources are on a regular publishing schedule. Some are issued each year, or even every month, while others are regularly updated every three or four years. With celebrities coming and going rapidly, it is obviously important to know the range of time covered by the parent work and its supplements. Many (although not all) biographical reference books are less than satisfactory because of no regular updating procedure.

Other Points. Are there photographs? Are there bibliographies containing material both by and about the subject? Is the work adequately indexed or furnished with sufficient cross-references? (This

---

[7]"Living on Borrowed Glory," *The (London) Guardian,* June 24, 1988, p. 29.

is important when seeking individuals connected with a major figure who may be mentioned only as part of a larger biographical sketch.) Is the work arranged logically? The alphabetical approach is usual, although some works may be arranged chronologically by events, birth dates, historical periods, or areas of subject interest.

Actually, in practice, few of these evaluative tests are employed. If a person is well known, the problem is not so much one of locating a source but of screening out the many sources for pertinent details. If the individual is obscure, usually any source is welcome.

Beware

Dealing as much with individual ego and pride as with accomplishment and fact, biographical reference sources can be great sources of income for what some call the "tin cup" brigades. These are people who literally moved into a community, established a biographical book of that community, and then charged individuals for an entry. These "mug books" are a far cry from the legitimate. Yet, ironically enough, historians are grateful for the information they provide of Americans, particularly in the nineteenth and the early twentieth century before profiling communities became an art.

The librarian should be aware that biography can be a source of illegitimate income. One example, and a familiar one, is the thousands of directories of high school and college students which include those with scholastic or sports achievement. A few are perfectly sound, but the majority are not. Numerous publishing companies, or tin cup artists, dupe parents and students by asking them to pay from $35 to $50 per entry (1988 prices).

The New York Times reports that the California Education Superintendent, Bill Honig, told schools in his state (1988) not to give information about their students to publishing companies, because "he was particularly concerned about solicitations sent to recent immigrants, who . . . might believe they were obligated to pay to have their child's name listed in the directories."[8]

Bells and red lights should flash when the publisher insists the honored person buy the book(s) before an entry is possible. This is a sure signal of a rip-off. Of course, even the most legitimate source often will suggest that the individual buy the book; but there is a great difference between "suggest" and "insist." For example, the

[8]Katherine Bishop, "A Warning on Student Directories," *The New York Times,* July 27, 1988, B7. The two other publishers named: *Outstanding High School Students of America* (Indianapolis) and *Outstanding College Students of America* (Washington).

honorable *Who's Who in America* will include a name without requiring that the individual purchase anything. At the same time a series of letters will suggest "this is your final chance to order (the work) because the publisher is now closing out the biography reservation segment of the 45th (or whatever) edition." In addition, the publisher offers "a special mahogany wall plaque that displays a certificate of recognition in your name." Well, all of this is perfectly legitimate, and may please those being included, but, again, neither the purchase of the book nor wall plaque has anything to do with acceptance or rejection in the *Who's Who in America.* Similar plans of attack are launched by almost all publishers. Most are the tried and true way of Americans in mining a dollar, but the illegitimate ones are simply "hands up."[9]

INDEXES TO BIOGRAPHY

> *Biography and Genealogy Master Index,* 2d ed. Detroit, MI: Gale Research Company, 1980, 8 vols. $975. 1981–1985 cumulation, 5 vols., $750. Annual supplements 1986 to date, $235 each (DIALOG files 287–288, $63 per hour).
>
> *Abridged Biography and Genealogy Master Index,* 1988, 3 vols., $375.
>
> *Almanac of Famous People* (formerly: *Biography Almanac*) 4th ed. 1989, 3 vols. $90.
>
> *Biography Index.* New York: The H. W. Wilson Company, 1947 to date, quarterly with annual cumulations. $135 (Online, Wilsonline $25–$45 per hour).

There are two types of indexes to biography. The first, represented by *Biography and Genealogy Master Index,* is a key to 7.5 million entries found in biographical dictionaries and directories such as *Who's Who in America.* The purpose is to reduce tedious searching of basic, generally current guides.

The second type of index, represented by *Biography Index* includes citations to biographies appearing in periodicals and selected

---

[9]A too-typical gross practice is to send, at random, postcards informing the recipient that a genealogical record of his/her family may be purchased for $30. This is no more than a printout of people with the same last name taken from phone books and/or city directories across the country. Sometimes called "The John Doe Album," the computer printout according to the publisher comes in a "leathered textured library edition, beautifully hard bound and gold stamped."

books. The purpose is to offer a key to biographical information about persons living and dead from a wide variety of general sources.

The first type would be employed for ready reference when the data type of information is required. The second would more likely be used to seek detailed information for a paper, research project, speech, or other presentation.

For example, a user who wished to find the address of Mary Doe would turn to the *Master Index* for sources of short data entries in the various biographical dictionaries indexed. The user who wished to write a paper on the achievements of Doe would need a fuller entry and would turn to biographical information in periodicals as indicated in *Biography Index*.

In an opening search, where not much is known about an individual, the *Master Index* would be preferred. If the person is well known to the searcher, and the essential facts are in hand, then one would go first to *Biography Index*. All of this is to say that the two basic reference works may be used separately or together, but they are the first steps in any biographical search.

There are approximately 7.5 million citations found in approximately 700 biographical reference works. Since 1985, the publisher has issued a new volume each year, and cumulates the annual volumes every five years. The work is arranged in a single alphabet by the last name of the individual. After the name come the birth and death dates, and then a key to one or more sources in which there is a short entry or essay about the individual. Famous people may have up to a dozen or more citations, but for the most part the citations usually number no more than two to three.

Among the 700 biographical works indexed are both data type (*Who's Who* variety) and essay type (*Dictionary of American Biography*). In the early years the focus was almost entirely on the data variety, but this changed as the publisher indexed more and more biographical sources. Most of the standard works published by the five largest biographical reference publishers are indexed in the *Master Index*.

There are several versions of the *Master Index*:

1. *Abridged* . . . . This includes the basic set, plus the supplementary volumes from 1980 through 1987, cut from 6 million to about 1.6 million entries. Some 115 current and much-used basic sources are analyzed. According to the publisher, the selection of biographical source material is based upon a nationwide survey of holdings of small- and medium-size libraries, e.g., only standard biographical sources are indexed. Updates are planned every five years.

2. *Almanac of Famous People.* In an effort to bring the set within the financial means of libraries, this work is only $90 for three volumes. The first two volumes have regular entries for about 25,000 people. The third volume offers numerous indexes from chronology to geography. Occupations are indexed as well.

3. Online, *Biography and Geneology Master Index* DIALOG provides a full work. If only a few searches are to be made each year, it is obviously preferable to the printed version. It is also somewhat more convenient, although one probably can find what is needed as fast, if not faster, in the Bio-Base.

4. Duplicating entirely what is found in the main set, the publisher offers six spin-offs. These are *not* needed when the main set is available, but may be useful for particular subject areas. They range from *Children's Authors and Illustrators* to *Historical Biographical Dictionaries Master Index.*

As useful as all of this may be for the librarian, the index is far from perfect. The publisher simply prints names as found in the sources. If, for example, Joe Doaks cites his name in this form in *Who's Who in America,* but prefers Joe Vincent Doaks in *Who's Who in American Rat Catchers* and Joseph V. P. Doaks in *American Businesspersons,* his name will be alphabetically arranged in three different ways. Of course, it could be three different Doakses, but the date of birth indicates that it is probably the same person. Just to make things confusing, the date of birth for the same person may vary, depending on which source was indexed. Also, there may be a simple listing of the same name, albeit with reference to different sources, four or five times.

There are several other indexes of this type, but they are more restrictive in that they are limited to particular areas. One example: *People in History* (Santa Barbara, Calif.: ABC-CLIO, 1987. 2 vols.). The nearly 8000 citations to biographical material are taken from the publisher's *America: History and Life* database from 1976 to about mid-1987. It is updated from time to time. There are brief abstracts, but not the full-length ones found in the index from which this service originated.

One answer to locating retrospective biographical reference sources is offered by the publisher K. G. Saur. The company sells a series of fiche (running in number from 1200 to 1800 individual fiche) which reprints standard sources. For example, *"The American Biographical Archive,"* includes 367 reference works in approximately 300 volumes. "All entries on an individual appear on the same fiche in chronological sequence by date of publication of the original source." This obviates the need of an index, or so claims the publisher. At any rate this costs $7800. Other sets move from the standard French and German works to Spanish and Italian. The cost goes as high as $12,000 per set. While perhaps useful, the librarian today might ask why it could not all be put online or on CD-ROM disks for less cost and easier access.

At times even the *Biography and Genealogy Mastery Index* fails—the name cannot be found. There may be many reasons to explain the omission. One may not be so obvious: The name may be of a literary character, and such names are not found in standard biographical guides of real people. If one suspects this to be the situation, numerous literary guides, as well as general encyclopedias, carry entries for everyone from Simon Legree to Holden Caulfield. Two examples: *Dictionary of American Literary Characters* (New York: Facts on File, 1990) has brief notes on over 11,000 personalities from American novels published between 1789 and 1980. *Characters in 20th Century Literature* (Detroit, Mich.: Gale Research Company, 1990) is another that considers characters from 250 novels. *Masterplots,* and its numerous spin-offs, is a third good place to seek a literary character.

The *Cyclopedia of Literary Characters* (Englewood Cliffs, NJ: Salem Press, 1990) is a key to 4000 characters in about 1500 novels. The four-volume set offers analytical descriptions that are tied to the 1963 *Masterplots II* family. Titles, authors, and characters are indexed. The descriptions, the key to the value of the *Cyclopedia,* are not brilliant, but they are accurate.

Biographies in Periodicals

Where information from periodical articles is required, *Biography Index* is the first choice. More than 2600 different magazines are analyzed for biographical material. This gives the user an extremely wide range of sources, which move from the extremely popular to the esoteric. The end result is rarely disappointing. When searched over several years, and the *Index* goes back to 1947, inevitably something turns up, and often that "something" may be quite detailed. Arrangement is by name of the person. An added bonus is that birth and death dates, nationality, profession and, of course, the citation to the periodical are given. Another most useful feature is the index by profession or occupation. Someone looking for material on an architect—not Frank Lloyd Wright—simply turns here, as would another individual looking for biographical data about dentists or zookeepers.

The index also covers some books, and particularly makes note of individual biographies and autobiographies, as well as collections. A nice touch is the inclusion of some, but certainly not all, fiction which has a well-known real figure at the center of the novel. The same is true of poetry, drama, etc. Obituaries are indexed, including those from *The New York Times.*

UNIVERSAL AND CURRENT BIOGRAPHICAL SOURCES

Universal biographical sources include those from all parts of the world, or at least those parts selected by the editors, and normally include both living and dead personalities. The result is a compendium of relatively well-known individuals.

Current sources may cover the same geographical area but narrow the scope by concentrating on people who are still active or who are only recently dead.

Biographical Dictionaries

Webster's New Biographical Dictionary, Springfield, Mass.: G. & C. Merriam Company, 1985. $21.95.

Before the advent of the *Biography and Genealogy Master Index,* the biographical dictionary was a first place to turn to identify, qualify, and generally discover basic facts about an individual. With that, one might go on to other works, or if nothing more was needed than a birth or death date, occupation, claim to fame, etc., the biographical dictionary might be quite enough. Today, in order to quickly find information about an individual, it is much faster to consult the *Master Index* first. Lacking that reference work, one might return to the dictionary, and it can still be used for ready-reference facts about famous people who are almost sure to be included.

By far the best-known and most used of the biographical dictionaries, *Webster's* gives brief biographies for about 40,000 people from the beginning of history through the early 1970s. The individual's primary contribution is noted, along with nationality, birth (and death) dates, and pronunciation of name. The majority, well over 80 percent of the listings, are deceased, and its primary, if not almost exclusive value, is for checking on persons who are dead. American and British subjects receive most space, with appropriate attention given to major international and historical figures.

Other reference works of this type are found in larger ready-reference sections, such as *Chamber's Biographical Dictionary* (rev. ed., London: Chambers, 1990), which lists 20,000 prominent people, with particular emphasis on British and American personalities. *The New Century Cyclopedia of Names* (New York: Appleton-Century-Crofts, 1954) is a three-volume work of some 100,000 names, including fictional and mythological characters.

Pseudonyms

Pseudonyms and Nicknames Dictionary, 3d ed. Detroit, Mich.: Gale Research Company, 1987, 2 vols. $230.

Covering all periods and most of the world, this is a listing of about 55,000 pseudonyms and nicknames from Johnny Appleseed (John Chapman) to Mark Twain (Samuel Clemens). Information includes birth and death dates, nationality, and occupation. When one looks up the pseudonym or nickname, there is a reference to the original name and the primary information. Cited sources are included, and these amount to over 200 basic biographical works. Arranged in a single alphabet, the guide is extremely easy to use. It is updated by two supplements which are issued between editions of the primary work.

Directory: The Who's Who Form

Who's Who in America. Chicago: Marquis Who's Who, 1889 to date, biennial, 2 vols. $375. (DIALOG file 234, $150 per hour.)

Who's Who. London: Black, 1849 to date, annual (distributed in the United States by St. Martin's Press, Inc.). $150.

International Who's Who. London: Europa Publications Ltd., 1935 to date, annual (distributed in the United States by Gale Research Company). $200.

Although the biographical dictionaries are primarily concerned with dead celebrities, the who's who directory forms list only the living, and, for that matter, only those in some outstanding position. Again, most of the who's who are indexed in the *Biography and Genealogy Master Index*.

The directories are among the most frequently used of the biographical sources. Common questions they answer: (1) Where does X live, or receive his or her mail? (2) What is X's age and position? (3) What has X written? (4) What honors does X claim? These are just a few of the typical queries.

The who's who directories vary in scope, and often in accuracy and timeliness, but their essential purpose is the same: to present objective, usually noncontroversial facts about an individual. The approach and style are monotonous; most are arranged alphabetically by the name of the person, with a following paragraph of vital statistics which normally concludes with the person's address and phone number.

The who's who aids may be classified by scope as international, national, local, professional or business, religious or racial, and so on, and is usually indicated in the title.

Information is normally compiled by sending a questionnaire to the candidate, who is then free to provide as much or as little of the requested information as he or she wishes. The better publishers check the returns for flaws or downright lies. Other publishers may be content to rely on the honesty of the individual, who normally has little reason not to tell the truth, although—and this is a large "although"—some candidates for inclusion may construct complete fabrications.

The American *Who's Who in America* has a long history of reliability. It is a source of about 79,000 names of prominent American men and women, as well as a few foreigners with some influence in the United States. As the nation's current population is over 250 million, how do the editors determine who is, or who is not, to be included? The answer is complex, usually based on the person's outstanding achievement or perceived excellence.

The inclusion-exclusion process is of more interest when the reputation and fame of a work, such as *Who's Who in America,* is purposely built upon selectivity of a high order. The natural question is one of legitimacy. Is the selection of Y based on Y's desire to be included (supported by willingness to buy the volume in question or, in a few cases, literally to pay for a place in the volume), or is it based on the editor's notion of eminence, where no amount of persuasion or cash will ensure selection? All works listed here are indeed legitimate; in them, one's way to fame cannot be bought. This is not to say there is no room for criticism. No one will entirely agree on all names selected or rejected in, say, *Who's Who in America.*

In the 1988–1989 edition the editors dropped such luminaries as Philip Roth, Ivan Lendl, Geraldo Rivera, T. Boone Pickens, James Reston, C. Everett Koop, Irving Kristol, Pat Robertson, Trini Lopez, and scores of others. How much of this was intent, and how much was oversight and failure to carry through on questionnaires by the editors is not clear.

On balance, the selection is adequate, if not brilliant. The data for entrants vary in length but not in style, as each fills out a standard form requesting basic information, including date of birth, education, achievements, and address. The form is used to compose the entry, and a proof of the entry is sent to the individual for double checking.

The set also includes a list of those who died and those who retired since the last edition, and a feature "thoughts on my life" is included in some entries. Here the notable figures are asked to reflect on principles and philosophies which have guided them through life. This can be inspirational, or downright disturbing, but it is an always-fascinating facet to otherwise straight directory-type information.

A third index volume is now available (from 1982 at $50), which lists the entries in *Who's Who in America* geographically by state, and then by city. A similar arrangement is found for those from Canada and Mexico. In the "professional area index" there are 16 broad subject headings (arts to unclassified specialties) which list entries by occupation. Unfortunately, the subject headings are much too broad, but this may improve with time.

A paperback four-volume junior and senior high school version of *Who's Who in America* became available in 1990. The work reduces the coverage to 6000 people, but also cuts the price back to a paper edition of $79, as contrasted with the hardbound price of $243. Another advantage, the size of the typeface is twice as large as in the main set, and there are no abbreviations.

Updated quarterly, the online *Who's Who in America* consists of the 97,000 records in *Who's Who in America* and the 15,000 records in *Who's Who in Science and Technology*. In time, the publisher will expand the database to include more of the who's who files. The online version, except for the cost, has several advantages over the printed works. First and foremost, there are over 40 different points of entry, from the person's name to his or her address, company, or other affiliation. The geographic possibilities are even more rewarding. For example, how many prominent Americans are women living in Chicago; or what is the ratio of successful attorneys in Los Angeles and San Francisco (as compared with the total number and those not found in the guide). Another advantage is that new names may be added each quarter, so one does not have to wait for the annual or the biannual printed volumes.

The publisher issues *Supplement to Who's Who in America* every other year so as to update the biennial set, but since the changes and additions are usually minor, this is not recommended.

An often-unforeseen consequence of listing in *Who's Who in*

America, and other major works, is that the requests for further recognition never cease. As one writer explains:

> Every month or two I receive invitations to be listed in other Who's Who–like compilations. I've gotten so many invitations, in fact, that I've stopped filling out the forms, with their requests that I list my "creative works" and "awards, honors, grants." I confess to throwing away the forms, along with the accompanying order blanks for commemorative plaques acknowledging my selection.
>
> Recently a letter informed me that the editors of Who's Who in Finance and Industry, having consulted "many publicly available sources," had "identified" me as a candidate for inclusion. I tried to think how I'd earned this distinction. Was I being honored for the adroit manner in which I bought 200 shares of a toy company called Worlds of Wonder Inc., for $25 each in 1986, and then sold the shares for 63 cents each in 1987? Or maybe it was the manful way I divulged this news, and that of other similarly lucrative investments over the years, to my wife and accountant.
>
> No matter—it's clear that my qualities transcend mere financial acumen. Just last week the mail brought word that I've been nominated for listing in 5,000 Personalities of the World.[10]

Who's Who was first published in Britain on January 15, 1849, fifty years before there were enough prominent Americans to make a volume possible here. During its first forty-seven years, *Who's Who* was a slim book of about 250 pages which listed members of the titled and official classes. In 1897, it became a biographical dictionary, and the 1972–1973 edition is close to 4000 pages. Selection is no longer based on nobility but on "personal achievement or prominence." Most entries are British, but it does include some notables from other countries. And in the past decade, it has put more and more emphasis on prominent scholars and professional people as well as political and industrial leaders among its 28,500 entries.

The British *Who's Who* is the only one which does not have a qualifier, i.e., Who's Who in *Siberia,* Who's Who in *America,* etc. Why? Because the British originated the form. The not too subtle point is that there is no need to go beyond *Who's Who.* It must be a select group of British, or it would not be the genuine thing.

Depending on size and type of audience served, most American public, university, and college libraries will have *Who's Who in America* and possibly *Who's Who*—"possibly" because the better-known figures apt to be objects of inquiry in *Who's Who* are covered in the *International Who's Who,* which opens with a section of names

---

[10]Jacques Leslie, "What's What with Who's Who," *The Wall Street Journal,* Aug. 4, 1988, p. 22.

of "reigning royal families," then moves to the alphabetic listing of some 12,000 to 15,000 brief biographies of the outstanding men and women of our time. The range is wide and takes in those who are prominent in international affairs, government, administration, diplomacy, science, medicine, law, finance, business, education, religion, literature, music, art, and entertainment.

Marquis issues *Who's Who in the World* (1970 to date, biennial) which lists about 31,000 names, or about 10,000 more than in the *International.* Interestingly enough, the amount of duplication is minimal, although the form and type of information is much the same in both.

Almost every country in the world has a similar set of "who's who" directories, that is, a basic work for the living famous and a set for the famous who have died. Most of these are published by reputable firms listed in the standard bibliographies such as *Guide to Reference Books* and *Guide to Reference Materials.* For example, there is *Canadian Who's Who* (Toronto: University of Toronto Press, 1910 to date, every three years). This includes a wide variety of biographical sketches from all walks of life, including businesspeople, authors, performers, and teachers.

One work which would be unnecessary if women were not treated as the second sex is *Who's Who of American Women* (Chicago: Marquis Who's Who, Inc., 1959 to date). A biennial dictionary of notable living American women, it follows the same general pattern as all the Marquis works. The seventeenth edition includes 27,000 women's names. The editor's breakdown of 1000 sketches indicated that, according to occupation, a woman's chances to earn an entry were best if she were a club, civic, or religious leader (9.6 percent of all biographies).

Minorities fare no better than women in the standard who's who. As a result there are separate directories. One example is *Who's Who among Black Americans* (Detroit, Mich.: Gale Research Company, 1976 to date, about every three years). This lists 17,000 people from all fields of endeavor. Entries include the standard type of material, and there are cross-references when needed. The "Occupational Index" lists most, although not all, of the names under 150 categories. There is a "Geographical Index" which needs to be improved.

ESSAY FORM OF BIOGRAPHICAL SOURCES

Current Biography. New York: The H. W. Wilson Company, 1940 to date, monthly except August. $48.

The New York Times Biographical Service: A Compilation of Current

Biographical Information of General Interest. Ann Arbor, MI: University Microfilms Intl., 1970 to date, monthly. Loose-leaf, $120.

Current Biography is the single most popular current essay-length biographical aid in almost all types of libraries. Issued monthly, it is cumulated, often with revised sketches, into annual volumes with excellent cumulative indexing. Annual emphasis is on around 200 international personalities, primarily those in some way influencing the American scene. Articles are long enough to include all vital information about the person and are usually relatively objective. The sketches are prepared by a special staff which draws information from other biographical sources and from the person covered in the article. Subjects are given the opportunity to check the copy before it is published and, presumably, to approve the photograph which accompanies each sketch. Source references are cited. Obituary notices, with due reference to *The New York Times Obituaries Index,* are listed for those who at one time have appeared in the work.

Thanks to the format and rather "catchy" photographs on the cover, *Current Biography* resembles a magazine which, literally, can be read cover to cover.

Each issue includes a cumulative index to past issues of the year, and with the twelfth number, the title is published as a hardbound yearbook. The yearbook adds a subject index by profession, useful for looking for leaders in various fields. A cumulative index to the yearbooks is issued every ten years, with paperback cumulative indexes issued between; e.g., as of 1990 there is a hardbound index for the years 1940–1985. Another feature in the annual is a list of current "biographical references." This serves as a convenient up-to-date checklist for purchases.

The New York Times Biographical Service serves the same purpose, and usually the same audience, as *Current Biography.* The essential difference is that *Current Biography* is staff-written with source references. *The New York Times* biographies are usually written by individuals who do not cite sources. Published each month in loose-leaf form, it is a first choice for any medium-size or large library. It includes obituaries and the "man in the news," and features stories from the drama, book, sports, and Sunday magazine sections. Each sheet is a reprint of biographical material which has appeared in *The Times.* The monthly section has its own index, cumulated every six months and annually. (The lack of current indexing is a real headache, and one must search up to 5 to 6 months of individual issues to find persons recently in the news. One might locate persons through the regular *New York Times Index,* but this, other than on-line, is late as well. The efficient way is to search for names where *The New York Times* is indexed on CD-ROM, such as *Newspaper Index* or *Newspaper Abstracts Ondisc.*) The sketches are often reports on controversial, less-than-admirable, individuals. Most of the reporting is objective. Incidentally, the monetary rewards to the authors are slim. They average about $75 per 500-word essay.

The deceased are dutifully listed under "Deaths" in the annual and online and CD-ROM versions of *The New York Times Index.* Usually, too, there are appropriate cross-references in the main index to the page lined in black. Also, for a retrospective key to such obituaries one might turn to the microfilm version of *The New York Times Obituaries Index, 1858–1978.*

No matter how large the cast of characters in these various biographical sources, someone is always missing. Counting on that, as well as introducing a new approach to the famous found in all sources, Gale Research Company launched a rival to the two standards in 1985. This is *Newsmakers* (1985 to date, quarterly), which considers about 30 to 40 people in each issue. All are presented in a uniform style, including numerous photographs. The fourth volume, labeled *Contemporary Newsmakers,* cumulates the three issues and adds another 50 entries to bring the year's total to 200 prominent people. Emphasis is on Americans, but there is a fair amount of international coverage.

Retrospective Essay Form

> *Dictionary of American Biography.* New York: Charles Scribner's Sons, 1974, 10 vols., eight supplements, 1977 to date, irregular. The set, $1300.

> *Dictionary of National Biography.* Edited by Leslie Stephen and Sidney Lee, 1885 to 1901; reissue, London: Oxford University Press, 1938, 22 vols. and supplements $1275 including supplement 9.

> *Notable American Women 1607–1950. A Biographical Dictionary.* Edited by Edward T. James. Cambridge, MA: Harvard University Press, 1971, 3 vols.; paper, $40; supplements 1980, 1983 paper, $13.

The fruitful use of these national, retrospective biographical aids depends on the librarian's or user's recognizing the nationality of the figure in question and the fact that all entrants are decreased. When the nationality is not known, it will save time to first check the *Biography and Genealogy Master Index* and its companion for historical figures, *Historical Biographical Dictionaries Master Index.* Where neither is available, one might turn first to a biographical dictionary, to an encyclopedia, or to the *Biography Index.* The latter may prove particularly productive when the name cannot be found in any of the sources noted.

The listing in either the *DAB* or *DNB* is a way of making certain that a person's reputation lives forever. The judgment of the work is the yardstick whereby everyone from historians to art curators measure the importance of an individual. Posthumous celebrity is the final accolade, although it often is bestowed on somewhat obscure, dimly remembered, politicians and sports figures.

The *Dictionary of American Biography* (or the *DAB,* as it is usually called), with its supplements, covers 18,000 figures who have made a major contribution to American life. Almost all are Americans, but there are a few foreigners who significantly contributed to our history. (In this case, they had to have lived in the United States for some considerable length of time.) Furthermore, no British officers "serving in America after the colonies declared their independence" are included.

About 3000 scholarly contributors add their distinctive styles and viewpoints to the compilation. As a consequence, most of the entries, which vary from several paragraphs to several pages, can be read as essays rather than as a list of connected but dry facts.

The original set and the supplements are indexed in a single volume, published in 1990 as *Dictionary of American Biography: Comprehensive Index.* The index is in six sections: subjects of the biographies, their birthplaces, schools and colleges attended, occupations, topics discussed within the biographical entry, and names of contributors to the biographical essays. There are numerous cross-references in each section, which makes the index easy to use. It is a required item for any library with the basic set and supplements.

The *Dictionary of National Biography* (or *DNB*) is the model for the *DAB*; and having learned how to use one set, the librarian can handle the other without difficulty. The *DNB,* approximately twice the size of the *DAB,* includes entries on over 36,000 deceased "men and women of British or Irish race who have achieved any reasonable measure of distinction in any walk of life." It also includes early settlers in America and "persons of foreign birth who have gained eminence in this country."

The 1981–1985 supplement, published in 1990, is unique in that it includes "names of those people you have looked up in the *DNB* and not found," according to the editor. This is a "catch-up" volume in that it includes some names not found in the earlier supplements. At the same time, the 380 entries do include recent dead such as the poet/librarian Philip Larkin and Indira Gandhi.

The original set, edited by Leslie Stephen, Virginia Woolf's father, includes short to long signed articles with bibliographies. Aside from the scope, it can be used in much the same way and for many of the same reasons as the *DAB*.

Both the *DNB* and the *DAB* are classics of reference service and marvels of scholarly research and writing. Leslie Stephen made the real point as to why the sets are so well read: "The most amusing book in the language is the *Dictionary of National Biography*. If anyone doubts what appears to me to be a self evident proposition, he has only to buy the work and to dip into it at odd moments."[11]

A *Chronological and Occupational Index to the Dictionary of National Biography* (New York: Oxford University Press, 1985) is primarily an index which divides the entries into 20 basic professional and occupational categories. There is a separate chronological listing for each category. This is a massive index (close to 1000 pages) to both the basic set and the supplements.

Notable American Women includes 1359 biographies of subjects who died prior to 1950, and the supplements add around 900 who died between 1951 and 1980. Inclusion is based on their "lives and careers (having) had significant impact on American life in all fields of thought and action." The long, signed biographies are similar to those in the *DAB* and *DNB*, and the author of each entry has special knowledge of the subject. In explaining who was included or excluded, the editors noted that the usual test of inclusion—being the wife of a famous man—was not considered. (The only exception is the inclusion of the wives of American Presidents.) Once more, the domestic skills of a woman were seldom considered, and no moral judgments as to a woman's being a criminal or an adventurer were used to exclude a name. There is an excellent 33-page introduction,

[11]John Ezard, "Cocky Confidence," *The Guardian Weekly*, Aug. 14, 1988, p. 12. Ronald Fritze, "The Dictionary of National Biography and Its Early Editors and Publishers," *Reference Services Review*, no. 4, 1988, p. 27. A brief history of the set, this puts particular emphasis on how it developed in the nineteenth century. By 1990 the publisher, Oxford University Press, was considering a total revision and rewrite of the set. The cost of the total revision is estimated at over $10 million. For a review of the new supplement, see *The Sunday Times* (London), March 25, 1990, p. H3. Humphrey Carpenter observes: "I think I've found the formula that guarantees entry. Time and again, in an article on some half forgotten academic or public servant, there appears the words: To this Dictionary he contributed the notice of. . . . Evidently the way to get in . . . is to write an entry for someone else."

which gives a historical survey of the role of women in American life; there is also an index of individuals grouped by occupations.

The biographical form which honors the dead and the worthy is found in almost all countries. A single example close to home is the *Dictionary of Canadian Biography* (Toronto: University of Toronto Press, 1966 to date, in progress). About every five or six years a new volume is issued, which covers a particular time period. For example, the twelfth came out in 1990 and features people from 1891 to 1900. The set has biographical sketches of educators, military figures, craftspeople, etc. Published in French as well as English, this is considered a definitive source of biography in Canada. A cumulative index to the first part of the series came out in 1991, which solved the problem of multiple indexing. Note, especially, the useful bibliographies. Subsequent volumes are in progress.

Newspaper indexes offer an excellent key to retrospective biography of both the famous and infamous. Some newspaper obituary columns, such as *The Times* of London and to a lesser extent *The New York Times*, have distinctive points of view about people who may not quite make the *DAB* or the *DNB*. At one time obituary notices were entirely flattering. No longer. Now the more detailed entries tend to add a sting to the death notice. *The Times* of London is uninhibitedly publishing articles on the passing of, among others, "A cuckolded poet, a rock promoter strangely addicted to collecting orang-utangs and an Italian writer striving to avoid becoming a bore." The editor points out that "an obituary should be an exercise in contemporary history, not a funeral oration."[12]

PROFESSIONAL AND SUBJECT BIOGRAPHIES

The interest of biography to almost everyone from the researcher to the layperson has not escaped publishers. Consequently, almost every publisher's list will include biographical works, from individual biographies to collective works to special listings for individuals engaged in a profession. The increase in the number or professions (almost every American claims to be a professional of sorts), coupled with the growth in education, has resulted in a proliferation of specialized biographical sources.

---

[12]Frances X. Clines, "British Paper Adding Sting to Death Notices," *The New York Times*, March 15, 1987, p. 13. It is pointed out, too, that the dead cannot sue for libel and their survivors can only do so "under an obscure provision in which an obituary proves so unbearably insulting as to provoke a criminal offense"--such as perhaps killing the obituary editor.

What was stated before applies here: The reliability of some works is questionable, primarily because almost all (and sometimes all) the information is supplied directly to the editor or publisher by the subject. Little or no checking is involved except when there is a definite question or the biographical sketch is evaluative. Entries tend to be brief, normally giving the name, birth date, place of birth, education, particular "claim to fame," and address. There are rare exceptions to this brief form. The H. W. Wilson Company series on authors features rather long, discursive essays. Most biographical works devoted to a subject or profession have mercifully short entries, however.

The primary value of the specialized biographical work is as a

1. Source of address
2. Source of correct spelling of names and titles
3. Source of miscellaneous information for those considering the person for employment or as an employer or as a guest speaker
4. Valuable aid to the historian or genealogist seeking retrospective information (if the work has been maintained for a number of years)

When one turns from the standard Marquis titles to other who's who titles, the list is as imposing as it is indicative of numerous professions. For example, there is a *Who's Who in American Music: Classical,* a *Who's Who in Real Estate,* and a *Who's Who in Aviation and Aerospace.* While all these are legitimate, there are nearly 500 biographical directories of a questionable reference value that are published irregularly in the United States.

The directory form has reached a point where almost everyone can qualify for at least one or even a dozen such listings. *The New Yorker* ran a cartoon in 1983 which shows a cowboy taking a letter out of a mailbox. The letter begins: "You've been selected to appear in the forthcoming edition of *Who's Who on the Lone Prairie.*" It is too close to the truth to be funny. Others represent the fragmentation of biography. An excellent example of this carried to extremes is the *Directory of Experts* (Washington: Broadcast Interview sources, 1984 to date, biennial). An alphabetical listing of people who are found on talk shows, it includes a subject, state, and tour index. The latter is for "national tours you can book for the future." The paperback is $23.45, which may be reasonable "to put you in touch with a specialist who knows the issue, can provide background information, and is available for interview."

Following are only representative examples of professional and subject sources. There are hundreds more. When conducting a search for a specific individual, it is usually much faster to begin with the *Biography and Genealogy Master Index* or one of its spin-offs. The exception is when the profession of the individual is known and it is obvious that he or she will be listed in one of the basic professional and subject biographical sources.

Librarianship

Directory of Library and Information Science. Woodbridge, CT: Research Publications, 1988 to date, biennial, 2 vols. $345. CD-ROM, American Library Association, $495.

The librarian interested in the career, background, education, or simply the age of a colleague will turn to what is, admittedly, a rather limited who's who for most public use. Still, it can be of great interest to librarians and to people dealing with them. The majority of the 43,000 short listings are from Americans who were asked to fill out a questionnaire.[13]

Most entries are from public libraries, library schools, and college and university libraries. There are few from special or school libraries.

Unfortunately, over 20,000 of the entries are no more than name, title, address, and in a few cases, a telephone number. These are people who are members of the American Library Association but who did not fill out the form asking for information. There are extensive listings of people involved with "information" including information brokers, television stars, and you name it. This is extraneous and of little value to anyone.

The second volume offers indexes by employer, specialty, and geographical location. The subject interests fall under about 1600 headings, and are useful for identifying would-be employees, authors of books and articles, speakers, etc.

Three things are wrong with this: (1) The price is much too high for the limited use of the set. (2) The inclusion of anyone connected with information expands the size and the price. (3) The

---

[13]This is more than triple the number of entries in the older *Who's Who in Library and Information Sciences* (Chicago: American Library Association, 1982). The older work, although dated, is preferable because it gives considerably more information about individuals.

indexes are useful, but not carefully enough generated. Any self-proclaimed expert is listed. Still, it is all we have.[14]

It may be difficult for a small- or medium-size library to justify purchase of the librarian's who's who and as stated before, the audience for it is, to say the least, limited.

There are numerous other works of this type, and although they are for large, or specialized libraries, they have no place in libraries with tight budgets. For example, a most useful source, but, again, of somewhat limited appeal is *The National Faculty Directory* (Detroit, Mich.: Gale Research Company, 1970 to date, 4 vols., $510) which gives brief information about more than 660,000 teaching faculty in some 3200 U.S. junior and senior colleges and universities. Obviously, this is a first choice for anyone dealing with faculty and for large university libraries. But for others? No.

Literature

> *World Authors, 1980–1985.* New York: The H. W. Wilson Company, 1990, 1000 pp., $80. Supplement: *World Authors 1975–1980,* 1985, 831 pp., $68. *World Authors 1970–1975,* 1979, 893 pp., $73. *World Authors 1950–1970,* 1975, 1340 pp., $90.

> *Contemporary Authors.* Detroit, MI: Gale Research Company, 1962 to date, irregular. (1990: 128 volumes) $97 each.

There are biographical essay collections for many subject areas. One of the most often consulted concerns writers and writing. Students use the library often for information on specific authors for class reports. When the author is well known, there is little difficulty. A good encyclopedia will give information, which can be supplemented by literature handbooks and periodical articles.

Another place to check to find information on a dead or a living author is the *Author Biographies Master Index,* 2d ed. (Detroit, Mich.: Gale Research Company, 1984), which alphabetically lists 300,000 different authors found in about 225 different sources. A

---

[14]See a letter to the editor by Louis M. Morris (*Library Journal,* December 1988, p. 11). Ms. Morris concludes: "OK. Nobody's perfect. After all, the publisher probably accepted input with no serious attempt to do any significant editorial job (just as we might expect from any good vanity press). But then to charge $345 (plus $10 shipping and handling) is to display a gall that rivals even—(an unnamed publisher in the library world known for such unprofessional scalping). How could the American Library Association allow its name to be sullied on the cover of the *DLIS?* The cost of the volumes would probably be a shameless waste of resources for any library committed to effective information service."

supplement (1986) adds another 200,000 citations to the main work. The same publisher's *Biography and Genealogy Master Index* is as useful. In fact, if the latter is available, the former really is not necessary because the larger index includes all the material found in the *Author Biographies Master Index.*

World Authors, issued by the Wilson Company, is one of the best-known series on authors. The series is useful because it includes not only the essential biographical information but also bibliographies of works by and about the author. The source of much of the material is the author, if living, or careful research if the author is deceased. Some of the entries are printed almost verbatim as written by the author and are entertaining reading in their own right.

An example of the series is *World Authors 1950–1970,* edited by John Wakeman, with Stanley Kunitz as a consultant. International in scope, the alphabetically arranged volume includes material on 959 authors, most of whom came to prominence between 1950 and 1970 or, for one reason or another, were not included in previous volumes. Entries run from 800 to 1600 words, with a picture of the writer and a listing of published works as well as major bio-bibliographies. The style is informative, and about half the biographies include autobiographical essays. The work periodically is updated.

The latest edition, edited by Vineta Colby, follows the style of the other volumes. Close to 320 biographical sketches are included of poets, novelists, dramatists, as well as philosophers, historians, and educators. Unlike earlier volumes, about one-third of the profiles here are prepared by the authors. The rest of the sketches are by experts.

Related titles in the H. W. Wilson series are *Twentieth Century Authors,* 1942, and the *Supplement,* 1955. Until publication of *World Authors,* these two titles were the basic sources of "current" information on writers. They now may be used to supplement *World Authors.* For deceased writers, Wilson has five author titles: *Greek and Latin Authors, 800 B.C.–A.D. 1000,* 1980; *American Authors, 1600–1900,* 1938; *European Authors, 1000–1900,* 1967; *British Authors before 1800,* 1952; *British Authors of the Nineteenth Century,* 1936. All these follow the style of *World Authors.*

Also, note that The H. W. Wilson Company publishes a series of related works from *Current Biography* (which often includes writers) to *World Artists 1980–1990,* and *Junior Authors & Illustrators.*

Looking ahead, an expert on the series comments:

The future of the Wilson Authors Series seems secure. Companion volumes to *World Authors* will continue to appear at five year intervals, adding to the over 8,700 profiles of authors. . . . The series has an unequaled reputation for accuracy and good writing, and continues to provide a service to scholars and lovers of literature through the inclusion of autobiographical sketches. The volumes are reasonably priced, the most expensive costing less than a single volume of *Contemporary Authors* . . . and may be afforded by small libraries where they often constitute the primary source of information about authors. . . . This is an endlessly fascinating and informative series.[15]

The Wilson series leaves a serious gap, in that the volumes are revised infrequently and do not offer access to newer writers. Also, the Wilson works disregard authors of more ephemeral titles. Here *Contemporary Authors* is of assistance.

Almost any published American writer is included in the *Contemporary Authors* volumes; the qualifications according to a publicity release by the publisher are that

> The author must have had at least one book published by a commercial, risk publisher, or a university press within the last three or four years. . . . Novelists, poets, dramatists, juvenile writers, writers of nonfiction in the social sciences or the humanities are all covered.

In fact, just about anyone who has published anything (this side of a vanity or a technical book) is listed. Newspaper and television reporters, columnists, editors, syndicated cartoonists, and screenwriters, are included.

The information is gathered from questionnaires sent to the authors and arranged in data form—personal facts; career data; writings; and "sidelights," which includes discursive remarks about the author and his or her work.

As of 1990, the 128 volumes included about 95,000 contemporary writers. This makes *Contemporary Authors* the most comprehensive biographical source of its type. Each volume has a cumulative index to the whole set. Unfortunately, the numbering system is totally confusing, and understood, if at all, only by the publisher. Fortunately, the indexes can be followed, after a bit of study, without too much difficulty.

Adding to the confusion, the publisher is revising the main set as *Contemporary Authors: New Revision Series*. In 1990 there were 28

---

[15]Gary Ferguson, "Lives of the Poets, Novelists, and Dramatists: The Wilson Authors Series. *Reference Services Review*, no. 3, 1988, pp. 41–42. Here is an excellent overview of the complete series, how it began, how it developed, and of the strong and weak points of the individual parts. Note the extensive bibliography.

volumes in print, and more are promised. This serves to update the biographical material in the earlier volumes.[16]

Of reference works on authors there seems to be no end. A cursory glance at *American Reference Books Annual* and *Guide to Reference Books* indicates the scope of what is by way of a cottage industry.

Take, for example, "The Scribner Writers Series." This series from Charles Scribner's Sons began in 1974 and has no indication of completion. Among the individual works: *American Writers, Ancient Writers, British Writers, European Writers, Science Fiction Writers, Supernatural Writers, Writers for Children,* etc. These range from a single volume to a set of 14 volumes, and cost from $75 to over $1000. Each offers individual articles on authors, periods, and styles, etc. All are authoritative, and well written. Most are on the American Library Association's "Outstanding Reference Sources" for any given year.

Science

Dictionary of Scientific Biography. New York: Charles Scribner's Sons, 1970–1980, 8 vols. $825. Supplement: 1990, 2 vols. $160.

International in scope, the *Dictionary of Scientific Biography* concentrates on famous scientists, now deceased, from all periods and countries. The work is called monumental by many; it took 17 years to complete. Not only are approximately 6000 notables covered, but the reader is given a history of science from antiquity to the mid-twentieth century. Most entries are two or three pages long. They take a critical perspective, and highlight the individual's contributions. Several entries (Louis Pasteur, Isaac Newton) run over 50 pages. Fortunately, the material is written with the educated layperson in mind, and most of it is comprehensible to the general reader. The two supplementary volumes expand the coverage to include persons who died from 1970 to about 1982. The second volume has a detailed index to both volumes which include more than 400 scientists.

---

[16]Gale Research publishes a great number of author biographical works, particularly in series. Among the works most often found in libraries are the library criticism titles: *Contemporary Literary Criticism*—covers novelists, playwrights, short story writers, poets, mystery and science-fiction writers, nonfiction writers, and screenwriters; *Children's Literature Review*—covers authors and illustrators of books for children, preschool to high school; *Classical and Medieval Literature Criticism*—authors from antiquity through 1399; *Literature Criticism from 1400–1800*—authors who died between 1400 and 1799; *Nineteenth Century Literature; Shakespearean Criticism; Short Story Criticism; Twentieth Century Literary Criticism.*

A related work: *American Men and Women of Science* (New York: R. R. Bowker, 1906 to date, irregular). The 1989–1990 edition consists of eight volumes at $650. The edition lists in who's-who style approximately 125,000 scientists who "have made significant contributions to their respective fields." A discipline index (volume 8) lists the entries under 160 subject headings from computer scientists to medicine and health.

SUGGESTED READINGS

Atlas, James, "Speaking Ill of the Dead," *The New York Times Magazine,* Nov. 6, 1988, p. 40. "These days no man is a hero to his valet—or a biographer." The biographer himself goes on to study the development of too much truth, too much interpretation in modern, full-length biographical studies. A certain amount of this has slipped, too, into the essay study found in numerous reference works.

Grogan, Denis, *Biographical Sources.* Chicago: American Library Association, 1988. Another case book where the student is offered problems in biographical reference questions and asked to solve the problems through a knowledge of basic reference sources—and common sense.

Homberger, Eric, (ed.), *The Troubled Face of Biography.* New York: Macmillan Company, 1989. Biographers are "asked to reflect upon their own practice and upon the state of biography today." The 11 contributors vary in content from the genuinely informative to the egotistical, but it is good reading.

"Landed Gents and Assorted Nobs," *The [London] Sunday Telegraph,* November 25, 1990, "Books," p. 5. In this interview, the editor of the *Dictionary of National Biography* establishes the qualifications for such a position. There are remarks, too, on the work that went into the 1981–1985 supplement, published in 1990.

Mount, Ferdinand, "The Late Great Show," *The Spectator,* April 7, 1990, pp. 29–33. In this review of the 1981–1995 supplement to the DNB, the critic examines the whole purpose of detailed essays concerning the dead. "The glimpses we get are often partial at best and tend either to skate over specifics or skirt the controversial." Other points are made in rapid fire. See, too, in the same issue (pp. 33–34) a witty evaluation of the linked biographical aid *Debrett's Peerage & Baronetage.*

Robinson, William C., "Adult Biographies Reviewed by Library Journal in the 1960s and 1980s." *RQ,* Summer 1990, pp. 540–553. Just how sexist are biographies? How well are various occupations and professions explained? What nationalities are favored, if any? In an effort to answer these and related questions, the Library and Information Science professor examines "all biographies reviewed in *LJ* in 1962 through 1965 and 1981 through 1985." The methodology would be suitable for similar projects. Need one add that a good three-quarters of the biographies are about men and fully over 94 percent concern the lives of whites?

Whittemore, Reed, *Pure Lives: The Early Biographers,* Baltimore: The Johns Hopkins University Press, 1988. This is a lively history of biography and its early practitioners from Machiavelli to early modern writers.

CHAPTER TEN
DICTIONARIES

Consider this summary of the *dictionary:*[1] It is a book almost everyone reads, but never reads through. "The plot is nonexistent, the ending shamelessly predictable and the style sets the standard for wordiness."[2] Millions of copies are sold each year.

It is no accident that the dictionary is a constant best seller, outpulling every nonfiction work except the Bible. And the dictionaries pretty well sell themselves, although some publishers advertise and tout that their edition is better than the others.

A recent Gallup poll shows that 90 percent of American households have a dictionary. In addition, another 20 percent own a crossword puzzle dictionary, and 8 percent claim a rhyming dictionary. One-third have a foreign language work.

The larger dictionary publishers offer a wide line; not only are there specialized works, but there are different versions of the basic dictionary. For example, Merriam-Webster not only has the popular *Webster's Ninth New Collegiate Dictionary* but three editions for younger

---

[1]Totally unconnected items in alphabetical order make up the dictionary. Where there is a "connection," the publisher may use the term *dictionary* in the title. *The Dictionary of National Biography*, for example, is in alphabetical order but has the connection of listing only the dead who are, to be sure, famous. Hence, *dictionary* in the title of a reference book does not necessarily refer to a language dictionary, but only to alphabetical order, and a central theme.

[2]N. R. Kleinfield, "The Dictionary as a Blockbuster," *The New York Times*, Sept. 18, 1988, p. 4F.

people, as well as the related *Webster's Concise Family Dictionary* and a paperback, *Webster's Vest Pocket Dictionary.*

Keeping pace with technology, publishers offer numerous dictionaries available as part of a software package for the home and office computer's word processing system. In addition, several major sets, including the *Oxford English Dictionary,* are online.

Ken Kister, the master of dictionary evaluation, cleverly points up the use of the dictionary for spelling, punctuation, meaning, syllabication (word division), and just about anything which makes it the indispensable reference work:

> For many of us, the English language is a vast, sometimes forbidding ocean of words, full of grizzly demons (or is that *grisly* demons?) lying in wait to confuse and confound. Is the word spelled *supercede* or *supersede*? Is it *double-duty* (with a hyphen)? Is it *on-line* or *online*? How do you pronounce *consortium*? What about *chemotherapy*? Is *Virgin Birth* capitalized or not? Is it *hordes* or *hoards* of people? Is *dockominium* a recognized word? Is *irregardless* an accepted word? What is the meaning of *emolument*? What did Robert Bork mean when, during the Watergate business, he said he had no desire to be an *apparatchik*? Can the words *egoism* and *egotism* be used interchangeably? Can it be that *presently* means both "soon" and "now"?[3]

Incidentally, the individual who knows all the right answers, who can be at home with the 15,000 or so words people employ (and can call on knowledge of 30,000 more when necessary), has mastered the art of verbal offense, or self-defense. A few carefully selected words may blunt a verbal attack and diplomatically win you points. More than one dictionary has been sold on the promise of close to instant, guaranteed articulation for the user.[4]

If nothing else, the dictionary indicates the reader's own, sometimes deplorable, knowledge of his or her native language. Dictionaries are far more effective instruments for inculcating linguistic humility than prayer books are for inculcating the spiritual variety. One may turn to the dictionary for the last word on spelling, pronunciation, meaning, syllabication, and definitions. Hardly a day goes by that the average person does not have need of a dictionary, if only

[3]Ken Kister, "The Big Dictionaries," *Wilson Library Bulletin,* February 1988, p. 38. The article (pp. 38–43) offers a summary of the author's tips on evaluating a dictionary.

[4]See, for example, Suzette Elgin's *The Gentle Art of Verbal Self Defense,* reprinted by Barnes & Noble, 1988. According to an advertisement by the reprint house, this work is "for anyone who's ever been pulverized by put-downs, rankled by reproaches, or irritated by insinuation." In other words (sorry), a type of intellectual's answer to someone on the beach kicking sand in your eyes.

to check the meaning of this or that word or to assist (on the sly) with a crossword puzzle.

What are the most common usage and grammar types of questions? Two New York English professors who operate a grammar "hotline" have this to say: "The standard queries include ones on hyphenation; which-versus-that; getting rid of legalese (using 'about' instead of 'with respect to', for instance, and eliminating words like 'therein'), and spelling."[5]

Scope[6]

The public is apt to think of dictionaries as representing only one category, but they cover almost every interest. Seven generally accepted categories are: (1) general English language dictionaries, which include unabridged titles (i.e., those with over 265,000 entries) and desk or collegiate dictionaries (from 130,000 to 180,000 entries); these are for both adults and children, (2) paperback dictionaries which may have no more than 30,000 to 55,000 words and are often used because they are inexpensive and convenient to carry, (3) historical dictionaries which show the history of a word from date of introduction to the present, (5) period or scholarly specialized titles which focus on a given time period or place, such as a dictionary of Old English, (4) etymological dictionaries which are like historical titles, but tend to put more emphasis on analysis of components and cognates in other languages, (5) foreign language titles, which are bilingual in that they give the meanings of the words of one language in another language, (6) subject works which concentrate on the definition of words in a given area, such as science and technology, and (7) "other" dictionaries include almost everything from abbreviations to slang and proper usage.

Compilation

How is a dictionary compiled from the written and spoken words that are its source? Today the larger publishers, from Houghton Mifflin to Merriam-Webster, Doubleday, and Simon and Schuster have substantial staffs and free-lance lexicographers. The *American*

---

[5]"Dialing for Scholars," *The New York Times,* July 25, 1984, p. B5. People can phone this grammar hotline for help with grammatical problems.

[6]Annie Brewer, *Dictionaries, Encyclopedias, and Other Word Related Books*, 4th ed. (Detroit, MI: Gale Research Company, 1988, 2 vols.) includes more than 35,000 titles. The compilation indicates the number of both English and non-English language dictionaries and related titles.

Heritage Dictionary offices employed a staff of over 40 people when the new edition of the desk dictionary was in preparation. *The Oxford English Dictionary* has an even larger part- and full-time staff.

The process differs from firm to firm, but essentially it is in two stages. The free-lance readers send in words taken from magazines, newspapers, and other sources. The newly coined words, or the variations on an older word (as for example the use of "hardware" in relationship to computers) are dutifully recorded on 3- by 5-inch cards, or, these days, entered in a computer's memory.

EVALUATION

For those who seek to evaluate dictionaries, the first rule is not to expect any dictionary to be perfect. Dr. Johnson said, "Dictionaries are like watches: the worst is better than none, and the best cannot be expected to go quite true." There is no perfect dictionary, and there never will be one until such time as the language of a country has become completely static—an event as unlikely as the discovery of a perpetual-motion mechanism. Language is always evolving because of the coining of new words and the change in meaning of older words. No single dictionary is sufficient. Each has its good points, each its defects.

The second rule should be self-evident, but is rarely followed: Consult the preface and explanatory notes at the beginning of a dictionary. The art of successfully using a dictionary, or any other reference book, requires an understanding of how it is put together. This is important because of the dictionary's constant use of shortcuts in the form of abbreviations, various methods of indicating pronunciation, and grammatical notations.

In dictionaries and other commonly used reference works, it is particularly important to read the preface and introductory material. Here one finds the rules employed for everything from determination of pronunciation to proper usage and spelling. As dictionaries vary from work to work, the preface is a necessary introduction to those differences which may cause confusion.

The single finest guide to dictionaries is the standard work by Ken Kister, *Best Dictionaries* (2d ed. Phoenix, Ariz.: Oryx Press, 1991). Here the same critical intelligence is applied to 1700 general and specialized works which is employed in his *Best Encyclopedias*. Most attention is given to the general work likely to be found in library and home. There is a splendid introduction which clearly identifies and outlines features of major titles. Electronic (machine-readable) forms are examined in detail. The latter part of the guide is devoted to subject dictionaries from art and architecture to transportation, as well as foreign language titles.

Two R. R. Bowker guides, *General Reference Books for Adults* and *Reference Books for Young Readers* cover dictionaries. Both have excellent sections, including comparative charts, on the basic titles discussed here as well as several other dictionaries. The best review of current dictionaries will be found in the "Reference Books Bulletin" of *The Booklist*.

Authority. There are only a limited number of publishers of dictionaries. The reputable ones include Merriam-Webster, Oxford University Press, Random House, Scott-Foresman, Doubleday, Macmillan, Simon & Schuster, and Houghton Mifflin—to name the larger, better-known publishers.[7] In specialized fields and other areas where dictionaries are employed, there are additional reputable publishers.

The reason that there are comparatively few general dictionary publishers is the same as that used to explain why there are so few working on general encyclopedias—money. A dictionary is an expensive matter. For example, the new edition of the Simon & Schuster's *Webster's New World Dictionary* (1988) took seven years to complete and a basic investment of well over $2 million. Over $9 million was spent on revising *The Random House Dictionary*.[8]

"Webster" in the title of a dictionary may be a sign of reassurance, and it frequently is found as the principal name of a number of dictionaries. Merriam-Webster Company, which bought out the unsold copies of Noah Webster's dictionary at the time of his death had the original claim to the name. For years, the use of Webster's name was the subject of litigation. Merriam-Webster finally lost its case when the copyright on the name lapsed. It is now common property and may be used by any publisher. Hence the name "Webster's" in the title may or may not have anything to do with the original work which bore the name. Unless the publisher's name is recognized, "Webster" per se means nothing.[9]

[7]Among these publishers, the clear leader is Merriam-Webster. The college dictionary goes through 5 or 6 printings each year and sells over a million copies annually.

[8]Robert Carter, "The War of Words" *Publishers Weekly*, Oct. 2, 1987, p. 33. Random House's vice president broke down the $9 million: $6 million on editorial development and plant; $3 million for paper, printing, and binding, and another $1 million for promotion.

[9]Webster's first dictionary was published in 1806. A *Compendious Dictionary of the*

A good illustration of using "Webster" to help sell a less than excellent dictionary is found in *Webster's New Universal Unabridged Dictionary* (New York: Dorset & Baber, various dates). This is a prominent work, which is advertised heavily in almost all Barnes & Noble and other bookstores, dealers, and catalogs. The advertisements claim it retails at $79.95, but is now "only $19.95" (1991) and the 2400 pages contain definitions of more than 320,000 words. It has appeared under a variety of titles by other publishers as well. No matter what the date on the title page, it is usually ten to fifteen years behind in including current words and definitions. Furthermore, definitions are poor, the history of words incomplete, if offered at all, the illustrations are dated, and the overall format an invitation to disaster. One would be wiser to invest in any of the standard desk dictionaries.

Vocabulary. Vocabulary can be evaluated in terms of the period of the language covered and the number of words or entries. Other special features may include slang, dialect, obsolete forms, and scientific or technical terms.

In the United States the field is divided between the *unabridged* (over 265,000 words) and the *abridged* (from 130,000 to 265,000 words) type of dictionary. Most dictionaries are abridged or limited to a given subject or topic. The two unabridged ones vary from about 460,000 entries for *Webster's* to 315,000 for *Random House.* The *Oxford English Dictionary* has 500,000 words but is not considered a general dictionary.

Most desk dictionaries, such as the much-used *Webster's Ninth New Collegiate* or the *American Heritage,* have about 150,000 to 170,000 words, considered more than sufficient for average use. How important is it for the average reader to have a volume which includes more than 100,000 words? There are many paperback dictionaries of from 50,000 to 85,000 words which serve the purpose of millions of people.

Currentness. Dictionary publishing is a never-ending affair. New editions are usually issued every seven to ten years, but hundreds of changes are usually made in each reprinting. These include adding

English Language had 37,000 entries. His *An American Dictionary of the English Language,* upon which later editions of Webster's are based, was published in 1828. With his death, the copyright was purchased, in 1843, by two brothers in Springfield, Mass., George and Charles Merriam. For a detailed history of this dictionary and other works, see the article on dictionaries in the *Encyclopedia Britannica, Macropaedia* volume.

new words, revising definitions of older words which have taken on new meaning, and dropping a few no-longer-used technical terms.

A quick check of a desk or unabridged dictionary which claims to be up to date should include the common, sometimes much over-used words, introduced into the language by television, radio, and film. For example, by the 1990s all dictionaries should include relatively new definitions of *poison pill, insider trading, cash cow* (all Wall Street terms); *Denver boot, couch potato, handler,* and *Ayatollah.*

Usually, there have to be eight or more occurrences of a word appearing in print before the word is considered for inclusion in a dictionary. In addition, the publisher must determine whether the word has been in use for more than two or three years. For example, the word *humongous* came into partial use in the 1960s on college campuses but dropped away a year or so later, only to be picked up and used again in the early 1980s by newspapers. It is now relatively common. After nearly 18 years, authorities decided it was here to stay, and so it is now in most dictionaries.

At Merriam's there are 17 lexicographers who spend a minimum of one hour each day hunting for words. This means pouring over newspapers, magazines, and books for unusual word usages. When a word qualifies, it is marked and handed to a typist who stores it both in the computer and in the familiar 3- by 5-inch card file. Some publications are more fruitful than others. A magazine like *People* can produce several hundred new words in each issue whereas a book will generally yield far fewer. When revision time comes, the staff will look at all the 10 to 15 thousand citations gathered each month and make their decisions. Because there are no hard-and-fast rules, selections are made by educated intuition and "feel."[10]

As of early 1989, the count of citations stood at over 14 million. Annually or biannually the dictionaries are updated using these citations. (A thorough, complete revision of most dictionaries is made only every 10 to 20 years). For example, in the 1989 edition of the college edition of G. C. Merriam Webster's dictionary, the publisher added such terms as *computer virus, couch potato,* and *glasnost.* Other publishers following somewhat the same procedures add the same terms and others.

Then there is the matter of what some call *teenspeak,* the special language of the teens which varies from generation to generation, from year to year, but is as constant as the winds of winter.[11] For

[10]Kleinfield, op. cit.

[11]Richard Bernstein, "For Teenspeak . . . " *The New York Times,* Aug. 25, 1988, p. A16.

example, by 1989 *like* was an equivalent of *say* to many youths, as in: "I just went up to him and he like (said) . . ." At one time in the 1960s it was *go* which replaced *say*. Some adults find this fascinating, others an encroachment on the language.

A good test of timeliness is to check whether words involved with popular music, from jazz to rap, are included. Music usually has its own distinctive vocabulary, and although the words may originate in a particular ethnic group, they often spread through professional musicians to the population as a whole. For example, *hip-hop* (the culture of rap) may include old slang (*bum's rush*) as well as totally new terms such as *dis*, meaning "to show disrespect," or the verb *lamp*, meaning "to take one's ease."[12]

In addition to the updates to regular dictionaries from time to time, new-word reference works appear. An example: *The Facts on File Dictionary of New Words* (New York: Facts on File, 1989, 176 pp.). Created primarily for reference librarians, this is a fine place to turn when all else fails, when one is seeking a common meaning of DINK (double income, no kids—an acronym). The compilation by Sid Lerner is hardly scientific, but it does cover words one is likely to hear on television for the first time or in the mouths of jargon fiends, from teenagers and librarians to scientists and sanitation workers.

Format. Before considering the standard in-print format, it is well to remember that today many dictionaries are available at the computer, usually in a package which allows the user to look up words for spelling or meaning. (This is discussed later in the chapter.)

Turning to the print dictionary, a major consideration of format is the binding of the book. Both individuals and libraries should purchase hardcover editions because the hard binding will withstand frequent use. Another consideration is how the words are arranged. Most dictionaries now divide the words among a great number of separate headwords. If a dictionary does not do this, and crams many items under a single entry such as *lay*, one must look for *lay* to find such words as *layout* or *lay-by*.

Important factors to be evaluated are print size and how readability is affected by spacing between words and lines of type, the

---

[12]Some publishers solve the problem of timeliness by issuing dictionaries of new words and meanings, e.g., *The New Words Dictionary* (New York: Ballantine, 1989), which contains more than 500 new words and phrases as well as new usages of old words.

use of boldface type, and the differences in type families. With the exception of some colored plates, most dictionary illustrations are black-and-white line drawings. The average desk dictionary has from 600 to 1500 illustrations, the unabridged from 7000 to 12,000.

Kister has a wise word to say about the use of illustrations in advertising of dictionaries. "Be skeptical of dictionaries with the word illustrated in their titles. "Illustrated" dictionaries are usually desk sized works that have been jumped up with a few thousand pretty pictures. Of course the price has also been jumped up, often from the $14.95–16.95 range to $34.95–49.95 or more."[13]

Encyclopedia material: Some dictionaries are a combination of facts found in an encyclopedia and a dictionary. To a certain extent all have some of these features in that they include sections, or work into the text, biographical and geographical data. Others, such as the second edition of *The Random House Dictionary of the English Language* go further and include additions such as those found in atlases. A better example is *The Oxford Reference Dictionary* (New York: Oxford University Press, 1986) which announces that it is "both a dictionary and a concise encyclopedia." There are only 75,000 words, or about half the number found in a standard college dictionary, and about 6000 articles. At close to $30 it falls between two basic reference works, and although good as far as it goes, it is better to simply get a good desk dictionary and, say, the paperback edition of the more complete *Concise Columbia Encyclopedia.* Buy an encyclopedia, buy a dictionary, but do not try to buy both in one because combinations never really work. Most of these are not acceptable, at least for a library. For an individual, on the other hand, it may be useful to purchase one of the better combinations—in this case: *The American Heritage Illustrated Encyclopedia Dictionary* (New York: Houghton Mifflin, 1987). This work has 180,000 good definitions, 2400 illustrations, an encyclopedia and an almanac—all for $55.

Spelling. Where there are several forms of spelling, they should be clearly indicated. *Webster's* identifies the British spelling by the label "Brit."; other dictionaries normally indicate this variant by simply giving the American spelling first, e.g., *analyze, analyse* or *theater, theatre.* Frequently two different spellings are given, either of which is acceptable. The user must determine the form to use. For example, *addable* or *addible, lollipop* or *lollypop.* (It is worth reminding both librarians and laypersons that explanations of such refinements

---

[13]Kister, op. cit., p. 41.

are found in the preface. Always, always, always, examine the preface.)

Etymologies. All large dictionaries indicate the etymology of a word by a shorthand system in brackets. The normal procedure is to show the root word in Latin, Greek, French, German, Old English, or some other language. Useful as this feature is, the student of etymology will be satisfied only with historical studies, such as Mencken's *The American Language,* to trace properly the history of a word and how it developed.

Definitions. Dictionaries usually give the modern meaning of words first. Exceptions include most older British-based dictionaries as well as the Merriam-Webster publications and *Webster's New World.* Without understanding the definition ladder, an unsuspecting reader (who has not read the preface) will leave the dictionary with an antiquated meaning. Also, the meaning may be precise, but it can lead to "circularity" in which words of similar difficulty and meaning are employed to define one another.

The quality of the definition depends on several factors. Separate and distinct meanings of words should be indicated clearly, and this usually is done by numbering the various definitions. The perfect definition is precise and clear, but in more technical, more abstract situations this is not always possible. What, for example, is the true definition of *love?*

Pronunciation. There are several different methods of indicating pronunciation, but most American publishers employ the diacritical one. In *Webster's Ninth New Collegiate* the pronunciation system tends to be quite detailed and, except for the expert, quite confusing. In the *American Heritage Dictionary* the process is much easier to understand. Again, look in the preface when in doubt.

All dictionaries employ the simple phonetic use of the familiar, that is, a person looking up *lark* finds the "r" is pronounced as in *park.* Regardless of what the person's accent may be, the transferred sound will be the same as that in *park.* Regional accents do make a difference in that *park* may be pronounced as "pock," "pawk," or even "pack." At the same time, the phoneticists consider variations such as the pronouncing of *tomato, potato,* and *economics* which differ from region to region, even person to person. In these cases, more than one pronunciation is noted as correct.

Syllabication. All dictionaries indicate usually by a centered period or hyphen, how a word is to be divided into syllables. The information is mainly to help writers and editors, not to mention secretaries, divide words at the ends of lines. There are special, short desk dictionaries which simply indicate syllabication of more common words without benefit of definition or pronunciation.

Synonyms. The average user does not turn to a general dictionary for synonyms, but their inclusion helps to differentiate between similar words. Some desk dictionaries indicate the differentiation and shades of meaning by short essays at the conclusion of many definitions.

Grammatical Information. The most generally useful grammatical help a dictionary renders is to indicate parts of speech. All single entries are classified as nouns, adjectives, verbs, and so on. Aside from this major division, dictionaries vary in method of showing adverbs, adjectives, plurals, and principal parts of a verb, particularly the past tenses of irregular verbs. Usually the method is clearly ascertainable; but, again, the prefatory remarks should be studied in order to understand any particular presentation.

Bias. Most dictionaries are quick to point out that certain terms or words are not socially acceptable because they are vulgar or have insulting ethnic overtones. Cultural prejudices against women in such words as *girl* for a grown woman took many years to overcome in dictionaries. No one seemed to question sexist aspects. Although this is changing, at least in part, dictionaries may continue to err.

Usage: The most controversial aspect of evaluation concerns how proper usage is or is not indicated. Today there is division between those who wish a dictionary to be *prescriptive* (i.e., to clearly and categorically indicate what is or is not good, approved usage) or *descriptive* (i.e., simply describe the language as it is spoken and written without any judgment as to whether it is acceptable by the common culture).

Dictionaries vary on how they handle usage. At one extreme is the work which says almost anything goes as long as it is popular (e.g., most of the Merriam-Webster dictionaries). At the other is the dictionary which is critical and gives rules of good usage (e.g., *Webster's New World Dictionary* from Simon & Schuster). In between is the "it depends" school which is more pragmatic than prescriptive or descriptive (e.g., *The American Heritage Dictionary*).[14]

---

[14]Roy Harris, "On a Sticky Wicket," *The Times Literary Supplement,* Oct. 6, 1988, p.

Deciding on what is acceptable or nonacceptable English is an ongoing debate. For example, Prince Charles of England joined in the discussion when he noted that the teaching of contemporary grammar is badly done. There is much more to his argument than dictionary indicators of what is or is not acceptable English. The fact is that proper grammar and acceptable usage cannot be separated. The prescriptive advocates believe that the increasingly pervasive sloppiness of writing and speaking goes back to a failure to apply rules.[15]

The descriptive school dominates American dictionaries and culture. This is not the case in numerous other places. For example, members of the French Academy fairly well dictate what will or will not be changed in the French language. They tend to prevail because tradition—nearly 400 years of such rule—is more important to some than possibly needed revision.

In the late 1980s the French schoolteachers called for simplification of French spelling. French writers and intellectuals strongly disagreed. They pointed out that the venerable French Academy has determined proper French since 1635. Any change "would be a disaster," said the novelist Françoise Sagan. She points out that French is "a superb language" and to tamper with it would be "extraordinary folly and stupidity."[16]

Lacking an Academy, Americans rely on their own good sense. This may not be enough, at least according to some critics such as Christopher Porterfield of *Time* (November 2, 1987, p. 86). He deplores the lack of attention to basic grammar. A champion of the prescriptive school, he argues that it is a mistake to have proper usage determined "by the heedless masses of people who rarely look at dictionaries, much less write them."

1082. Although *prescriptive* and *descriptive* are common terms, Harris says that it is by no means clear to endorse the curious distinction, popular among linguists, between 'prescriptive rules' and 'descriptive rules'. If ever modern linguistics needed to put their own metalinguistic house in order it is surely here. The odd expression *prescriptive rule* is a tautology, while the even odder expression *descriptive rule* is nonsensical. Rules *are* prescriptive, and descriptions are *not* rules. Any inquiry into language which does not recognize this basic dichotomy is doomed to confusion from the start."

[15]"For Teaching New British Grammar . . ." *The New York Times,* June 12, 1989, p. B9.

[16]"Tilting at the Mother Tongue: In France the Purists Bristle," *The New York Times,* Dec. 28, 1988, p. 1. Note that the *Times* considers this of enough interest to put it on its first page—probably the only newspaper in America with such a claim.

Closely associated with the democratic tenet that everyone has the right to speak the way he or she wishes, the descriptive school does not "buy" tradition or proper usage in all situations. Although English is the global lingua franca (about 600 million have it as a first or second language), there are many criticisms about its improper use.

What makes anyone's English "correct"? Some say an answer is impossible. There are too many variables from a definition of correctness to the meaning of semantic competence. Different social and cultural situations offer their own rules.

UNABRIDGED DICTIONARIES

Webster's Third New International Dictionary. Springfield, MA: Merriam-Webster Inc., 1961. 2752 pp. $79.95. Supplements, 1976 and 1988, various paging, each $10.95.

The Random House Dictionary of the English Language, 2d ed. New York: Random House, 1988, 2510 pp. $79.95.

Today there is only one unabridged dictionary of the English language. This is *Webster's Third New International.* One may count *The Oxford English Dictionary* (*OED*) in this category, but it really is more concerned with etymology than definitions, and is not meant to be an everyday working dictionary. *The Random House Dictionary* may come close to being unabridged, but its 315,000 entries puts it somewhere between Webster's with 472,000 words and the typical 150,000-word desk dictionary.

As there is no choice, the library buys the *Webster's* and supports it with the *OED,* several desk dictionaries, and special dictionaries. Despite the publishing date (1961), the *Webster's* is essential. Each new printing includes some new words, or variations on definitions of older words. See, for example, recent computer, political, and sociological terms. Most will be included, if not in the main work, at least in the two supplements which add about 22,000 words to the basic 450,000 in the primary volume.

Noah Webster had been involved with publishing dictionaries through the early nineteenth century. It is important to stress that 1909 was the date of the first current series of *unabridged* titles. A second edition came out in 1934 and a third in 1961. A 1990 dictionary has several copyright dates: 1961, the date of the original revision, and later dates—usually every five years—which imply some revisions since 1961. However, the work is primarily the original 1961 edition.[17]

Since it is an unabridged dictionary recognized as an authority, many claim it should be prescriptive and lay down the verbal law. It does not. It is descriptive, and sometimes it is difficult, despite labels, to pinpoint the good, the bad, or the indifferent use of a word. Also, it has such an involved scheme of indicating pronunciation that most people are helpless to understand how to pronounce anything.

Originally published in 1966, *The Random House Dictionary* came out again in 1988 with the challenge that it, and it only, was the most up-to-date unabridged dictionary. For the moment, there is no argument that this is one of the best "big" dictionaries. The publisher claims 315,000 entries and 2500 illustrations. There are added features, such as concise, yet quite practical, bilingual dictionaries in French, German, Spanish and Italian, almost 30 pages of full-color maps, and the usual style manual.

Although not as large as *Webster's,* the new *Random House* has the distinct advantage of being relatively current. Approximately 50,000 new words were added or revised for the second edition (the editor notes that the last word to be included was *glasnost).* Among the new terms, or new shades of definition one finds *greenmail* and *golden parachutes,* in business; *user friendly* and *string theory,* in science; *disinformation,* in government; and the *underclass* and *yuppies* in sociology. A *mole* is now more than an animal. It is a spy who burrows into the enemy's secrets. Expletives are in more common use, and the four-letter words are everywhere. These are normally identified as "vulgar."

But one looks, without much help, for some guidance in the use of the word *hope* as a modifier. The dictionary is descriptive. Disputes about *hopefully* are noted, and other embattled terms are described as such. It accepts the word *infer* in its accepted meaning "to draw a conclusion" and also as a synonym "to imply" or "to suggest," but adds that the distinction between the two words is "widely observed."

Definitions are clear and use words likely to be understood by the average person. Many entries conclude with helpful synonyms and antonyms. Although the philosophy is descriptive, there are nu-

[17]According to William Llewellyn, Merriam-Webster's president, there are no plans for a Fourth New International, "but M-W aggressively keeps up with the language. They have almost 14 million citations on file and add between 100,000 and 120,000 new citations each year," according to Robert Carter, in "The War of Words," *Publishers Weekly,* Oct. 2, 1987, p. 28. This was in 1987, but by 1990 the rumor was that a new edition is nearly complete. So why deny it? To sell the Third of course.

merous notes which tip off the reader as to the advisability of employing a given word, e.g., "nonstandard" or "slang" are clear warning signs.

Attention is given to *etymology*, or the history of a word's development in that the date a word first entered the language usually accompanies each word. Pronunciation instructions are easy to follow, and often there are notes explaining how the pronunciation of a word may have changed.

Weak points include the failure to give sensible verbal illustrations of the word. Most of these examples are from the editors' imaginations and not from actual texts. Sometimes the result is simplistic to a fault. Also, one may question the wisdom of the publisher in trying to make it more than a dictionary by expanding encyclopedia features such as biographical data, reproductions of major historical documents, and the 30-page atlas.

Another difficulty of both dictionaries is weight. *The Random House* comes in at slightly over 13 pounds, as does *Webster's*. Neither is the type of dictionary one is likely to carry from room to room.

Both are reasonably priced, and the Random House often is discounted. Barnes & Noble, for example, offered it at $64.95 only a few weeks after it appeared at $79.95. In its first year of publication, The Book of the Month Club offered it "for only $15 with membership."

DESK (COLLEGE) DICTIONARIES

The American Heritage Dictionary of the English Language, 2d College Edition. Boston: Houghton Mifflin Company, 1982, 1568 pp. $17.95.

Webster's New World Dictionary of the American Language, 3d ed. New York: Simon & Schuster, 1988, 1600 pp. $17.95.

Webster's Ninth New Collegiate Dictionary, 9th ed. Springfield, MA: Merriam-Webster, Inc., 1983, 1693 pp. $17.95. CD-ROM, Washington, DC: Highlighted Data, $200.

The Random House College Dictionary, New York: Random House, 1984, 1600 pp. $17.95; paperback, 1989, $11.95.

These are the four most often found dictionaries in libraries and in the home. They are all good, and all have strong and weak points. "Best" and "better" depends on personal preference. They all are priced the same and have much the same number of words;

they are all authoritative and relatively current. (Which is best? See the comparison made at the end of this section.)

The core of the dictionary publishing business is the familiar desk or college version. It normally includes from about 150,000 to 175,000 words; it has the familiar illustrations; and offers added material such as short biographical and geographical notes. The definitions are written for those with a college education, although they can be used by almost all age groups and by anyone who has basic literacy.

These four primary college or desk dictionaries, by these four publishers are accepted standards. Any dictionary of this type by another publisher is highly suspect.

The four account for sales of about 2 million hardcover copies each and every year. Shorter paperback versions of some are available, but are not all that popular.

American Heritage stresses prescriptive entries, and the usage notes are useful to help guide the average person seeking to find whether this or that word may be used in polite society. This is determined by a panel, and the collective result is a valuable guide for laypersons. The notes summarize the sometimes differing views of the panel and are well worth reading.

Definitions are clear and are particularly good in using simple, easy-to-understand words. The revised edition has about 15,000 new words (25,000, if one counts the new geographical and biographical entries), and the 160,000 entries represent an excellent selection. The dictionary is outstanding for its more than 4000 illustrations.

In the first edition, editor William Morris took pride in the fact that this was one of the first desk dictionaries to include slang and four-letter words. Since then, it has been a regular policy of almost all other desk dictionary publishers to include them as well. While the revised edition follows the same guidelines, there is a special school edition of the work which eliminates the four-letter words.

The *American Heritage* work is the best single desk dictionary for detailed etymology and gives details on the linguistic sources of most words. By contrast the *Webster's* (both titles) are incomplete and much briefer.

Now in its ninth edition, *Webster's Ninth New Collegiate Dictionary* is based on the unabridged *Third.* It has about 155,000 words and 600 illustrations. It reflects the philosophy of the larger work and places considerable emphasis on contemporary pronunciation and definitions. As in the larger work, the philosophy is descriptive, although with the ninth edition there is more emphasis on usage notes (fully explained in the explanatory preface). "Substandard" is the warning for the use of *ain't*, and this is followed by a short paragraph that discusses the current use of the word. In this case it is noted that "although disapproved by many and more common in less educated speech, *ain't* is used orally in most parts of the U.S." When the four-letter words are explained, and major ones are included, the usage note is "considered obscene" or "considered vulgar."

Webster's Ninth New Collegiate is the country's most popular dictionary. The revised edition of 1983 was on *The New York Times'* best seller list for over three years, and the current work continues to lead all others in sales.

There are passable line drawings, although in number they do not come close to those found in the *American Heritage Dictionary.* The history of words is usually shown, and, in fact, an added feature since the 1980s is the inclusion of a date when the word first appeared in the language. Until now, no desk dictionary had this type of information.

The pronunciation system remains a problem. The symbols employed are listed in full inside the back cover, and a shorter version appears at the bottom of each right-hand page. The problem is that the whole is extremely complicated and it takes a special section, "guide to pronunciation," to try to explain the process to readers. The overall result is less than satisfactory.

Although the maze of pronunciation symbols may be puzzling, the definitions are improved. Derived from the unabridged version, the definitions are considerably more lucid and simplified. They are still given in chronological order, with the modern meaning last. For example, *explode* begins with the labeled archaic definition "to drive from the stage by noisy disapproval."

Geographical and personal names are not included in the main alphabet, but are separate features in the appendixes, a habit now followed by other dictionaries. The appendixes include words and phrases, as well as foreign colleges and universities.

Although there are various CD-ROM and software packages that feature dictionaries, *Webster's* is one of the few desk works that stands by itself on a CD-ROM. It has serious drawbacks, however: The price alone is $200 (as compared to about $18 for the print version), and in a simple test by this author it was found that a word could be located as fast, if not faster, by using the printed work. There are, to be sure, some positive features, such as the ability to rapidly search cross-references and, even more valuable, a voice-over that pronounces the particular word. One may also use large print, if desired.

Webster's New World Dictionary of the American Language is not from Merriam-Webster, and often the two works are confused. This Simon & Schuster *Webster's* is not a Merriam-Webster product, but it is equally reliable. It is one of the few with "Webster's" in the title, which can be so judged.[18]

A total revision of the desk dictionary was made in 1988, about 17 years after the previous edition. Partial revision has been made biennially, as is done by all publishers of standard desk dictionaries. The publisher claims that there are now 170,000 entries, 5000 new definitions (since the 1984 edition) and about 800 less than exciting black-and-white illustrations.

The *New World* is aptly named because its primary focus is on American English as it is spoken and written. There are particularly good definitions which are closely related to current speech. The definitions are in historical order, not by the most common current understanding of the word.

A star preceding an entry indicates an American word or expression. There are some 11,000 of these. Meaning is illustrated with made-up sentences and phrases. Pronunciation is clear, and a key is found in the lower corner of every right-hand page. There are only a few—about 800—illustrations, but these are at least adequate.

Of the three, it is by now the most prescriptive, even more so than the *American Heritage*. It is favored by *The New York Times*, as well as Associated Press and United Press International. Given this type of recommendation, it has won many readers.

Based on the second edition of *The Random House Dictionary of the English Language*, the college edition has about 170,000 words and some 1500 illustrations. The illustrations are about the only point where the desk dictionary surpasses its three rivals. The typeface is not as clear; the definitions are adequate, but not up to the others; and the editors favor the descriptive rather than prescriptive.

Comparison

These are the four desk dictionaries found in most libraries and millions of homes.

---

[18]As noted earlier, the term *Webster* is not copyrighted, and numerous publishers use it to hide sometimes inferior works, or, in this case, a quite excellent dictionary. The quality varies, but in 99 percent of the cases the Simon & Schuster's *Webster's* is the only reliable work to use the name. See *General Reference Books for Adults* (New York: R. R. Bowker, 1988) where there are at least 18 other dictionaries using *Webster*. Most of these are inferior or cut-down versions.

The standard publishers' dictionaries are periodically revised, and all are authoritative. Differences are essentially those of format, arrangement, systems of indicating pronunciation, and length of definitions. All include synonyms, antonyms, etymologies, and limited biographical and gazetteer information. Price variations are minimal.

The natural question is Which is best, and the answer depends primarily on personal need. All have about the same number of words, and all meet the evaluative tests of excellence.

Kenneth Kister votes for the *Webster's Ninth New Collegiate* and *Webster's New World*. *The New York Times* recommends the *New World* for its staff, and the author favors *Webster's Ninth*.

One of the better comparisons of the standard desk dictionaries is offered by the "Reference Books Bulletin":

> Other desk dictionaries comparable to *Webster's New World Dictionary* are *The American Heritage Dictionary*, second college edition, *The Random House College Dictionary*, and *Webster's Ninth New Collegiate Dictionary*. While all have a similar number of entries, each has its distinguishing features. *American Heritage* has a great number of photoillustrations, clear and inviting typeface, and a very accessible style in its introductory guide to the English language. *Webster's Ninth* in some cases offers a clearer, more precise definition than do its competitors. In addition, it is unique in that it dates the first use in the language for many words. . . . *Random House*, while suffering in comparison from less clarity in its typeface and in some of its definitions, offers the most illustrations (with the exception of *American Heritage*). *Webster's New World* is strong in Americanisms, typeface readability, and ease of comprehension of its definitions.[19]

Considering the similarities among the four including price and number of words, there is not all that much difference. The wise librarian will have all four.

Reduced-Word Dictionaries

There are many dictionaries which are limited to under 60,000 words. Many of these are available in paperback and from the same publishers of the standard desk works. Others are from equally reliable firms. For example, the *Oxford American Dictionary* (New York and London: Oxford University Press, 1986) has only 30,000 words. *The Concise Oxford Dictionary of Current English* from the same publisher has 50,000 words, and there are other versions from Oxford.

[19]*The Booklist*, March 1, 1989, p. 1119.

CHILDREN'S DICTIONARIES

Macmillan Dictionary for Children. New York: Macmillan Company, 1987, 784 pp. $13.95.

Scott Foresman Beginning Dictionary. Glenview, IL: Scott, Foresman, 1988, 832 pp. $16.50.

Webster's Elementary Dictionary. Springfield, MA: Merriam-Webster, Inc., 1986, 600 pp. $10.95.

The World Book Dictionary. Chicago: World Book, 1983, 2 vols. $79.

There are as many, if not more, dictionaries for children as for adults. The reason is easy to see: there are many school libraries and all of them require not just one dictionary, but different ones to fit different grade levels. It is, in a word, a lucrative market for publishers.

Are they of equal worth? It is the same story as for adult works. A few publishers are responsible for the more accepted titles. And these few are generally the same ones who issue the adult dictionaries. World Book, Scott Foresman, and Macmillan are exceptions in that they concentrate on children and young people's dictionaries.

The works are usually graded for preschool through elementary grades; for junior high school or equivalent; and for high school. The obvious rub is that by junior high school, students should be able to use adult desk dictionaries and not need special works for their age group. Obviously some teachers (and librarians) do not agree anymore than some parents do. If they did, there would not be the specialized dictionaries for younger people. A case can be made for elementary grades, and most would agree that at this level at least, the younger dictionary is preferable to the adult work.

The four listed here are the ones most often found in school and public libraries along with the standard adult works in grades beyond elementary. They are 4 of almost 50 possibilities. Many of the 50 are spin-offs of the basic three plus titles from the four adult publishers. For example, Macmillan has about 10 related works. On the other hand, World Book has only the single title.

The *World Book Dictionary* has 225,000 entries. This makes it the "unabridged" dictionary for children and young people. It has from 125,000 to 200,000 more words than its rivals. The dictionary follows the familiar Thorndike-Barnhart system of using definition words which are within the grasp of the reader. One does not have to turn to other entries to find the meaning of words used in a definition. The definitions are models of clarity, although a sophisticated adult is likely to find many of them much too simple. The format is good, and the illustrations, although not up to the number in the *American Heritage*, are at least clear and placed properly.

The problem is the price. One may buy an excellent desk dictionary that contains about 150,000 to 175,000 words for about $17, and *Webster's Third New International*, with about twice as many words is only $79.95, the same price as the *World Book* entry. Nevertheless, if a dictionary must be purchased for children and young adults, it is a first choice.

World Book does publish a reasonably priced work, the *Childcraft Dictionary*. The 900 pages cost $25, and the 1989 revised edition has 11,000 entries, many of which are complemented by the 1000 color illustrations that are quite suitable for its elementary-grade users. It is an ideal work for children from about seven to eleven years of age.

Scott Foresman publishes a series of dictionaries which include volumes for the elementary grades through high school. The beginning version for elementary grades 1 to 5 is typical, and is based on the Thorndike-Barnhart system. The beginner's dictionary relies heavily on illustrations, about 75 percent of which are in color. Some words have histories set off in a different-colored ink. The whole is in a pleasing format and is as much for instruction as for definitions.

Librarians often favor the *Macmillan Dictionary* over all the others because: (1) It has 30,000 entries for grades 2 through 6, although it may be used by younger or older students. (2) It has 1500 illustrations in color. (3) It uses simple easy-to-understand definitions with numerous illustrative phrases and sentences. (4) Its pronunciations, given at the end of the definition, are clear. (5) It contains added materials such as maps, lists of presidents, etc.

All this adds up to a work a trifle too elementary for some, and it lags in including new words which may be used regularly on, say, MTV. Nevertheless, because it is so easy to use and so easy to understand, librarians have found many children prefer it.

Equally an opinion winner among librarians is *Webster's Elementary Dictionary*. It is somewhat similar to the Macmillan entry in terms of number of entries, ease of definitions used, etc. On the other hand, and this is a major difference, the publisher relies on quality rather than condescendingly appealing to a special age group. The result is a true junior type of adult work rather than a specialized dictionary for children.

Which is best among the numerous children's dictionaries? To reach a consensus, much depends on whether the work is used in a classroom, in a home, or in a library. Among the titles listed here one could not go wrong in selecting one or two, depending on purpose and age of the prospective user.

A children's version of the *American Heritage* work, by the same publisher, claims 35,000 entries and 700 illustrations. This is *The Lincoln Writing Dictionary for Children* (Boston: Houghton-Mifflin, 1988). It differs from others in that it uses numerous examples from well-known writers for children. It suggests proper usage for basic words and explains problems involved with some words and phrases. It has some 600 encyclopedic length articles which discuss grammar and related matters.

The Writing Dictionary is one of a series published by Houghton Mifflin for children. Others that are equally attractive and useful include: *The American Heritage Picture Dictionary* (preschoolers); *The First Dictionary* (primary grades); *Children's Dictionary* (grades 3 to 6) and *The Student's Dictionary* (grades 6–9).

HISTORICAL DICTIONARY

> *The Oxford English Dictionary,* 2d ed. New York: Oxford University Press, 1989, 20 vols. $2500.[20] CD-ROM; publisher, 1988. $950.

Of all the dictionaries of the English language, the *Oxford English Dictionary* (begun as the *New English Dictionary on Historical Principles*) is the most magnificent, and it is with some justification that H. L. Mencken called it "the emperor of dictionaries." The purpose of the dictionary is to trace the history of the English language. This is done through definitions and quotations which illustrate the variations in the meaning and use of words.

The dictionary defines over half a million words and supports the definitions and usage with some 2.4 million quotations. In *Webster's New World Dictionary* the etymology of *black* takes 5 lines, whereas in the *OED* it takes 23 lines. The word *point* in the *OED* consumes 18 columns and *put* accounts for 30 columns. (This is an

---

[20]The publication of the second edition brought the critics out in force. Numerous stories appeared about the event in British and American papers. For those interested in the problems, debates, and the history of the second, see, for example: Geoffrey Hill, "Common weal, common woe," *Times Literary Supplement,* April 21, 1989, p. 411; Anthony Burgess, "Taking Their Word for It" *The (London) Observer Magazine,* March 18, 1989, pp. 32–39.

observation of fact, not a criticism. After all Webster's is in one volume, while the *OED* is in 20.)

The *OED* does not employ usage labels, but it does indicate whether a word or a phrase is "slang" or "coarse." Both labels are found because the decision was made in 1970 to at long last print, define, and explore the history of four-letter Anglo-Saxon words.

By the mid-1980s the publisher decided to automate the whole of the *OED*. The text was converted to a database. The cost came to over $10 million. The expense, partially shared by Canada and various corporations, resulted in the second edition.

Librarians should realize that the second edition is little more than a combination of the older work, plus four supplements. The original 13-volume printed set was completed in 1933, and from 1972 through 1986 a four-volume supplement was published which, among other things, updated material in the original work and added new words, including the four-letter variety. With the publication of the second, the editors added only another 5000 words and meanings. Some of the new words and terms added to the *OED* include *artsy-fartsy, diskette, endangered, fax, bed and breakfast, fast track, basket case,* and *plastic money.*

The new work has the advantage of incorporating the four supplementary volumes into a single set. The earlier, somewhat difficult pronunciation system has been converted to the International Phonetic Alphabet system. And the whole is published in a new, easier-to-read format.

The dictionary expert Ken Kister, among others, raises the questions: Is the interfiling and an added 6000 words really worth $2500? Would the library be better off waiting for an even more improved work? The library that has the original set and the four supplements might hesitate. (For that matter, the original set costs slightly more than $1200 in print, and is still a best buy when compared with $2500.)[21]

The CD-ROM version has two different forms:

1. The CD-ROM version of the 12 volumes, less the supplements.

---

[21]"Reference Books Bulletin," *The Booklist,* June 1, 1989, p. 1701: "The big question for libraries owning the first edition and its four supplements is whether they should spend $2500 on the second edition. Libraries where the OED has seen heavy use and needs replacement will welcome the opportunity to buy the second edition. Many libraries will want it for the new material, the convenience of one alphabet, and the fact that the pages are easier to read. Still others may decide to wait for further revision in the twenty-first century."

2. The CD-ROM version of the 20 volumes, i.e., new edition, 1991. This replaces the earlier 1980s CD-ROM version.

Now that the dictionary is in machine-readable form, it can be updated at will. Online, the user has access to the latest vocabulary changes and additions. Sound is promised eventually so that one can hear how a word is pronounced. Illustrations, heretofore not included, may be part of the new work both online and in revised printed editions.

Another advantage of the online use is that the searcher is able to create a custom-made glossary. For example, a command will allow one to have a printout of common—and not so common—terms employed in reference services, information science, or, for that matter, all of library and information science. One can also search for appropriate quotations from the history of the word(s).

Does everyone need such access to the Oxford online? Let Richard Gray give the obvious reply:

> The answer is almost certainly no. The demands that most people make of a dictionary are simple and uni-focal. It is only when a dictionary user begins to take a Boolean approach to language and its components that the immense advantages of a computerized database become evident. Hence for the user who wants to find the definition of a single adjective, a traditional dictionary is adequate; but for the user who wants to relate a whole class of adjectives to suffixal forms or to date of appearance in the language or to derivation from parent languages (e.g., Norman-French, Anglo-Saxon, Middle Latin), a machine-readable dictionary is essential.[22]

MACHINE-READABLE DICTIONARIES

As the *OED* indicates, dictionaries lend themselves to the computer; they are available in several forms:

1. Spelling checkers and basic words for computer software word processor programs. These programs have been around for many years now, and there are many to choose from. For example, *Choice Words* is an 80,000 word version of the *Webster's Ninth New*

---

[22]Richard Gray, "The New Oxford English Dictionary, and the Uses of Machine Readable Dictionaries," *Reference Services Review*, no. 4, 1988, p. 93. For a detailed explanation of types of searches possible, see "Online with the English Language," *The Wall Street Journal*, Sept. 12, 1988, p. 16, and Richard Bowers, "The Oxford English Dictionary on Compact Disc," *Electronic and Optical Publishing Review*, June 1988, pp. 88–91.

Collegiate Dictionary augmented with a thesaurus. It sells for $99. It is useful as one needs understanding of a word which cannot be defined. It can be called up in the computer screen without reference to a book.[23]

2. Electronic spelling dictionaries which are software and 6- by 4-inch hardware in one unit. There are now scores of these, but the most reliable are the ones which can claim to include entries from *Webster's Ninth New Collegiate Dictionary*. For example, there is the "electronic spelling dictionary" for $72.95 which has 80,000 words from the basic dictionary. According to an advertisement for Hammacher Schlemmer: "If you spell the word correctly (by punching typewriter keyboard keys), the 4-MHz microprocessor confirms your spelling; if you spell the entry incorrectly, it offers a list of correctly spelled alternatives. A special crossword puzzle feature lets you enter a word with missing letters then supplies a list of completed words that fit the pattern." More expensive ($225 to $300) complex handheld microprocessors include added words, synonyms, etc.

3. CD-ROM disks and online. Several dictionaries are online as part of larger units of information such as Compuserve. But the most successful, useful dictionary online is the one which offers translations. An example: "Smart Translators" which performs automatic translation of technical terms from English into French, Spanish, Italian, or German.

SPECIALIZED DICTIONARIES

There are hundreds of specialized and subject dictionaries. Almost every discipline from economics and law to sociology and zoology has its own specialized work. A cursory check of the *American Refer-*

[23]"Let Your Fingers Do the Research," *Business Week*, Aug. 27, 1990, pp. 90–91. By now there are countless variations of the word processor and dictionary. All of the major dictionaries are available as part of the growing software for writers. Houghton Mifflin, for example, offers the *American Heritage Dictionary* on a disk, along with other features. The cost is $89.95. Then, too, there is Frankline Spelling Ace ($50) which displays the correct spelling of 80,000 words to the Frankline Language Master 4000 ($300) which gives voice to 83,000 words for pronunciation and includes a thesaurus, word games, etc. Two other examples: Poetry Processor ($90) automates the scanning of lines to check metrical structure, simple rhyme, cadence, and format; Newman's Electronic Rhyming Dictionary ($60) suggests internal and slant rhymes. Both, of course, are for poets, and there are templates for virtually every poetic style from sonnets and haiku to sestinas. According to the publisher, the systems allow the poet to get the mechanics out of the way and to concentrate on thought and emotions. This is in the take it or leave it department, with most poets choosing the latter.

ence Books Annual, as well as *The Guide to Reference Books,* will clearly indicate the scope of the subject dictionary. For example, there is a *Dictionary of Modern Legal Usage* (New York: Oxford University Press, 1988) which includes an entry, "Lawyer, derogatory names for" and lists such items as jailhouse lawyer and ambulance chaser.

Among the most common specialized dictionaries, which cross every subject field and are found in most libraries, include: slang, synonyms, and antonyms, usage, abbreviations, and foreign language—among others.

American Regional Dictionaries

> *Dictionary of American Regional English* (DARE). Cambridge, MA: Harvard University Press, 5 vols.; vol. 1, 1985, $66; vols. 2 to 5, in progress.

While the *OED* remains the "bible" of the linguist or the layperson tracing the history and various meanings of a word, it is not the best place to go for correct usage, at least for Americans. English-speaking Americans and English-speaking Britons actually come close to using two different languages, the latter, of course, being recorded in the *OED*. A decision was made that in the *OED* supplements more attention would be paid to American words, particularly as most of these are now familiar to Europeans or to viewers of American television and films and readers of American magazines. In fact, since 1970, the *OED* supplements are equal to, if not better than, many American dictionaries at providing careful definitions and the history of new and slang American words.

In any discussion of the history of the American language, there is one outstanding work which many have enjoyed reading, literally from cover to cover. This is Henry Mencken's *The American Language* (New York: Alfred A. Knopf, Inc., 1919 to 1948). In three volumes, the sage of Baltimore examines a very large proportion of all American words in a style and manner that are extremely pleasing and always entertaining and informative. The initial one-volume work of 1919 was supplemented with two additional volumes. All are easy to use, as each volume has a detailed index.

Planned for completion in the mid-1990s, the *Dictionary of American Regional English* assembles colloquial expressions and their meanings from all 50 states. The monumental project began in 1965, and specially trained workers spent five years interviewing nearly 3000 Native Americans in over 1000 communities. In addition to the interviews, material for the *Dictionary of American Regional*

English, often referred to as *DARE,* has been gathered from countless printed sources including regional novels, folklore journals, newspapers, and diaries.

There are and will be countless efforts to keep DARE current by recording new words and phrases in the English language. An outstanding example: *Third Barnhart Dictionary of New English* (New York: The H. H. Wilson Co., 1990). This defines and, more important, traces the history of new words from *body mike* to *bomfog.*

Crossword

The Random House Cross-word Puzzle Dictionary. New York: Random House, 1989, 1093 pp. $19.95.

Crossword purists say it is not fair to consult a dictionary. Still, when one is stuck and frustrated, the crossword puzzle can be solved by turning to dictionaries for synonyms and antonyms, or to this guide. The clues, i.e., the typical entries, are listed in alphabetical order with the key words to fill in the boxes. In addition, there are numerous sections scattered throughout which offer quick facts on everything from family to presidents. Little is left to chance, and an experiment indicates that from 50 to 70 percent of the queries put to the reader in a typical crossword puzzle can be answered here.

Slang

Wentworth, Harold, and Stuart Flexner, *Dictionary of American Slang,* 2d supplemented ed. New York: Thomas Y. Crowell Company, 1975, 766 pp., out of print.

Chapman, Robert L., *Thesaurus of American Slang.* New York: Harper & Row, 1989. 500 pp. $22.50.

The Thesaurus of Slang. New York: Facts on File, 1988. 435 pp. $40.

Until a few years ago, most of the vulgar, four-letter words simply were not included in dictionaries. Today even the desk dictionary includes the common words and expressions. Most are labeled, and usually as "offensive."

These dictionaries also list and define words that describe people who are physically or mentally lacking (*loony, fatty*); slang terms for religious or ethnic groups (from *WASP* to *wop*); designations for women (*doll, tomato*); slang terms for homosexuals, etc. All these terms should be in a dictionary, and should always be clearly labeled to show that they are far from acceptable.[24]

Today the committee of the "Reference Books Bulletin" considers a dictionary remiss if it refuses to include such terms—carefully labeled, to be sure—as vulgarisms or unacceptable. Other reviewers, aside from those evaluating children's works, take much the same attitude.

The library needs dictionaries of slang because: (1) Most dictionaries do not indicate the variations of meaning of given slang terms or words, and few trace their history, which is as much a part of the history of a nation's popular culture as are its primary figures and events. (2) Readers often come across expressions which are not defined well in an ordinary dictionary. (3) Authors often look for words which will convey the background, class, or occupation of a given character, and the slang dictionary is a fine place to double-check such words. (4) Just plain curiosity and interest in the language will lead anyone to pause and enjoy the wild imagination of people able to conceive of the 22,000 different slang words in Wentworth and Flexner.

General in scope, Wentworth and Flexner's *Dictionary of American Slang* gives definitions which are supplemented by sources and one or more illustrative quotations. It is accepted in libraries, and certainly by all scholars. The particular merit of the work is its broad general approach to all aspects of the culture, from the slang of space scientists and FBI agents to the jargon of stripteasers and Madison Avenue advertising tycoons. Where possible, the history of the term is given, with the approximate date when the slang entered the written (not the oral) language.

The *Thesaurus of Slang* is a reverse dictionary in that it translates 12,500 standard English words into 150,000 slang equivalents. Arrangement is alphabetical, with the most current and widely used slang equivalents normally given first. There is no effort to define, as in Wentworth and Flexner, although the basic derivation is built into the equivalent standard English word. For example, if one wishes to find slang for *distill*, the compiler offers everything from *moonshine* and *cook* to put *in a nutshell*. Another thesaurus, based on

---

[24]For a detailed analysis of how dictionaries handle these type of words, i.e., whether to clearly label them as biased, see Robert Pierson, "Offensive Epithets in Six Dictionaries," *Reference Services Review*, Fall 1984, pp. 41–48. One of the earliest recorders of slang was the Englishman Eric Partridge. He has numerous works in this field. After Partridge's death Paul Beale issued a summary of his findings in *Partridge's Concise Dictionary of Slang and Unconventional English* (New York: Macmillan, 1990). Here, though, the emphasis is on British words.

the revised Wentworth and Flexner is Chapman's *Thesaurus of American Slang.* This has an extensive index whereas the previous work has none. The two complement each other nicely.

The work by Wentworth and Flexner are updated in Robert Chapman's *New Dictionary of American Slang* (New York: Harper & Row, 1986). Based on the authors' original dictionary, this work includes about 20,000 entries with considerable repetition from the first title. There are now fewer military words, but a greater number of slang expressions for drugs. Words are marked "taboo," "never to be used," etc. This is a resource for relatively current expressions, but in no way replaces the Wentworth and Flexner effort.

Synonyms and Antonyms

Roget's International Thesaurus, 4th ed., New York: Harper & Row, 1979, 1455 pp. $14.95.

Roget's Thesaurus of English Words and Phrases, rev. ed. London: Longman, 1987. 1254 pp. $20.

Webster's Collegiate Thesaurus, Springfield, MA: Merriam-Webster Inc., 1976, 944 pp. $14.95.

Webster's New Dictionary of Synonyms, rev. ed., Springfield, MA: Merriam-Webster Inc., 1980, 942 pp. $14.95.

A book of synonyms often is among the most popular books in the private or public library. It offers a key to crossword puzzles, and it serves almost everyone who wishes to increase his or her command of English. There are several dictionaries giving both synonyms and antonyms in English, but the titles listed above appear more often in libraries. Certainly, the most popular and best known is the work of Peter Mark Roget (1779–1869), a doctor in an English mental asylum. He began the work at age 71 and by his ninetieth birthday had seen it through 20 editions. (The term *thesaurus* means a "treasury," a "store," a "hoard"; and Roget's is precisely that.) His optimistic aim was to classify all human thought under a series of verbal categories, and his book is so arranged. There are approximately 1000 classifications; within each section headed by a key word, are listed, by parts of speech, the words and phrases from which the reader may select the proper synonym. Antonyms are usually placed immediately after the main listing. Thus: "possibility/impossibility"; "pride/humility."

The advantage of this grouping is that like ideas are placed together. The distinct disadvantage is that *Roget* offers no guidance or annotations; and an overzealous user may select a synonym or an antonym which looks and sounds good but is far from expressing what is meant. Sean O'Faolain, the Irish short story writer, recalls giving a copy of Roget's to a Dutch-born journalist to improve his English, but the effect was appalling. For example, the journalist might have wished to know the synonym for *sad*. He would have consulted the index and found four or five alternatives, such as "painful"; "gray"; "bad"; "dejected"; and, surprisingly, "great." When he turned to the proper section, he would have found two- or three-hundred synonyms. Unless the user has a clear understanding of the language, *Roget's* can be a difficult work.

There are at least a dozen titles which freely use Roget's name. (Like *Webster*, the name *Roget* cannot be copyrighted and is free to any publisher. Many of the dozen titles are little more than poor, dated copies of the master's original work.)

The genuine Roget (from that original work) was published first in the United States by Thomas Crowell in 1911. Longman began work on a new edition in the late 1980s, but with each printing, minor additions and changes have been made. Harper & Row's *Roget's* is organized in the original way, i.e., by concept. The work sells about 175,000 copies each year in hardcover and close to 45,000 in paperback. This is the most popular thesaurus on the market.

The best, current edition of Roget is the London revision. The obvious advantage is that it is new, and new words and changes in meaning are included. The 1987 revised edition, for example, includes new words in business and politics, such as *creative accounting* and *insider trading*. It follows, too, the pattern set down in the major revised edition of 1962. Then, as now, groups of related words follow one another in a logical sequence so that the mind is "led by easy transitions from one nuance to another without distraction" (to quote the publisher). There is a detailed index and excellent cross-references. All and all it is the best of the genuine Roget's now available.

Most versions of Roget's are in alphabetical order, not arranged by concept. This is a "reverse dictionary," i.e., it allows one to ask and find the answer to such a question as "What is the synonym for *sloppy?*" or "What is the precise word to describe a *kindly person?*" The catch is that one may suffer a mental block and be unable to look up a related word.

Aside from *Roget's International*, the most popular book of synonyms is *Webster's Collegiate Thesaurus*. Here the 100,000 entries are arranged alphabetically. After each main entry there is a definition (a useful device) and then a list of synonyms. This is followed by related words and, finally, by a list of antonyms. Sometimes quotations are employed to make it clear how words should be used.

Webster's is updated with each edition, and the work is as current as almost any now in print. However, its primary claim to popularity is its ease of use. Some would say it is too easy and totally ignores the purpose of the original Roget's but nevertheless the *Webster's* should be found in libraries.

Webster's New Dictionary of Synonyms is another version of the *Collegiate.* It has fewer words, but the arrangement and the approach is much the same. The work is particularly helpful in discriminating between what, at first sight, appear to be similar words. There are scores of other books of synonyms, although the average library or individual would do quite well with only those listed here.

The other versions include *The Random House Thesaurus: College Edition;* the *Reader's Digest Reverse Dictionary. Bernstein's Reverse Dictionary* (New York: Times Books) still, the original Roget's and the *Webster's* efforts are by and large the best for the library and the home.

Usage and Manuscript Style

Fowler, Henry Watson, *Dictionary of Modern English Usage,* 2d ed. rev. by Sir Ernest Gowers. New York: Oxford University Press, 1987, 725 pp., $22.95; paperback (1983), $9.95.

Strunk, William, Jr., and E.B. White, *Elements of Style,* New York: Macmillan, 3d ed. 1979, 97 pp., paperback, $8.95.

Webster's Dictionary of English Usage. Springfield, MA: Merriam-Webster, 1989, 980 pp. $18.95.

Turabian, Kate. *A Manual for Writers of Term Papers, Theses, and Dissertations,* 4th ed. Chicago: University of Chicago Press, 1987, 300 pp. $20; paperback, $7.95.

Even in the era of computers, word processors, videocassettes, and data banks, "the urge to put a sentence together sensibly, even lovingly, still engages the attention of students, teachers, and professional wordsmiths. . . . To scholars, Fowler's has been the standard that other books on usage have had to look up to."[25] Found in every library, Fowler's guide to good English continues to sell at a steady clip of about 5000 copies a year, and the paperback version more than doubles the number.

[25]Herbert Mitgang, "Fowler Classic on Language Translates to Paper," *The New York Times,* Sept. 6, 1983, p. C12.

Fowler deals extensively with grammar and syntax, analyzes how words should be used, identifies clichés and common errors, and settles almost any question that might arise concerning the English language. The dictionary, and the revision by Sir Ernest Gowers, has a special flavor treasured by all readers. Fowler commented on practically anything that interested him, and the hundreds of general articles can be savored for their literary quality, in addition to their instructional value.

Strunk and White is one of the few books on grammar and writing that can be read for pleasure. *The Elements of Style*, first published in 1959, but now in a paperback edition, is a concise guide for those who want the right rules while learning the skill of writing with simplicity and grace. The work is by now a fabled reference guide. It is distinguished as much for its ease of use as for its good sense. As a staff member of *The New Yorker* magazine, E. B. White practiced what he preached. He gives the impression that anyone can learn to write as well as he by following the rules in his manual. That may not be quite right, but the well-organized guide does make it possible for the user to find an answer to almost any puzzle of proper usage in a given situation.

Webster's Dictionary of English Usage offers direct advice and clear instructions as to proper usage. The word expert William Safire claims this is the "one of the great books on language in this generation."[26] The author is inclined to agree with Safire, as are most other critics. It is highly recommended for all libraries as an up-to-date, easy-to-follow guide. It will answer the vexing problems of usage, particularly when employed with Fowler.

Arranged alphabetically from "a, an" to "zoom" it is extremely easy to use. The editors tend to follow the prescriptive school, as does the publisher, but there is a discussion of different points of view. See, for example, the ubiquitous "ain't" and some 10 columns of discourse with scores of illustrative quotes. (There are 20,000 such quotations used throughout to emphasize this or that point of usage.)

Another fascinating aspect of usage concerns English as spoken by sections of minority groups in America. For example, students whose language is BEV (black English vernacular) find that standard English can be a barrier. The problem is that what is acceptable in one's own particular culture may be different from what is acceptable in the working world. At one extreme are those who view BEV

---

[26]William Safire, "Shades of Gray/Grey" *The New York Times Magazine*, July 16, 1989, p. 9.

as a civil right, so much so that a study of it may be part of the curriculum. At the other extreme are those who attack it for being little more than badly mastered English.[27]

America may well be embarked upon a policy of bilingualism that will recognize and accept foreign languages (and most particularly Spanish) together with English. Former Senator and language expert S. I. Hayakawa headed a national public interest organization at the end of the 1980s to establish English as an official language via a constitutional amendment. But many, including leading Hispanics, are fighting this effort both nationally and locally.

There are numerous other dictionaries and handbooks of good usage, but because the particular rules governing use tend to change rapidly (at least if one is of the descriptive school and is influenced by television, radio, or pop music), it is best to have the latest, authoritative guide about. For background and for sometimes opposing opinion, another choice is *Harper's Dictionary of Contemporary English Usage* (New York: Harper & Row, 1989).

A *Manual for Writers*, or "Turabian" as many librarians call it, is the bible of both trade and scholarly book editors as well as writers. It is not a book on word usage, although many of the rules and examples are useful in determining which word or style to employ. It answers questions on how to prepare footnotes and how to edit a manuscript; it also discusses rules concerning punctuation, spacing, and indexing. There are discussions of how to cite nonprint material, the meaning of cataloging in publication, and even how an author should phrase a letter when sending a publisher a manuscript.

Abbreviations and Acronyms

Acronyms, Initialisms, and Abbreviations Dictionary, 14th ed. Detroit, MI: Gale Research Company, 1990, 3 vols. $208.

The basic guide in this field is the Gale publication. It is in three volumes. The first volume has over 480,000 entries for acronyms, initialisms, and related matters. These are listed alphabetically, and the full meaning of the term is then given. Most of the focus is on the United States, but basic acronyms from western Europe are included. The second volume is really two softbound sup-

---

[27]Eleanor Orr, *Twice as Less.* (New York: Norton, 1988). Written by a high school mathematics teacher, this work suggests a compromise which takes the best (and the acceptable) of Black English vernacular and works it into the curriculum with standard English. Along the way the author points up the problems involved.

plements issued between editions. They provide about 15,000 new acronyms in two sequences, by acronym and by meaning. The third volume is a "backward," or "reverse," companion to the first volume, i.e., one looks up one of the 480,000 entries to find the acronym. For example, one would turn here to find the acronym for the American Library Association—ALA. A smaller version is the *Concise Dictionary of Acronyms and Initialisms* (New York: Facts on File, 1988). Compiled by a librarian, S. W. Miller, this cuts the massive Gale listing back to 3000 entries. The compiler rightfully thinks they represent answers to the more common reference queries about terms found in newspapers, crossword puzzles, and daily reading. Arranged in alphabetical order, the terms are all from the English-speaking world. A helpful addition: brief annotations which explain the new, the difficult-to-understand, or the uncommon entry such as airport coding (DET, LAX and P- to list three). The great advantage of this work is cost: $22.95 as compared with over $600 for the considerably more ambitious Gale publication.

Comparatively, DeSola's *Abbreviations Dictionary* (New York: Elsevier, various editions) has 180,000 entries and is twice as expensive, i.e., about $50 as opposed to Miller's for $24. The catch: It does not have the useful explanatory annotations and simply has too many terms for daily use. A closer competitor and much used, again, though, without explanatory material is the *Webster's Guide to Abbreviations* (Springfield, Mass.: Merriam-Webster Inc., various editions) which has about 8000 entries.

Subject Dictionaries

Dictionaries devoted to specialized subject fields, occupations, or professions make up an important part of any reference collection. This is especially true in the sciences. General dictionaries tend to be stronger in the humanities, weaker in the fast-changing scientific fields. Consequently, there are a vast number of scientific dictionaries, but relatively few in the humanities.

Subject dictionaries explain particular meanings for particular words or terms for professions, occupations, or areas of subject interest. Otherwise, of course, most of the material might be found in the unabridged dictionary, or desk dictionaries which are regularly updated and show an interest in adding new terms.

The major question to ask when determining selection is: Does this dictionary offer anything that cannot be found in a standard work now in the library? It is surprising, particularly in the humanities and social sciences, how much of the needed information is readily available in a general English dictionary.

While all evaluative checks for the other dictionaries apply, there are also some special points to watch:

1. Are the illustrations pertinent and helpful to either the specialist or the layperson? Where a technical work is directed to a lay audience, there should be a number of diagrams, photographs, or other forms of graphic art, which will make it easier for the uninitiated to understand the terms.
2. Are the definitions simply brief word equivalents, or is some effort made to give a real explanation of the word in the context of the subject?
3. Is the dictionary international in scope or limited chiefly to an American audience? This is a particularly valuable question for the sciences. Several publishers have met this need by offering bilingual scientific dictionaries.
4. Are the terms up to date? Again, this is a necessity in a scientific work, somewhat less so in a social science dictionary, and perhaps of relatively little importance in a humanistic study.

Many of the subject dictionaries are virtually encyclopedic in terms of information and presentation. They use the specific-entry form, but the entry may run to much more than a simple definition.

The thin line between necessary technical language and unnecessary jargon is one which disturbs. Within highly developed areas of the hard sciences and technology, new words and phrases are necessary to describe what is found on equally new frontiers. Technical terms and/or jargon is less necessary and acceptable in the humanities or much of the social sciences.

Jargon, another way of describing barbarous language, is unnecessary. It is used primarily to give the appearance of profundity and complexity to concepts that are rather easy to understand and ordinary when explained clearly. The library field has its share of such chatter and indecipherable writing.

So-called *doublespeak*, a jargon variation, is used by government and business to obfuscate. For example, "At the Gas Research Institute in Chicago, they have decided that it is inappropriate to use the term low-cost gas. In the future it will be cost competitive gas supply, making marginally priced resources more cost competitive."[28]

---

[28] *Quarterly Review of Doublespeak*, July 1988, p. 1. The 12-page newsletter, published

Foreign Language Dictionaries (Bilingual)

The Cassell's series, all published by The Macmillan Company, different editions and dates, various pagination, e.g., *Cassell's French Dictionary; Cassell's German Dictionary; Cassell's Italian-English, English-Italian Dictionary;* etc. Price range: $10.95 to $21.95.

Guinagh, Kevin, *Dictionary of Foreign Phrases and Abbreviations,* 3d ed. New York: The H. W. Wilson Company, 1982, 288 pp. $38.

Most readers are familiar with the typical bilingual dictionary which offers the foreign word and the equivalent English word. The process is then reversed with the English word first, followed by the equivalent foreign word. For other than large public, academic, and special libraries, the bilingual dictionary is usually quite enough. For that purpose the Cassell's entries are standard, familiar desk dictionaries (issued in England under the Cassell imprint, here by Macmillan). Most have gone through numerous editions and revisions by many editors. Pronunciation is given clearly enough for even the amateur to follow, and the equivalent words are accurate. Definitions, of course, are not given. Most dictionaries usually include slang words, colloqualisms, idioms, and more common terms from various subject areas. The number of main entries varies from 120,000 to 130,000.

There are several other reputable publishers of basic foreign language dictionaries. Collins of England (distributed here by Rand McNally), Charles Scribner's Sons, Simon and Schuster, and Oxford University Press, as well as Cambridge University Press, are only a few of the better-known, reliable publishers of works which range from Arabic to Swahili.

The person who simply seeks a common foreign word or phrase is likely to find the answer in almost any desk dictionary. These are either part of the main dictionary, or set off in a special section. When it comes to more sophisticated, specialized words, the choice is either to turn to a bilingual dictionary or to a work such as Guinagh's. Here one finds definitions for more than 5000 abbreviations, words, phrases, quotations, proverbs, etc. All the entries are in a single alphabet, with cross-references when appropriate, to other languages. The languages covered include French, Italian, Greek, German, Spanish, and Latin.

by the National Council of Teachers of English, documents the slaughter of the language.

Larger and specialized libraries will have dictionaries of other countries. Larousse is the venerable French publisher of dictionaries (and encyclopedias). University libraries are likely to have several of the Larousse dictionaries such as the *Petit Larousse en Couleurs,* a common title found in most French homes.[29] Equally basic dictionaries from other countries will be purchased.

In the next decade or so, translation from a foreign language to English may be a routine reference process. The dictionaries will remain, but for rapid translation, say of a business letter, one will simply turn to a computer. Computers are able to translate, but only roughly, not only individual pages of material, but individual words.

CD-ROM

Meanwhile, how about 12 foreign languages on a CD-ROM disk. NTC Publishing Group offered this in 1990 for $950. Called *Languages of the World,* the disk includes 7 million words and 18 dictionaries; it is also a complete multilingual approach. One may find definitions, translations, and synonyms. Most of the focus is on business, education, and science and technology, although common words are included, too. One is given an instant translation of an English word into one or all of the foreign languages (Chinese, Danish, Dutch, Finnish, French, etc.). It works the other way as well, so one may translate an English technical term into Spanish, Swedish, etc. Definitions and synonyms are provided.

SUGGESTED READINGS

Amato, Kimberly, and Karen Moranski, "Oxford English Dictionary: CD-ROM and Second Edition," *Reference Services Review,* Spring 1990, pp. 79–81, 86. A short overview of both the second edition (in print) and the CD-ROM version which requires "extensive and intensive one on one assistance prior to and while conducting searches." The implication is clear: Except for use by experts there are many standard reference books which are easier and quicker to use in print format.

Burchfield, Robert (ed.), *Studies in Lexicography.* New York: Oxford Clarendon Press, 1987. The editor of the supplement to the *OED* includes 10 articles focusing

---

[29]Larousse was founded in 1852, and their dictionaries are to France what Webster's are to the United States. In 1990, according to Larousse, they made the worst mistake in company history: A new edition of the 1700-page *Petit Larousse* claimed that some highly poisonous wild mushrooms are harmless. All copies of the dictionary had to be recalled. For details see: "Deadly Error Halts Sales of Larousse," *The New York Times,* Aug. 29, 1990, C10.

primarily on the lexicography of the English language. There are pieces on Old English by E. G. Stanley; English homonyms by L. V. Malakhovski; and Yakov Malkiel's discussion of Romance etymologies in English dictionaries and related items.

Cmiel, Kenneth, *Democratic Eloquence.* New York: William Morrow, 1990. In this study of popular language from 1776 to 1900, the author explores the arguments for and against prescriptive and descriptive approaches to speech. The way a gentleperson is supposed to talk and write has changed drastically. Dictionaries first were prescriptive, but by the turn of the century leaned in the direction of sanctioning new styles of popular speech. The book is based on wide reading and is fully documented.

Fritze, Ronald, "The Oxford English Dictionary: A Brief History," *Reference Services Review,* Fall 1989, pp. 61–70. A well-researched history of the *OED* by a history professor. It is particularly useful for the massive amount of background information. See, too, the Shenker piece.

Gray, Richard, "Sources of Etymological Reference in the English Language," *Reference Services Review,* Summer 1986, pp. 9–17. A discussion of the development of etymological dictionaries with some wise comments about their strengths, weaknesses, and use.

Grogan, Denis, *Dictionaries and Phrase Books.* Chicago: American Library Association, 1988. As in others in this series, this includes case histories which teach the student the ins and outs of basic dictionaries and related works. Again, though, this is an English text, and some of it may be not quite that applicable for American students. Still, it is an excellent approach to learning about the day-by-day use of dictionaries.

Kaiserlian, Penelope, "Kate Turabian's Manual—A Best Seller for Fifty Years," *Scholarly Publishing,* April 1988, pp. 136–143. The "Emily Post" of scholarship is discussed, as is her book which now (1989) has reached sales of over 5 million copies. Mrs. Turabian died at age 94 in 1987 after serving as Dissertation Secretary at the University of Chicago for 25 years.

Lamb, Annette, "Webster's Ninth New Collegiate Dictionary," *CD-ROM Librarian,* September, 1990, pp. 33–36. In this brief discussion of a typical dictionary on CD-ROM, the author points out the benefits and the drawbacks. What is true of *Webster's* is equally true of the countless other versions on CD-ROM. Price is the primary difficulty—usually five to eight times higher than the printed version.

Shenker, Israel, "Annals of Lexicography: The Dictionary Factory," *The New Yorker,* April 3, 1989, pp. 86–100. This is by far the best, single article on the revised *OED.* Informative as it is witty and scholarly, the piece gives detailed data on the history and the present condition of the set. It is a pure delight to read.

Stacey, Michelle, "At Play in the Language," *The New Yorker,* Sept. 4, 1989, pp. 51–74. While this is a profile of the man who traced the history of "O.K.," it is also a well-written explanation of the various steps taken to discover the background of a given word or phrase. The article, too, considers the arguments for prescriptive and descriptive. Allen Walker Read, the subject of the sketch, is on the descriptive side.

CHAPTER ELEVEN
GEOGRAPHICAL SOURCES

M any Americans are geographically illiterate. One survey, for example, found that nearly 20 percent of Americans 18 to 24 years old could not find the United States on a world map.[1]

One can understand why there is constant need for updating and improving the geographical sources in the library—any type or size of library. People, ignorant of where to find London, Paris, or even New York are in dire need of reference assistance. Moreover, in our fast-paced world even people who know their way around maps need help because geographical boundaries and names of places change constantly.

Survey after survey continues to confirm a Gallup finding of mid-1988: Close to 11,000 adults from the United States and western Europe and Japan were asked to identify 16 places on a map. The average American could find only 7, while the average Swede located 12. Many Americans had trouble identifying the Pacific Ocean, not to mention the Persian Gulf.

> "This reinforces the urgency of National Geographic's long term commitment to improve geographic teaching in our classrooms. Our adult population, especially our young adults, do not understand the word at a time in our history when we face a critical economic need

[1]"Finding New Ways to Make Geography Exciting," *The New York Times,* Aug. 3, 1988, p. B6. This is the same survey considered below, i.e., the one conducted by the Gallup poll for the National Geographic Society.

to understand foreign consumers, markets, customs, foreign strengths and weaknesses," said the president of the National Geographic Society.[2]

Given this situation, the reference librarian should be willing and anxious to assist with geographical questions. Furthermore, a strenuous effort should be made to keep the geographical sources current, easily available to users (they are not, too often, because of their awkward size), and a major part of reference services.

An interesting sidelight is the revelation made in the late 1980s that the Soviet Union for 50 years faked many of its own maps. The process started out for an understandable reason in 1940. Fearing a German invasion, the Soviet hierarchy ordered cartographers to literally locate towns and roads in the wrong places—this, of course, to confuse the invaders. It worked.

> Field Marshal von Rundstedt wrote: "I realized soon after the attack was begun that everything that had been written about Russia was nonsense. The maps we were given were all wrong. The roads that were marked nice and red and thick on a map turned out to be tracks, and what were tracks on the map became first-class roads. Even railways that were to be used by us simply didn't exist. Or a map would indicate that there was nothing in the area, and suddenly we would be confronted with an American-type town, with factory buildings and all the rest of it."[3]

After World War II bureaucratic inefficiency and mistrust of the United States resulted in the continued practice of moving towns and roads here and there on the maps. The "approved" maps were distributed right up until the mid-1980s, when orders were given to return to true cartography.

DEFINITIONS AND SCORE

Geographical sources may be used at the mundane level ("Where is it?"), or in a more sophisticated way to help clarify linkages between human societies. Reference librarians are familiar with both

[2]"Americans Falter on Geographic Text," *The New York Times,* July 28, 1988, p. A16. In similar surveys reported in this story, "One in 10 said the United States was a member of the Communist bloc organization," and "more than a third could not calculate the distance between two designated cities, given a mileage scale." See also "2 Superpowers Failing in Geography," *The New York Times,* Nov. 9, 1989, p. A20.

[3]"Faked Russian Maps Gave the Germans Fits," *The New York Times,* Sept. 11, 1988, p. 30. See, too, the front-page story on this in the *Times* for Sept. 3, 1988.

approaches. The first, and the more common, is the typical question about where this or that town is located, the distance between points X and Y, and what type of clothing will be needed to travel in Italy in December. Moving away from the ready-reference query, one becomes involved with relationships concerning climate, environment, commodities, political boundaries, history, and everything else with which geographers are deeply interested.

When she is asked to quickly identify a city or a country, the reference librarian has little difficulty matching the question with a source. The correct answer usually is in an atlas, an individual map, or a compilation of geographical data. Asked to establish the elements common to the Philippines and Ethiopa, she must turn to both geographical sources and related works which, in this case, might range from the *Statesman's Yearbook* and an encyclopedia to the periodical and newspaper indexes for current events. Then, too, she would wish to search the geographical texts and individual economic and political historical studies.

Once one embarks on trips which go beyond the ready-reference desk, the geographical sources become more complex. This chapter is not concerned with that aspect of the subject. Due to space limitations and the scope of the text, it is limited to basic geographical sources.

Geographical sources are generally graphic representations which allow the imagination full reign. Indeed, many of them are works of art, and they provide a type of satisfaction rarely found in the purely textual approach to knowledge. They often are used for decorating, e.g., see "Maps That Aren't for Getting Somewhere" (*The New York Times*, March 29, 1990, p. C6). As one fan puts it: "There's really nothing else in that price category that gives you the impact on a wall that a map does."

Geographical sources used in ready-reference works may be subdivided into three large categories: maps and atlases, gazetteers, and guidebooks.

Maps and Atlases. A map is, among other things, a representation of certain boundaries of the earth (or the moon and planet as well) and we generally think of them as on a flat surface. Maps may be divided into flat maps, charts, collections of maps in atlas form, globes, etc. Cartographers refer to these as *general* maps, i.e., for general reference purposes.

A physical map traces the various features of the land, from the rivers and valleys to the mountains and hills. A route map shows roads, railroads, bridges, and the like. A political map normally limits itself to political boundaries (e.g., towns, cities, counties, states) but may include topographical and route features. Either separately or together, these three types make up a large number of maps found in general atlases.

Cartography is the art of mapmaking, and a major headache of cartographers is achieving an accurate representation of the features of the earth. This task has resulted in various projections, i.e., the effort to display the surface of a sphere upon a plane without undue distortion. Mercator and his forerunners devised a system, still the best known today, based on parallel lines; that is, latitude (the lines measuring the "width" of the globe, or angular distance north or south from the equator) and longitude (the lines measuring the "length" of the globe, or angular distance east or west on the earth's surface). This system works well enough except at the polar regions, where it distorts the facts. Hence on any Mercator projection, Greenland is completely out of proportion to the United States. Since Mercator, hundreds of projections have been designed; but distortion is always evident—if not in one section, in another. For example, the much-praised azimuthal equidistant projection, with the North Pole at the center of the map, indicates directions and distances more accurately, but in other respects it gives a peculiar stretched and pulled appearance to much of the globe.

In late 1988 the National Geographic Society met the challenge by changing its standard projection (in use since 1922) for one developed by Arthur H. Robinson, one of the nation's most respected cartographers. The distortions are fewer with his approach. The Soviet Union and Canada shrink to a truer relative size. Under the old system the USSR was depicted 223 percent larger than it is in reality. It is now represented as only 18 percent larger than its real land mass.[4]

Combining maps from Bern and Oxford, the *Peters Atlas of the World* (New York: HarperCollins, 1990) is unusual on two counts. First, it is international in that editions of it are available in almost all western countries including, after 1990, the United States. Second, and more important, the some 180 pages of maps are what is known as the *Peters Projection*. This form of projection is an effort to

[4]"The Impossible Quest for the Perfect Map," *The New York Times*, Oct. 5, 1988, p. C1. This is a discussion of the problems involved in cartography as well as a clear explanation of the new National Geographic system for its world maps. Rand McNally uses the Robinson Projection, while Hammond leans toward the heart-shaped Bonne Projection. Still others prefer the Peters Projection. Computers are likely to introduce even more approaches in the 1990s.

represent the curved surface of the earth in two dimensions. The 100 pages of colored topographic maps show Europe, the United States, and China, for example, in proportion to their real size on the face of the globe. In addition there are 245 thematic world maps which cover climate, religions, population, sports, etc. The index is barely adequate for a $50 atlas.

The only relatively accurate graphic representation of the earth is a globe. The need for a globe in a reference situation is probably questionable. It is certainly desirable to have one; however, the reference librarian who has had occasion to use a globe instead of a map to answer particular reference questions is rare indeed.

The average general map gives an enormous amount of information for the area(s) covered. Cities, roads, railroads, political boundaries, and other cultural elements are indicated. The physical features, from mountain ranges to lakes, are depicted. Relief is usually indicated by shading and contrast or color.

Libraries will primarily purchase *atlases,* or collections of maps. Libraries with larger holdings will include flat or sheet maps such as those distributed by the National Geographic Society or the traditional state and regional road maps.

Details on other types of maps may be found in a number of textbooks concerned with map librarianship. See, for example, Mary Larsgaard's *Map Librarianship* 2d ed (Littleton, Colo.: Libraries Unlimited, 1987).

Another large group of maps are termed *thematic,* in that they usually focus on a particular aspect of geographical interest. Reference here is usually to historical, economic, political, and related matters which may be shown graphically on a map. An example: *The Times Atlas of World History.*

Gazetteers are geographical dictionaries, usually of place names. Here one turns to find out where a city, mountain, river, or other physical feature is located. Detailed gazetteers will give additional information on population and possibly leading economic characteristics of the area.

Guidebooks hardly need a definition or introduction; they furnish information on everything from the price of a motel room in Paris or Kansas to the primary sights of interest in New York or London.

There is no equivalent *Books in Print* for maps, but *The World Map Directory* (Santa Barbara, Calif.: Map Link, 1988 to date, irregular) comes close. The directory indicates maps available from the publisher, who also is a map vendor. Over 46,000 are listed, and there is a good index. The coverage is international, and the scope takes in all types of maps from city plans and atlases to topographic and thematic.[5]

EVALUATION

The same standards apply for university map collections, and medium to large public and special libraries and will provide a useful guide for both beginners and experts. The Standards are published by the Special Libraries Association, Geography and Map Division. The 1987 ten-page publication is available, too, in the *SLA/ G&MD Bulletin* for June 1987. It gives detailed instructions and suggestions on how "to create, study, evaluate or reorganize" a map library.[6]

There are several major points to consider in map evaluation that differ from book evaluation. Because maps and atlases depend on graphic arts and mathematics for presentation and compilation, a librarian is called on to evaluate them with a type of knowledge not usually important in book evaluation.

Buying Guides

The best relatively current guide to popular atlases is the *General Reference Books for Adults,* which, as with encyclopedias and dictionaries, gives detailed information on each of the works, as well as useful preliminary information on evaluation.

Still reliable, although now somewhat dated is Ken Kister's *Atlas Buying Guide* (Phoenix, Ariz.: Oryx Press, 1984). After a lucid discussion on evaluating atlases, Kister offers descriptive and evaluative comments on 105 titles. This is followed by a handy set of charts which compare the various works. Each section considers the same basic points, and it is easy to see where one atlas is better (or worse) than another.

From time to time, the "Reference Books Bulletin" in *The Booklist* offers reviews of just-published atlases, such as the "World Atlas Survey," December 1, 1990, pp. 769–773. The Geography and

---

[5]See *Guide to Reference Books Guide to U.S. Map Resources,* 2d ed., Chicago: American Library Association, 1990. This has comprehensive information on 975 map collections with an excellent 128-page index.

[6]Marsha Selmer, "Standards for University Map Collections: The Rationale, History, and Method," *Special Libraries Association, Geography and Map Division Bulletin,* June 1988, pp. 10–18. This article gives useful background on the important standards.

Map Division, Special Libraries Association, issues the bulletin which frequently has articles of interest to librarians. Contributors cover new atlases, books, and related material in each issue.

Publisher

Map printing is a specialized department of the graphic arts; while simple maps can be prepared by an artist or draftsperson, more complicated works require a high degree of skill. More important, their proper reproduction necessitates expensive processes which the average printer of reference works is not equipped to handle. As with dictionaries and encyclopedias, the specialized skills needed and the resulting expense narrow the field of competent cartographic firms down to a half dozen or so. In the United States, the leading publishers are Rand McNally & Company, C. S. Hammond & Company, and the National Geographical Society. In Great Britain, the leaders are John G. Bartholomew (Edinburgh) and the cartographic department of the Oxford University Press.

With commercial sales of maps at about $200 million a year, it is a lucrative business. The largest publisher is Rand McNally, although as it is privately controlled there is no way of knowing its actual size or profits. A German firm, Langenscheidt, is considered second in volume of sales, followed by Simon & Schuster (a Paramount Communications publisher), which brings out the Mobil Road atlases among others. Hammond is next, with the National Geographic Society coming up near the end.

When the cartographic firm's reputation is not known, it is advisable to check through other works it may have issued, or in a buying guide. The mapmaker may differ from the publisher, and in the case of an atlas both should be checked.

Scope and Audience

As with all reference works, the geography section must represent a wide variety of titles for many purposes and, in a public or school library, for the appropriate age groups. Essentially, it is a matter of scope. Some atlases are universal; others are limited to a single country, or even a region. Other maps, even within a general work, may be unevenly distributed so that 50 percent or more of the work may give undue attention to the United States or Canada, ignoring the weight of the rest of the world.

Scale

Maps often are classed according to scale. One unit on a map equals a certain number of units on the ground, i.e., 1 inch on the map may equal 10 or 100 miles on the map. The detailed map will have a larger scale. The scale is indicated, usually at the bottom of the map, by a line or bar which shows distances in kilometers or miles, or both.

Geographers use map scale to refer to the size of the representation on the map. A scale of 1:63,360 is 1 inch to the mile (63,360 inches). The larger the second figure (scale denominator), the smaller the scale of the map. For example, on a map which shows the entire United States, the scale may be 1:16 million (1 inch being equal to about 250 miles). This is a small-scale map. A large-scale map of a section of the United States, say of the northwest, would have a scale of 1:4 million. In the same atlas, the scale for Europe (and part of Russia) is 1:16 million; but for France (and the Alps) it is 1:4 million.

The scale from map to map in a given atlas may vary considerably, although better atlases attempt to standardize their work. The standardization is determined both by the size of the page on which the map appears as well as the effort of the publisher to use the same basic scales throughout.

Currency and Standardization

Slow, yet-constant, evolution in place names, as well as their spelling can prove difficult for cartographers. New names may or may not stick, "Cambodia stayed Cambodia, despite an official preference for Kampuchea. Saigon is now firmly Ho Chi Minh City. Peking—or was it Peiping?—became Beijing and Szechwan became Sichuan."[7]

In an effort to resolve these problems in the United States, the Board on Geographic Names was established about 100 years ago. Originally the purpose was to establish names for settlements, mountains, and other geographical features in the United States, but as the years passed the board's mandate was extended. It now includes standardizing all foreign and domestic names for use by federal agencies on maps and in periodicals. By extension, the board influences the commercial mapmakers. In seeking to standardize foreign

---

[7]"Myanmar and the River of Time," *The New York Times,* June 25, 1989, p. 26. The editorial was prompted by the decision of Burma to change its name to Myanmar.

names, the board works with similar groups in other Western countries.

The work of the foreign names committee of the board is the most arduous. Many rules are fixed; others, subject to change. For example, living persons cannot be used for place names; a feature can be named for a deceased person, but only when deemed in the public interest; and no derogatory names may be used.

There are ongoing and sometimes dramatic changes that should be recorded in new atlases. A perfect example is the 1990 reunification of Germany. No longer "east" or "west" as shown on most maps, the single country requires a new designation. This change alone, if not shown on a map or atlas, is an excellent clue to its currentness.

Reputable mapmakers follow a revision policy similar to that of encyclopedias. They are continually revising as they reprint. Normally, this is clearly indicated by: (1) the copyright date on the verso of the title page and (2) revision date, with some indications of revision. Much of this is an act of faith because the publisher may offer a new copyright and/or revision date, yet leave most of the maps untouched. The wise librarian will go beyond the publisher's date and check to see if the name, say, of the major third-world city or town actually has been changed; or if the new preferred spelling for a Chinese river is used.

Format

When one considers format, the basic question is simply: Can I find what I want easily on the map, and is it as clear as it is legible? The obvious problem is to print a map in such a way that it is easy to read a mass of names which cover a densely populated area. It is one thing to clearly print maps of the north and south polar regions, and quite another to be able to arrange type and symbols so that one can find a path from point to point in a map of the areas around New York City, Paris, and London.

The less that has to be shown, the more likely the map will be clear and easy to read. The actual number of points represented on the map is a major editorial decision.

Color. The chief value of color is to enable different classes of data to be related to one another and to show distinctions among details. On physical maps, color clarifies approximate height by hatch lines, hill shading, and special cross sections. The success or failure of color depends on careful consideration in printing. Where colors bleed over, where the color for a town does not correspond with the outline of the town, the librarian can be sure that the map was poorly printed.

Symbols. As important as the choice of colors is the selection of symbols. A standard set of symbols for roads, streams, villages, cities, airports, historical sites, parks, and the like is shown on most maps. While these legends are fairly well standardized in American maps, they vary in European ones. Consequently, the symbols should be clearly explained on individual maps, or in an atlas, at some convenient place in the preface or introductory remarks.

Thematic mapmakers have a considerable problem with symbols, and here the variation from map to map and country to country will be significant. The problem becomes complicated when a number of different subjects are to be displayed on a single map. Frequently, the task is so complex that the map becomes illegible. Hence, in the case of thematic maps, it is best to have different maps indicating different items, such as population, rainfall, or industry, rather than to use a single map for all.

Projections. All maps are distorted. For example, on some, the land surface of China may be smaller than that, say, of the United States; or Siberia may appear larger than the whole of the Yukon territory and Alaska. Normally, an atlas will use a number of projections to overcome distortions and to indicate the degree of distortion in a map.

Grid Systems. Latitude and longitude are the essentials of any map; they are particularly helpful for locating a special place on the map. These are further subdivided by degrees, minutes, and seconds: $45°12'18''$N, $1°15'$E, for example, is the location of a certain French town. The advantage of this system is its ultimate accuracy, but it has the distinct disadvantage of being a number of such length as to be difficult to remember from index to map. Consequently, most maps also are divided into grids or key reference squares. Index references are then made to these squares, usually by letter and number—E5, D6, and so on—with the page number of the map.

The usefulness of a map may be evaluated by the size of the grid system. Obviously, if lock square covers more rather than less area it will be more, rather than less, difficult to pinpoint a place.

Type. There is clearly room for considerable improvement in the design of lettering on most maps. Even the best of them often use typefaces developed for display or book texts, not specifically for maps. The normal procedure is to use a scale that indicates large places by large type, medium ones by medium-sized type, and so on.

Binding. Because of its large trim size and the weight of pages being turned, an atlas needs a sturdy binding and one that allows the book to lie flat when opened. When the book is lying flat, the entire map should be visible and not hidden in part of the binding. Unfortunately, this is not always the case, and the fault is too frequent given of the relatively high prices of most atlases.

Marginal Information. Each map gives certain basic information, usually in the margin. A quick way of ascertaining the worth of a map is to check for this type of data. It should include, at minimum, the scale (inclusion of both a bar and natural scale is desirable), the type of projection, and in the case of thematic maps, the symbols and significance of the colors. In an atlas, the meaning of the general symbols may be given in the preface or introduction, which should include the date of printing, the dates of revision, and other such data. Normally, directional symbols are not given in an atlas, it being understood that north is at the top of the map. On single sheets, there should be a compass rose indicating direction.

The Index

A comprehensive index is as important in an atlas as the maps themselves. A good index is in alphabetical sequence and clearly lists all place names that appear on the map. In addition, there should be a reference to the exact page; the exact map; and latitude, longitude, and grid information. A page number alone is never enough, as anyone who has sought an elusive town or city on a map lacking such information will testify. The index in many atlases is really an excellent gazetteer; that is, in addition to basic information, each entry includes data on population and country.

Other useful index information will include, among other things, pronunciation and sufficient cross-references from spellings used in a foreign country to those employed by the country issuing the atlas or map; e.g., Wien, Austria, should be cross-referenced to Vienna, and the entry for Vienna should say "*see* Wien."

A check: Try to find four or five names listed in the index on the maps. How long did it take, and how difficult was the task? Reverse this test by finding names on the maps and trying to locate them in the index. Difficulty at either test spells trouble.

How many world atlases does the average library need? An average would be from 10 to 15, with at least one or two new atlases purchased each year, if they are updated. Larger collections will number world atlases close to a hundred.

Publishers update their atlases after each census. The round of new editions appeared in 1990–1991. Still, the basic configuration for the atlases does not change, and what is outlined here will be much the same for the next editions. Speaking, for example, of a recent atlas, the "Reference Books Bulletin" observes, "This atlas, standard on library shelves, is—except for the front matter—little changed since last reviewed (eight years ago). The maps have been updated to reflect name and boundary changes."[8] Much the same may be said of almost all "new" atlases, at least those revised between the ten-year censuses.

In addition to overall quality, atlases may be divided in several ways such as, major-size atlases, intermediate (medium-size) adult atlases, etc. That procedure is followed here, with the largest ones considered first.

MAJOR-SIZE WORLD ATLASES

The New International Atlas. Chicago: Rand McNally Company, 1990. 568 pp. $150.

Times Atlas of the World: Comprehensive Edition. London: Times Newspapers Limited, 8th rev. ed, 1990, 522 pp. $160 (distributed in U.S. by Times Books: Random House).

The *Times Atlas of the World* is the best single-volume atlas available.[9] That it happens to be the most expensive is chiefly because such meticulous care has been taken, with emphasis on large-scale, multiple maps for several countries and attention to detail and color rarely rivaled by other American atlases.

The volume consists of three basic parts. The first section is a conspectus of world minerals, sources of energy and food, and a variety of diagrams and star charts. The atlas proper comprises about 123 double-page eight-color maps, the work of the Edinburgh house

---

[8]"Reference Books Bulletin," *The Booklist,* June 1, 1988, p. 1659. The review is of the 1987 *Rand McNally Cosmopolitan World Atlas.*

[9]*The Times Atlas* is a first choice of almost all libraries. It is also a shelving headache because the large format (12 × 18 inches) will not allow for normal storage.

of Bartholomew. This is the vital part, and it is perfect in both typography and color. The clear typeface enables the reader to easily make out each of the enormous number of names. A variety of colors is used with skill and taste to show physical features, railways, rivers, political boundaries, and so on. A remarkable thing about this atlas is that it shows almost every noteworthy geographical feature from lighthouses and tunnels to mangrove swamps—all by the use of carefully explained symbols.

The Times Atlas is suited for American libraries because, unlike many other atlases, it gives a large amount of space to non-European countries. No other atlas matches it for the detailed coverage of the Soviet Union, China, Africa, and Southeast Asia, lands not overlooked in other atlases, but usually covered in much less detail. A uniform scale of 1:2,500,000 is employed for most maps, but is changed to 1:850,000 for the United Kingdom. Maps of the larger land masses are supplemented with smaller, detailed maps which range from maps of urban centers to maps of the environs of Mt. Everest.

The final section is an index of over 210,000 place names, which, for most purposes, serves as an excellent gazetteer. After each name, the country is given with an exact reference to a map.

The Times Atlas comes in a shorter version: *The New York Times Atlas of the World*, 2d rev. ed. (New York: Times Books, 1990, various paging, $49.95). This has many of the same features, certainly the same maps, as the more expensive, larger edition. However, it is a smaller work and instead of 210,000 names in the index, it has half as many, about 100,000.

The New International has 160,000 entries in the index and 300 good to excellent maps. A team effort of international cartographers, the atlas strikes a good balance between the needs of American readers and those in other countries. The scales are large with most countries at 1:6 million to 1:3 million. The maps tend to be double-paged and are models of legibility. The "birthday-cake-icing" material (from essays on the climate to thematic maps) is mercifully missing. The main focus is on maps of extraordinary quality.

Larger libraries will want both atlases. If a choice has to be made, *The Times Atlas* would be first; although the *International* would be a close second. *The Times* has the reputation and is expected to be found in major libraries. *The International*, on the other hand, is more current. If both cannot be had, the solution is to buy *The Times* and "update" it with several intermediate current-sized atlases.

Intermediate- to Small-Size Atlases

Gold Medallion World Atlas, rev. ed. Maplewood, NJ: Hammond Incorporated, 1990, 672 pp. $85.

Citation World Atlas, rev. ed. Maplewood, NJ: Hammond, Incorporated, 1990, 394 pp. $29.95.

National Geographic Atlas of the World, 6th ed. Washington: National Geographic, 1990, 425 pp. $80.

Rand McNally New Cosmopolitan World Atlas, rev. ed. Chicago: Rand McNally Company, 1990, 344 pp. $55.

The Medallion World Atlas is the largest of the numerous atlases issued by Hammond. The atlas is the work horse of the line, with 324 pages of maps and over 148,000 entries in the index. The maps are heavily biased in favor of the United States and Canada, and here the energy is well spent in that the scale, features, and legibility demonstrate a solid command of the art of cartography. Critics sometimes are hard on the aesthetic qualities of the maps. True, they are not up to Bartholomew, yet they certainly are clear and easy to follow. Also, thanks to the North American bias, they often give details, at least state by state and province by province, not found in other atlases. There are maps of states, for example, which show everything from the topography to distribution of agriculture and population. Another excellent feature: each map has its own gazetteer, including state, county, and city population figures. Of somewhat dubious value is the added material. A library with thematic atlases hardly needs these additions.

Hammond, like Rand McNally and other cartographers, builds atlases around a basic set of maps. The more expensive volumes include more items in the index and also more less-than-necessary thematic and encyclopedic material. At the other end of the price scale one finds precisely the same maps, but shorn of the extras. This is pretty much what separates the intermediate-size atlases from their big brothers.

A case in point is the *Citation World Atlas.* This is an abbreviated version of the *Medallion,* with an abbreviated price: $29.95 as contrasted with $85. The *Citation* has 26,000 entries in the index as compared with *Medallion's* 100,000. There are other differences, and yet the maps are precisely the same. Again, the United States is emphasized with individual maps for most states, and there are a number of thematic maps, although the *Citation* lacks the 160 pages of historical mapping found in the *Medallion.* Given the general excellence of the maps, if not the balance of coverage, and the lack of extraneous materials, this is a "best buy" for the average librarian or home.

The *National Geographic Atlas* has much in addition to maps. It is quite attractive, at least to many people and school children. Here one finds numerous thematic maps and discussions of world resources. Divided by continent, the 180 maps are introduced in each section by an encyclopedia-like article on the various countries. The maps, while clear and easy enough to read, fail to indicate more than rudimentary aspects of relief. Another negative aspect is found in the 155,000-entry index where there are no coordinates of latitude and longitude. Finally, there is too much emphasis on American interests, sometimes to the neglect of proper attention to third-world countries. The atlas does have its strong points, including large scales, good-sized pages, and the aforementioned extensive index. It is favored by many who want something more than just an atlas.

The *National Geographic* magazine is a familiar source of maps. The separate, folded maps are by now a familiar addition to numerous issues. These are usually removed from the magazines and filed by the librarian.

The *Rand McNally Cosmopolitan* has approximately 300 maps on a scale of from 1:3 million (1 inch equals about 4.75 miles) to 1:16 million (1 inch equals about 250 miles). The 12 largest metropolitan areas in the United States benefit from the larger scale. Heaviest emphasis, as might be expected, is on American maps. About 82,000 entries are in the general index, and these help to locate political names and physical features. The facts and text material found in the nonmap sections are in another index. This is a standard atlas found in almost all libraries and can be as useful for ready reference materials on countries as the maps themselves. Note, too, that Rand McNally, unlike Hammond, employs different maps in its various atlases.

In a class by itself is the Rand McNally *Goode's World Atlas,* a basic item in many schools. Of all the atlases it may be the most familiar. It has a serviceable index (36,000 entries) and close to 400 (sometimes less than astonishing) maps. As it is a part of the curriculum, it is updated frequently, i.e., the eighteenth totally revised edition appeared in 1990. And at under $25, it is the best buy for smaller libraries.

There are countless variations of intermediate to small atlases. Take, for example, the *Desk Reference World Atlas* (Chicago: Rand

McNally, 1990). This sells for a modest $18; it has 346 pages of good maps and an index of some 30,000 place names. Between the sections is a modest encyclopedia of 200 pages filled with tables and facts pertaining to geographical queries. Designed in the same format and size as a desk dictionary, the idea is to use it as a supplement to that reference work. Not a bad notion, but the problem is that while the two volumes may look good together on a shelf, the 6- by 12-inch desk dictionary page size is not ideal for maps. The result is a workable atlas, but one libraries can do without.

It is interesting to know that often Rand McNally produces maps for other publishers who then sell the resulting atlas under their own name. This is more the rule than the exception. The reason is that there simply are not that many map publishers in America, or for that matter in the world, and most publishers who want an atlas to their credit turn to the major map makers for help. Two examples: (1) *Reader's Digest Atlas of the World* (New York: Reader's Digest Assoc., 1990) where the maps come from Rand McNally and, in addition, from several other international cartographers. The editorial material primarily is from the Reader's Digest group.

An even better example is (2) *The World Book Atlas* (Chicago: World Book, 1990, 432 pp.). This is an example of how an encyclopedia publisher has modified the work of two map publishers. The atlas is made up of the United States and Canada map section contents of the Rand McNally *Cosmopolitan Atlas,* with some thematic maps from the same publisher's *Goode's World Atlas.* World maps are taken from an Italian atlas, *The Great Geographical Atlas.* Normally the atlas is marketed along with the encyclopedia, although it can be purchased separately.

Appealing to younger people and the curriculum needs of schools, the first 100 pages have the format of the encyclopedia with such illustrated sections as "looking at the earth's features," "understanding maps," and 30 pages of thematic maps. The actual atlas runs from pages 97 to 288, followed by an index with slightly over 34,000 entries. The maps are up to Rand McNally's high standards as found in *Goode's* and the *Cosmopolitan.* The Italian maps are equally good.

The volume is particularly suited to its audience, and for once the inclusion of encyclopedia information is quite appropriate. Also, because of its medium-range price ($69) it is a good purchase for the average home.

GOVERNMENT MAPS[10]

U.S. Geological Survey. *National Atlas of the United States.* Washington: Government Printing Office, 1970. 417 pp.

Conservatively, at least 90 percent of maps published each year originate from government sources. This wide variety of materials provides detailed mapping of almost every area of the world, with particular emphasis on the United States. Many of the items are available to the public and are found in libraries.

Although out of print and in need of revision, the *National Atlas of the United States* remains an impressive and still much-used reference work in the libraries that have a copy. The oversized 14-pound volume has over 335 pages of maps and a 41,000-entry index. "General Reference Maps" make up the first part, and these are on a scale of 1:200 million with urban areas at 1:500,000 and certain other areas at 1:1 million. In addition, there are a great number of "Special Subject Maps" which cover the thematic aspects of the country. Themes range from economics to demography and contain some of the best information available. Again, they are in need of revision. There is a valuable section on administration maps which show various districts and regions.[11]

The U.S. Geological Survey (USGS) has a continuing publishing program whereby many librarians routinely receive maps as issued. The maps are detailed, covering elevation, vegetation, and cultural features. The National Mapping Division of the USGS provides mapping information to the library as does National Cartographic Information Center for the USGS. Libraries may learn about these various publications through the USGS's *New Publications of the Geological Survey* and *A Guide to Obtaining Information from the USGS. The Monthly Catalog of United States Government Publications* is another source, and, from time to time, maps appear in *U.S. Government Books,* a quarterly listing of more popular publications.

Maps for America: Cartographic Products of the U.S. Geological Survey and Others, 3d ed. (Washington: Government Printing Office, 1988) is revised every four to five years. It contains maps, plus considerable background information on cartography and related matters.

---

[10]For an excellent discussion of government maps see Mary Larsgaard, *Map Librarianship* (2d ed. Littleton, CO: Libraries Unlimited, 1987). She offers a clear explanation of current government mapping programs and distribution.

[11]A crude update of the *Atlas* is provided in the 1986 publication by Macmillan of *Atlas of the United States.* It includes much the same information with 1980 data, but the maps are poor and there is no index.

Of all the USGS series, the topographic maps are the best known, the most often used. The maps show in detail the physical features of an area, from streams and mountains to the various works of humankind, and are of particular value to the growing number of hikers and others who enjoy outdoor activities. Libraries have a separate collection of these maps and take particular pride in offering them to the public. They are sold by map dealers throughout the United States and are available directly from the USGS, National Mapping Program at Reston, Virginia.

Local and Regional Maps

In evaluating a local map, the requirements are usually threefold. First, the map should be truly local and should show the area in detail. Second, it should be large-scale. Third, it should be recent. Although all these requirements may be difficult to meet, an effort should at least be made to keep the local collection as current and as thorough as possible.

The United States Geological Survey topographic maps, mentioned in the previous section, are ideal local maps. Thousands of these are issued covering every region and area in the United States. One will inevitably find the detailed map needed for either an urban or rural area among those in this series.

Local state and city government departments are a good source of maps. State and provincial offices issue them, usually to encourage tourism. Chambers of commerce usually have detailed city maps as well as considerable information on the city itself. The most direct way for a library to get such material is to send a request to the chamber of commerce in the desired city or town.

In tracing the history of state government atlases Peter Ives observes that there is a "gathering of many freakish creatures within the book kingdom. Tall, fat, thin, sleek, scruffy, bland and colorful, they reflect the secondary American political entities in a wide variety of texts and coverings."[12]

THEMATIC MAPS AND ATLASES

Historical Atlas of the United States. Washington: National Geographic Society, 1989, 289 pp. $59.95.

The Times Atlas of World History. Maplewood, NJ: Hammond Inc., 1989, 360 pp. $85.

---

[12]Peter B. Ives, "State Atlases by State Agencies: An Historical Survey," *Government Publications Review,* March/April 1988, p. 114. The author shows the major works, state by state.

Rand McNally Commercial Atlas and Marketing Guide. Chicago: Rand McNally & Company, 1976 to date, $150 (1990). Annual price varies.

The thematic or subject map is usually limited to a specific topic or related topics. Almost anything with a geographic focus may be the subject of such a map but thematic mapping of a specific topic is not always available. It may be hard to find a map showing the exact topic for the exact area, and often for an exact time period. There are so many possibilities that at best only a fraction are ever mapped. At the same time, for the average library there are a suitable number of thematic maps and atlases available. Those listed here are representative of a much larger number which can be located by consulting the *Guide to Reference Books, American Reference Books Annual,* and, of course, geographical bibliographies.

An outstanding, descriptive list of thematic maps will be found in *The Map Catalog* (New York: Random House, 1987). There are chapters on 49 specific types of maps from land, sky, and water guides to maps for treasure hunts and bicycle rides. Excellent illustrations and appendixes give detailed advice on how to obtain maps from various government agencies.

Although each thematic map listed is a separate publication, many general atlases include thematic maps. These can range from climatic and primary-industry maps to those concerned with soil and mining. Unfortunately, they are rarely detailed enough for more than superficial overviews. For details and more current data, one should turn to a specific thematic work.

Historical maps may settle more than one argument. In *The Two Gentlemen of Verona,* Shakespeare has Proteus travel from Verona to Milan by boat. A modern-day map shows that this is impossible. But a map of the 1483–1499 period shows a series of canals, once designed by Leonardo da Vinci. Even though the two Italian cities are not connected by water, the canals come quite close—within 40 miles of each other—so a substantial part of the trip could have been by boat as Shakespeare claims.

Discussing the *Historical Atlas of the United States,* the "Reference Books Bulletin" gave it a prize sendoff with:

This magnificent new *Atlas* is a fitting commemorative volume for the 100th anniversary of the National Geographic Society. It encourages browsing and will delight laypersons as well as the most discriminating professional geographer. Its 287 oversize pages (12 by 18 inches) are full of maps, timeliness, historical charts, and new and historic photographs that provide a visual panorama of every aspect of American life from hot dog stands to house types. All told there are 380 maps (most in color) done on four varying scales ranging from 1 inch to 300 miles to 1 inch to 900 miles, 450 photographs, 80 graphs, and 140,000 words of text.[13]

It is the first commemorative atlas of United States history in over 50 years. But only about one-quarter of the volume is maps. The remainder is a pleasant, illustrated summary of history, statistics, and just plain flag waving. This is magnificent material for the classroom and for poring over at the dining room table, but it is hardly up to standard for a true historical atlas.

Updated every five or six years, *The Times Atlas of World History* shows parallel historical events, cultural activities, and social movements in parallel development in Europe, Asia, Africa, and the Americas. The maps are large, easy to read, and placed in such a way that one may trace the history of an event, individual, or, more likely, a movement that is developing. The atlas has an excellent index and a useful glossary of unusual historic terms.

There are scores of historical atlases. The best known, at least in past years, was William Shepherd's *Historical Atlas* (9th ed., New York: Barnes & Noble, 1964). A rival of later vintage is the *Rand McNally Atlas of World History* (Chicago: Rand McNally & Company, 1987). Both cover world history, Shepherd's from about 3000 B.C., and the Rand McNally title from pre-history, i.e., about 40,000 B.C. Outline maps indicate developments. There are 240 in Shepherd, although they are not all the full-page size of the 115 in the Rand McNally work. The latter has essays and is designed for the general audience; Shepherd has no essays and is prepared for students. In terms of ready reference, Shepherd is preferable, not only because of the additional maps, but because there are far more place names in the index—a ratio of about seven (in Shepherd) to one (in Rand McNally).

Updated, revised, and always in print are scores of similar thematic atlases. Some are concerned only with the Bible: *The Harper Atlas of the Bible, The Macmillan Bible Atlas, The Reader's Digest Atlas of the Bible, Facts on File's Atlas of the Bible.* Each has a different approach.

The value of the *Rand McNally Commercial Atlas* is that it is revised every year, and for the library which can afford to rent it (it is rented, not purchased), the *Atlas* not only solves the problem of adequate United States and Canadian coverage, but solves it in the best form possible.

The *Commercial Atlas* accurately records changes on a year-by-year basis. All information is the most up to date of any single atlas or, for that matter, any reference work of this type. It is an excellent

---

[13] *The Booklist,* May 1, 1989, p. 1513.

source for current statistical data, and the first 120 pages or so offer (1) regional and metropolitan area maps, (2) transportation and communication data, (3) economic data, and (4) population data. Most of this is listed by state and then by major cities with codes that clearly indicate the figures.

The largest single section is devoted to "state maps and United States index of statistics and places by states." Here one finds the state maps. The statistical data, arranged by state, follows. This includes such things as principal cities and towns in order of population, counties, basic business data, transportation, banks, and post offices by town. It is followed by briefer data for Canada and the world. The system is a trifle awkward and is another case where an online or CD-ROM access would be most welcome (see next section).

Astronomy and Air Photos

> *The Cambridge Atlas of Astronomy.* 2d ed. New York: Cambridge University Press, 1988, 432 pp. $90.

Now that space is a consideration in our worldview, it is necessary to have atlases and maps which clearly show aspects of astronomy of interest to both laypersons and experts. There are several good to excellent guides, of which the Cambridge entry is one of the best. Here one finds detailed maps of the planets, satellites, and related areas of the universe. In addition, the publisher provides over 350 color and 420 black-and-white photographs, many taken in space. The text is clear, nontechnical, and current. It is an ideal place to start for any imaginary (or, for that matter, real) trip to the stars.

If there is a need to see an aerial view of almost any place on this earth, one may turn to the government. By now more than 6.5 million separate pictures from downtown Detroit to African road networks are available. This mapping is from nonmilitary government satellites orbiting around the earth up to 500 miles out in space. The file is maintained in South Dakota, and inquiries may be sent to the EROS data center, Sioux Falls, S. Dak. 57198. One may purchase a single black-and-white aerial shot for $5 or go as high as $800 for a 40-inch, enlarged, color infrared print.

CD-ROM/Computer

With a breakthrough in graphics and photographs for textual CD-ROMs, it is now possible to envision the day when most geographical material will be available on CD-ROM.

The Electromap World Atlas (Fayetteville, Ark.: Electromap Inc., 1990 to date, annual, $160) is one of the first CD-ROMs available, and is sure to be followed by entries from the major publishers. The disk contains 239 full-color county, regional, topographical, and statistical maps including every county and most dependencies in the world. Updated annually, it is a modest $160.

Compton's electronic encyclopedia allows one to focus on a map and then call up articles related to the country, area, city, or community. This is equivalent to IBM's PC USA, a computer program that permits the user to "point and shoot" at the map via a mouse. The screen automatically calls up information about the point from government and history to natural resources and agriculture. Another program offered by IBM is called PC Globe. Numerous other companies offer similar products each year.[14] Geographic information programs are now relatively common. For example, Atlas Graphics is software that allows one to analyze data and link it to a specific location. This permits someone to find the right neighborhood to open a pizza outlet or an opera house.

The same type of program was used for the 1990–1991 census. The information in machine-readable form gives "unprecedented access to information about customers and citizens. The government sells its Census data, and that data, plugged into a geographic information program, will help companies determine sales opportunities."[15]

MapInfo offers software which allows one to zoom in on a continent, country, state, city, and small section of a city right down to a particular block or point. It can be used to keep track of everything from sewer lines to manhole covers.

A hand-held gadget by Interstate Travelmate is a small computer with 30,000 places on the nation's major highways, from restaurants and gas stations to motels and hospitals. A few simple commands and the $99.95 guide gives data on numerous places within a 50-mile radius of any spot on an interstate highway. Similar map devices are to be offered on automobiles allowing one to avoid traffic jams and map out a quick way from X to Y point.

GAZETTEERS

Webster's New Geographic Dictionary, rev. ed. Springfield, MA: Merriam-Webster, Inc., 1985, 1408 pp. $19.95.

In one sense, the index in any atlas is a gazetteer, that is, it is

---

[14]"Trips through Geography and Time," *The New York Times*, April 3, 1990, p. C9.
[15]"When Maps Are Tied to Databases," *The New York Times*, May 28, 1989, p. F10.

a geographical dictionary for finding lists of cities, mountains, rivers, population, and the features in the atlas. A separate gazetteer is precisely the same information, but usually without maps. Why, then, bother with a separate volume? There are three reasons: (1) Gazetteers tend to list more names; (2) the information is usually more detailed; and (3) a single, easily managed volume is often welcomed. Having made these points, one can argue with some jurisdiction that many atlas indexes often have more entries, that they are more up to date, and that they contain a larger amount of information than one finds in a gazetteer. The wise librarian will first consider what is to be found in atlases before purchasing any gazetteer.

The number of gazetteers and indexes presently found in good atlases, the expense to prepare them, and the limited projected sales probably account for the lack of interest by many publishers in gazetteers as a separate group. The fact or argument that most information sought by the layperson can be found in even greater detail in a general or geographical encyclopedia does not increase the use of gazetteers. Their primary value is as a source for locating places possibly overlooked by a standard atlas and for use as informal indexes.

There are three American gazetteers found in almost every reference section. The most used is *Webster's New Geographical Dictionary*. This has 47,000 entries and over 200 maps. The work is easy to consult, and the information, while quite basic, gives specifics on where a given place is located. It can be used for many other purposes, including checking the spelling and pronunciation of place names. More detailed information is given here than in atlases on states, such as date of entry into the United States, motto, chief products, etc. The entries for countries follow the same detailed presentation, but for most place names, the entry is short and primarily useful for location.

Unfortunately, the second work is now so far out of date that it is of limited use. This is the *Columbia Lippincott Gazetteer of the World* (New York: Columbia University Press, 1952, 1962). The initial work and the 1962 supplement have over 130,000 entries, or almost seven times the number found in *Webster's*. Whereas the latter constantly revises their dictionary, Columbia has chosen not to do so, and it must be used with that in mind.

Chambers World Gazetteer (New York: Cambridge University Press, 1988, 845 pp.) is the most current, but it has only about 20,000 entries as compared to more than double the amount in *Webster's*. The obvious advantage is that it lists such names as Chernobyl (not in its rival). Also, the entries are more lengthy in *Cham-*

bers. The major disadvantage is that some place names are given only once or twice whereas they may be found five or six times in *Webster's.* The two titles complement each other, and one might begin with *Chambers* first and then turn to *Webster's* for more or missing data.

TRAVEL GUIDES[16]

American Automobile Association. *Tour Book.* Washington: American Automobile Association, various dates, titles. Free to members.

The purpose of the general guidebook is to inform the traveler about what to see, where to stay, where to dine, and how to get there. It is the type of book best carried in one's pocket or in the car. Librarians frequently find these works useful because of the vast amount of details about specific places. Atlases and gazetteers are specific enough about pinpointing locations, yet rarely deal with the down-to-earth facts travelers require.

The American Automobile Association numbers its members in the millions, and it is estimated at least 45 to 50 percent of middle-class American drivers belong to the association. It issues regular tour books which cover the states, either individually or in groups. For example one book is devoted to Florida, while another considers Georgia, North Carolina, and South Carolina. The books are divided into two primary sections. One part, arranged alphabetically by city or town, points out the primary points of interest. The second section, arranged in the same fashion, lists motels, hotels, and restaurants.

The AAA guides are particularly good for certain parts of the nation where local access assistance is almost nonexistent. There are, for example, many other guides on how to get around New York, Chicago, and San Francisco, but few for smaller communities, particularly in the middle of the country. Here, again, the AAA guides are useful.

---

[16]The really successful guides are described with considerable verve by the author, Harold M. Otness, "Wanderlust and Fireside: Building a Travel Collection," *The Library Journal,* May 1, 1988, p. 33. Otness writes an annual feature for *LJ* on guides, e.g., "The Sins of Going Further," in the May 1, 1989, issue (pp. 39–40). Updates, but only descriptive and not critical, are provided time to time in *Publishers Weekly,* e.g., see "Going places" in the Jan. 22, 1988, issue (p. 26) and "A roundup of 1988 travel books, (p. 35). The feature is included each year, about the same time, in *Publishers Weekly.*

Although constantly being updated, these and other guides cannot be trusted for such details as prices of hotels or meals. Experts say to add 15 to 20 percent to almost any price given, particularly when travel is outside the United States.

Increasing pressure to bring the guides to the bookshelves earlier and earlier in the travel season means that much of the information may be a year or so old. Even though the cover reads "1990 Guide to . . . ," the data are most likely to have been gathered in 1989 or even earlier.

With the primary focus on the United States, the AAA guides are of very limited use in other parts of the globe.[17] Specific sign posts are needed, particularly ones which are not only descriptive but evaluative. For example, the world-famous *Michelin* "Red" (hotels/restaurants) and "Green" (sights) guides give evaluative information for most of the countries of the world. (Published in France, these are available in English in the United States via Michelin Publishing, Spartanburg, S.C.)

Just how many guide books are there? From 550 to 650 new travel books covering every part of the globe and meeting every need are published each year in the United States alone. The number is much the same for western European countries. *Going Places: The Guide to Travel Guides* (Cambridge, Mass.: Harvard Common Press, 1989) evaluates over 3000 guides. After an introduction to the genre, it divides the guides by geographical areas. The short annotations are descriptive and evaluative. An appendix lists travel magazines and newsletters.

Suggested Reading

Carey, Susan, "Putting Baedeker Back on Track," *The Wall Street Journal,* Sept. 3, 1987, p. 34. The brief history and the future for the world's best-known travel series, the Baedeker guides. They began publication in 1835 and had a reputation for ultimate accuracy, e.g., the Germans used the guide to Norway to draw up plans for attacking that country in 1940.

Harley, J. B. (ed.), *The History of Cartography*. Chicago: University of Chicago Press, 1987 to date, 6 vols., in progress. This gigantic intellectual effort will fill the lamentable void which has escaped scholarship—the detailed history of map-making and its historical sweep. The first volume covers cartography in prehistoric times and in ancient and medieval Europe and Egypt. The second

---

[17]Actually, the American Automobile Association does offer guides to Europe and other parts of the globe, but these are rarely detailed enough for most travelers. One might turn to the equivalent group in, say, England or France for assistance.

volume covers Asia. Subsequent works, scheduled at two-year intervals, will consider the Renaissance up to and including the late twentieth century.

Otness, Harold, "Going Plating/Stealing Maps from Libraries," *Western Association of Map Libraries Information Bulletin,* August 1988, pp. 206–210. The problem of map theft is discussed: "A high percentage of library thefts are committed by insiders" and "one cannot expect convicted library thieves to be incarcerated for long, regardless of how many convictions." The author demonstrates ways of checking theft other than by having the local police at the library door.

Rockwell, Ken, "Privatization of U.S. Geological Survey Mapping: Implications of Map Libraries," *Bulletin, SLA Geography and Map Division,* March 1989, pp. 26–29. A map librarian examines a government plan to privatize mapping and decides it is bad. "Loss of depository access, imposition of copyright restrictions and fees, and unreliable services are strong possibilities."

Steinhauer, Jennifer, "With Computers, Mapmakers Are Redrawing the World," *The New York Times,* December 2, 1990, p. F5. This article is a discussion, in easy to understand terms, of how computers are used by modern mapmakers. There is some attention, too, given to various types of projections and to the so-called electronic navigators employed in automobiles.

Weide, Janice, "Electromap World Atlas," *CD-ROM Librarian,* July/August 1990, pp. 27–32. In this discussion of a CD-ROM map system, the author not only evaluates the particular work but explains other points which anyone interested in CD-ROM geographical source evaluation will find of value.

CHAPTER TWELVE
GOVERNMENT DOCUMENTS

What is a government document? It can be the 48-page *Pocket Guide to Baby-Sitting* or *The Congressional Directory*. It can be *The Senate Legislative Procedural Flow* or *The Code of Federal Regulations* or the 10-page pamphlet *Cockroaches: How to Control Them*. Reference librarians constantly use the *Statistical Abstract of the United States* and turn to various sources for business statistics generated by the government and its many agencies. To answer the question "What is a government document?" one must reply "A treatise on almost any subject."[1] Name the subject, and the chances are there is a government document that tells what it is or how to handle it.

Government documents are not all legal, technical, or how-to-do-it approaches to existence. They come in many different forms, from reports on arms to studies of tulip growing. But they do have one thing in common, and that is *numbers:* In 1990, the Superintendent of Documents sold over 90 million copies of publications.

A *government document* is any publication that is printed at government expense or published by authority of a governmental body. Documents may be considered in terms of issuing agencies: the congressional, judiciary, and executive branches, which include many departments and agencies. In terms of use, the documents

---

[1]Since it was established in 1865 as the sole printer of documents, the Government Printing Office has cataloged and published 3.5 million works. About 25,000 are still in print.

may be classified as: (1) records of government administration, (2) research documents for specialists, including a considerable number of statistics and data of value to science and business, and (3) popular sources of information. The form may be a book, pamphlet, magazine, monograph, microform or almost any media.

While this discussion mainly concerns federal documents, state, county, and municipal governing bodies issue publications that are also a major concern of any library.

Some of the mystery surrounding government documents will be dispelled if one compares the government with the average private publisher. The latter may well issue a record of government action, although normally the commercial publication will be expressed in somewhat more felicitous prose, along with editorial comments. The simple purpose of the U.S. Government Printing Office is to furnish documents that may be considered useful for research.

The vast labyrinth of public records calls for expert librarians. There are private librarian investigators who work independently to find a specific document. For example, one such group has clients who "include foreign governments, corporations, labor unions and law firms. The trick, they say, is knowing where to look in the archival mazes. The information can be in anything from a law to records in a 10K [referring to the annual report that publicly held companies must file with the Securities and Exchange Commission]. Documents are a mother lode when it comes to information."[2]

Bibliographical control and daily use of documents in reference work often is difficult and requires expertise beyond the average experience of the reference librarian. Nevertheless, there are certain basic guides and approaches to government documents which should be familiar to all librarians.

ORGANIZATION AND SELECTION

The organization and selection of government documents in all but the largest of libraries is relatively simple. Librarians purchase a limited number of documents, usually in terms of subjects of interest to users, such as the *Statistical Abstract of the United States*. If they are pamphlets, they usually are deposited by subject in a vertical file. If books, they are cataloged and shelved as such.

The reference librarian normally will be responsible for the

[2]Barbara Gamarekian, "There's Gold in Archival Labyrinth," *The New York Times*, Jan. 19, 1988, p. A24.

acquisition of documents. Confusion is minimal because government documents are rightly treated like any other information source and shelved, filed, or clipped like other media.

When one moves to the large or specialized libraries, the organizational pattern is either a separate government documents collection or, as in the smaller libraries, an integration of the documents into the general collection. Even the large libraries tend to partially integrate government documents with the collection, although complete integration is rare. About one-third of large libraries have totally separate collections.

The justification for separate collections is that the volume of publications swamps the library and necessitates special considerations of organization and classification. There are other reasons; but on the whole, it is a matter of the librarian's seeking to find the simplest and best method of making the documents available.

The separate documents collection isolates the materials from the main reference collection. The reference librarians are inclined to think of it as a thing apart and may answer questions with materials at hand rather than attempt to fathom the depths of the documents department. If patrons are referred to the documents section, the librarian there may attempt to answer questions that might be better handled by the reference librarian.

Evaluation

There are no problems with evaluation of government documents; there are no choices. One either accepts or rejects, say, *The Statistical Abstract of the United States.* The government has no competitors, and evaluating such a document in terms of acquisitions is as fruitless as commanding the seas to dry up. Many government documents are unique and no one, but no one, is going to challenge them with another publication. The *Congressional Record* more or less dutifully records the words and actions of Congress each day. There is no possibility of (and no gain to) anyone's publishing another version of that.

Still, there are some matters pertaining to government documents which the librarian and the layperson may consider.

Cost. The government first began its massive publishing program as a service, and works were sold either at cost or even below cost. This is no longer the case. Now, thanks to appropriation cuts and a new budget philosophy, the documents are supposed to pay for themselves. This does not always happen, but the pricing policy is reflected in the individual prices of items.

Government documents formerly distributed free or at low cost have been eliminated or given to a private publisher. In 1982, for example, the Government Printing Office initiated a policy of offering for sale only those publications with an anticipated sale value of $1000 or more.

The all-time best seller, *Infant Care*, not too long ago cost 20 cents. By 1990 the 67-page document, which has sold over 18 million copies since 1919, was more than $5. Another best seller, consistently in the government's "top 10," gives details on septic tanks. This, too, went from a few cents to several dollars.

Timeliness. Current information is a valuable feature, particularly in the statistical reports and with the present methods of keeping up with scientific and technological advancement. Many publications are issued daily or weekly. Still the problem remains as to the frequency of indexing or abstracting; e.g., recently the *Monthly Catalog* has been almost five months behind the material published.

Range of Interest. The range of interest is all-encompassing. No publisher except the government has such a varied list.

GOVERNMENT INFORMATION POLICY

Essentially the government's publishing program is an effort to furnish documents to keep the citizens informed of its activities. In addition, it publishes works (from how to grow strawberries to how to fight terrorists) which improve the life quality and ensure the health and safety of its people.

With noncontroversial issues, there is rarely a problem about the distribution of government documents. The difficulty arises when some individual or branch of the government resorts to checking the free flow of information. During periods when government becomes more closed and less open, it appears to operate as an oligarchy and less as a democracy. Taking on the guise of omniscience and omnipotence, it favors secrecy and a close watch on information.

What has this to do with government documents? Everything—when the effort is to hide information rather than to make it public.

Problems change along with changes in administrations, but, in general, government documents provide a lightning rod for trouble. Reviewing critical issues which involve reference librarians working with such documents, one may quickly spot the difficulties.

1. *Censorship* works in either a direct (overclassification of documents as secret) or indirect (attempts to privatize, raise the price of, or otherwise make fewer documents available) way. In general, conservatives tend to favor privatization. Liberals believe in getting out as much information about the government and its activities as possible—at government expense.[3]

2. *Lack of skilled librarians* works to cancel out even the best government documents acquisition system. All too often the librarian does not use a government document when it would answer a question, or where it is used, it is the wrong one.

3. *Lack of availability* of documents would not seem a difficulty, particularly as they can now be had in various forms from the traditional printed form to CD-ROM to online, but it is a potential headache. More and more documents are only available electronically, and not in print. This requires the library to be ready technologically, but the librarian often cannot meet this requirement.

4. *Inadequate central indexing.* Bibliographic control is an old story, but growing worse. The paradox is that there are now more and more indexes and bibliographical keys to government documents, but as fortunate as we are to have modern technological tools, what we really need is ready access by means of one or two channels, including the library's own online catalog.

All this boils down to what some call a "federal information policy."[4] The policy is looked upon in many ways, as favorable or otherwise, often depending upon one's political views, vested interests, or basic trust or mistrust in authority of any type. It is an area open to vast amounts of conjecture, discussion, writing, and includes, of course, elements other than those listed in the four points cited above.

There is an obvious conclusion: "The breadth of issues relating to federal information policy suggest[s] that it is important for information professional[s] to become involved ... by (among other things) being informed about the issues."[5]

---

[3] *Government Publications Review,* vol. 5, no. 5, 1988. Nearly the entire issue is given over to federal information policy, including proposals for privatization.

[4] Kathleen Eisenbeis, "U.S. Government Information Policy," *Journal of Education for Library and Information Science,* Fall 1988, p. 96.

[5] Marilyn Moody, "Government Information" *RQ* Summer 1988, pp. 479–483 offers a wide-ranging discussion on these and other problems. Almost every issue of *Library*

Documents to the People (Chicago: American Library Association, 1972 to date, bimonthly) is a newsletter and watchdog for preserving the Freedom of Information Act. It includes news on government documents, abstracts of ERIC titles, notices of new commercial indexes, and much material of value to reference librarians.

ACQUISITION

Once a document has been selected for purchase, its acquisition is no more difficult—indeed, often somewhat easier—than that of a book or periodical. Depository libraries have a peculiar set of problems, but for the average library, the process may be as follows:

1. Full information is given in the *Monthly Catalog* and *U.S. Government Books* on methods of purchase from the Superintendent of Documents. Payment may be made in advance by purchase of coupons from the Superintendent of Documents. In the case of extensive purchases, deposit accounts may be established.

2. Some documents may be obtained free from members of Congress. However, as the supply of documents is limited, the member of Congress should be notified of need in advance. It is particularly advisable to get on the regular mailing list of one's representative or senator to receive publications.

   Issuing agencies often have a stock of publications which must be ordered directly from the agency. These are noted by a plus sign in the *Monthly Catalog* and frequently include valuable specialized materials, from ERIC documents to scientific reports.

3. There are government bookstores which sell documents. In addition, some larger private bookstores sell the documents or at least the books dealing with the popular subjects from space to gardening.

Journal, Wilson Library Bulletin or the *American Libraries* has some mention of government documents and changes in policy. See, for example, the editorial in *Library Journal* (Nov. 15, 1989, p. 4) "Liberate Federal Information." By the 1990s a new twist had developed: charging processing fees to groups that collect government documents for use by researchers. The U.S. Supreme Court ruled that such fees cannot be charged. "Private Researchers Backed over U.S. in Clash on Documents," *The New York Times*, March 20, 1990, p. A18. See, too, in the same newspaper (July 12, 1990, p. D2), "Congress Unit Assails U.S. Information Policy." This report urges greater access to scientific and technical data.

4. A growing number of private firms now publish government documents; for example, the *CIS/Index* offers a complete collection of the working papers of Congress on microfiche. Most of the publications are highly specialized and expensive, and are reviewed in a number of the reviewing services mentioned earlier.

Depository Libraries

In order to ensure that the documents are freely available, the government early established points where they might be examined. These are called depository libraries.

Since the Printing Act of 1895, modified by the Depository Act of 1962, approximately 1370 academic, public, and special libraries have been designated as depositories for government documents. The law was modified in 1972 and 1978 to include law school libraries and court libraries. The depositories are entitled to receive publications free of charge from the Superintendent of Documents. While few of them take all the government documents (the average is about 54 percent of what is published), they at least have a larger-than-average collection. The purpose is to have centers with relatively complete runs of government documents located throughout the country.

About two-thirds of the depository libraries are academic, whereas public libraries account for about 20 percent of the total. The "remaining percentage (less than 14 percent) consists of federal, state agency, court law, historical society, medical and private membership libraries."[6] In each of the 50 states there is one depository library which accepts *every* unclassified government publication.

The basic problem faced by all but the largest of the depository libraries is the volume of material. Much of it is of limited use, and a good deal is nothing but raw data and statistics employed to support arguments or gathered more for the sake of gathering than for any specific purpose. The volume problem may be solved by putting most, if not all of the documents online or in optical disk formats. This will solve the space difficulties as well as, to a lesser extent, the problems of organization. Whether the packaged forms will do anything to improve the quality of the searches for this or that bit of information or data is an unanswered question.

[6]Peter Hernon and Charles McClure, "GPO's Depository Library Program: Building for the Future," *Library Journal*, April 1, 1988, p. 52. An excellent background article on the whole system, as well as suggestions on how the program may be improved.

GUIDES

Morehead, Joe, *Introduction to United States Public Documents*, 3d ed. Littleton, CO: Libraries Unlimited, Inc., 1983, 309 pp., paperback, $19.50.

Schwarzkopf, Leroy, *Government Reference Books*. Littleton, CO: Libraries Unlimited, Inc., 1972 to date, biennial, $47.50.

The basic textbook in the field is the Morehead volume, which is revised about every four years. It is a nice combination of facts about individual reference works and a clear, concise explanation of how the government manages to publish documents. Thanks to the superior organization and fine writing style, the textbook is easy to read. Both the beginner and the expert will find considerable assistance here, and it is the first place to turn when puzzled about some mysterious aspect of the acquisition, organization, and selection of government documents. It should be noted that the author is a frequent contributor to periodicals and for a number of years has been the editor of the government documents column in *The Serials Librarian.*

Government Reference Books is a two-year roundup of basic reference books, many of which are not familiar to either the layperson or the expert. Here they are arranged by broad subject, i.e., general, social sciences, science and technology, and humanities. The documents are then indexed by author, title, and subject. Each is fully described. About 1500 to 2000 titles are annotated every two years, and it has become a habit to star those which the editor believes are of particular importance to smaller- and medium-size libraries. Carefully edited and easy to use, the Schwarzkopf bibliography augments the standard sources and now stands as the Sheehy-Walford of the government documents field.

There are several guides for large depository libraries. Among the most useful is John Andriot's *Guide to U.S. Government Publications* (McLean, Va.: Documents Index, 1959 to date, irregular). Here documents are arranged by agency, and there are descriptive annotations for frequently issued titles. The volume ends with an agency and title index. Although the guide is far from complete and contains some errors, it remains a repository of hard-to-find information. (The Andriot work is confusing, however, in that it has been issued in multiple volumes and microfiche over the years. The last edition [1990] is a single 1200-page volume.)

GOVERNMENT ORGANIZATION

United States Government Manual. Washington: Government Printing Office, 1935 to date, annual, 904 pp., paperback. $20.

U.S. Congress Joint Committee on Printing, *Official Congressional Directory.* Washington: Government Printing Office, 1809 to date, biennial, 1625 pp., paperback. $15.

All federal, state, and local governments issue documents. The nature of those publications depends upon the particular organizational patterns of the issuing body. There are various guides and textbooks which explain the activities of these groups, but the best overall one for the federal government is the *United States Government Manual.*

The basic purpose of the *Manual* is to give in detail the organization, activities, and chief officers of all government agencies within the legislative, judicial, and executive branches. Each of the agencies is discussed separately, and the units within each organizational pattern are clearly defined. Occasionally, charts and diagrams are employed to make matters a bit clearer. The style is factual, yet discursive enough to hold the interest of anyone remotely involved with such matters.

Directory data are given for each agency. This includes the telephone number, address, names of officials, and addresses of regional offices for the major departments. There are several indexes, including one by subject. A useful feature of each year's issue is the list of agencies transferred, terminated, or abolished. Full particulars are given. This, by the way, is a justification for holding several years of the *Manual* on the shelves. All too often, someone will want information on a certain agency which can be found only in earlier editions.

There are guides, too, from private publishers. Two typical ones: The *Federal Fact Finder* (Washington: Washington Researchers Publishing, 1987 to date, annual) is a listing of telephone numbers and addresses of most of the federal agencies, including subdivisions. Also, a subject guide is offered by the *Washington Information Directory* (Washington: Congressional Quarterly, 1980 to date, annual). Here one can find 17 basic subject divisions and, under each, the primary and secondary government agencies, departments, sections, etc. Basic data are given for each, including background information on its role in government. Note, too, that numerous private organizations are included.

Congress

Issued every two years, *The Congressional Directory* includes biographies of members of Congress. The 20 sections include data, too, on Supreme Court Justices, names of foreign representatives and consular offices in the United States, and the chief officers of departments and independent agencies. It is a type of "who's who" of government, along with the essential addresses, phone numbers, and even maps of congressional districts. Despite efforts to curb the size of government, each year the *Directory* grows. It is now over 1600 pages and seems to grow about 300 to 400 pages every two years. The increase is not all due to government. The list of journals which are accredited to the congressional press galleries is about 125 pages long, up over 15 percent since the mid-1980s.

The drawback: matters change quickly in Washington and the *Directory* comes out biennially. It cannot be trusted, for example, to have the latest information on committee assignments or members of the press corps, both of which are included. One might think it would be current when first issued, but it can be up to six months behind official publication date.

What should be done? Turn to the private publisher, e.g., *Congressional Yellow Book* (Washington: Monitor Publishing Co. 1980 to date, quarterly) or *The U.S. Congress Handbook* (McLean, Va.: Congress Handbook, 1979 to date, annual). Both of these have information similar to what is found in the *Official Congressional Directory*. The difference is that they are current. There are several other similar guides. An example: Congressional Quarterly's annual *Politics in America* (Washington, DC: Congressional Quarterly, 1980 to date, annual.) This is a state-by-state listing with biographical information on each member of Congress. There are useful data on each state.

Where does one find information on former members of Congress no longer listed in the *Congressional Directory*? If relatively well known, they will be listed in such sources as the *Dictionary of American Biography* (if deceased) or in a good encyclopedia. But for short, objective sketches of all senators and representatives who served from 1774 to 1988, the best single source is *Biographical Directory of the American Congress, 1774–1989* (Washington: Government Printing Office).[7] There is a handy first section which includes officers of the executive branch, i.e., the cabinets from George Washington

---

[7]For a discussion of the much-improved, better-edited, and carefully written 1989 edition, see "Revising 200 Years of Misinformation," *The New York Times*, Dec. 23, 1988, p. A18.

through the second administration of Ronald Reagan. There is also a chronological listing by state of members of the First through the Ninety-first Congress. The bulk of the volume is an alphabetically arranged entry of members of Congress, as well as resident commissioners, delegates, and vice presidents. A short "who's-who" type of entry is used for each name, including place of burial.

Among the most-used directories and biographical sources for members of government, at both the national and local levels, is *Who's Who in American Politics* (New York: R. R. Bowker Company, 1967 to date, biennial). This work gives information on 25,000 individuals at the federal, state, and local level. The "who's-who" data includes office held and current address as well as basic biographical facts.[8]

Executive and Judiciary

Kane, Joseph. *Facts About the Presidents,* 5th ed. New York: The H. W. Wilson Company, 1989. 419 pp. $45.

Questions concerning the presidents are answered in considerable detail in almost any encyclopedia as well as in the basic guides to government discussed in this chapter. Still, Kane's work is one of the easiest to use because it offers the facts in a consistent fashion. The first section of the standard reference guide has a chapter on each of the presidents, including family life. A bibliography is included.

Possibly of more use, at least for ready reference purposes, is the second part, which is a comparative guide. Here one finds everything from the number of children to the last words. Also, there are facts on the office itself from legal problems to the cabinet officials.

There are similar directories and sources of background information for the executive and judiciary branches. Many of these are from private publishers and are listed in Morehead's guide and other places.[9] Most of the major offices are covered in the previously discussed congressional directories.

---

[8]For an overall view of Congress and its operations, the best single manual for laypersons is *Congress A to Z* (Washington: Congressional Quarterly, 1988, 612 pp. $75). The encyclopedia is written for the general public and can be used in high schools.

[9]A useful summary of the basic guides is found in "United States Government Guides," "Reference Books Bulletin," *The Booklist,* Feb. 1, 1988, pp. 910–912.

CATALOGS

> U.S. Superintendent of Documents. *Monthly Catalog of United States Government Publications.* Washington: U.S. Government Printing Office. 1895 to date, monthly, $185. (DIALOG file 66, $35 per hour.) CD-ROM: Pomona, CA: AutoGraphics, 1976 to date, monthly. $1750.

There are a few bibliographies on government documents used in almost all libraries. Large institutions tend to rely on the *Monthly Catalog of United States Government Publications* both as a finding device and catalog as well as a source of information for purchase. Arrangement in the *Monthly Catalog* is by the classification number of the Superintendent of Documents, which amounts to an index by issuing agency; that is, most documents issued by the Library of Congress will be listed under that agency name—most, but not all. Special classification situations arise when documents are arranged under a main entry other than the organization that issued the document. Hence, it is always wise to check the indexes and not to rely on the document being under the likely agency, department, and so on.

Full cataloging information is given for each entry, and so the user can generally tell much about the contents from the descriptors. There are four major indexes: author, title, subject, and series and reports. For reference, the subject and title indexes are the most useful. The subject and author indexes list the documents by their full title.

Most government documents are listed under a corporate entry in the card catalog, rarely by title or by subject. A *corporate entry* is a listing under the name of the government body responsible for its issue. For example, a corporate government entry will be under the country (United States), state (Minnesota), city (St. Paul), or other official unit that sponsored the publication. Thus someone requesting a publication about foreign affairs would probably first look under the U.S. Department of State. Since there are vast numbers of government agencies, it is frequently difficult to remember the proper point of entry.

Another problem is that usually people ask for a government document by its popular name, not by the Superintendent of Documents classification or its official title. For example, The Senate Nutrition Subcommittee released a report, "Dietary Goals for the United States." How does the librarian locate it by its popular name or, for that matter, the follow-up report on the same subject by the

Surgeon General's office? Popular names are now used in the title index of the *Monthly Catalog,* either with cross-references or by themselves. However, there never seem to be enough of them, and so when this fails, *Popular Names of U.S. Government Reports* (Washington: The Library of Congress, various dates) should be tried. This is frequently updated and contains reports listed alphabetically by popular name.

Although it is a basic finding tool for government documents, the *Monthly Catalog* does not index the majority of them. Estimates vary, but only about two or three out of every ten documents now come from the Government Printing Office. The remainder, therefore, are not in the *Catalog.* It also does not index periodicals and the material therein.

Documents are not included in the *Monthly Catalog* for a number of reasons, although the most common one is that they are issued outside of the Government Printing Office and printed or otherwise made available somewhere besides the GPO. Other reasons for nonentry include secrecy and failure of a given section, office, or department to use the GPO or otherwise send a copy of a document for cataloging.

Other governments follow much the same bibliographic control. For example, Canada offers *Government of Canada Publications Catalogue* (Ottawa: Canadian Government Publishing Center, 1953 to date, weekly and quarterly). This is a listing of Canadian departmental and parliamentary documents, which range from the esoteric to the popular.

Online/CD-ROM Services

"To many online searchers government databases are the workhorses of the information industry: the files are large, they cost little to access and they provide a multitude of varying users with information."[10] As with the majority of government-sponsored databases, the *Monthly Catalog* online is available from most of the database vendors. It offers a relatively inexpensive way of searching (because, of course, of the government support) and is familiar to almost every reference librarian. Whether one employs DIALOG or other vendors, the coverage goes back only to 1976. About 2500 new items are added each month. It is somewhat more up to date than the current printed version.

[10]Diane H. Smith, "Online Government Databases," *Database,* June 1988, pp. 56–62. The author gives a brief survey of the basic databases in government.

Beginning in 1990, Online Computer Library Center (OCLC), the bibliographical network now found in most libraries, offers GOVDOC, a cataloging service which generates MARC tapes or catalog cards for everything distributed through the federal depository system. Then, too, OCLC may be employed to locate a government document.

The *Catalog* is available in other forms, including CD-ROM. In fact, almost all the government indexes and services are now available, from one or more companies, on CD-ROM. *The Monthly Catalog* may be purchased annually, for example, from The H. W. Wilson Company, for $995, or monthly from Auto-Graphics for about double the price, $1750. For most libraries, the monthly update is preferable and well worth the added cost.

AutoGraphics covers the period from July 1976 to date and offers several levels of searching from author and title to subject. Although it has faults, it is easier to use than thumbing through the printed version of *The Monthly Catalog*.

Another approach is offered in other libraries. Here the *Catalog* is mounted in a microfilm reader, similar in appearance and use to that used for *Business Index* and *Magazine Index*. One simply scans the film for the necessary title, author, agency, etc. It is virtually done automatically in the machine. A full ten years of the *Catalog* is mounted. Each month the film is replaced as it is updated. One may search June 1985 to June 1991 in one place, at one machine. The cumulation is in two main parts: alphabetical by author and title; and alphabetical by subject. In addition there is a *Sudoc Number* (i.e., a Superintendent of Documents number, or a *government document number* as it is sometimes called) and a Report Number index.

Catalogs for Smaller Libraries

U.S. Superintendent of Documents. *U.S. Government Books.* Washington: U.S. Government Printing Office. 1982 to date, quarterly. Free.

―――. *New Books.* 1982 to date, bimonthly. Free.

―――. *Subject Bibliographies.* 1975 to date, irregular. Free.

Turning to a more manageable type of bibliography, *U.S. Government Books* is an annotated listing of about 1000 popular and semipopular documents for laypersons and professionals. The bibliography, of approximately 60 pages, is presented like a magazine and almost every one of the entries includes a picture. It is a persuasive sales tool as well as a source of information. For small- to medium-size libraries, it is an ideal buying guide. Also, thanks to its pleasing format, it will be of interest to many laypersons, and it should be made available for easy inspection.

A related free government document selection aid: *Consumer Information Catalog* (Pueblo, Colo.: Consumer Information Center, 1970 to date, quarterly, free). This lists and annotates pamphlets and booklets concerned with everything from automobiles (the first subject heading) to hobbies and travel.

New Books is a drab 25-page listing of new publications. Listed under 20 broad subject headings (agriculture to transportation) it simply lists the title, date of publication, number of pages, Superintendent of Documents number, and price. There are no annotations, although often the title is descriptive enough. This is primarily for the person who handles government documents in the library and is useful as a checklist. One major help, though, is the highlighting of two or three documents on the cover, as for example, "Conditions of education . . . page 6," "Desktop publishing guide . . . page 16," etc.

Subject Bibliography, as the title indicates, stresses documents in a specific area. There are now close to 300 areas, and they cover material on everything from air pollution to zoology. Many of the entries are annotated. The guides cover a wide variety of interests and levels of interests. A listing is available from the Government Printing Office.

For the library seeking information on government periodicals, the best single source is *Price List 36.* Government Periodicals and Subscription Services (Washington: Government Printing Office, 1974 to date, quarterly, free). This is an annotated listing of over 500 publications, the majority of which can be classified as periodicals.

There are layperson's guides to basic government documents, and new ones appear each year, as do new editions of older titles. One example will suffice to indicate the type, most of which are outlined in Morehead's guide and/or *American Reference Book Annual.* Typical of the group: William Bailey's *Guide to Popular U.S. Government Publications* (2d ed. Englewood, Calif.: Libraries Unlimited, 1990) divides much used documents into 75 broad subject areas. Full bibliographic data are given for each item and there are brief descriptive notes. There is title index and a superior subject index.

An extremely useful, selective list of from 100 to 150 government documents is chosen each year by the Notable Documents Panel of the American Library Association. Basic federal, state, and even international documents are selected. These are likely to be most used in answering topical reference questions. The annotated list appears in numerous journals including *Library Journal* for May 15 of each year.

Almost all the periodicals which carry reviews of books from time to time consider government periodicals. *The Booklist,* for example, has a regular annotated selection section. *Library Journal* and *Choice,* as well as the *Wilson Library Bulletin* and *American Libraries,* all feature articles and reviews.

Joe Morehead has a regular column on documents in *Serials Librarian,* and *RQ* has different experts. *Government Publications Review* (New York: Pergamon Press, 1973 to date, bimonthly) considers federal, state, and local materials, and each issue normally has three to five scholarly articles about government documents.

GOVERNMENT IN ACTION

> *CIS Index to Publications of the United States Congress.* Washington: Congressional Information Service, 1970 to date, monthly. Service: $600 to $2200 per year. (DIALOG file 101, $90 per hour.) CD-ROM: publisher, 1970 to date, quarterly. $1190 to $4870.

> *CQ Weekly Report:* Washington: Congressional Quarterly 1945 to date, weekly. Libraries: rates on request. Summarized in *Congressional Quarterly Almanac,* 1945 to date, annual. $195. (Online: Congressional Quarterly, rate per hour varies.)

There are numerous indexes to government documents, and only the basic ones are considered here. For those who wish additional information on these and other indexes, see John Ross's *How to Use the Major Indexes to U.S. Government Publications* (Chicago: American Library Association, 1989). The 64-page, $10 booklet offers a step by step, easy-to-follow way of getting through six major indexes. It particularly is useful for the beginner.

Turning to the indexes, one of the most frequently used is the *Index to Publications of the United States Congress,* usually called the *CIS/Index.* The *Monthly Catalog* lists only complete congressional documents; the *CIS/Index* analyzes what is *in* those documents, covering nearly 900,000 pages of special studies, bills, hearings, and so on each year.

Published by a private concern, the *Index* averages between 150 and 200 pages a month in loose-leaf form. It is in two parts: (1) The index section offers access by subject, author, and title. This section is cumulated quarterly, and there is an annual. (2) The summary section gives the full title of the document and includes an abstract of most of the items indexed.

There is a complete system for the library that can afford to purchase all the indexed materials. These are made available by Congressional Information Service (CIS) on microfiche. The user locates the desired item in the index and, through a simple key system, finds the microfiche copy.

As one of the most comprehensive of document indexes, although limited to the activities of Congress, the *CIS/Index* is a blessing for the reference librarian seeking information on the progress of a bill through Congress. Popular names of bills, laws, and reports are given, as well as the subject matter of those materials. In addition, an index covers the same material by bill number, report number, and so on. Hearings are covered as well as the names of witnesses, committees, and the like, and so the librarian can easily keep up with the development of legislation.

The comprehensive nature of the *CIS/Index* is such that, with a little practice, the reference librarian will feel fully capable of tracking down even the most elusive material. It is an exemplary index and abstracting service of current materials. (In time, of course, it will be equally useful for retrospective searching.)

The CD-ROM version, as often is the case, considerably eases the difficulty of searching. Called "Congressional Masterfile," it is divided into two sections. The first is an invaluable retrospective guide covering documents from 1789 to 1969. Depending on type of library, subscription to printed version, etc., the price of this is from a low of $9092 to a high of $32,000. The basic Masterfile is updated by Masterfile 2, which carries on from 1969 to date. Again the prices vary.

The searching is made easy due to a clear menu system which leads the user through various paths to the documents. The user may search by standard index terms, congressional session and data, the name of a witness, the title of a hearing, committee print, serial set, etc. A considerable amount of information—as in the printed work—is given on the screen. Often this is more than enough so that the user does not have to turn to the actual documents.

Valuable as it is, the CD-ROM is only updated quarterly. This is fine for most people, but for others the online daily and weekly update is considerably more useful.

The *CQ Weekly Report,* a much-used reference aid similar in some ways to a congressional version of *Facts on File,* is *not* an index but a summary of the week's past events, a summary which is often sufficient either to identify a government document to be later found in a specialized work or to answer in one step a reference query.

Each issue analyzes in detail both congressional and general political activity of the week. The major bills are followed from the time they are introduced until they are passed and enacted into law (or killed along the way). A handy table of legislation shows at a glance where the bills are in the Congress. Cross-references to previous weekly reports allow easy access to material until the quarterly index is issued and cumulated throughout the year.

The *CQ Almanac* is a handy reference work for almost all libraries. The annual divides the work of Congress into eleven subject areas (from environment and health to transportation and law), and then summaries are given of each bill suggested or passed in the various subject categories. Most of the material is analyzed objectively. In addition there is a handy summary of Supreme Court decisions and data on presidential messages. Thanks to a splendid index, it is the ideal reference work in the area it covers.

Another publication from the same firm is *Editorial Research Reports*. There are 48 issues a year which objectively summarize one current topic of interest in a 6000-word essay. The reports may run from gun control proposals to the shortage of doctors. There is an index to each issue as well as a cumulative index. Another feature: added reference sources and readings for each topic discussed.

A competing weekly index found in larger libraries is the Commerce Clearing House's *Congressional Index* (Chicago: Commerce Clearing House, 1937 to date, weekly). This, as the *CQ Weekly Report,* is an excellent place to trace the status of house and/or senate bills as well as all the activities of the Congress in session. The cumulations include subject and author indexes as well as a list of public bills and resolutions with brief summaries of content and history.

Fielding Questions

Typical questions concerning government documents may be answered in the aforementioned reference works.

1. "I am looking for information about a congressional hearing."[11] Turn to the *CIS Index* which covers subjects and titles as well as other points of access such as the name of the committee.

[11]When someone desires a new law, normally a "hearing" is held before Congress

a. Lacking the *Index,* or for hearings of several years ago, turn to *The Monthly Catalog* where the subject, title, and committee involved offer access.

b. *PAIS (Public Affairs Information Service)* offers a subject approach to most major hearings, but not all, and it is highly selective. Note, too, that PAIS will index periodicals and some books and reports *about* the hearings, and so for background information this is most useful.

c. Other sources include current newspapers (usually online) such as *The New York Times Index* or online periodicals in the subject area.

2. "What is happening to the bill which guarantees three little pigs for every family in America?" Here one might turn to the *CIS Index.* A more current, somewhat easier to follow approach is offered by the *CQ Weekly Report.* This traces the development of the bill into a law. See sections "on the floor" and/or "in committee." See, too the excellent status tables of important legislation which includes the votes as well. And see the entries in (1) above for additional information, particularly as the progressing bill is viewed by the public and by officials outside of Congress.

3. "Where can I find a current law?[12] It just became law." Laws are cumulated at the end of each session of Congress in volumes called *Statutes at Large* (1789 to date). Later the laws are organized in a more detailed fashion and become part of the *U.S. Code.* Current laws are in the *Statutes* and those of some standing are in the *Code.* While the full law may not be given, the content is reported,

---

(either/or both House and Senate) to determine the wisdom of the proposed law. Expert testimony is given. Also, hearings are heard to clarify a public issue such as the Iran Contra hearings, to examine the appointment of officials, etc. Hearings are familiar to an estimated 30 million people who watch C-Span (the cable television network). This channel often gives full television coverage of Senate and House hearings about a given issue and debates about new proposed laws.

A *report* is the result of the hearing and the recommendations of the legislative body. This accompanies the proposed new law i.e., the *bill* as it goes to the full House and/or Senate.

[12]When the bill is passed either by both houses of Congress or by one (as procedure dictates), it becomes a "law." Of course, many hearings do not result in either a report or a bill or a law; and numerous bills are killed or vetoed by the President before they become law. Actually, if it really did "just" become law, it probably would appear only in what is called "slip law" form, i.e., an unbound pamphlet which has not been cumulated and bound as part of the *Statutes at Large.* These normally are identified by public law number and filed as such according to their reference government document section. (See Morehead for full background information on this outline.)

often with its implications, in the *CIS Index, CQ Weekly Report* and the other reference works listed for (1) above.[13]

These steps will result in finding 90 to 95 percent of the answers to questions put to the reference librarian about ongoing federal legislative activities.

Technical Reports, Conference Proceedings, etc.—NTIS

Published scientific material is difficult enough to find, but an even greater challenge is to locate the work which has only limited publication (mimeographed or duplicated) or which is simply buried in another work. This is the situation with the typical report or conference proceeding.

By now the reader is familiar with the effort of ERIC to control the social sciences report literature, but an even greater challenge is to control the vast output of scientific, technical reports. To some degree this challenge is met by the National Technical Information Service (NTIS). It consists of the *Government Reports Announcements* (Springfield, Va.: National Technical Information Service, 1946 to date, semimonthly) and *Government Reports Index* (1965 to date, semimonthly).

The two services are really one. The announcement section includes abstracts of about 70,000 reports each year. By 1990 the total number was well over a million. They are divided into 26 major subject areas and then subdivided. Produced by local, state, and federal government agencies, as well as by individuals, private, and for-profit groups, the reports cover a wide spectrum of interests, including much material in the social sciences. In fact, NTIS and ERIC interchange some report information and there is a limited amount of duplication. The *Index* includes subject, personal and corporate author, contact number, and access/report number. Annual cumulations may be purchased separately.

---

[13]*The Congressional Record,* the daily record of the proceedings of Congress, has a section on the "history of bills and resolutions." This is too difficult to use because of bad indexing, and most librarians rely on other sources such as the *CIS Index. The Record* is another major government document which includes and excludes material dictated by members of Congress. For brilliant (not to mention amusing) discussions of this document, see Joe Morehead's "Congress and the Congressional Record," *The Serials Librarian,* September, 1987, pp. 59–70. See, too, "Conflicting Accounts of Words in Congress," *The New York Times,* October 20, 1990, p. 46.

Beyond the passing of laws there is *interpretation* of law. This can involve highly specialized training, but for a general, yet useful, approach to one aspect of this, see Judith Ohles, "A Quick Guide to Finding United States Supreme Court Cases," *Reference Services Review,* Spring 1989, pp. 81–83.

NTIS is backed up by documents on microfiche, which may be on standing order selectively through the Selected Research in Microfiche program (SRIM). Standing orders are for subject, category, agency, or descriptor. The library may also order individual documents on microfiche or in printed form as needed.[14]

The same people who publish the *CIS Index* use a similar approach with *Current Events Transcripts Service* (1988 to date quarterly, $2395). With an index and on microfiche the publisher offers access to interviews, press conferences, major speeches, and congressional hearings. A weekly index gives access to these events by name and by subject and includes a chronological key. Even though the publisher offers the index by itself, it has little meaning without the microfiche. Most of the material is hard to find anywhere else. While not for the general collection, it is a marvelous innovation for the person doing serious, detailed research.

Periodical Indexes

> *Index to U.S. Government Periodicals.* Chicago: Infordata International, 1970 to date, quarterly. $410.

There are a number of practical indexes which make some effort to index government periodicals and documents selectively. The best known, most often used, is the *Public Affairs Information Service Bulletin,* followed by *Resources in Education,* published by the U.S. Educational Resources Information Center (ERIC).

The librarian looking for material should turn to the *Index of U.S. Government Periodicals,* which indexes close to 200 titles. Actually, there are about 2000 periodicals and serials currently available from the federal government and probably several times that number from agencies and sections not found in Washington.

The smaller number of titles indexed is not a drawback, in that many of the 2000-plus government periodicals and serials are so specialized as to be of little use to more than a few people locally and, except in a depository library, not likely to be readily available. While primarily used by subject, the index does provide an author

---

[14]NTIS is available from many vendors online, and Silver Platter offers it on CD-ROM (four year archival and quarterly update, $3,750). For background information on the entire system see Stuart Weisman, "Computer Information Products at NTIS," *Reference Services Review,* no. 1/2, 1988, pp. 17–24.

For a detailed description of NTIS, see: "Library Reference Service Provided for NTIS Products and Services ..." *Government Information Quarterly,* no. 2, 1986, pp. 117–32. And for plans for privatization of the service: Marc Levin, "Government for Sale ..." *Special Libraries,* Summer 1988, pp. 207–214.

index which is useful to check for what has been published by an agency, bureau, or department. The index has proved particularly useful for searches involving the sciences and social sciences.

If one seeks information about the individual titles indexed, there are several places to turn. Obviously the first is to look at the periodical itself. Beyond that: (1) *Magazines for Libraries* (6th ed., 1989), has a separate section devoted to government journals. The annotations are both descriptive and evaluative. (2) *Government Reference Serials,* by LeRoy Schwarzkopf (Littleton, Colo.: Libraries Unlimited, 1988 to date, biennial), arranges the serials by broad subjects and offers excellent annotations of close to 600 publications. (3) There are 183 serials listed and annotated in the self-descriptive title of content, *Business Serials of the U.S. Government* (Chicago: American Library Association, 1988).

STATISTICS

U.S. Bureau of the Census. *Statistical Abstract of the United States.* Washington: Government Printing Office, 1879 to date, annual, 980 pp. $30; paperback. $25.

Historical Statistics of the United States, Colonial Times to 1970. Washington: Government Printing Office, 1975, 1979, 2 vols., reprinted, 1989. $58.50.

Statistics are concerned with the collection, classification, analysis, and interpretation of numerical facts or data. Statistical questions begin with "How much?" or "How many?" Depending on whether the query is motivated by simple curiosity or by a serious research problem, the reference librarian can go to the hundreds of reference works dealing peripherally or exclusively with statistical data as sources of possible answers.

The reference librarian's most difficult problem remains one of identifying a source for an answer to the esoteric, specialized statistical query; almost as hard is translating the query into the terminology of the statistical source. Given the numerous sources and the specialized terminology, it is no wonder that in larger libraries the expert in statistics is as important as the subject bibliographer. Normally, this librarian is located in the government documents or the business section. Statistical reference work is highly specialized; this text will indicate the basic general sources with which the beginner should be familiar.

The federal government, followed by state and local governments, provides the greatest number of statistical documents. A number of agencies issue them regularly, and they are an important source of forecasting in the private sector.

Statistics Sources (Detroit, Mich., Gale Research Company, 1962 to date annual) in the 1991 two-volume edition lists more than 42,000 sources of statistics under 20,000 subject headings. To be sure, not all of these are issued by the government, but the major American government sources are listed, as are sources for 186 nations of the world.

There are a number of general guides and indexes which will help even the most statistically unaware librarian through the maze. Although not all these are published by the government, the majority rely on government statistics.

How reliable are the statistical data? If they come from standard federal and major state agencies, data are likely to be quite reliable, although there are always exceptions. Most errors are caught, but international data are likely to be more error-prone because, among other things, of the legal constraints imposed on the collection agencies. The parent organizations of the agencies that collect and disseminate international statistics heavily influence the accuracy and validity of the data presented for consumption. They may be less than ideal because of political constraints or because the governments simply do not have the funds for extensive statistical data.

It is one thing to gather statistics, quite another to understand and interpret them. Is there anyone who has not heard the saying, "Statistics lie"? Statistics are as much an art as a science. Numbers mean little unless they are interpreted properly. And that is precisely what makes many of the statistical works published by the government so baffling. Rarely is proper guidance given to help interpret what they mean.

One example: Each year the federal government publishes a report on mortality rates for Medicare patients at nearly 6000 hospitals. The 14-volume report covers 10.5 million cases and shows which hospitals have an "excessive" death rate determined by the number of deaths among a given number of patients. As one official puts it, information is power, and power drives change for improvement in medical care.

The validity of the data is annually challenged by the American Hospital Association, the American Medical Association, and the General Accounting Office. Why? Because in spite of the massive study, the mortality rate of a given institution can be skewed by factors not taken directly into account by statistics. Despite correlations "proven" in the statistics between death and hospital care, despite the exhaustive nature of the statistics, the findings are open for debate. The same may be said of almost all statistical reports, from the modest to the exhaustive.

The primary problem librarians have with statistics is that few are certain on how to dig out the information. Librarians are, as one critic puts it, "innumerate," the mathematical analogue of functional illiteracy. "The rampant innumeracy of . . . the educated public in general is appalling, and since this . . . does lead to muddled personal decisions, misinformed governmental policies and an increase in susceptibility to pseudosciences of all kinds, it's not something that can be easily ignored."[15]

Statistical Guides

The Statistical Abstract of the United States is the basic source of American statistical data in any library. Filled with 1500 tables and charts, the work serves to summarize social and economic trends. The guide is divided into 34 major sections—from education and population to public lands—with a detailed 40- to 50-page index which takes the reader from abortion to zoology.

Despite the good index, the 500,000-plus statistics are not always easy to comprehend. There is a need to formulate the statistics in such a way that they are easier to understand. There is, for example, need for clearer explanations of the figures. Reference librarians should study each edition with care.

Historical Statistics of the United States has been revised over the years. The present edition includes data for more than 12,500 time series such as grouped in tabular form. It gives comparative figures on statistics, ranging from the average wage over the years to the number of residents in a given state or territory. Most material is on the national level, but a few sections cover regions and smaller areas.

The majority of Western nations follow the pattern established by the American government in issuing equivalents of the *Statistical Abstract* and specialized statistical information. For example, England has *Annual Abstracts of Statistics* (London: Her Majesty's Stationery Office: 1854 to date). On an international level the best-known equivalent is the United Nations *Statistical Yearbook* (New York: The United Nations Publications, 1949 to date, annual) which covers basic data from over 150 areas of the world. The information

[15]John Paulos, "The Odds Are You're Innumerate," *The New York Times Book Review,* January 1, 1989, p. 16.

is broken down under broad subject headings ranging from population to transportation, and no effort is made to single out units of government smaller than national.

There are both government and private corporate published reference works that deal with popular national statistics. Facts on File, for example, publishes an *Almanac of the American People.* The 1990 edition, which relies heavily on government data, is noteworthy for lists. Here are lists of favored snacks, recreations, medical problems, television programs, and government spending trends.

For an overview of data, one of the best single sources is *The World in Figures* (Detroit, Mich.: Gale Research Company, 1976 to date, biennial). The 300 pages cover statistical data under two major sections—the first in worldwide groups, such as "World Education" or "World Tourism" and the second is a breakdown by nations under five major areas of the world. Lists of primary sources are clearly given, the figures are relatively easy to follow, and there are numerous graphs. The data are more up to date and easier to follow than in United Nations statistical summary volumes.

Indexes

The three indexes to statistics are published by the Washington-based Congressional Information Services. Price depends on institutional budgets, varying from $850 to $2200 per index but averaging about $1500 a year.

American Statistics Index, 1973 to date, monthly.

Statistical Reference Index, 1980 to date, monthly.

Index to International Statistics, 1983 to date, monthly.

(All are available on CD-ROMs from the publisher, 1989 to date, quarterly. Price varies, and ASI online via DIALOG, about $90 an hour.)

These indexes follow a basic pattern: (1) Issued monthly, they have a quarterly index and are cumulated, with an index, annually. When searching, generally, one should begin with the annual index to get a sense of subject headings and general arrangement. (2) The index, a separate section or volume, refers the user to the document in the main work. Material is indexed by subject, title, issuing agency, primary individuals involved with the document, etc. Each document or series is abstracted, and there is complete information about the issuing agency and the necessary background about the statistics. The entries in the main section are arranged by accession number. Each document is within a particular issuing agency. (3) Almost all the documents are available, as with ERIC and similar services, in microfiche. Each abstract is keyed to the proper microfiche item. In addition there is a Superintendent of Documents classification number to help locate the hard copy.

Given this type of detailed support system, the librarian has a marvelous set of tools for answering almost any statistical question. The indexes are extremely easy to use, particularly as they have such detailed abstracts. There is no problem in locating the documents themselves. Actually, the abstracts often are enough to answer many research questions other than the most involved.

The three cover distinct areas. The *American Statistics Index* indexes and abstracts almost every statistical source issued by the federal government. This includes the contents of over 800 periodicals. It provides entry to close to 10,000 different reports, studies, articles, and the like.

Its twin, *Statistical Reference Index,* indexes and abstracts state documents. It does *not* include federal material. It *does* include many nongovernmental statistics, as well. These range from those issued by private concerns and business to nonprofit organizations and associations.

The *Index to International Statistics* includes major governmental statistics from around the world. There is particular emphasis on western European countries, including the European Community. It is an excellent source of United Nations statistical data. As in the other indexes, periodicals are analyzed (in this case about 100). Almost all the publications are in English, albeit there are some in other languages when there is no English equivalent.

Although only the ASI is available online, all three of the services come packaged on a single CD-ROM called *Statistical Masterfile.* Issued by the publisher, the quarterly service has the same microfiche backup, and offers sophisticated boolean search patterns. The disk has the tremendous advantage of allowing the user to search three services at once instead of each separately. At the same time the user may search the individual indexes separately. Then, too, there is an invaluable "category" index that analyzes the data in terms of age, income, states, type of legislation, etc. All and all, the CD-ROM version is superior to the printed format and much easier for the layperson to master. The drawback is the same as for most CD-ROMs—it is quarterly instead of monthly, and the cost is high. Price is based on the size and the budget of the library, but the annual CD-ROM goes from $1020 to $4275. The rate is lower when the library already subscribes to the print version. The two-disk retrospective set (covering 1973–1988) is $7000.

Statistical information is hardly limited to these three indexes. One may wish to consult the previously discussed *CIS/Index*. Other valuable data will be found in the basic indexes such as *Public Affairs Information Service Bulletin; Business Index; Business Periodicals Index;* and any service which regularly reports on the activities of government and business, such as *Predicasts.*

CD-ROM and Online

Both CD-ROM and online offer shortcuts through the masses of statistical data. It is easier, even for the beginner, to search for a specific bit of information on a CD-ROM version of, say, *American Statistics Index,* than to do a detailed search of the printed work.

Almost all the basic statistics from the government (federal to state and local) are now on CD-ROM or online. Other than those mentioned, there are such services as Government Statistics on CD-ROM offered by Slater Hall Information Products of Washington. This is a group of services from *County & City Statistics* to *Current Business Indicators,* which are CD-ROMs issued by the federal government. The *County & City* CD-ROM is typical. It costs $1200 and is updated irregularly. The data cover over 1000 cities and counties. It has statistics from crime and education to retail trade and housing.

STATE AND LOCAL DOCUMENTS[16]

> *Book of the States.* Chicago: Council of State Governments, 1935 to date, biennial, 500 pp. $42.50.
>
> *Index to Current Urban Documents.* Westport, CT: Greenwood Press, 1972 to date, quarterly. $250.
>
> U.S. Bureau of the Census, *County and City Data Book.* Washington: Government Printing Office, 1952 to date, every 5 years, 996 pp. $30.

[16]A singularly useful guide to state publications is offered by the guru of the subject, Margaret Lane. Her *Selecting and Organizing State Government Publications* (Chicago: American Library Association, 1987), covers any question either the beginner or working librarian may have about the subject. She offers an excellent overview, too, of basic bibliographies in the field.

———, *State and Metropolitan Area Data Book*. Washington: Government Printing Office, 1979 to date, biennial. 760 pp. $28.

U.S. Library of Congress, *Monthly Checklist of State Publications*, 1910 to date, monthly. $26.

At the state level, there is no entirely satisfactory bibliographical tool that lists the majority of publications. Of considerable help is the *Monthly Checklist of State Publications*. Prepared by the Library of Congress, it represents only those state publications received by the library. Arrangement is alphabetical by state and then, as in the *Monthly Catalog*, by issuing agency. Entries are usually complete enough for ordering, although prices are not always given. There is an annual, but not a monthly, subject and author index. The indexes are not cumulative. Periodicals are listed in the June and December issues.

The most comprehensive index and bibliography of local publications will be found in the *Index to Current Urban Documents*. This covers a wide variety of material from pamphlets issued by the various city agencies to annual audits and reports. It is supported by a microfiche collection which is tied to the main index.

The County and City Data Book is a mass of statistical information. Here one finds data for each county in the United States, as well as for close to 1000 cities with populations of over 25,000. Page after page provides information on everything from income levels to weather and types of jobs in various communities.

The Bureau of the Census publishes another similar work in the *State and Metropolitan Area Data Book*. Under more than 2000 different subjects one can trace statistical data for each state and major metropolitan area. This ranges from education and housing to employment and crime.[17]

The aptly named *Book of the States* is valuable on three counts. First, there are standard articles on issues such as reapportionment, consumer protection, rights for women, and the like. These are updated with each new volume. Second, there are reviews of trends, statistics and developments at both the local and federal level which have, or will have, a strong influence on state government. Third, it has relatively current information on names of principal state of-

---

[17]A related work: *The Municipal Year Book* (Washington: ICMA, 1933 to date, annual). A fundamental source of data on small to large urban centers, this appears in six parts. It gives the latest information on such things as salaries, profiles of individual cities and counties in tabular form (arranged by state), and directory listings which give the names of seven leading officials in all U.S. cities with over 2500 people.

ficers. The wealth of data makes it an invaluable reference work for almost any type or size of library.

U.S. Census

A word about the census. Data collected by the U.S Bureau of the Census are the statistical backbone of most of the works considered in this section. Where specific census data are required there are three basic approaches. First, one should turn to *American Statistics Index*. Second, other business and related indexes (from *Predicasts* to the *CIS/Index*) will analyze census material. Third, for a detailed description of the various files and reports there is the *Bureau of the Census Catalog* (Washington: Government Printing Office, 1946 to date, annual). Although this has changed in form and format, essentially it arranges news and information about statistical data by subject, from agriculture to trade. There is a detailed index which allows one to locate material by a specific area.

Most of the statistical data found in reference works, including those considered in this chapter, are based on the last *Census of Population*. The 10-year overview is the single best and most expansive source of information of its type in the world.

These data find their way into printed reference works and are part of major databases. The Census Bureau has its own online database, called CENDATA (DIALOG file 580). This is divided into 16 main subject sections which include both economic and population data. Most of the parts of the file are updated regularly by ongoing census and Bureau of Labor—among others—figures.[18]

SUGGESTED READINGS

Baber, Carolyn, "Recent Literature on Government Information," *Government Publications Review*, March/April 1990, pp. 167–172. This annual feature offers current material (usually no more than one year old) on all aspects of government documents and information policy. The citations (without annotations) are arranged under broad subject headings. This is an excellent place to turn for current articles, as well as a limited number of books, on government publishing.

[18]"Census in the Age of Information," *The New York Times*, Jan. 2, 1990, p. 1, A17. A detailed article on the census, its methods, and its uses. See also Diane Crispell, "The World of Demographic Data," *Database*, April 1987, pp. 36–43. Useful as a summary of basic databases employed in demographics, e.g., "any data that pertain to people ... the number of five-year-olds in kindgarten, the proportion of men with incomes of $50,000 or more, the number of hours teenagers watch TV," etc.

Conable, Gordon, "The FBI and You," *American Libraries,* March 1990, pp. 245–248. During the late 1980s the FBI investigated several libraries to determine who checked out what. Part of this investigation centered on librarians who took exception to the FBI's approach. The article provides a method of determining from government records whether an individual was investigated. It is a primary, close-to-home example, with basic procedures, about government documents and the Freedom of Information Act.

"Development Brief: The Human Condition," *The Economist,* May 26, 1990, pp. 80–81. This is a brief explanation of the much-quoted, much-used United Nations Development Program study of standards of living in various nations. Its *Human Development Report 1990* offers a new way of viewing statistical studies. Along the way it tells the reader much about the world in which one lives.

Hardie, Lelane, "Depository Versus Nondepository Status: A Look at the Costs," *RQ,* Summer 1989, pp. 455–458. What is the cost of a library (in this case the Kalamazoo Public Library) to withdraw from the depository system and purchase only documents which are needed? The question is not so important as the in-built explanation of the depository system and how it operates in a particular library. The conclusion: Despite costs the system is "on balance a great bargain."

Miller, Tim, "Information Capital on Capitol Hill: Online in Congress," *Online,* September 1989, pp. 17–24. A discussion of how congressional information needs are met by "a force of librarians, analysts, and staffers." Many of them use online services. The most frequently employed are NEXIS and LEXIS. Research requests continue to rise as the service functions more economically.

Plum, Terry, and Hans Raum, "Monthly Catalog on CD-ROM," *Choice,* September 1989, pp. 59–60. A brief survey of the CD-ROM possibilities of a major government bibliography. Much of the evaluation is applicable to other CD-ROM products.

Smith, Donald, "The Rhetoric of the Weekly Compilation of Presidential Documents," *Government Publications Review,* May/June 1989, pp. 213–217. A relatively new information service for distributing Presidential materials is examined and found wanting. The analysis shows just about everything which can go wrong with an ill-planned government document, including the ability of the editors "to control what version of history will appear in the government documents section of the library."

INDEX